THE LEGITIMIZATION OF VIOLENCE

Also by David E. Apter

AGAINST THE STATE: Politics and Social Protest in Japan (*with Nagayo Sawa*)
ANARCHISM TODAY (*co-editor with J. Joll*)
AN INTRODUCTION TO POLITICAL ANALYSIS
CHOICE AND THE POLITICS OF ALLOCATION
COMPARATIVE POLITICS: A Reader (*co-editor with H. Eckstein*)
CONTEMPORARY ANALYTICAL THEORY: A Reader (*co-editor with Charles Andrain*)
GHANA IN TRANSITION
IDEOLOGY AND DISCONTENT (*editor*)
THE MULTINATIONAL CORPORATION AND SOCIAL CHANGE (*co-editor with L. W. Goodman*)
POLITICAL CHANGE
POLITICAL DEVELOPMENT AND THE NEW REALISM IN TROPICAL AFRICA (*with Carl G. Rosberg*)
THE POLITICAL KINGDOM IN UGANDA: A Study of Bureaucratic Nationalism
POLITICAL PROTEST AND SOCIAL CHANGE: Analyzing Politics (*with Charles Andrain*)
THE POLITICS OF MODERNIZATION
RETHINKING DEVELOPMENT: Modernization, Dependency and Post-Modern Politics
REVOLUTIONARY DISCOURSE IN MAO'S REPUBLIC (*with Tony Saich*)
SOME CONCEPTUAL APPROACHES TO THE STUDY OF MODERNIZING NATIONS
WANG SHIWEI AND WILD LILIES (*co-editor with T. Cheek*)

The Legitimization of Violence

Edited by

David E. Apter
Professor of Political Science and Sociology
Yale University

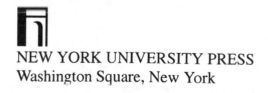

NEW YORK UNIVERSITY PRESS
Washington Square, New York

This book is printed on paper suitable for recycling and made from fully managed and sustained forest sources.

First published in the U.S.A. in 1997 by
NEW YORK UNIVERSITY PRESS
Washington Square
New York, N.Y. 10003

Library of Congress Cataloging-in-Publication Data
The legitimization of violence / edited by David E. Apter.
p.   cm.
Includes bibliographical references and index.
ISBN 0–8147–0648–7
1. Political violence.   2. Violence—Religious aspects.
I. Apter, David Ernest, 1924–
JC328.6.L44   1996
303.6—dc20   95–52769
                                         CIP

Printed in Great Britain

Contents

Preface

There is nothing new about political violence. It is the original sin of politics. How to prevent it, how to establish and maintain both a system of order and order itself is, after all, what most of politics is about. The overthrow of tyrannical systems and regimes, the desire for a separate and independent state, the tendency to impose one's religious beliefs on others, to establish state religions and ideologies, to intrigue and gain access to power by devious as well as institutional means, are all as old as the human group. Indeed, history is a virtual chronicle of political violence either from above or below, for or against the state, and as drama, spectacle, and power. It is a chronicle which can be read in many different ways, from the standpoint of the victim as well as the perpetrators, the tragic and the heroic, and both the evil and the good that lives after them.

The essays presented here are interpretive. They represent efforts to "read" political violence in hope of revealing aspects of it not usually included in more conventional approaches to the subject. We have also tried to read it through different disciplinary lenses. The authors of these essays themselves represent a wide range of disciplinary as well as analytical perspectives: anthropology, history, sociology, political science. What drew them together was a common concern with political violence as a problem. All wrestled with how to interpret their field studies by means of a common analytical framework – discourse analysis, an approach which, as will become readily apparent, works in some cases more successfully than others. In the long course of the project two extremely stimulating week-long seminars were held in Geneva where drafts of the papers were presented, criticized, and repeatedly amended.

The entire enterprise, which we refer to as the "Legitimization of Violence Project", was held under the auspices of the United Nations Research Institute for Social Development (UNRISD). However, it began at Magdalen College, Oxford, in spring 1988 where Professor Apter delivered the Wayneflete Lectures in which he laid out some of the ingredients of a discourse theory of political violence. The then President of Magdalen, Professor Keith Griffiths, suggested that applying it comparatively to case materials might be a good way to evaluate the utility of such a theory. It was at his suggestion that UNRISD came to provide an opportunity. This book and a second volume by Professor Andre du Toit of the University of Capetown in South Africa, which analyses the South African

vii

case, are the result of the attempt. We leave it to the reader to decide, and hopefully debate, the virtues and failings of such an approach.

As to the studies themselves, a few words are in order about their selection since there is, unfortunately, what might be called a wealth of examples on which to draw. We used several criteria. First, we wanted cases that represented three predominant and different types of violence (or combinations of them): extra-institutional protest, terrorism, and revolutionary insurrection. Secondly, we preferred those where political violence had gone on for quite a long time, some of them several generations, but for one reason or another were losing momentum, or where possibilities for negotiated settlement, however dim, were beginning to appear on the horizon. Finally, we selected some examples where discourse theory seemed to work best and also worked least well.

All of us who had the opportunity to participate in this project wish to thank Dr Dharam Ghai, the Director of UNRISD, and his colleagues for their imagination as well as their patient support and encouragement of a project which at times must have seemed not only novel but perplexing. We also wish to thank Professor Bruce Kapferer for his detailed comments on drafts of these essays.

Notes on the Contributors

David E. Apter is Henry J. Heinz II Professor of Comparative Political and Social Development, and Chairman of the Council of African Studies at Yale University. Among his books are *Ghana in Transition, The Political Kingdom in Uganda, The Politics of Modernization, Choice and the Politics of Allocation* (winner of the Woodrow Wilson Award of the American Political Science Association), *Against the State* (with Nagayo Sawa), and *Revolutionary Discourse in Mao's Republic* (with Tony Saich).

Paul Arthur is Professor of Politics at the University of Ulster specializing in Peace and Conflict Studies. Among his publications are *The People's Democracy, 1968–1973* (Belfast, 1974) and *Government and Politics of Northern Ireland* (Longman, 1980, 2nd edn 1987). He is currently working on Anglo-Irish relations and the nature of political mediation.

Malcolm Deas is a Fellow of St Antony's College, Oxford. He was one of the founders of the Oxford Latin American Centre and has several times been its Director. He has been visiting and writing on Colombia for three decades, and his collected essays on the country's history and politics have recently been published in Bogotá under the title *Del poder y la gramática*.

Carlos Iván Degregori is an anthropologist from the University of Ayachuco (Peru). Formerly, he was Professor at the University of San Marcos and Director of the Instituto de Estudios Peruanos, both in Lima. He has done extensive research on social movements, ethnicity and violence. The English translation of his book *El sugimiento de Sendero Luminoso* is forthcoming.

Bruce Kapferer is Professor and Chairman of the Department of Anthropology, University College, London University. Among his books are *A Celebration of Demons*, and *Legends of People, Myths of State: Violence, Intolerance, and Political Culture in Sri Lanka and Australia*.

David Moss has been Professor of Contemporary European Studies (Italian) at Griffith University, Brisbane, since 1992. In 1993 he was

ix

Visiting Fellow at All Souls College, Oxford. Trained as a social anthropologist, he has written on many aspects of contemporary Italian society and politics, including poverty and inequality, political violence, responses to HIV/AIDS, and banditry and pastoralism in Sardinia. His publications include: *The Politics of Leftwing Violence in Italy, 1969–1985*, *Action on AIDS: National Responses in Comparative Perspective (1990)*, and *Italian Political Violence: The Making and Unmaking of Meanings*. He is currently writing a study of patronage in Italy since 1870.

Elizabeth Picard is Professor of Comparative Sociology at the Institute of Political Studies and the Department of Political Science of the University of Paris 1, Sorbonne. She has a research appointment in political science at the Centre d'Études et de Recherches Internationales of the Foundation Nationale des Sciences Politiques. Her books include *Liban, État de Discorde*, which has been translated as *Lebanon: The Shattered State*. She has also edited *La Question Kurde*, and *La Nouvelle Dynamique au Moyen-Orient*.

Bradden Weaver attended the College of William and Mary and Yale University. He has served as US Senate and Congressional aide and has interned at the German Bundestag and the US Embassy, Bonn. He has also studied at the Wilhelms University, Münster, on a Rotary International Scholarship. In 1992–3 he worked as a Robert Bosch Fellow at the German Foreign Ministry and the Berlin Senate Chancellory. While in Berlin he did research on the resurgence of xenophobic violence and rightest extremist organizations. He is the author of "Rightest Violence as a Youth Phenomenon" in the Robert Bosch Foundation publication *German Unification at the Crossroads*.

Michel Wieviorka is Professor of Sociology at the École des Hautes Études en Sciences Sociales. He is Director of the CADIS (Centre d'Analyse et d'Intervention Sociologiques). He published, in English, *The Making of Terrorism*, *The Arena of Racism*, and, with Alain Touraine and François Dubet, *The Working-Class Movement*. He has worked on social movements, race and political violence and is now finishing research on post-totalitarian Russia. He is Editor of *Les Cahiers Internationaux de Sociologie*.

1 Political Violence in Analytical Perspective

DAVID E. APTER

I CONTEMPLATING VIOLENCE

To speak of "contemplating" violence is perhaps a contradiction in terms. Too shocking, too saddening, too infuriating and often too pious or passionate, it is, even under the best of circumstances, a phenomenon difficult to approach neutrally. Political violence conjures up the massacres of the innocents in Rwanda, Southern Sudan, East Timor, the drizzly parade of funerals in Northern Ireland, the tortures and trials of captives on public display by terrorists, the violation and mutilation of women in Bosnia. Even where the intents are heroic, as in the case of the Zapatistas in Chiapas, or in the context of such successful struggles for freedom as in South Africa, the attending loss of property and blood leaves behind the unfinished business of retrievable anger. The more so because not even the most successful movements realize their aims quite on their own terms. Among its most negative effects is the reinforcement of prejudiced boundaries. For political violence not only divides people, it polarizes them around affiliations of race, ethnicity, religion, language, class. It turns boundaries in the mind into terrains and jurisdictions on the ground. As an editorial in the *New York Times* put it: "In no previous age have people shown so great an aptitude and appetite for killing millions of other people for reasons of race, religion or class."[1] Those who are not victims become voyeurs. Even the best-intentioned movement suffers the effects of Foucault's paradox, i.e. the hegemonic consequences of the liberating project. Perhaps worst of all, where it becomes self-sustaining and of long duration, people accept it, live with it, and survive in a world gone dull, nasty, brutish and short.

The tragedies of political violence are compounded because so many political movements continue to sustain both the principle of violent struggle and the struggles themselves – often for long periods – so that violence generates its own objects. It creates interior meanings. Seeking the moral moment in the cannon's mouth it ritualizes death as sacrifice, turns martyr-

1

dom into testimony. When death is the measure of devotion to noble causes, even the victims become co-conspirators if they accept it as some historical necessity. It is one way for political violence to become legitimized.

Of course, political violence is not all of a piece. It varies in its objects, its methods, its rationale, its organization. Even under the best circumstances it remains morally ambiguous. Like the evil to the good it can represent the dark side of politics or its most shining project. It can serve as a terrible over-simplifier, and with a terrifying finality. It can lead to virtual dehumanization, bestiality. The epithet if it becomes the negativizing substitute for a living person, may lead to that person's murder. Martyrs of the Hamas or the Party of God regard the Israelis they are ordered to kill as "pigs, or monkeys", their followers honouring the killers at the moment of their death. So too the Tutsi have been demonized by the Hutu in Rwanda, and we see the reality invoked by the terminology; smashed people, their bodies hacked, oozing blood, grotesque displays of limbs or sexual parts. Such scenes are elsewhere in venues as diverse as airports as well as churches, cities as well as villages and as often among people who know each other as intimates as well as aliens. Which suggests how complex the connections between the need for violence and the need to exorcise it, and both within movements as between them and the rest of society. A great deal of political violence centres around boundaries, violation and perversity, sexuality, the uses of rituals in murder, and choreographing of death including what Greenblatt calls "filthy rites".[2]

People do not commit political violence without discourse. They need to talk themselves into it. What may begin as casual conversation may suddenly take a serious turn. Secret meetings add portent. On public platforms it becomes inflammatory. It results in texts, lectures. In short it engages people who suddenly are called upon to use their intelligence. Political violence then is not only interpretive, it engages the intelligences in ways out of the ordinary. It takes people out of themselves.

Such things occur in particular in the condensed and miniaturized world of the underground where the "cell", the microbiological unit for the reconstruction of the world, serves as a metaphor for a return to the origins of life – the Ur-unit stripped to its most fundamental. Hence the uses of violence are in some measure reflexive of the organization of violence, especially where a movement becomes the primary unit of primary obligation (replacing family or all other affiliations). In these regards, the more one focuses on political violence itself the more rather than the less bizarre it becomes. It requires a Bataille to probe these properties. They defy ordinary rationality.

Yet take one step back and look again, this time through the prism of developmental history. It becomes difficult to ignore the heroic side of political violence. Reallocations of wealth, moral teleologies of human betterment, doctrines of how to realize it, these are also inseparable from political violence. It would be hard to envisage the evolution of democracy or for that matter the English, French, and American revolutions without such violence and indeed fears of its potentiality. The list of reforms which were successfully pushed and prodded by confrontational violence is a long one. Nor can violence be completely separated from institutional politics. The right to organize, and the actual organization of trade unions, or civil rights required a certain tandem connection between political violence and the ballot box, extra-institutional protest movements and political parties. It takes confrontation outside the law to make the law itself. Few basic changes in the content and scope, logic and practices of liberty and equality occur peacefully, contained within the frameworks of institutional politics.[3]

In this respect violence as a form of political exceptionalism lurks just outside the institutional door. For this reason alone political life generally has great potentiality for the kind of symbolic density that challenges to order invoke almost instantaneously. Indeed, the least important part of politics is of the tin horn and self-advertising variety. Moreover, what is hidden under the surface, or one should say the superficial conduct of government business and party politics, is not only the hard bargaining of highly professionalized politicians, but what might be called the real underlying the ostensible. Actual politics is based on conventional wisdom, transparency in common sense, and the need to act on the basis of the reasons people give for what they do. Political violence not only challenges conventional wisdom, tears away at transparency, and creates quite other reasons for what they say and do. The real becomes the unreal.

But what then is the real? There is the reality of the act itself. There is the reality of its organization, the work of those who are hidden – the work out of sight. There is the real of the "unmasking discourse", which locates through the acts some higher moral purpose, some transcending goal, some overcoming project which will work simultaneously for the individual and for the community. It is in this sense that political violence generates not "communitarianism", a thin word, but a discourse community, a "thick" condition.

Of course, a great deal depends on what interests are represented by the acts themselves. Discourse becomes important as a way of connecting moral principle and interests. Hence the discourse constitutes a boundary between the acceptable and the unacceptable interest. Those acceptable need to reinforce principle. It is in the mutual reinforcement of principle and interest that discourse becomes both conceptually, and on the ground, self-reflexive, legitimizing, and no matter how reprehensible the act, not a matter of the "event" alone. In this context acts of violence are never innocent. Nor are the victims, the targets: businessmen, political leaders, journalists, etc. Each becomes a role rather than a person. A surrogate for the system may be destroyed. Hence, even the most horrifying acts may be perpetrated in the pursuit of some higher purpose. Extremism is testimony of provocation.

This does not mean to suggest that one can correlate the outrageous act with some presumed degree of outrage. Any more than it is to suggest that there is some threshold of tolerance beyond which people explode. Indeed, it is quite remarkable how passive most people remain when confronted with situations beyond their control. For the most part outrage, frustration at some long-festering situation, hopelessness and degradation lead at best to random acts. But when people do try to take control, and by means of interpretive action, then the iconography of violence, the choreography of confrontational events, the planning of actions based on interpretation and interpretations deriving from actions becomes a process. The process enables one to shuttle back and forth between violent acts and moral binaries. Each change in the latter and the frame of the former shifts, as with the eye of a camera. Yet, in retrospect, what remains after all is said and done is a photograph – death on a flat plane.[4]

But the plane does not stay flat. On the one hand it is quite remarkable, considering how ubiquitous political violence has become, how often confrontational events can be healed or at least papered over, as, in a troubled way we see happening in the negotiations between the PLO and Israel (despite desperate efforts by the Hamas and other organizations to rip them apart). Even conflicts of the long durée eventually succumb to a peace process. Negotiation may have to wait a long time, as indeed most of the cases here illustrate. Political violence may have to go through its cycle, from chance events, to protest, to confrontation, to interpretive discourse, quite often passing through intergenerational political violence, to arrive at negotiated solutions. This is the case with the Sendero Luminoso since the capture of its top leadership. The Red Brigades have been relatively inactive since the mid-1980s. The IRA, despite lapses, has declared itself for peace and is engaged in negotiation with British and Irish authorities. Shi'a violence in Lebanon has been transferred to Gaza and the West Bank. A precarious and uneasy truce has failed to hold in Sri Lanka. But political violence is declining among the Basques. The two exceptions are Neo-Nazism which remains the dangerous shadow not yet bigger than a man's hand, and violence in Colombia, which has become a permanent politics of vengeful and enforced circulation of money, power, and women.

On the other hand even settled controversies leave little room for complacency as events in former Yugoslavia or Southern Russia suggest. There always remains some residue of retrievable anger, which, if it breaks out in violence again, can be mobilized by the appropriate discourse, its re-enactment usually worse than the original. If it is the case that such events occur twice, the second time is not farce, Marx to the contrary, but virulence.

Which is hardly surprising considering that political violence feeds on divisions, makes them into fundamentals and elevates even trivia to the level of loyalties. It polarizes affiliationally and doctrinally. It feeds on intolerance by making race, ethnicity, religion, language, class, doctrine, nationality, etc., decisive in "reordering". It separates actors and audience, victims and voyeurs, but reunites them again on its own terms. It is the original sin of politics. How to prevent it, how to establish and maintain both a system of order and order itself is at bottom what politics is about, its ultimate *raison d'être*.

As should be clear from these remarks, we distinguish political violence from violence in general. Most violence is random if not criminal. Political violence disorders explicitly for a designated and reordering purpose: to overthrow a tyrannical regime, to redefine and realize justice and equity, to achieve independence or territorial autonomy, to impose one's religious or doctrinal beliefs.[5] Boundary smashing goes together with boundary resetting. Just as there are reasons of state, so there are reasons of the anti-state. Indeed it is as an anti-state which gives a social movement its rationale as a "discourse community".[6] The key to political violence is its legitimacy.

Sendero Luminoso is a good example. Outrageousness in its truth claims it is ruthless in the disjunctive break it seeks with "normalcy". Its inversion is double, against the bourgeois capitalism of the urban areas and the "Indianness" of its rurals. It insists on a revolutionary logic in which peasants are the class with radical chains. Hence they can no longer be "Indians". They are redefined as peasants. They must think like peasants according to the Maoist, as modified by Leader Guzmán. If not they are against both their history and their destiny. The penalty is death. Many have paid it.

That said one must not lose sight of the fact that in its time nothing was more radical than republicanism. Similarly with liberalism, and the emphasis on equalitarianism, a concept made more feasible by both the idea and possibilities of developmental growth. So, too, were doctrines critical of them when they became "hegemonic"; anarchism, socialism, communism. In turn these doctrines have themselves been subject to the schismatic, prone to divide along lines of contending sub-discourses. Today they have largely been replaced by repatriated fundamentalism, much of it, in the case of a redemptive Islam, brought back to Egypt, the Sudan, Algeria and elsewhere from the Afghan wars. Indeed, radical versions of redemptive Islam have replaced developmental socialism and rejected liberal capitalism. In the case of Algeria the most militant fundamentalists claim the right to rule based on electoral principles, while publicly proclaiming their intent to abolish democracy if they win power.

Whatever the mode and the principles so embodied, what makes these important is not their status as doctrines but as discourses – fictive and logical reconstructions of reality. Each inversionary movement generates its own discourse by means of which it defines its principles, goals, and establishes boundaries which give rise to outrage when violated or penetrated. The more totalizing the discourse the more aspects of social and political life it embraces, the inversionary accomplishment being celebrated in art, literature, theatre. As with the Jacobins they may change the calendar, redefining history and time. So too with Futurism, Constructivism, and so on up to Fluxus and other such expressions. Not a few movements generate an explosion in artistic life as service to revolutionary aims.

Perhaps the final individual act, a way of dying happily, brilliantly, going off with flair, to act with drama and artistry, is martyrdom. The excitement of the act is sexual as much as political, the body as weapon. And afterwards the mourners. On one side are the families and friends of the victim-victimizer and on the other those of the victim-surrogate. One celebrates martyrs as part of a social text. In Northern Ireland one can read their names on the stones in every county. They appear like saints' days on calendars, faces hooded, arms at the ready, So too in radical Islam. These events remind us of the close connection between killing and sexuality – which suggests how it is that acts in themselves become meaningful.

II   ANALYSING POLITICAL VIOLENCE

Analysing violence is almost as ubiquitous as the acts themselves. Despite the difficulties of dealing with so complex a phenomenon, or perhaps because of it, the extant literature is huge. A number of works have been standard, philosophical ones, like Arendt on revolution; historical descriptions, like Laqueur and Wilkinson on terrorism; and a very large literature on social movements such as Tilly on social mobilization, Hobsbawm on political movements, Gurr on rebellion, and Tarrow on collective action.[7] Some of this literature takes a "diagnostic" view. Applied to autocracies, political violence becomes self-legitimizing, an expression of the natural desire for freedom and liberty. In democratic societies, political violence suggests institutional weaknesses and blockages, or normative insufficiencies, injustices, or inequities, i.e. wrongs to be righted. The diagnostic view suggests that political violence results when offended interests seek their outlets by means outside the rules of the game. It is a rational phenomenon, no different generically speaking than normal politics except in terms of its means. So political violence can be examined in terms of theories of bargaining, coalition, and rational choice. Tactics and strategies become subject to cost-benefit forms of analysis.[8]

A second strand in the literature deals with political violence as individual pathology. Those engaging in violence are likely to be in some sense "pathological". For example, in any movement, those most prone to the use of violence have some kind of personality problem. Experience shows that it is usually the wrong people who bring up the right issues – the troublemakers, malcontents, those quickest to meddle, to take on the grievances of others as their own, the most presumptuous, those lacking self control, common sense propriety and the institutional respect necessary for the responsible exercise of citizenship.[9]

A third strand in the literature treats political violence as social pathology. The pathological condition may arise out of asymmetries of power and access, of classes, of systems of political economy like capitalism or socialism. Most large theories of change, structuralist, institutionalist, Marxist, coalitional, see it as a consequence of social pathologies, systemic faults. Some see it as an inevitable progress of history: democracy replacing monarchy, capitalism replacing mercantilism, socialism replacing capitalism, or today, in some countries, capitalism replacing socialism.[10]

The social pathology approach lends itself to cases and comparisons. Perhaps the most studied is the French Revolution. Materials on it alone would fill several large libraries. Susceptible to infinite revisionisms, reworked again and again, each generation sees in it a preferred interpretation. So much so that coding and decoding the themes of the French Revolution have provided the prisms through which subsequent revolutions have been viewed.[11] Indeed, it has provided many of the ingredients for the examination of political violence more generally, a fund of remarkable and original interpretive ideas – iconographic as in the work of Crane

Brinton, as spectacle by Mona Ozouf, as metaphor in the work of Dorinda Outram to name only a few.[12]

So much so that Jacobinism, and the Paris Commune became the model revolution not only for those analysing revolution but making it as well. A good example is Leon Trotsky's monumental study of the Russian Revolution. One could argue quite plausibly that the genesis of the French Revolution remains the bedrock for a good many mainstream theories of comparative revolution.[13] One thinks in this connection of the work of J. L. Talmon, Barrington Moore Jr or Theda Skocpol.[14]

It is not a big jump from the social pathology literature to radical therapy as in the work of Fanon for whom political violence purges dependency, exorcises deeply internalized inferiorities, frees one from remaining an accomplice of foreign and colonial authorities who impose on mind, spirit, and body. Such theory owes as much to Marx as to Freud. Other "therapies", descending more directly from Marxism (including Leninism and Maoism). The putative descendants of Marx see in revolution the rectifying course of material history. Revolutionary necessity is the restorative to social health. Smashing the bourgeoisie becomes the precondition to the healing, and liberating, solution. This emphasis on the beneficial effects of violence on the social body was shared by both a Sorel and a Sartre who provided the stepping stones for others desiring to trace the uncertain route from Marxism to anarchism all the way up to Situationism, and beyond. The beyond that is of modern nihilism, form, taboo, and language smashing; violence as spectacle, as in the work of Bataille or Debord or the Fluxus movement.[15] Indeed with this evolution both language and discourse becomes more important than less because language itself, perceived as hegemonic, as a form of hierarchy, itself becomes the object of violence.[16] (This was particularly the case for the Situationists, or the militants of the "generation of '68" in Paris.)[17] Violence becomes a way of challenging hegemonic discourses, the power of the abstract conceptualizers who use knowledge as power, or as in Foucault to challenge abstraction in the service of professionalism and expertise.[18] As already indicated, of the various modes of political violence, the most intellectually substantial treatment has been about revolution, the entry point for theories about violence which consider revolution the cure for social pathology. Terrorism, while it has received more than its fair share of attention, has a much less intellectual pedigree. Much of the preoccupation with it is in terms of deterrence. It too has a diagnostic dimension. It treats political violence as deviant behaviour. Pathology is not social but individual.

The problems then do not lie with society or the state, but with the individuals who cannot properly fit into it. Since one needs to find ways to fit such people in – especially since it is business and political figures who become vulnerable, targeted by terrorists – a good deal of the literature is practical.[19] It is about how to deal with and dispose of terrorists.[20]

Information about terrorism and terrorists has been deposited in worldwide archives, collected by government secret services, psychologists, lawyers, jurists, university professors, and political officers. It is also collected by professional students of terrorism in their "cells" in such research centres as the Rand Corporation (where computer print-outs spew out information in the gnomish language of relative deprivation, rising expectations, or the J curve of authoritarianism). Data banks, survey materials, classifications, terrorist profiles, case histories are used to establish techniques, legislative and other strategies, and instructions on the use and protection of informants. There is also preoccupation with techniques, the use of fibre optics for surveillance, linguistic analysis of threat credibility, new methods for the tracing, screening and detecting of weapons.

Theories abound, conceptual modelling, bargaining and indemnity frameworks, communications models, deterrence and negotiation techniques, organizational analysis, "futuristics", role playing, gaming, not to speak of public opinion surveys to correlate public support for governments under threat. The terminology associated with its analysis is bewildering, whether by pychologists using group dynamics, role analysis, and organizational theorists using gaming, or as adaptations of frustration–aggression theory.[21]

Countermeasures have been internationalized. There is the virtually instantaneous exchange of information across national jurisdictions. A variety of instruments for regional co-operation have been established, the Club of Berne (1971), the Trevi Group (1976). Today there are many others, the Club of Vienna, the French–German Operational Group, and of course the Council of Europe Convention on the Suppression of Terrorism. Indeed, the study of terrorism has become a virtual growth industry.[22]

Several recent journals devoted to its analysis have shown considerable theoretical ambition.[23] For the most part, however, the focus is on gathering hard data on events, personalities, and situations, and by police agencies, think tanks, and specialized organizations concerned with prevention.[24]

There is also a very large literature on extra-institutional protest movements, i.e. those that favour confrontational episodes which will rally and mobilize public support for groups whose claims and intents fall largely on deaf political ears, especially given the concatenation of coalitional forces within majoritarian and pluralist democratic systems. The materials are very diverse but fall under the category of social movements, emancipatory movements, communitarianism, etc. Extra-institutional protest differs from both revolution and terrorism in so far as its violence is tempered by the desire to generate larger clienteles and public support. The strategy of violence is in part to garner sufficient sympathy to force dominant parties to pay attention to matters obscured by coalitional interests and dominant policy agendas. Political violence tends to be a choreography using different modalities of civil disobedience. Its major emphasis is on the articulation and fine-tuning of rights. Among its more familiar forms are struggles to organize trade unions, enlarging the spheres of individual and civil rights, women's suffrage, and today everything from protecting Amazon Indians and Australian Aborigines to saving spotted owls.[25] Its tactics include protest marches, hunger strikes, takeovers of public spaces, buildings, occupation of factories or universities.[26] Issues range very broadly, and intertwine with normal politics. The Greens are a good example. What began as a fringe of the student movement in the 1960s in Germany, developed into a number of extra-institutional protest movements both in Europe, the United States, and Japan. In the German case, and not without great internal debate between the Realos and the Fundamentalists, it transformed itself into an institutional political party.[27]

Thus extra-institutional political movements using confrontational tactics are associated with protests on behalf of minorities: enlarging the rights of women, protection of gays, or other groups, characteristically and systematically disadvantaged by the institutions of government, society, law and its application, and the administration of rights, including, in the United States, anti-abortion movements which define the foetus as an unborn child and the doctor engaging in abortion a murderer. No matter how radical its objectives extra-institutional protest tends to be reformist rather than disjunctive in its consequences if not in its objectives.[28]

It is common for a given movement to combine extra-institutional protest with an underground wing using terrorism, aiming to create a revolutionary disjunction. Such combinations allow different strategies and modalities of action by different parts of the same organization. This aspect of political violence is perhaps the least understood and the most poorly studied.

III   OUTLINES OF A DISCOURSE THEORY

However one considers these and other approaches to the analysis of political violence, discourse theory draws on quite different sources for ideas. Its themes derive from a very diverse literature, scholars as diverse as

Levi-Strauss and Roland Barthes on mytho-logics, Pierre Bourdieu on symbolic capital, Paul Ricoeur on sin and re-enactment, Guy Debord on spectacle, Frederic Jameson on magic realism, Terry Eagleton on drenched signifiers, Peter Brooks on narrative, Henri Lefevre and David Harvey on space as meaning and time, a Bataille and surplus – a surplus of signifiers embodied in the violating act, Jean Baudrillard on simulacra, and most important, phenomenologists like Gadamer who treat discourse as intentionality – one could go on. All have important things to say about the relationship between discourse and its components and discourse communities and their formation. Spectacle, voice, leadership, and the sheer choreography of violence take on quite different proportions when examined in these contexts.

Whatever else can be said about them, such ideas are quite opposite to rational calculation and different from those which emphasize both "opportunity" and political mobilization, or theories of justiciable claims.[29] Nor is it simply the product of armchair theorizing. It has also developed out of empirical work in field settings.[30]

Discourse starts with events which serve as a basis for more reasoned interpretation. Such interpretation is a process. It employs certain ingredients, paradigm or example (exemplars), syntagm or propositions, doctrines, systematic organized treatises, myth and theory, magic (or fantasy) and logic, metaphor and metonomy, narrative and text, retrieval and projection.

It is by such linguistic alchemy that what begins as spontaneous outbreaks, riots, demonstrations, or for that matter street violence becomes self-sustaining. Without discourse such events, no matter how long-festering some people's anger or heavy the burden of social grievances, may explode like fireworks, burn brightly for a moment, only to sputter and go out. It is when events are incorporated into interpretive discourses embodied in discourse communities, that political violence not only builds on itself, but becomes both self-validating and self-sustaining. For those involved all one's activities are redefined in terms of the needs and obligations of the movement itself. So a movement depends on violence to sustain its organization and the means of satisfying its needs.[31]

The analytical inspiration for such an approach derives from the model "mytho-logic" of Plato's Republic. In Plato, a logic of truth supersedes the understanding of appearances and where that logic leaves off myth comes in.[32] It is perhaps the first example of what might be called the narrative reconstruction of reality.[33] More modern versions include the mytho-logics of a Levi-Strauss or a Roland Barthes in which one begins with myth and ends with logic. Themes of disordering and reordering are recounted and rendered in events. Such discourse starts concretely enough.

A tale is told, a myth created. Some triggering or focal happening which might ordinarily hardly cause comment suddenly stops time and resets it. There is a sudden beginning and end. Then meanings become loaded, cumulatively, the event "thickens" symbolically. It serves as a lightning rod for a wide variety of experiences. Recounted stories makes for sociability. Collectivized, stories have consequences when, as myths they purport to be history, as history they are reinterpreted as theories, and as theories they make up stories about events. In politics, truth-telling and story-telling are part of the same process by which it becomes possible to interrogate the past in order to transform the future. When violence is the form which this interrogation takes, events become endowed with a surplus of signifiers. There is a troping of facts. Events become metaphors, as part of a narrative process and metonyms for a theory. The result is what might be called collective individualism. Individuals convey their individual stories to reinforce a collective one and draw down in interpretative power more than they put in. In short, the "overcoming project" is both individual, the individual transforming the self, and collective; the movement overcoming negative circumstances in the form of some major disjunctive transformation.[34]

Such transformations are moral moments. They punctuate history. They convert time into space. They form into a kind of symbolic capital which, powerful for the moment, can enable people to accomplish more than they thought possible, to transcend themselves, and to commit themselves to the collective enterprise. By the same token such conditions foster splitting, betrayals, and conflicts within which are both personal and personalized. Other events are recounting to build up a narrative in which such ingredients as loss, depatrimonialization, dispersion, diasporization, dispossession, constitute a fall from grace, locking the fate of the individual with the group so defined, and deriving fictive truths from the narrative reconstruction of reality. When such truths become the basis for redemptive and transformational projective solutions, a logic is provided. It is in making the connection that agency comes in.

Agency is that power to retrieve the past in the present through storytelling, and transform it into a logic of outcomes. As Walter Benjamin put it: "Death is the sanction of everything that the story-teller can tell. He has borrowed his authority from death".[35] And most of the stories render the inexplicable explicable. What may look like bad luck, fate, misfortune, is shown not to be chance but the design of the powers that be. By rendering the events of a predicament the predicament becomes general. One finds oneself in the account, as pariah, a stranger in one's own land, a marginal, powerless, vulnerable, a victim, etc.

Which suggests that if there is power in recounting it takes a truth-teller to consolidate it. The story-teller may be an Odysseus figure, a wanderer in exile who gains in wisdom and after many trials comes home to reclaim the patrimony. Or, the leader may become "the source", the father or mother of the country, the phallocrat, all guns, weapons, uniforms, the putative fertility figure. But to consolidate a myth, to make it a mytho-logic, one requires a cosmocratic figure, a latter day Socrates, the Buddha within the Tantric circle (there are many representations). It is such a figure who finds the logic of truth in the narrative, the myths recounted by the story-teller creating a space for theoretical explanation. Or if not a cos-mocrat, the agent may be prophetary, a vehicle for a voice higher than his or her own. Indeed, the story-teller, the phallocrat, the cosmocrat and the prophet may combine in the same person. Culling from the multiple expe-riences of those in negative predicaments, incorporating violent events and circumstances in narrative and text, not only is a discourse created but so is a form of capital, a monopolistic capital of truths and virtues, of logo-centric closure. It produces a conveyance, people giving over a piece of their minds to the collective, enabling them to draw down more power than they give up. There is power in this. It is the power of discourse. We will call it symbolic capital.

What are its conditions of possibility? Such transformations work best where there is an agora, forum, a public space which can be filled by people as "addressees" responding to an "addressor". In the exercise of orality the sound of the voice is as important as the content of the words. But equally these sounds need to be transcribed as texts, as writing. It is here where we find the greatest variation between movements, the quality of the texts, their intentions, and what kind of future solutions they project.

But texts themselves have to be read. Here too we can distinguish between movements. The most inversionary require textual analysis leading to exegetical bonding. The texts must be studied. Not only the words but the word patterns become important. Key terms are drenched in symbolic density. One learns, repeats, and both as prayer and hermeneuti-cally, in the search for hidden meanings. The readers become chosen, a chosen people privileged to know a superior truth. Exegetical bonding is thus one way to establish moral superiority.[36]

One can argue then that the importance of discourse is threefold. Given the right circumstances discourse represents a translation of violent events into a social text. In the process symbolic capital is generated and move-ments become monopolistic. Political violence becomes self-validating and self-sustaining. Language takes on such social force that it touches the ordi-nary with exceptionalism. And not only language itself but body language, oratory, the sound of the voice, the tone of the words, the spell of the signifiers. Orality becomes penetration, a reaching into as well as outward. It touches the private parts of individual experience. As writing, as text, the process of inscription becomes important as method. Interpretation is transformed into epistemology, a mode of revelatory or logical truth. In these terms discourse as political violence and political violence as discourse constitute disruptive interventions in the taken-for-granted world of causes, effects, and probabilities. It is then that words can kill. In the beginning is the act not the word. But word follows closely behind.[37]

In these ways discourse theory enables one to deal with the peculiar and complex connections between violence and ethical beliefs, boundary and boundary violation. It applies best to the activities of inversionary movements, particularly those which resist the conversion of principle into interest and negotiated settlements. The best examples are those where violence is interpreted as meaningful, inversionary, transformational, redemptive, and based on themes of loss, deprivation, vulnerability, marginality, functional superfluousness, victimness, as represented in individuals and groups constituting a "negatized others". But such theory does not apply equally well to all cases. Many types of movements use political violence as a form of exchange, a market in which vectors of force and intimidation rather than the rules of the market prevail and where the object is the pursuit of money and power. In the first instance, where discourse is involved, exchange involves the exchange of meaning. The modes of meaning, or the ingredients which we have described, can be put into diagrammatic form. Each of the components relates to the other. The paradigmatic is represented in myth, which contains elements of magic, which involves metaphoric representation, within narratives which retrieve the past. In turn, projections are embedded in texts, for which events serve as metonymies, to define a logic, embodied in a theory, which is itself syntagmatic. These modes of discourse are employed in going from episode to a "mythologiques" by means of which symbolic capital is produced.

We are now describing a recreated world, a world of real events (many of which are horrific) out of which is derived an invented one – one in which the past literally comes alive in the present. One feels history as blood coursing through the veins. The magic is reproduced in spectacles, deadly theatre and on stage. The logic seems to emerge from the facts of the narrative, its truth value irresistible. Here are some of the working ingredients of this "mythologiques".

These constitute the ingredients we work with in analyzing inversionary discourse. Add to them such contextualizing concepts as terrain, mobilization space, exegetical bonding, and simulacrum, and a dynamic which converts history into purpose, purpose into truths, and truths as logic, and we have the main elements of a discourse theory of political violence.

Structural (abstraction)

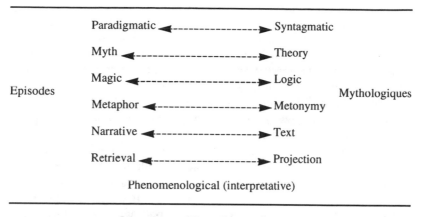

	Paradigmatic ◀----------------▶ Syntagmatic	
	Myth ◀---------------------▶ Theory	
Episodes	Magic ◀---------------------▶ Logic	Mythologiques
	Metaphor ◀------------------▶ Metonymy	
	Narrative ◀------------------▶ Text	
	Retrieval ◀------------------▶ Projection	

Phenomenological (interpretative)

Ingredients of inversionary discourse

Of course, not all political violence is of the nature, as some of the cases here show. Some are what they seem to be, competitive exchanges of power by armed force. They represent the opposite of inversionary discourse, involve no changes in meaning and represent what can be called a violence exchange model. Both models then constitute a spectrum as follows:

IDM   VEM
Inversionary Discourse Model .... Violent Exchange Model
        Symbolic capital   Economic capital

The Model Spectrum

The closer to the IDM end of the spectrum the more totalizing, radical and disjunctive a movement – an inversion of meaning. The closer to the VEM end of the spectrum, not meaning but prestige, power, and wealth are exchanged. The first model is logocentric – it generates symbolic capital. The second is econocentric – it exchanges economic capital. Together, they constitute a continuum along which cases of political violence can be distributed.

IV   SOCIAL MOVEMENTS AS DISCOURSE COMMUNITIES

Before suggesting where the cases in this book fall along this continuum we need to show how, indeed, discourses become embodied in movements which in turn form into discreet discourse communities. We can start with the following propositions. The more inversionary the discourse, the more powerful the symbolic capital, and the more interior such a community becomes and the more willing it is to define its role in terms of rupturing the *doxa*, or shattering and replacing the commonsense of ordinary life. To disrupt routines, to make the ordinary reprehensible, the more moral the goal the easier it is to justify violence as a means of replacing the "is" with the "ought". Just as in Plato logic creates the space for myth, so in inversionary discourse communities myth creates the space for logic. The inversionary discourse defines the "over-determined" moment, to use Althusser's term, and the discourse community is obligated to realize it,[38] which identifies what is the "proper" as distinct from the improper use of violence.[39]

Historians like Hayden White and François Furet have shown how powerful narration becomes in such contexts. It transforms events into fictive truths. By means of the "poetic troping of facts", as White calls it, experiences become symbolically dense, to serve as drenched signifiers.[40] By treating acts of violence as ingredients of narrative, and as well a basis for logical projection, the myth, the moral and the logical intertwine. Embodied in texts that define both a negative pole and a logic of transcendence, sin and redemption, re-enactment as described by Ricoeur,[41] the effect is to turn a discourse community into a chosen people.

Once begun violence develops within its interiority, its own rationality. It sets itself apart and above the rest of society often in the name of those most marginalized. The interpretations and explanations need not be convincing to outsiders but to insiders, followers and supporting clienteles. With validity claims condensed, interests elevated to principle as moral imperatives, organization becomes everything. Rules become binding obligations, categorical imperatives. Transgressors are expelled, made to suffer punitive outrage, the more publicly the better. Such condensed attributes produce their own internal dangers to a movement. They represent potential lines of cleavage. They threaten internal polarization. They personalize difference. Which is why such movements are subject to frequent splitting.

Political movements using violence are also prone to what can be called abstract personalism. It is typical for leaders to make some direct contact with the humblist member and idealize him or her. Not always, but very often it is the marginal who represents the true soul of the people, or the race, or embodies wisdom. The leader's role is to seek it out, to find it, and generalize it within the framework of the myth. What abstract personalism does is to enable leaders to use intimacy and remain aloof all at the same time.

The more inversionary movements will select particular violent events to serve both as turning points and as metaphors which signify connections between the body of the victim and the body of the state, the social body. Codes are established in which in the considered rage at the body politic *viol*-ence equals *viol*-ation. Complicity in loss and suffering may itself only be exorcised by means of violent acts: the uprising of Fanon's black colonials, Foucault's prisoners, madmen, homosexuals, Sartre's anti-intellectual intellectuals, the list is endless.

How a discourse community is formed is thus bound up with the way the discourse is created. In the case of inversionary discourses, such communities tend to be of the last-shall-be-first, variety, or Hegel's masters and slaves.[42] In so far as a dominant history has "erased" their's, what is recounted is an anti-history, a history obliterated by victors, the retrieval of which is itself a way of legitimating violence. The retrieving of revelatory past events provide authenticity and a certain resonance to present ones.

So considered, political violence is an extreme form of interpretative action.[43] The discourse establishes its own communicative fields within which political movements are defined and around which boundaries are established.[44] Organized by means of political and social movements invoking their own legitimizing principles they aim to alter prevailing boundaries, moral and territorial. Political violence is among other things a state of mind impelled by its own hyper-reality and imposed on normal political life.[45] In short, retrievals lead to projection and political violence acquires its own rationality.[46]

To recapitulate, retrieved events and projected solutions are signified and validated as metaphors around which is constructed a narrative of fictive truths, and metonyms for logical truths, theories, or doctrines. In so far as the first is mythic, i.e. the recounting of symbolically significant events in a story with fantastic ingredients, the second is textual, written, 'writ-ualized', read, studied, as with biblical and other sacred writings, or constitutional and legal texts, or the selected works of the instrumental Marxists, Lenin, Mao, and their putative descendants.[47]

Today, as Marxism and its variants have become discredited, or at least gone out of fashion, political violence has taken a neo-ecclesiastical turn. The revival of fundamentalist religious movements is found everywhere. Whereas in Marxism the goal was transformational, the ecclesiastic mode is redemptive, its logic revelatory, its texts biblical. These are the visible transcripts in which truths validate violence. Hegel's masters and slaves are less inverted than saved.

V CASE MATERIALS

A brief word is in order about the case materials before actually turning to them. The arrangement of the essays follows the "exchange" or reciprocity continuum outlined above, which puts symbolic capital at one end and economic capital at the other. The first is logocentric, the second econocentric. The first involves the forced exchange of meanings. The second the forced exchange of money, power, women, and revenge.

All to some degree have engaged in violent acts. In almost all of them, violent acts have served as testimonials to moral claims – claims to a higher legitimacy, rectifying, i.e. the righting of perceived injustices, redemptive, or the salvation of the damned, the penalized, the victim, or the "negativized other". They have enjoyed a certain durability, sustaining themselves organizationally over time, and in some cases intergenerationally. They have had to weather internal factionalism and negotiate crises of leadership. Finally, each of these movements has developed their own "need" for violence. That is they show how violence creates movements, develops its own functions, generates organization and intentionality and, by so doing, becomes a thing in itself, and not easily susceptible to mediation even when its terms are met. Indeed, some movements, if they gain their objectives "lose" as movements. That is, their rationale disappears. A fifth is a more comparative concern. Each represents a type of movement for which it is a surrogate, whether predominantly extra-institutional protest, seeking broad public support through confrontational acts, revolutionary, mobilizing oppositional forces for the forcible overthrow of the state, or terrorism, in which small bands use acts of violence to render the state impotent, turn citizens into bystanders, and force the state to engage in violent retaliation which undermines both its credibility and legitimacy.

Each explores the interior views of those engaging in violence, tracing their evolution, claims, purposes, and aims. All show how violence begets discourse and discourse begets violence. In this regard we regard discourse as a crucial factor in when, or not, violence will be used. It is discourse about them which makes violent events into ingredients in and of interpretation. It is discourse that transforms triggering events into sustained political violence.

It is "exchange" by means of violence which links the cases analytically but shows their differences. Each invokes rather different "discourses" around which they construct the rationale for their movements, and define their aims in terms of predominantly secular or sacral criteria. We have already mentioned that the Sendero Luminoso stand in for a variety of others, from Sri Lanka to India, and which draw inspiration from Maoism. Myth, text, narrative and logic derivative of Mao's doctrines of peasant revolution have been "adapted" by a slightly comic opera "cosmocratic" figure to Peru. At times intensely violent, it also connects, although distantly, to radical Jacobinism and the radical and projective "yearning" embodied originally in the Paris Communes. The implosion of the Russian, the econocentrism of present day China, the deterioration of the Cuban revolutions has left a radical vacuum in to which Sendero has stepped, as the putative carrier of world revolution, the last and purest torch-bearer for the still unrealized final Marxist revolution.

Equal, at least in presumptuousness, was the Red Brigades in Italy which, for a time, played a cat and mouse game with the Italian state which it tried to make stupid and incompetent by daring acts which left the authorities helpless. It also revealed the corruption at the core of the state, a critique which was not as wrong as the solution. The Red Brigades, as a movement, represent other similar ones, like Baader-Meinhof (Red Army Fraction), and Action Directe. These came to regard themselves as the last pure crystalline structure, the radical residue of the "generation of '68", the others having become compromised and corrupted. For the Red Brigades, the story-telling includes a classic tale of betrayal, the proletariat betrayed by the Italian Communist Party. The hegemonic enemy represents world capitalism. Loss is double, the product of the proletariat to a hegemonic bourgeoisie, and the domination of that bourgeoisie, and the state itself, by NATO, the chief instrument of the American military–industrial complex. Terrorism is necessary to up-end the state and reclaim the national patrimony, returning it by means of revolution to its rightful owners.

Neo-Nazism is of course not entirely a German or Austrian phenomenon. It has its counterparts in Belgium and France, not to speak of the United States where a good many of the texts, such as they are, are printed. The logic is "scientific". It repeats the old themes of racial inequalities to create a biocentric model. In this it differs from Italian fascism.

There is denial – of history, and especially the Holocaust. Its retrievals, nostalgia, yearning, too have to do with the double loss, of Wilhelminean or Imperial Germany, and Hitler's, a desire to conquer, triumph, and by the same token, exterminate the pariahs, Jews and gypsies, and immigrant foreigners, Poles, Turks, Iranians, etc.

The IRA, although entirely secular in its objects, combines sacral defining elements, Catholicism, with a somewhat reluctant unity with an Irish Republic most consider reactionary. As a movement it combines extra-institutional protest movements and the struggle against discrimination (in its civil rights campaign) with projective political solutions which are practical rather than transformational. It rescues itself from "terrorism" by insisting that its armed bands are soldiers and the struggle itself an anti-colonial war. It is also interesting because of a "diaspora" factor, like Palestinians in relation to the PLO, or for that matter Jews in relation to Israel.

Both Sri Lankan and Lebanese Shi'ah show the complexities of so called religious fundamentalism, the dangers of using such overkill terms too loosely, and how, from the interior world of violence, how "rational" their violent encounters are. Finally, both Basque nationalism, despite its long historical pedigree, and violence in Colombia, are about money and control, the first as separatism, the second more or less as a self-perpetuating system of violent exchange within the larger framework of a rather fragile, but tenacious, democracy.

In presenting these cases we stress historical context which is particularly relevant to a theory in which retrievals are important. There is of course "historians' history". In this case it is used to examine "fictive history", the stories and myths people use to "order" the events of their lives and circumstances, and historians' history with its careful reconstruction of events. We use the latter to show, where possible, how the former occurs.

Despite their variations each movement poses the question of how to regard the validity of its claims. Each seeks to justify violent means by means of self-validating ends.[48] In short, each in its different way shows how political violence is legitimized. For each violence is a testimonial to its necessity.[49] Each is a surrogate type of political movement, revolutionary insurrection, extra-institutional protest, terrorism, or combinations thereof, and in several contexts, transformational, redemptive, separatist, nationalist, etc.

VI   VIOLENCE AS A POST-MODERN CONDITION

What kinds of conclusion can we draw both from the present approach and the cases to which it has been applied? Each is winding down its violent operations. Are there similarities in the way this process occurs? How is it that after years of reciprocal violence which simply reinforced symbolic capital the process is reversing? Why is it, in other words, that principles hitherto non-negotiable can suddenly turn into interests for bargaining as, indeed, is happening in Northern Ireland and possibly Sri Lanka, and functional boundaries become more important than the ethnic, religious, linguistic, doctrinal ones that have been the source of such bitter controversy? Do such transitions depend on gaining new advantages by means of pluralist and consociational linkages? Or does violence, at some point, reach a point of no further returns? These are difficult questions, in part because when peace and negotiation begin to occur it all seems so self-evident that many wonder what all the fighting was about. For example, today it is difficult for people to even recall what the Biafran War was about. Similarly, revolutionary discourses which were so passionate in places like El Salvador and Nicaragua have simply eroded.

Negotiation does indeed break out, and in the same kind of rashes that political violence does. Which brings us back to the question of discourse. There are discourses of negotiation just as there are discourses of political violence. One question is when and how the latter takes over from the former. Another is whether or not resolution of political violence eliminates the first discourse or whether it continues to lurk under the surface, an anti-history readily mobilizable, waiting for the right retrieving circumstances. Finally there is the question of what those right circumstances might be, how to recognize them, and how to head them off before violence returns. And finally, of course, what of the future: more political violence or less?

Obviously we cannot deal with these matters here and now. But the last problem, the question of future predispositions to violence requires some speculation if not answers. The question of mediation is in some measure at least dependent on developmental opportunities as well as recognition of grievances, rights, and putting an end to discriminatory practices. But the larger question is the extent econocentric solutions based on the exchange of economic capital can work in the absence of real economic growth and development. If so, then the question of political violence, for whatever reasons, and however interpreted, using whatever discourses, is related to the prospects for economic growth and the equitable distribution of material benefits as well as the power to define equity and make appropriate allocations.

If developmental prospects improve will political violence go down? The above analysis would suggest that even if developmental prospects improve political violence will not necessarily go down in any particular situation. But more important, if developmental growth produces negative consequences, it is virtually certain that political violence will continue and become worse.

What are some of the structural changes in the nature of developmental processes which might predispose people to violence? Unless the following "post-modern development predicament" can be somehow resolved the prospect is that it will get worse instead of better. That predicament can be described as follows. Modern developmentalism is based on the premise of unlimited growth, the universalization of the market, and more and more effective access to and participation in economic, social and political institutions. Growth plus equity of allocation constitutes order. Equity is a product of the workings of the political market place, the institutions of party government and accountability of decision-making. We have seen that it is also in part violence-driven, leading to reform when movements do not challenge the fundamental structure of law or the constitutions. Violence- or policy-driven, political development is intrinsically linked to economic development, their "systems" being mutually linked within a double market.[50] Despite instabilities, the result is a moving equilibrium based on growth and reallocation.

Today, the productive process has changed in important ways which make for institutional stickiness, coalitional stalemates, and in particular declining responsiveness to those with the least power and the most need. There are several structural reasons for this. One does not need to lay the blame on politicians of bad faith, although one might in particular cases.

Among the several negative structural tendencies of post-modern growth are several which constitute social pathologies not dealt with in the literature described above. Some of their features are more clearly marked in the United States and Great Britain, than other industrial countries, but the problem is a general one. The first is the changing composition of the labour force. There is a increasingly serious problem of unemployment among some groups turning into unemployability – an underclass problem, or what we will call here a "marginality" problem. It is in part a consequence of changes in the character of innovation leading to growth itself. These factors, among the negative consequences of post-modern development, are driven by enhanced design changes, innovations which produce improved productivity by means of the application of new forms of knowledge. Industrial outputs changed. New technologies and modes of production are increasingly capital-intensive. This produces rising social overhead costs as labour-intensive industries are displaced and workers are either absorbed in lower-paying service jobs, or become marginalized.

Design innovation is essential if a society is to successfully compete in the economic market and have the wherewithal for making appropriate policies. But one social effect is to create a marginalized class, functionally superfluous, taking more out of the productive system than it puts in. Another effect is the emergence of a functionally significant élite which, the more efficiently it does its job, the greater the degree of marginalization it is likely to produce. In turn this generates a variety of responses within the middle spectrum which is more and more pulled in both directions. It must pay the tax on growing social overhead costs. And increasingly it resists reform which, no matter how required in social terms, becomes in real terms for individuals more and more zero-sum.

In so far as rising social overhead costs can be paid for only by increasing productivity, the greater the degree of growth, the more necessary it is to raise productivity, increase the quality of innovation, which by default intensifies the original contradiction. What might be called the predisposition to violence is thus linked to the spectre of superfluous man, i.e. those expelled from the functional roles of society.

Typically those so "expelled" are the insufficiently educated, those lacking work discipline, and those discriminated against (blacks and Latinos in the U.S.; Algerians in France; blacks, Asians, and others in Britain; Turks in Germany, etc.) A permanent condition of marginality produces sub-cultural patterns in some ways similar to the rest of society in terms of highly valued forms of prestige and wealth, but since they are barred from getting them by normal means, tend toward random violence rather than political violence. Marginals are "different" and not only in terms of access to money and power or even styles of life. The sociology of this underclass itself tends to be violent. Conditions with it are characterized by high personal risk and vulnerability. Victims of such a condition frequently gamble with violence. Risk is, after all, a representation of order as odds.[51]

Most of all there is the danger that marginality and functional polarization can also lead to conceptual differences. Between the functionally significant and the functionally superfluous then not only is there institutional inadequacy, but linguistic blockage, deafness at the top to the voices at the bottom, and under the worst of such circumstances a disappearance of the subject: invisibility. It is this which generates a social pathology which might be called a growing predisposition to violence – a predisposition brought about by modern development and which, in the sense that it increases the likelihood of violence, is post-modern.[52]

The more so because those living under high-risk conditions tend to think in metaphorical terms, equivalences of experiences. It is a way of thinking connected to quick identification of circumstances, learning on the basis of experiences, identities and mimetics. The world of functional élites is based on abstraction. To the extent that this is so, the latter becomes both a condition of hierarchy and a form of hegemony, as Foucault and others have pointed out.[53] Schooling and other remedial programmes fail because for the most part they validate failure. Hence, among the negative effects of development is a growing conceptual gap, the one using restricted codes the other extended, a condition which has nothing to do with intelligence. Indeed marginality can produce an extraordinary degree of intelligence, not to speak of organizing ability.

These processes do not apply only to industrial countries. Indeed, they are of infinitely greater magnitude in countries like Brazil or Mexico. And as for Africa, the circumstances there have been steadily worsening for over a decade. Whole countries are more marginal today than they were at independence from colonialism. Such situations provide the raw materials, and in abundance, for the recounting of loss, of specifying grievances, of deprivations of life and liberty, the stuff of story-telling, the playgrounds for cosmocrats and prophets, and the mytho-logics on which violence depends.

Nor will democracy seem too appetizing under such circumstances either, if, in a context of capitalism as a key to growth, inequalities of magnitude grow. For just as socialism has been discredited by its expropriation by a bureaucratic class and failed miserably at an economic level, so capitalism results in the individualization of risk in a context of marginality and functional superfluousness. If, indeed, new discourses should arise, inversionary in character, which do not consider the market as neutral or objective allocational mechanism, then the stage will be set for a new round of attacks on democracy itself.

Nor are there good solutions for the general predicament. The market must be skewed away from equity demands and towards the functional requirements of growth if the results are not to be disastrous. But if, as a result, coalitional stickiness makes the political market-place insufficiently responsive then institutions of democracy will come under attack. In this sense one can raise the question of how far, under the best of circumstances, capitalism as a system and liberalism as a polity can go in the direction of equality. In the past it was development itself which made it possible for faith to override despair. But today, at least among those penalized by the way growth actually works, it is quite the other way around. Despair overrides faith, or at least faith in rationalistic and developmental solutions. Which opens the door for both cynicism about what is and an even greater innocence about what might be. Hence post-modern development predicaments lead to post-modern kinds of discourses, a kind of radical magic realism, which expresses itself both in the turn to religion, to fascism, and to fundamentalism.

The point being that there is a dearth of good solutions to the problems of post-modern development so that political violence leads to discourses which become more and more bizarre. We are heir to such bizarreness in the not so distant past, of movements whose "rationality" was a form of non-rationality, of magic realism and simulacrum, Nazism perhaps being the ultimate case in point with its "logic" of biological mastery and extermination. Religious alternatives may also be quite as bizarre, and they are flourishing where they can gain a foothold. Where older social movements aimed at eliminating barriers to opportunity, or the compensation of victims of economic or social conditions beyond their control, or the fine-tuning of prevailing but inadequate notions of justice and equity, hence enlarging their scope and coverage, today's movements have fewer prospects.

Without suggesting some one-to-one correspondence between negative conditions and political violence, what is happening today and developmentally, increases the possibilities for violent discourse. It provides new venues for story-telling, myth-making and logical projections. It speaks to the collectivization of individual risk, and the creation of symbolic capital among whose for whom economic capital is hard to come by. It revalidates ethnicity, religion, race, language, and doctrinal, as ways of defining redeeming projects, discourses and their communities.

Which brings us back to the beginning, and the question of what kind of individual pathologies are produced by such social pathologies. In our terms, individual pathologies are not psychological twists but real conditions which people experience and suffer very concretely, but more or less as individuals. That, indeed, is what vulnerability, loss, depatrimonialization, dispersion, displacement, diasporization, and negativization as the "other" is all about. These are some of the ingredients which help explain when and why the gap between a general structural predisposition to political violence and the real thing. To bridge the gap one needs, in addition to the spark, the reasons for it. Discourse theory addresses the question of why, under similarly negative structural conditions, political violence occurs in one case and not in another. For even a cursory look at events of violence would suggest that there is no one-to-one correspondence between suffering and an explosive reaction. It remains impossible to identify, for example, thresholds of intolerability, breaking-points beyond which violence is inevitable.

One should not lose sight of course that each political movement will have its own very real and concrete objectives, like the Bosnian Serbs, or other autonomist and separate movements, or proselytizing goals, as with Algerian fundamentalists. But a lot more goes on under the surface of such goals including the search for copeable jurisdictions and a craving for intimacy. But if the territorialization of projected solutions lacks the means for necessary developmental improvements, no here-and-now logic of outcomes will work for long. Hence, while political violence may become even more commonplace, and overcoming-projects proliferate (not least of all in former socialist countries), no good projective solutions are in sight.

Which raises finally the question of democracy and its future. We are now in a celebratory mood about it. It has won over its chief enemies. The old (and stabilizing) polarization is gone. But the reports of its success may be premature. This is not to be critical of democracy. It is not only the best political alternative we know. It is also the only system with open-ends although the rule of law is not only a means but a set of ends in itself, and the foundation for civility, of respect, rights. It is the only system which offers the prospect of continuous self-mediating and self-improving policies according to the rules of incremental and orderly change.

It also requires a self-monitored self-restraint and a self-generating individual dignity. The problem is that for those for whom dignity, through no fault of their own, is hard to come by, civility virtually non-existent, respect a travesty, and above all where democracy falls short of its defined responsibilities, political violence becomes a common and frequent recourse. It is a truism that where people despair of improving solutions, they become more inclined to tear down the institutional framework itself.

We have said that political violence, although a fluctuating phenomenon within democracy, has at every step accompanied its evolution, and with on the whole improving results. Which is why we have argued that in some respects democracy is violence-driven.[54] But if the structural contradictions suggested above are likely to worsen rather than improve, then democracy will itself become vulnerable, and to both increasing political violence and simplistic and unworkable solutions. These are circumstances under which political violence becomes endemic. Indeed, the wave of revolutionary, terrorist and extra-institutional protest movements which occurred in Argentina, Chile, Bolivia, Brazil, El Salvador, Nicaragua, and virtually throughout Latin America in the 1960s, 1970s and 1980s were mainly a result of the kinds of conditions described here. They came to an end in part because Marxist and post-Marxist solutions became discredited – the demise of the Soviet Union – as much as actual repression by armed force and state power. Nor have they the integralist or fundamentalist alternatives that we now see in so many parts of the Middle East and elsewhere. Algeria is the most tragic example in which, denied access to power by the one democratic election held since independence which they won, movements like the Movement Islamique Armée (MIA), with its extremely militant armed wing, the Armée Islamic due Salut (AIS), not only is locked in bitter fighting with the government, but also with its less radical counterpart, the Front Islamique due Salut (FIS). The predisposition to violence caused by extreme

marginalization, functional superfluousness, polarization, also, in such countries, leads to associations and, indeed, includes membership with doctors,
lawyers, professionals of all kinds, many of whom come from the functional
élite, and many of whom formerly were Marxists and radicals of one persuasion or another. This is particular the case in Egypt where the two strongest
groups, Gama'a al-Islamiya, whose spiritual godfather is Sheikh Omar
Abdel-Rahman, and al-Jihad, have spread their influence from Northern
Egypt to Cairo, and of which the popular and often secret mosques serve as
the equivalents to the pubs in Northern Ireland, nuclei for militant congregation. Similarly primed is Turkey, which for so long so determinedly secular
since the days of Kemal Ataturk is experiencing the same kind of functional
polarization just described. One could go on citing examples, Kashmir for
example, Darjeeling, the list is virtually endless. Which raises some pretty
fundamental questions. Will political violence become more doctrinally religious as developmental solutions, both liberal and socialist, become more
visibly inadequate? Will the creation of discourse communities, inversionary
in character, generate greater political uncertainty posing even greater challenges to both civil society and the jurisdiction of the state? Will the elevation of tensed boundaries into points of friction require some setting limits to
pluralism and if so how and by whom is this to be accomplished? Will the
market come to represent disembodied cruelty and become the focus of
antagonism? Will political violence, in so far as it has been incorporated
into the epic recounting of the democratic accomplishment, continue to
serve as a source of moral replenishment? Will both fundamentalism and
market-driven developmental innovation lead to the reinvention of socialism? Or will people so despair of all solutions that if they mobilize at all it
will be for the short term, and for very specific ends, or single-issue politics?
There are many questions and few answers. Perhaps it is the dearth of good
answers which leads people to political violence because, if our analysis is
correct, it supplies answers of its own.

NOTES

1. *New York Times*, 26 January 1995.
2. Perhaps one of the most interesting cases was the Mau Mau uprising in
   Kenya prior to independence. For the concept of inversionary and emancipatory movements, see David E. Apter, "Democracy and Emancipatory
   Movements: Notes for a Theory of Inversionary Discourse", *Development
   and Change*, vol. 23, no. 3 (July 1992) pp. 139–74.

3. One thinks, for example, of Chartism in England, or struggles over the right to organize, to establish trade unionism, the universal franchise, protection of the poor, on up to civil rights, environmentalism, etc.

4. We will refrain from making moral judgements. It is to the ingredients of such discourse that we want to draw attention rather than dwelling on the admittedly very important matter of "good" versus "bad" discourses. On this score the observer must make his or her own judgements. But one might say much the same kinds of things that apply to arguments over just and unjust wars. See Michael Walzer, *Just and Unjust Wars* (New York: Basic Books, 1977).

5. See J. W. Gough (ed.), John Locke, "A Letter Concerning Toleration", in *The Second Treatise on Civil Government and A Letter Concerning Toleration* (Oxford: Basil Blackwell, 1948).

6. On the concept of "discourse community" see David E. Apter and Tony Saich, and David E. Apter and Nagayo Sawa, *Against the State* (Cambridge, Mass.: Harvard University Press, 1984). Both are field studies in which empirical analysis centred on the problem of how discourses of violence are created in a context of violence.

7. See Hannah Arendt, *On Revolution* (New York: Viking, 1963); Walter Laqueur, *The Age of Terrorism* (Boston, Mass.: Little, Brown, 1987); Paul Wilkinson, *Terrorism and the Liberal State* (New York: New York University Press, 1986); Charles Tilly, *From Mobilization to Revolution* (New York: Random House, 1978); Ted Robert Gurr, *Why Men Rebel* (Princeton, N.J.: Princeton University Press, 1970); Sidney Tarrow, *Power in Movement* (Cambridge: Cambridge University Press, 1994).

8. See, for example, Dennis Chong, *Collective Action and the Civil Rights Movement* (Chicago, Ill.: University of Chicago Press, 1991).

9. Work on politically violent personalities goes back to Adorno and associates and their work on 'The Authoritarian Personality', as well as studies of psychological warfare. See T. W. Adorno *et al.*, *The Authoritarian Personality* (New York: Harper, 1950). See, for example, William E. Daugherty and Morris Janowitz, *A Psychological Warfare Casebook* (Baltimore, Mo: Operations Research Office, The Johns Hopkins University Press, 1958).

10. Among the difficulties of using such forms of "system analysis" is the reification of the discourses which each represents.

11. See Tamara Kondratieva, *Bolcheviks et Jacobins* (Paris: Payot, 1989).

12. See, in particular, Crane Brinton, *The Jacobins* (New York: Russell and Russell, 1961), Mona Ozouf, *La fête révolutionnaire, 1789–1799* (Paris: Editions Gallimard, 1976), and Dorinda Outram, *The Body and the French Revolution* (New Haven, Conn.: Yale University Press, 1989). See also, Frederick Brown, *Theater and Revolution* (New York: Viking Press, 1980).

13. Marxist scholarship for a time established itself as the standard interpretation not only for the French Revolution but also revolutionary historiography more generally and particularly in terms of class struggles and the evolution from capitalism to socialism. Historical materialism is compelling in so far as it converts time into space, and space into a simulacrum for the world-as-it-is-becoming. Powerful enough to foster its own myths, orthodoxies, and revisionisms, it has served as a theory of "over-determination" of the superstructures, as in Althusser's examination of Leninism. For an

excellent analysis of the "discourses" of the French Revolution, i.e. the role and content of its discourse, and the discourses used to analyse it, see Roger Chartier. *The Cultural Origins of the French Revolution* (Durham, N.C.: Duke University Press, 1991).

14. See J. L Talmon, *The Origins of Totalitarian Democracy* (London: Secker and Warburg, 1955), Barrington Moore Jr, *Social Origins of Dictatorship and Democracy* (Boston, Mass.: Beacon Press, 1966), and Theda Skocpol, *States and Social Revolutions* (Cambridge: Cambridge University Press, 1979).

15. We cannot do more than hint at some of the very different kinds of literature relevant to political violence, either as exhortation or as analysis, or quite often both. See, for example, Georges Sorel, *Reflections on Violence* (Glencoe, Ill.: The Free Press, 1950); Jack J. Roth, *The Cult of Violence* (Berkeley, Calif: University of California Press, 1980); Franz Fanon, *The Wretched of the Earth* (New York: Grove Press, 1968); and Jean-Paul Sartre, "Foreward", to Jean Genet, *The Thief's Journal* (New York: Grove Press, 1964). See also Guy Debord, *La société du spectacle* (Paris: Éditions Gerard Lebovici, 1987); Roland Biard, *Histoire due movement Anarchiste en France 1945–1975* (Paris: Éditions Galilee, 1976); Jean-François Martos, *Histoire de l'internationale situationniste* (Éditions Gerard Lebovici, 1989); David J. Brown and Robert Merrill, *Violent Persuasions: The Politics and Imagery of Terrorism* (Seattle, Wash: Bay Press, 1993); Ozouf, op. cit.

16. See Michel Foucault, *Discipline and Punish* (New York: Vintage Books, 1979).

17. See Ken Knabb (ed.), *The Situationist International Anthology* (Berkeley, Calif.: Bureau of Public Secrets, 1981).

18. See Celeste Michelle Condit and John Louis Lucaites, *Crafting Equality* (Chicago, Ill.: University of Chicago Press, 1993).

19. Terrorism involves small clandestine groups. Its typical strategy is to make the state appear absurd. Small groups commit individual acts of violence against persons and property, supported by clandestine clienteles. This lends itself to data-collection and manipulation using descriptive variables.

20. Political violence of course involves spectacle. It relies on the use of the media, the outrageousness of the act serving as a triggering mechanism of violation. Through such triggering techniques even small bands can appear to paralyse governments, render the state absurd, helpless, its officers ridiculous and vulnerable rather than hegemonic and remote. It tries to force the state, especially the democratic state, to violate its own principles. It depends on both a kind of grim humour and also on the effects of generalized fear. Small inputs of violence yield publicly significant consequences including withdrawal behind walls in what becomes a garrison state. Its acts are also signifiers of its goals in a ballet in which the public is forced to choose between fear of the state and fear of the movement. Ends and means become difficult to disentangle. If successfully prolonged, terrorism from below generates terrorism from above with both engaging in killing, torture, murder, and death. Hence, terrorism aims at the rupturing of normalcy at its most normal, in the street, the bank, the university, the railroad station, the pleasure yacht, the Olympic games, etc. It seeks to convert state trials into trials of the state and citizens into bystanders rather than supporters of the

•

state. Any ordinary role is complicit, a potential surrogate for the state so that anyone can be a victim, a "valid", target, thus contributing to the idea that society as constituted is dis-ease, that is poisoned, and its supporters uneasy about its validity as a state. For this reason, perhaps, terrorism has become far more feared in the abstract than in the concrete, for in fact the number of actual deaths from terrorism is relatively small.

21.　See, for example, "Direct, Displaced, and Cumulative Ethnic Aggression", *Comparative Politics* (October 1973) pp. 1–16; Hans Toch, *Violent Men: An Inquiry into the Psychology of Violence* (Chicago, Ill.: University of Chicago Press, 1969); and Ronald D. Crelinsten, "International Political Terrorism A Challenge for Comparative Research", *International Journal of Comparative and Applied Criminal Justice*, vol. 2, no. 2 (Winter 1978) pp. 107–26. See also Walter Reich (ed.), *Origins of Terrorism, Psychologies, Ideologies, and Theologies, States of Mind* (New York: Cambridge University Press, 1990). The most important works using relative deprivation theories are W. G. Runciman, *Relative Deprivation and Social Justice* (London: Routledge and Kegan Paul, 1966) and Ted Robert Gurr, op. cit.

22.　See Clark McCauley, "Terrorism Research and Public Policy", in *Terrorism and Political Violence*, vol. 3, no. 1 (Spring 1981).

23.　See in particular *Cultures et conflits* (Paris: Harmattan) and *Terrorism and Political Violence* (London: Frank Cass). There are many other such journals.

24.　A good deal of the systematic analysis of political violence, from espionage to the development of terrorist psychological profiles, the use of gaming, the collection of quantitative data, etc., has focused on terrorism in its various guises.

25.　See Charles F. Andrain and David E. Apter, *Political Protest and Social Change; Analysing Politics* (London: Macmillan, 1995).

26.　Indeed, the ubiquitous of such movements today has won them a curiously ambiguous place within the framework of "normal" politics. Some theorists, such as Alain Touraine, consider them as new social actors, permanently engaging government but episodic in their organization and aims. See Alain Touraine, *La voie et le regard* (Paris: Seuil, 1978) pp. 246–7.

27.　See Werner Hulsberg, *The German Greens* (London: Verso, 1988).

28.　Although its rhetoric can be sufficiently inflammatory to incite killing, as in the cases of doctors and staff of abortion clinics in the US.

29.　For a very different and alternative approach involving rational choice see Dennis Chong, op. cit.

30.　See Apter and Sawa, op. cit., and Apter and Saich, op. cit.

31.　Or, as Gellner puts it, commenting on Descartes: "We speak, therefore the daemon exists. Our power of speech and the recognition of meanings, hence of thought, depends on principles and structures not generally accessible to us. Hence we take them on trust, and are in no position to underwrite the soundness of what and how we think." See Ernest Gellner, *Legitimation of Belief* (Cambridge: Cambridge University Press, 1974) p. 16.

32.　Plato in the Republic treated discourse as the ultimate expression of sociability, the foundation of the city, which depends on the ordering characteristics of discourse as a logical vehicle for the derivation of truth and justice.

Order, in this sense, is the application of discourse in ways designed to make explicit erosive and corrosive actions which depart an ideal pattern, and from the moral and structural harmony which can only be produced by the just society. For Plato decay and an insufficient understanding of the power of discourse went hand in hand. Such an insufficiency of knowledge led to the fractious state, divided by interests and with no group capable of the high-mindedness that truths provide. In this regard, by providing a logic for discourse, and a myth for its reinforcement, Plato offered the first "mytho-logic" as a theory of the state. For a discussion of this see David E. Apter, "The New Mytho-Logics and the Specter of Superfluous Man" in D. E. Apter, *Rethinking Development* (Newbury Park: Sage Publications, 1987). On the concept of "revolutionary Platonism" see Apter and Saich, op. cit.

33. See David E. Apter, "The New Mytho-logics and the Specter of Superfluous Man", pp. 295–324. See also, David E. Apter, "Yan'an and the Narrative Reconstruction of Reality", in Tu Wei-Ming (ed.), *China in Transformation* (Cambridge, Mass.: Harvard University Press, 1994) pp. 207–32.

34. See Jerome Bruner, "The Narrative Construction of Reality", *Critical Inquiry*, vol. 18, no. 1 (Autumn 1991) pp. 1–21.

35. See Walter Benjamin, *Illuminations* (New York: Schocken Books, 1969) p. 94.

36. For the detailed examination of how discourse theory of this kind works see Apter and Sawa, op. cit., and David E. Apter and Tony Saich, *Revolutionary Discourse in Mao's Republic* (Cambridge, Mass.: Harvard University Press, 1994). Both these are empirical studies out of which discourse theory as used here was developed.

37. See J. L. Austin, *How to do Things with Words* (Oxford: Oxford University Press, 1962).

38. See Louis Althusser, *For Marx* (New York: Vintage Books, 1970).

39. Lenin was more concerned to establish the appropriate use of state terrorism. See V. I. Lenin, *The Proletarian Revolution and the Renegade Kautsky* (Moscow: Foreign Languages Press, 1952). See also Leon Trotsky, *Terrorism and Communism* (Ann Arbor, Mich.: University of Michigan Press, 1964).

40. See Jerome Bruner, "The Narrative Construction of Reality", op. cit., pp. 1–21.

41. See Paul Ricoeur, *The Symbolism of Evil* (Boston, Mass.: Beacon Press, 1967).

42. For an analysis of such movements using ecclesiastical discourses, see Alexandre Koyre, *Mystiques, spirituels, alchimistes due XVI siecle allemand* (Paris: Gallimard, 1971), and Christopher Hill, *The World Turned Upside Down* (London: Penguin Books, 1972).

43. See W. J. T. Mitchell (ed.), *The Politics of Interpretation* (Chicago, Ill.: University of Chicago Press, 1982).

44. This is quite different, of course, from the way Habermas would have it. See Jurgen Habermas, *The Theory of Communicative Action* (Boston, Mass.: Beacon Press, 1981) vol. 1.

45. Specific acts become critical both for what they retrieve as turning points from which there is no going back. Examples drawn at random might be the taking of the Bastille, the October Revolution, the Sharpeville massacre in

South Africa, the Homestead Strike for the American labour movement, the 4 May 1919 movement in China, etc. These kinds of events are virtually endless, and include innumerable "black Thursdays" or "bloody Sundays". In short, commemorative events are located which do not stand alone, however, but which are retrieved from an anti-history to take their place as history itself and as acts which are re-enacted in subsequent events.

46. See Bernard Yack, *The Longing for Total Revolution* (Princeton, N.J.: Princeton University Press, 1986).

47. Mao's Little Red Book had many imitators, Khadafi's Green Book, Nkrumah's Black Book, or the Little Blue Book of the Peruvian revolution. See, in particular, Kwame Nkrumah, *Axioms of Kwame Nkrumah* (London: Thomas Nelson, 1967).

48. It is mainly in the context of democracy that political violence retains virtuous qualities: the liberty, equality, and fraternity of the French, the self-evident realization of life, liberty and the pursuit of happiness, etc. The British revolution, the Glorious Revolution of 1688, although more reticent in articulating them, in principle shares the same values. The revolutions that accompanied each constitute universal claims, the moment of their accomplishment redefining time as well as space with each in turn a new Rome, a new Jerusalem, or a new Athens.

49. "Good" violence has been, and today continues to be, defined in terms of democracy.

50. See David E. Apter, *Choice and the Politics of Allocation* (New Haven, Conn.: Yale University Press, 1971).

51. It is also the case that not only are sectors of a population becoming marginalized and functionally superfluous in highly industrial countries like the U.S. and Great Britain, but certain countries as well. For example, most African countries are today far more marginalized in their relationships to the industrial world then they were at independence from colonialism.

52. See William Julius Wilson, *The Truly Disadvantaged* (Chicago, Ill.: University of Chicago Press, 1987.

53. See Michel Foucault, *Discipline and Punish* (New York: Vintage Books, 1979).

54. See Tarrow, op. cit.

2 The Maturation of a Cosmocrat and the Building of a Discourse Community: The Case of the Shining Path

CARLOS IVÁN DEGREGORI

I INTRODUCTION

In the introductory essay a continuum was laid out at one end of which was placed a logocentric model with its emphasis on the violent and disjunctive exchange of meaning, the extreme expression of which was described as symbolic capital. At the other end was an econocentric model in which no exchange of meaning occurred but an exchange of money, power, and women. In the first instance, violent exchange refers to a radical disjunctive conflict by means of which the taken-for-granted pattern of power and the general understanding of the nature of political and economic life is to be ruptured and replaced with a entirely different structure of thought, a different logic of outcomes, and a millennial teleology. The actual violence is intrinsic to the exchange, with political violence legitimized not only by the virtue of its ends but the necessity of the outcomes. Such a movement is not simply on the side of history, it is its agent.

In the case of the Shining Path in Peru, we have an excellent if derivative example of a movement operating in this manner. We might even call it a case of revolutionary Platonism, and for several reasons.[1] First the logic becomes reified as a reality. Secondly, the texts and teachings of Carlos Abimael Guzmán, would-be cosmocrat, a self-styled radical Socrates known as the Fourth Sword of Marxism, chairman of the Communist Party of Peru, produced a number of texts which became virtually sacred documents. Finally, in these documents an outcome is outlined the ambition of which is a timeless and perfect order based on justice.

Known as Presidente Gonzalo, and in the tradition of Mao more than Lenin, he is the philosopher-king of the movement, even though since his capture in September 1992 he has transferred the sceptre to others. Now a "guest" of the Direccion Nacional Contra el Terrorismo (Dincote), he seems a quite different person in his striped prison garb from the feared author of *Gonzalo Thought.*

Which raises three interesting questions: How did such a movement come into being? How did the party get taken over by neo-Maoists like Guzmán? How did a party which had little or no significance come to have such an impact on Peru? (The three questions are interrelated.)

Founded in 1930, the Peruvian Communist Party (PCP) was never particularly important. In the department of Ayacucho, nestled in the south-central Andes, there was a Regional Committee of the PCP, but the name was in fact a pompous misnomer for a tiny and unimportant nucleus. In the early 1960s, the polemic between the Soviet and Chinese Communist parties shook the PCP. Stressed by the struggles between the "Pekingeses" and the "Muscovites", it split in two in 1964. The pro-Chinese PCP "Bandera Roja" (Red Flag) fraction known for being faithful to Mao Zedong's script, rejected the so-called "pacifism" of the pro-Soviets and proclaimed the need for a "protracted people's war" which would surround the cities from the countryside and use peasants as its principal force.

The Ayacucho Regional Committee sided with Bandera Roja. In 1962, a young communist militant, a graduate in law and philosophy from the University of Arequipa, had arrived in Ayacucho and begun working as a professor in the local university. By the time of the party split, this young militant, Abimael Guzmán, was already in charge of the Regional Committee. After the split, Guzmán was named head of Bandera Roja's military commission.

This was no arbitrary assignment. Ayacucho was one of Peru's poorest departments, with one of the greatest proportions of rural population – an ideal setting for the peasant war championed by the Maoists. Furthermore, since Guzmán's arrival, the Regional Committee had ceased to be a small circle of nostalgics. Between 1963 and 1966 it strengthened its work in the university and led the creation of the Ayacucho Federation of *Barrios*, the People's Defence Front, and the Departmental Peasant Federation. Though the latter organization had little representation, the former two urban groups achieved a high degree of legitimacy during the second half of the 1960s.

But the unity of the "Pekingese" did not last long. Soon, the Communist Youth began an "internal struggle" against Bandera Roja's leadership.

One sector of these young communists, who in 1968 broke away to form the Communist Party of Peru "Patria Roja" (Red Fatherland), asked Guzmán to lead them, but he refused. The professor had his own plans. In fact, after his election as regional leader in 1963, Guzmán formed in Ayacucho a "red fraction" which began to develop its own project, doubtless with the ultimate goal of taking over the entire party (PCP, 1988). But in 1968 while the professor was visiting China, which was living through the most heated years of the Great Proletarian Cultural Revolution, Bandera Roja's national leadership launched a preventive strike against the "red fraction".

Clearly, Guzmán's absence at the outset of the internal confrontation made success easier for his rivals, who managed to isolate the Ayacuchanos and keep them from winning converts in other party bases. Even in the heart of the "red fraction's" territory, Guzmán's rivals managed to win over the few peasant bases in the pompously named Ayacucho Departmental Peasant Federation. Towards February 1970, the new division was consummated, leaving the red fraction cornered in urban Ayacucho, especially in the university. Guzmán then turned to building his new alternative: the Communist Party of Peru "Sendero Luminoso" (Shining Path), whose central goal was the "reconstitution" of the ancestral Communist Party, which had been destroyed by opportunists of the left and the right.[2]

Throughout most of the 1970s, Guzmán led a regional political force with only a few minor nuclei in Lima and elsewhere. Nevertheless, towards the end of 1976, Sendero decided that conditions were ripe for the start of the people's war. After a meeting of its Central Committee in April 1977, "dozens of cadres were sent to the countryside to fill the strategic needs of the people's war..." (PCP, 1988, p. v). In 1979 the national leadership decided that the task of "reconstituting" the PCP had been completed and that they had made themselves into "a new kind of party". This party was one capable of destroying the old state and installing a People's Republic of New Democracy which would move without interruption into socialism and beyond it, through successive cultural revolutions, to communism.

And so it was that on the night of 17 May 1980, in the small Ayacucho village of Chuschi, a group of youths burst into the office that held the voting lists and ballot boxes for the national elections scheduled for the next day. The young militants burned the lists and urns in the public square. The event was buried beneath the avalanche of news about Peru's first presidential election in seventeen years. Both the government and all the political forces, including the Marxist parties in the United Left Front, brushed off the incident because at the time Sendero was still a small regional organization. It had, for instance, no presence in the great social movements and national strikes that between 1976 and 1979 shook the nation and helped drive the country's military rulers out of government and back into their barracks. Even Sendero's influence in Ayacucho's university and its People's Defence Front was badly eroded. Until it began its armed actions, Sendero's backbone was overwhelmingly made up of professors, university students, and rural teachers.

Nevertheless, twelve years later, the Communist Party of Peru (Shining Path), which celebrates that now-distant 17 May as the start of the "people's war" in Peru, had become the most important armed movement in contemporary Peruvian history. It is also, surely, the most unique of its kind to appear in Latin America in recent decades. Between 1980 and 1982 Sendero grew at a dizzying pace in Ayacucho's rural areas. In response to its advance, in 1983 and 1984 the armed forces unleashed a brutal counter-offensive that left 5,000 people dead, most of them civilians, in a territory with less than 500,000 inhabitants. Yet Sendero managed to survive and break through the wall around it. It opened new fronts, particularly in the central Sierra and in the Huallaga Valley, the world's largest producer of coca leaf, and in Lima as well. In 1986 it overcame the massacre of almost 300 of its members being held as accused terrorists in Lima's prisons. In January 1988 it held its first Congress. A short time later, now baptized "Presidente Gonzalo", Abimael Guzmán granted a lengthy interview to his party's official newspaper (Guzmán, 1988). The following year, Sendero began to speak of the transition to a "strategic equilibrium" in its war against the "old state".

By 1990, in the twilight of Alan Garcia's government (1985–90), 32 per cent of Peru's national territory and 49 per cent of its population were under military control in areas declared "Emergency Zones" (Peruvian Senate, 1992). Hyperinflation verged on 60 per cent per month, and the economic crisis was wreaking havoc on the population and destroying the state with even greater efficiency than the subversives themselves. In that year's elections, the discredit of all the political parties brought the triumph of Alberto Fujimori, a political outsider whose harsh neoliberal economic adjustment threw more than half the population into extreme poverty. "Let the strategic equilibrium rock the country more", proclaimed Sendero. It decided to speed up the war's pace and move the axis of its actions from the countryside to the city, increasing its pressure on the capital city of Lima.

In 1992 the Senderista offensive reached its high point. Peasants, organized in anti-Senderista "civil defence committees", were murdered by the dozens in Ayacucho and other Andean departments. In the cities, the murder of grassroots leaders and local authorities suffocated and paralysed the social organizations, already greatly weakened by the economic crisis. The explosion of powerful car bombs, both in middle and upper class districts and in poor zones, "Beirutized" Lima. The bombs and murders allowed the success of the so-called "armed strikes" with which Sendero immobilized and panicked Lima, a chaotic and starving metropolis of more than 7 million inhabitants, one-third of the nation's population, in whose poorest neighbourhoods 100,000 war refugees crowded together.

Concern now began to go beyond Peru's borders. There was talk of Senderista or pro-Senderista circles in Bolivia, Chile, Argentina, and Colombia. In March, the U.S. Congress held hearings on the situation in Peru. In them, Assistant Secretary of State for Latin America Bernard Aronson warned of the danger of "the third genocide of the twentieth century" if Sendero triumphed. Shortly thereafter, a Rand Corporation report announced the possibility of Lima's being surrounded and the government's collapsing (McCormick, 1992).

As if to prove McCormick right, on 22 and 23 July a ferocious armed strike swept Lima. Sendero's cells celebrated with a toast to "the consolidation of the strategic equilibrium" and began preparations for the start of the "Sixth Grand Military Plan", which would bring them to "struggle for power throughout the country".

Shortly before, on 5 April 1992, Peru's besieged democracy had stumbled, shoved from behind by President Alberto Fujimori himself, who with armed forces backing closed Congress and placed himself at the head of a "government of national reconstruction". Pressured by international public opinion, the U.S. and the Organization of American States (OAS), Fujimori found himself forced to convoke elections for a Constituent Congress, which were seriously threatened by Sendero. Meanwhile, Sendero's plans seemed to advance like clockwork, as Lima, lost in a sort of fatalistic paralysis, waited for the new wave of terror.

And then, on the night of 12 September, Abimael Guzmán and a good many members of Sendero's top leadership were captured without firing a shot.[3] Literally from one day to the next, a vast feeling of relief swept Peru, touching every corner of its social and geographical diversity, its depth a direct inverse proportion of the fear and demoralization that had gripped the country until 12 September.[4]

After a few weeks of confusion, and despite ongoing police blows that landed the majority of its Central Committee in jail, Sendero once again began to escalate its military actions trying to carry out Guzmán's final directive. In police custody, awaiting the trial that would condemn him for life to an island prison, Guzmán had delivered a speech warning his followers to advance their Sixth Grand Plan.

However, a year after, on 1 October 1993 came a new surprise. During a speech at the United Nations General Assembly, President Alberto Fujimori disclosed a letter sent by Abimael Guzmán asking him for peace talks. The move was totally unexpected coming from the leader of a party that had built its identity around violence and one that considered negotiations a synonym of treason.

Sendero's answer came as soon as its badly battered logistic apparatus allowed them. In a *Declaration* dated 7 October, the new Central Commmittee rejected the letter as a "clumsy and ridiculous hoax". However, in the following weeks new letters and TV speeches by Guzmán himself proved that the call for peace was not a deceit. By early 1994 Sendero split into two fractions. One accepted Guzmán's new turn; the other decided to keep on waging protracted war. But any possibility to reach strategic equilibrium has disappeared. Sendero's military actions have gone back to the level of 1981.

This surprising collapse shows that Sendero's fate was inseparable from Guzmán's. For beyond its military strength and ideological cohesion, Sendero is, like no other party in Peruvian history, a discourse community forged by and centred around a cosmocrat.

In the following pages we will analyse how the now-prisoner's political personality branded Sendero's history from the start, and in recent years managed to project itself over the entire nation. We will first review the factors that made it possible for this untimely Peruvian Maoism to emerge successfully. We will briefly outline the predisposition to violence born of Peru's economic structure, history, and political culture. Based on these predispositions, we will be able to see how Sendero Luminoso, with Abimael Guzmán as their cosmocrat figure, produced a primitive accumulation of symbolic capital which allowed it to become a "discourse community". This community allowed certain marginalized sectors, not the country's poorest but indeed functionally superfluous, to collectivize their risk and so become willing to die and to kill in the name of an "overcoming project". They did so within an organization which, by their own definition, has turned into a "war machine", able effectively to channel their pain, now become rage. That is why the request for peace talks had such a devastating and definitive impact on Sendero.[5]

To develop my argument, I use concepts which David Apter presents in the introduction to this volume.

II THE STRUCTURAL CONTEXT

In the past half century, the type of capitalist development which took place in Peru accentuated the breaches between Lima and the rest of the country, between the coast and the highlands, between rich and poor, and between the *criollo*, *mestizo*, and indigenous populations. Geographical, regional, class and ethnic gaps widened to make up a "tendentially" marginal pole: provincial-rural-Andean-poor-*mestizo*/indigenous. I would underscore the word "tendentially", with a tendency towards, because not all those who belong to this pole are in fact functionally superfluous. Moreover, though indeed Sendero sprang up precisely *there*, it was not an indigenous peasant movement, a tributary of the Andean millenarianism which in past centuries was the motor behind rebellions like those of Tupac Amaru and Tupac Ccatari.[6]

Sendero emerges from the encounter, in the University of Ayacucho during the 1960s, between a *mestizo* provincial university élite and a youthful social base which was also provincial and either *mestizo* or *cholo*.[7] The former were professors, the latter university students. Favre (1984) described the process somewhat more brutally as the meeting between a lumpen intelligentsia and a *cholo* milieu which had not resigned itself to life on the margins of society.

Why *mestizos*, intellectuals, and youth? Why in the Andean region of Ayacucho? Let us begin by answering the second question.

The pattern of growth designed to strengthen the internal market, of industrialization through import substitution, which predominated in Latin America after the Second World War tended to favour urban actors over rural ones, industrialization over agriculture. In Peru's case, the result was the economic and social debacle of Andean Peru, where until mid-century inefficient oligarchical landowners had dominated. The internal market/populist model (Cavarozzi, 1991) simply left them on the sidelines, allowing the massive peasant land seizures between 1958 and 1964 to deliver the death blow to a system unable to adapt to the new demands of the market. But several factors conspired against the consolidation of a new class of small and medium rural property owners to replace the old system of landlords and serfs. First, the development model fuelled the massive migration of the most dynamic rural sectors to the cities. The impoverished "notables" of the small cities sent their sons to the capital, and the peasants who might have been most apt to become *kulaks* followed.

From 1969 on, the reformist military government (1968–80) tried to fill the vacuum left by the old landowning élites with the most radical agrarian reform in South America. But the reform only hastened the breakdown of Andean society. It reverted the tendency to divide large landholdings and develop a peasant economy. Instead the government formed huge agricultural production co-operatives which functioned under state oversight. When, after 1975, the military government went into a crisis which at a deeper level announced the crisis of the internal market/populist matrix, the great associative enterprises were left like semi-abandoned and demoralized garrisons, scattered in the power vacuum left by the state's retreat from the countryside.

Different actors leapt forth to fill this relative vacuum: the agrarian bourgeoisie of some coastal valleys; drug traffickers in ever-expanding sections of the high jungle; new local powers – merchants, lawyers, police – which tried to continue plundering the highland peasants; peasant organizations including self-defence patrols (*rondas*) and federations, which confronted and competed with the new powers; non-governmental organizations; churches; leftist parties; and Sendero Luminoso.

At stake was the building of a new order. Sendero's growth over the past decade can thus be seen as the violent construction of a totalitarian order amidst the ruins of the old oligarchical order, in competition with a state which, after the 1978–80 transition to democracy and the exhaustion of the internal market/populist model, proved incapable of sweeping away those ruins and building a modern and democratic system. Sendero also competed with the disorderly efforts of social organizations and political parties to build more democratic orders on a local or regional basis.

But we must not get ahead of ourselves. What we want to emphasize here is how the development model marginalized the agriculture and the Andean societies which for centuries had played an important role in the Peruvian economy and politics.

Ayacucho was one of the departments to be hit hardest and earliest by this kind of development. From very early on, Ayacucho had played an important role in Peruvian history. Between the seventh and eleventh centuries, it was the seat of the first Andean empire, the Wari. During the Inca Empire (fifteenth to sixtenth centuries), one of the Inca state's few urban-bureaucratic centres was located there and given control over a vast region. During colonial times, the mining of mercury for the silver mines at Potosi, coupled with feudal agriculture, artisanry, and mule-driving, brought the region's golden age. Churches, monasteries and mansions were built in the regional capital, then called Huamanga. The city was the seat of a bishopric and of the viceroyalty's second university, which was founded in 1667 and baptized San Cristobal de Huamanga. The decline of the Huancavelica mercury mines affected the region, but it was able to maintain its territorial articulations and its relevance through agriculture, cattle raising, manufacturing, and trade.

Capitalist development after the late nineteenth century, and most clearly during this century, had a negative effect on the region. Ayacucho possessed no resources of interest for foreign or domestic capital; nor did it give rise to an economic pole with sufficient endogenous dynamism to link it with leading sectors of the national economy. The university's closing towards the end of the last century was the first warning bell. By the 1930s, the region was in absolute decline. During the 1970s, the region covered by the old colony of Ayacucho, today divided into three departments (from north to south Huancavelica, Ayacucho, and Apurimac), was the poorest in the country. And of the ten poorest provinces in the country, three were in Apurimac, one in Huancavelica, and two in Ayacucho–Cangallo and Victor Fajardo, precisely where Sendero began its armed actions in 1980.

In order to explain the regional situation, in addition to poverty we must keep in mind the landowner exploitation, the serf-like oppression, and the ethnic discrimination that flourished there: an archaic structure where until the 1950s caste stratification divided the population into lords and serfs, *mistis* and Indians.[8] But neither poverty nor oligarchical oppression suffice to provide us with a mechanistic explanation for the violence, particularly the kind of violence, that devastated the region.

Yet even though Ayacucho and its neighbours formed the most depressed region within Peru's unequal and centralist development, they were not exotic pockets nor "zones of refuge". As early as the 1915–40 period, according to Urrutia *et al.* (1988), the Ayacuchanos were exploring ways to escape their crisis: the sale of land by landlords to merchants and public officials, as well as to peasants from neighbouring communities and even serfs from the haciendas themselves; the construction of a railroad line that would link Ayacucho to the capital, which in the end was never built; a somewhat more successful highway-building effort; the colonization of the jungle areas of the Apurimac River in the north-eastern part of the department, areas which by the 1970s had become the department's only dynamic rural zone and to which the coca crop spread during the 1980s; migration, which until mid-century was practically the only hope of escape from a miserable and oppressive situation,[9] and education.

Increasingly as the century went on, along with chapels, roads, and irrigation canals, "communities built schoolhouses and either asked the authorities or themselves paid for a teacher" (Urrutia *et al.*, 1988). Not only the peasant communities, but even the hacienda serfs fought for their children's education (see Diaz Martinez, 1969; Ortiz, 1968). According to Norman

42   *The Legitimization of Violence*

Gall (1974), during the 1960s the number of primary school students in Ayacucho grew at a rate of 13.6 per cent annually, compared with 5.3 per cent nationwide.[10] And if primary and secondary educational advances were noteworthy, at the university level the growth was spectacular.

The local university had been closed in 1885, amidst the national débâcle that followed Peru's defeat in the War of the Pacific (1879–83). By the middle of this century, demands for its reopening had intensified, especially among the region's middle classes. Finally, in 1959 this longing was fulfilled and the university opened its doors once again. From the start, it seemed determined to be something more than just another university. A decade before Peru's other universities, it adopted more modern structures: credit systems, semester courses, tests of aptitude rather than of knowledge for admission. The university also sought to be of service to its region by training rural engineers, acquiring experimental funds, building a ceramic factory, and carrying out research programmes. To support its plans, the university obtained significant foreign support, especially from the European countries (see UNSCH, 1977; Degregori, 1990). In general it was viewed with admiration and esteem by the majority of the population. At the same time, young professors from around the nation flocked to San Cristobal. Among them we find Abimael Guzmán and many of those who around 1963 made up the "red fraction".

San Cristobal's reopening was part of a national trend. Between 1960 and 1970, the number of universities in Peru grew from seven to thirty, while the number of students shot up from 30,000 to 110,000. But in Ayacucho, the growth of the university-educated population sped up until it nearly doubled the national average: 501.6 per cent versus 256.3 per cent.[11] The 229 registered students of 1959 had quintupled by 1966, when the university faced its first crisis. A year earlier, unrest had swept the region as the Castroite guerrillas of the Movement of the Revolutionary Left (MIR) and the Army of National Liberation (ELN) established an armed group in the Ayacucho province of La Mar. The government saw San Cristobal as a centre of subversion and tried to suffocate it economically by cutting off its funding.

The rector turned to the social forces of Ayacucho to fight for an adequate budget. His plea won the backing not only of neighbourhood associations, craftsmen, and market women, but also of medium- and large-scale merchants, professional guilds, and even some members of the Superior Court. In this manner, a very concrete set of circumstances allowed the university to turn its economic and ideological weight into political power. At the prompting of the most politicized sectors, especially the Abimael Guzmán's "red fraction", a majority of the participants agreed that the struggle transcended the university walls. The group decided to form the People's Defence Front of Ayacucho, the first of its kind and the forerunner of those which by the middle of the next decade would spring up around the country. Soon after, San Cristobal won the restoration of its funding, and the victory consolidated the newborn organization, which from 1966 to 1969 experienced a true golden age.

The 1960s thus represented a decisive rupture in Ayacucho's history. The university's reopening produced a social earthquake that came amidst the decline of the region and of its traditionally dominant classes. Taking advantage of that decisive moment, with the oligarchical landowning caste beating a retreat and the new bureaucratic and commercial sectors linked to the state's expansion yet to arrive (they would do so during the 1970s, during the first phase of the military government, although in some ways the university itself was a sort of contradictory advance guard of that expansion), during the 1960s a new élite based in the university and the Defence Front seized its chance and became a sort of alternative power in Ayacucho. The new counter-power was feared and respected by the traditional local powers and even by the central powers. And at its heart the "red fraction" was sprouting.

During the 1966 crisis, the university had proven through practical experience the strength its popular backing gave it. It then plotted a strategy of rapid growth. By 1969, just three years later, the university population had once again doubled. It doubled again by 1974 and reached a demographic peak in 1977 with 7,600 students. By 1981, of twenty-four departments Ayacucho held eleventh place in population with a university education. During those years, university students represented 10 per cent of the city's total population. If we consider only the over-15 population, the figure exceeds 20 per cent of the total. And if we include secondary students, the figure becomes extraordinary. Gall (1976) calculates that university and secondary students made up one-fourth of Ayacucho's total population in 1972.

We must consider the high school students because they played an important role during those crucial years. The contrast with other departments is noteworthy. After the late 1950s, throughout much of the Andes there was a multiplication of peasant organizations invading the great traditional landed estates. But in Ayacucho the social movement of greatest impact was not a peasant struggle for land, but the struggle for free education waged in 1969 by the high school students of Ayacucho and Huanta, the department's second city, some 50 kilometres north of the capital.

In March 1969, the military government passed a Decree Law cutting back free secondary education, a right that had been in force since 1953.[12]

Throughout the country, parents' associations protested the measure. In a few isolated places there were demonstrations and fleeting takeovers of school buildings. But only in Ayacucho and Huanta did the protest become massive and involve other social sectors.

For two months, the region experienced a crescendo of agitation. A Secondary Student Front was organized in Huanta and on 1 June it decreed an indefinite general strike in the schools. Two weeks later, the movement spread to the high schools of Ayacucho, where the United Front of Secondary Students (FUESA) was formed. Finally, the state's response set off the explosion. On 21 June police flooded Ayacucho's central market with tear gas. The market, whose gates the market vendors had closed, was filled with shoppers and vendors.

That day the demonstrations, which had until then been basically student demonstrations, spread to include much of the population. That night several leaders of the People's Defence Front were arrested. At dawn on 22 June, thousands of students and *barrio* dwellers took over the city. The next day, thousands of peasants invaded Huanta. The government sent special forces to repress the movement. The repression left over ten people dead and hundreds wounded, but even greater than the loss of human life was the impact the movement had in the regional *imaginaire*.

In both cities, the movement was highly spontaneous; in Huanta almost entirely so and in Ayacucho significantly so. The university was on vacation, and the "red fraction" was wrapped up in the tensest moment of its internal struggle within Bandera Roja. Their miscalculation of the student strike's importance was so great that the night before the city was taken over, when police had already teargassed the market and disorder was spreading throughout the city, the fraction's leadership met in the home of one of its members, without taking any security precautions. They paid dearly for their mistake when, upon leaving their meeting, several of them were arrested, including Abimael Guzmán. Nevertheless, though they had underestimated the Ayacucho movement, the fraction had been present in it.

To summarize, in the one hand the movement voiced the enormous importance the region placed on education as a channel through which the new generations hoped to become functionally relevant. In Ayacucho's case, it underscored the Defence Front's high degree of legitimacy. In Huanta, where the imprisonment of the peasants' legal advisor sparked the social explosion, it also highlighted the weight of *mestizo* professionals linked to the peasantry.

But most important of all, as we said above, was the movement's impact on the regional *imaginaire*. The student strike and the repression which followed seem to have condensed profound historical tendencies and struck highly sensitive chords. In the years that followed in Ayacucho, *everyone* had a story to tell about the events of June 1969. They were inversionary tales, many of them telling the extraordinary actions of the elderly, women, children, or Indians, people who "by nature" are subordinate. Let us look at only a few examples, taken from a doctoral dissertation written three years after the events (Castillo, 1972) and from a literary journal called *Narración*, edited by intellectuals who at the time were close to the "red fraction". Castillo (1972) recalls: … the daring of an old woman who, under full fire and while the bullets which had killed a child and a father from San Juan Bautista were still smoking, with her slingshot forced the police to retreat.

Narración preferred chronicles and testimony:

Ayacucho, 6/21/69. From the New Bridge, a child with a slingshot flings rocks at the police. One of them fires his rifle and takes the child's life. Another child, brother to the fallen one, runs the length of the bridge to the corpse, but is struck down by another rifle shot.

Huanta, 6/22/69 (an old man's testimony). "Oh, girl, my courage returned that day. My wife, clinging to me, crying, 'What are you going to do, you'll only be cannon fodder, don't go out.' And I, to console her, said, 'My time for dying has already passed, dear, after 87 years death has forgotten about me.' Lost among the people who were running towards the *Plaza de Armas*, I mixed with the peasants. Then the bullets began. The women, with their babies, at their husbands' sides, and the bullets knocking them down by twos, by threes, with machine gun fire. As one fell, another ran to help him and – a bullet for him, sir! Like corncobs the dead and wounded piled up in the park, and the peasants said, 'Soon they'll run out of their bullets!' And they kept on offering their bodies to the bullets, throwing stones and slingshots … ."

There had been episodes of violence like that of June 1969 in the past, but this time the conditions were better for them to become events full of meaning. In the Ayacuchanos' accounts, it could be seen that out of certain events you could build myths with fabulous, magical, extraordinary traits, and in this way open a "space" for logical explanatory theories to fill (Apter, 1992). The red fraction and its leader, Abimael Guzmán, would be the agents to work out this explication throughout the 1970s and to build an "overcoming project".

III   THE SYMBOLIC CONTEXT

A number of factors made it easy for Sendero Luminoso to concentrate on elaborating a mytho-logic and forming a cosmocrat, Abimael Guzmán, capable of transforming myth into a logical discourse which "opened" the minds of his young students to possibilities which hitherto had seemed out of reach. I will mention here a few of these factors. The adverse results of the internal struggle within Bandera Roja reduced Sendero to a regional group and even cost them their few peasant bases, which remained with "Bandera Roja". Almost simultaneously, the repression of the free education movement and the long imprisonment of the main leaders of the People's Defence Front (captured in June 1969), weakened that organization, which would never recover the strength and the legitimacy it had enjoyed until 1969. The military government also aided the Front's decline with its reforms, which modernized the country and even "semi-feudal" Ayacucho, whose capital city grew and consolidated into a commercial and bureaucratic centre.[13] Relieved of the responsibility for solving the concrete problems of important social bases, Sendero found it easier to set aside extra-institutional protest that sought to force the state to listen, and concentrate instead on building a "revolutionary overcoming project" which sought to destroy it.

At the same time, we must also keep in mind the key moments in the evolution of the "cosmocrat". The first was his trip to China in 1967–8 at the high point of the Cultural Revolution, "the greatest political event humanity has seen" (PCP, 1991, p. 2), when the young Red Guards raised the flag of the Little Red Book to "bombard the bourgeoisie's general headquarters", embedded in the very leadership of the party. The youth, the book, the internal enemies – these were all familiar elements for Professor Guzmán, who at the time was a protagonist in the baroque internal struggles of the "Pekingese" groups. From prison, he would recall the trip to China with some nostalgia and great pride:

> I was in China in 1967, in the most advanced political school on earth. The pride that as a communist one can have in being able to nourish oneself on such highly solid theory. For me, it left an indelible mark. I learned a great deal. The party, as I have often said, owes immensely to the Chinese Communist Party, immensely. It has marked us to our depths for all the future . . . . (Guzmán, 1993)

A second key moment may have been the imprisonment he suffered in 1969, and then again in 1970. Perhaps it opened his eyes to the possibilities that closed universes offer for condensing meaning and consolidating the faithful. Admittedly, this possibility is conjecture, but I base it on Sendero's highly important work with imprisoned militants during the 1980s. At the same time, his untimely imprisonment, at the most heated point in the internal struggle, seems to have prejudiced him against the spontaneity of the masses. Thus, though it is true that at certain levels mass action was to be encouraged and praised, it was critical that the party regulate and direct their actions because: "What is fundamental for Maoism is power...[therefore] the Party should and must direct absolutely everything. Everything, with no exceptions" (*El Diario,* no. 616, 21 January 1992, p. 9).

And there is also the personality of the future cosmocrat himself. In a book written by a friend, we find the following description, which quite possibly had been discussed with the Senderista leader and corresponded with his self-image:

Abimael Guzmán must be unique among revolutionary intellectuals, one who comes to Marxism not for ethical reasons, as an existential search or cathartic therapy to overcome certain obsessions, but by the path of reason, after a fiery struggle in his own spirit between idealism and materialism.   (Gutierrez, 1988, pp. 256–7)

And even before that, "Abimael Guzmán's adolescence and youth were a secret, tenacious, unbending, ardent adventure in thought" (Gutierrez, op. cit.).

The combination is worthy of note. From the start, Guzmán tried to distinguish himself categorically from romantic, impassioned leaders such as, perhaps, Che Guevara. Guzmán also distinguished himself, and the words carry a hint of disdain, from those who "come to" Marxism as "cathartic therapy". From the beginning, Guzman emphasized "the path of reason", an emphasis directly linked with Sendero's likewise obsessive emphasis on the scientific nature of Marxism. Contradictorily, however, in the same paragraph Guzmán appears entangled in fiery struggles and ardent adventures. His combat is like that of the old Church Fathers, whose spirits (and bodies) were the field over which devastating battles between good and evil were fought; or like the mystical poets, consumed by a spiritual love for the Divine.

All told, a fascinating character. A somewhat chubby professor wearing thick glasses, so outwardly calm, so conservatively dressed. Taking his daily stroll through Ayacucho's *Plaza de Armas*, he gave no clue to the fires burning within him. His was, indeed, an "adventure in thought", whose first great chapter would be written throughout the 1970s.

Defeated in Bandera Roja's internal struggle and stricken by the repression of June 1969, at the opening of the decade "in all of Peru there were fifty of us, totally and fully dedicated" (Guzmán, 1993). Guzmán and his battered followers began their spiritual long march and sought refuge in the University of Ayacucho, where they would build their Andean Yan'an. While doing so they enjoyed, precisely between 1969 and 1973, undisputed sway over the university, in whose administration they held decisive influence. Abimael Guzmán himself was the university's personnel director at the time, in charge of all professors and employees.

In 1971 and 1972, Sendero's cadres formed the "Mariategui Centre of Intellectual Labour" and, with Guzmán leading them, plunged into an exhaustive study of the Marxist classics, especially the works of José Carlos Mariátegui.[14] While they did not live in caves, they did meet semisecretly after working hours in the university's classrooms and laboratories.

Against the current of other Peruvian Marxist groups, which in those years were instead trying to leave the universities and "go to the masses", Sendero concentrated itself within the university. They found theoretical justification for this shift by defining the military regime as "fascist". According to their analysis, the popular sectors which in its early years lent majority support to the government were misled by fascism. All of the Peruvian left in one way or another also succumbed, as did the university student movement. The University of Ayacucho, with Sendero Luminoso inside, thus appeared as the final bastion of anti-fascist resistance in Peru. Under this analysis, they found it legitimate to hole up in the university and even to accept that, as university authorities, their leaders apply the "fascist university law" passed by the military government in 1969. It is not arbitrary for us to say that their real reason was the need to protect both the party, in its moment of greatest weakness, and its "head", then engaged in an "adventure in thought". Their adventure in some ways resembled those of the medieval monks sheltered in their monasteries, trying to save Western knowledge (in this case Marxist–Leninist orthodoxy) or to find a philosophical touchstone (the overcoming project), while around them everything collapsed before the onslaught of the barbarians (the "fascist" government).

In the years that followed, that nucleus of professors became the first link in the chain that would one day link the cosmocrat at one end with the peasantry at the other. University students, among whom Sendero intensified its proselytizing, formed the second link in the chain. Here Sendero found favourable conditions for its efforts. First, its audience grew after 1969, as the university's growth rate accelerated and a thousand new students began entering each year. Among the incoming students were many who as high-schoolers had led the free education movement. To many of these, Sendero seemed the principal trustee of the 1969 experience.

Using their hegemony among the university authorities, Sendero concentrated its professors in the courses of the so-called "Basic Cycle"[15] and adapted the curriculum to its needs. Soon, a course on Historical Materialism replaced the Introduction to Social Sciences, Dialectics of Nature replaced Biological Sciences, and Dialectical Materialism filled the philosophy and even the physics courses. Before long, similar courses entered the curricula for different degrees, especially the social sciences and education, where Sendero centred its greatest efforts.

But beyond, and in addition to, its own efforts and situation during the 1970s, Sendero's discourse was echoed by a significant sector of the student body. During the 1970s Marxism–Leninism, or classical Stalinism, which was still the mould for Sendero's discourse, spread like wildfire not only in Ayacucho but in state universities throughout the nation. In another work, I called this phenomenon "the handbook revolution". The texts of the Soviet Academy of Sciences, with authors like Politzer and the Chilean Martha Harnecker, as well as the Peking Foreign Language Editions, were widely distributed among professors and students, creating a kind of common sense that favoured the expansion of a proposal like Sendero's beyond Ayacucho's borders during the 1980s.

IV   THE WORD IN THE TEXT/THE TEXT IN THE WORD

The handbook revolution was helped along by the way in which took place the aforementioned massification of Peruvian universities. The academic decline was accelerated thanks to what Lynch (1990) calls "massification without a project". As the élites defected, retreated, or moved to new private universities, they left behind a vacuum in the national universities that the handbooks would fill. But to our way of seeing, there were even deeper reasons for the extreme diffusion of these handbooks. Allow me to take, by way of explanation, a brief historical digression.

As is often the case in Peru, we must return to the beginning and recall the Cajamarca ambush in 1532, when the Inca went to meet the Spaniards. The Spanish chaplain Father Valverde came forward with a book in his hands. It was the Bible, and Valverde told Atahualpa, "This is the word of God". The Inca lifted the book to his ear, heard no words, and threw the book to the ground. By profaning the sacred book, Atahualpa "justified" the Conquest.

From the beginning, then, mastery of the Spanish language, reading, and writing were the instruments of domination. There thus emerged a society based on deceit, made possible among other factors by the ruler's monopoly over the Spanish language, reading, and writing. Since then, Peru's conquered peoples have swung between resignation and rebellion. Of course, these are two idealized extremes, when in reality the two states often blend together and even join in a contradictory mix. The concept "resistant adaptation" (Stern, 1987) identifies many of these intermediate situations.

Resignation is even internalized in myths. One, recalled by Marzal (1979, p. 12), says that the *mistis* are creation's *chanas*, God's youngest children and therefore the most indulged. God has given them the gift of speaking Spanish and of reading and writing, which is why they can "do as they please". Their domination is arbitrary, and in the words of Gonzalo Portocarrero (1993), it is a "total domination".

The other attitude is of rebellion, which in turn swings between two idealized extremes: on the one hand, Andean culture's retreat into itself and rejection of the West; and on the other, the appropriation of the conquerors' instruments of domination. Both variants can be traced back to the sixteenth century (Degregori, 1990). What interests us, however, is the predominance during the twentieth century of the second form of rebellion, which seeks to appropriate for itself the rulers' instruments of power. Among those instruments, education was key. Wresting from the *mistis* their monopoly on knowledge was the Andean equivalent of Prometheus stealing fire from the gods, thus destroying one of the bases of their "total domination".

As this century has advanced, the drive by the Andean population to conquer education has proven exceptional. Peru moved from fourteenth place among Latin American countries in 1960 to fourth in 1980 in terms of educational coverage. Meanwhile, among the approximately seventy nations which the United Nations labels "countries with medium levels of development", the average percentage of 18- to 25-year olds with secondary or higher education rose from 17 per cent in 1960 to 52 per cent in 1980. Over the same period in Peru, however, the percentage rose from 19 per cent to 76 per cent. This drive for education greatly surpassed the state's efforts and indeed fought against a current of state withdrawal from education. After the mid-1960s, the state's relative investment in education began to decline (Degregori, 1990). I would posit, as a hypothesis, that the impetus towards education was stronger among the Andean populations than among the lower class *criollos*.

But what do the people of the Andes seek in education?[16] Certainly they seek very pragmatic weapons for their democratic struggle against the *mistis* and the local powers. They want to learn reading, writing, and arithmetic. But in addition to these, they also seek the *truth*. Shortly after the uprising for free education, gathering material for his thesis on the movement, Aracelio Castillo (1972, p. 272) asked a Huanta peasant leader how he saw the peasants' situation. The leader replied:

> Compared with the abuses of earlier times, sure, things are a little better now. But he [the peasant] needs to be taught, he needs someone to orient him, he needs courses...to see if that way he can progress, free himself from slavery, from deceit. Otherwise, he'll go on being poor and exploited.

Education thus meant "freeing oneself from deceit", and can therefore take on explosive characteristics. At the height of the free education movement, a communiqué from the Ayacucho People's Defence Front declared: "The military junta has abolished free education because they know perfectly well that when the sons of the workers and peasants open their eyes, their power and wealth are in danger" (Castillo, op. cit., p. 205).

Thus education is seen as victory over deceit and, consequently as a rebellion and a threat to the dominant classes. But although the struggle for education has obvious democratizing effects at the social level, it does not necessarily imply the advance of democratic ideas in the political and cultural spheres. If we return to the testimony of the leader from Huanta, for example, we recall his saying that the peasant "needs to be taught", and "needs someone [implicitly an outsider] to orient him". The old hierarchical order is thus transferred to the relationship between the teacher (*mestizo-urban*) and the student (peasant-indigenous). Thus education may massify without substantially breaking down the concepts of traditional society.

When Castillo (op. cit., p. 272) asked the same leader what aspirations he would wish for the peasants of Huanta, the real complexity of peasant goals shone through:

> The greatest aspiration is progress for the people in the countryside. It would be, well, that their helpers, or rather their guides, orient them to achieve progress, to my way of seeing, to avoid the vices the peasants have, like liquor, coca, cigarettes. If they carry on with those vices we will never get a better life.

It was thought the link between ignorance and vice was the heritage of oligarchical ideology, but here we see that it can also form part of the peasant's outlook, where a powerful yearning for progress mixes with the demand for a conservative moral order (rejecting liquor, coca, cigarettes) and the need for a *guide* who will lead them to that goal.

Given this expressed need for an external guide, the emergence of a *caudillo*-teacher like the one who leads Sendero Luminoso becomes less surprising. Based on this testimony, it also becomes easier to understand Sendero's moralizing posture, its punishment of adulterers and drunkards. Nor need we be surprised by the boom the Marxist manuals enjoyed in the national universities. These were the children of the deceived, the young provincials with Andean backgrounds, streaming into the universities. There they found a simplified and more accessible version of a theory – Marxism–Leninism – which defined itself as the only "scientific truth". This science proposed a new but strictly hierarchical order in which they, having entered into the party and its truth, could pass from the base to the apex of the social pyramid (as well as the pyramid of knowledge, since they were university students).

It is worth asking if in that great need for order and progress – in a context where elements of traditional hierarchy remained – we cannot find *one* of the roots of Sendero's contradictory religious scientism, in which "the ideology of the proletariat ... is scientific, exact, all-powerful".[17] As its official documents state, it is "all-powerful because it is true" (PCP, 1988a, p. ii). Perhaps here we also find one of the roots of the personality cult and the sanctification of the cosmocrat: the *caudillo* is the embodiment of education and thus is the guide, the truth, virtue incarnate.

If, in general, for the Andean peasants who flung themselves into the conquest of "progress", basic education meant breaking the deceit, their children and grandchildren who made it to university would have to go further and search out, by dint of great effort, something beyond truth: *coherence*. Why? For many in Peru, but especially for Andean peasants, a school is a sort of "cargo cult". A book written by Juan Ansiòn (1989) shows that, to begin with, schools in Andean communities are a kind of "black box", a technological package-deal imported from beyond the Andean world, whose contents are unknown. The peasants do not really know what is inside, or how the box works; it is a kind of capsule of modernity placed in the village square, a place where children learn the secret mechanisms that will allow them to get on in today's world, especially the urban world. There thus grows a kind of superhuman expectation about the power of education.

But the children or grandchildren who reach the university feel that modernity seems to come to them in threads, in tatters, in shreds. That is how modernity reaches us all in Peru, but this vision of a fragmented world seems sharpest among young, provincial university students of peasant background in places like Ayacucho. There, the modernizing element was not an economic agent, whether mining, industry, or commercial agriculture, but fundamentally an ideological one: the university.

With no important material correlate, the feeling of achieving only shreds and tatters deepens and seems to become too agonizing. The young find themselves in a no-man's land between two worlds: the traditional Andean one of their fathers, whose myths, rites, and customs they no longer fully share; and the Western, or more precisely, urban-*criollo* world, which rejected them as provincials, *mestizos*, Quechua speakers. The young demand a world view that can both replace the traditional Andean one they no longer share, and be more accessible than the many and complex theories offered by the social sciences and philosophy. And in Ayacucho in the 1970s, they believed they had found what they were looking for in that rigid ideology which claims to be the sole truth and which gives the illusion of absolute coherence: Marxism–Leninism–Maoism.

This is and was the youthful fringe that joins Sendero Luminoso. They seek truth and coherence, and when they think they have found them, they are capable of the greatest violence in order to defend and impose them.

V

This sensation would seem to be shared by large numbers of young Peruvians in different regions, but in Ayacucho it appeared at its most unadorned. Moreover, while at most universities the students found only handbooks and professors who limited themselves to the academic diffusion of Marxist–Leninist ideas, at the University of Huamanga there formed a Maoist intellectual nucleus which gelled not only into a political party but into a discourse community. There they found, not only the books which taught that near-secret truth, but also flesh and blood people and an organization which offered an identity to those for whom the traditional Andean identity of their parents was no longer enough. These youths gained the possibility of becoming part of that new, all-powerful entity: the party "guided by the ideology of the Marxist–Leninist proletariat".

According to Senderista theory, it is not necessary that the proletariat exist in a given place. It is enough for the proletarian *idea* to arrive, and in Huamanga the idea was already embodied, incarnate, in a cosmocrat –

Abimael Guzmán. Sendero's posters give a central space to the professor in his suit and glasses, a book in his hand. Nowhere in Marxist tradition is there another leader whose intellectual character is so strongly emphasized, even as he is depicted surrounded by guns and flags, and with the red sun in the background.

We have tried to place, historically and culturally, the new generations of provincial *cholos* and *mestizos* acquiring education. Now we must do the same with the provincial *mestizo* intellectual nucleus that formed Sendero's leadership. We have thus far seen only a few of the personal characteristics of their top leader. But in order to understand the kind of "discourse community" being born in Ayacucho during the 1970s, it is important to place them historically and culturally as a social stratum.

In countries like Mexico, the *mestizos* managed to come from the epicentre of national identity. The Mexican Revolution early in this century became the new foundational myth which placed them at that epicentre. Peru had no similar event, and though the market and the state progressively changed interethnic relations, and certain *mestizo* sectors won more protagonistic roles, others remained, tense and tortured, between the *criollo* and the indigenous worlds.

Until the middle of this century, in general the *mestizos* tended to appear uprooted. For authors close to indigenism, *mestizos* were and continued to be the offspring of a rape (Macera, 1986). In any case, this was the stratum where perhaps the greatest structural grief, and thus the greatest potential rage, accumulated. Drawing a comparison between *mestizo* and Andean music, the *mestizo* writer and anthropologist Josè Maria Arguedas (1968, p. 7) stated:

> The *mestizo* songs of grief and loss are much more intimate and terrible. The *mestizo* suffered the scorn of the *criollo* and the Indian. One remedy for this ill was to flee one's hometown. And the wound this forced and cruel flight caused was more heartrending, more in need of violent expression, than the communal and almost epic – and to express it with an inappropriate but very expressive term, the racial – sense of oppression, not uncompensated, which the *mestizo* did not feel.

We could say the same of intellectual and political life. Provincial *mestizos* felt themselves unfairly disdained by the *criollo* élite, especially the Lima élite. They felt robbed of a central place in the country to whose Andean and indigenous heart they felt themselves closer than were the *criollos,* who were more oriented towards Europe, or now the United States, than to their own country. They likewise maintained an ambiguous relationship with the indigenous population. Within the stratified traditional society that prevailed until mid-century, they were unquestionably superior to the Indians. But at the same time, they felt better able to understand and represent them than the *criollos*. Let us turn to literature to explain ourselves.

Todas las Sangres is a "total novel" written in 1964 by José Maria Arguedas, the most distinguished Peruvian novelist of the generation just prior to Mario Vargas Llosa. Its principal characters are two landowning brothers, Don Bruno and Don Fermin. Don Bruno is a traditionalist. In his way, he loves "his" Indians and wants to "protect them" from the impact of modernization. Don Fermin, by contrast, wants to modernize them the capitalist way. Arguedas (1964, p. 20) puts the following phrase in Don Fermin's mouth: "with our Indians I shall get past the wall that the capitalists of Lima have put around me".

Let us now imagine a third brother, a lost son of the Aragon de Peralta family, who did not appear in *Todas las Sangres*, perhaps because he was an illegitimate child. In any case, he is poor. Not blond like his brothers, he is somewhat dark-skinned instead. He too wants to modernize the Indians, over whom he feels he has as great a claim – if not greater – than his two brothers. After all, he is closer to the Indians racially and perhaps also in his life experiences. Moreover, material wealth doesn't matter so much to this third son, for he is an intellectual.

I am referring to the petit-bourgeoisie provincial *mestizo* intellectual from whom most of Sendero's original core sprang. If Fermin relies on his economic capital, this third brother relies on his symbolic capital, which he plans to accumulate using the rhetoric of Marxism–Leninism–Maoism, rather than the millenarianism rooted in pre-Hispanic Andean tradition. Sendero achieves a sort of religiosity, but through what we could call an "excess of reason". The Senderistas are the last children of the Age of Enlightenment who, two hundred years later, lost in the Andes, have converted science into religion. They take on Marxism–Leninism in such a way as to convert it into a "divine cult of reason".[18]

It must thus be stated clearly that the provincial élite that formed the initial nucleus of Sendero leaders was neither the first nor the only to do so, but rather formed part of a long tradition of provincial élites opposing Lima's oligarchical centralism. In the first half of this century such people tended to adopt indigenist positions. From the 1920s onward, but especially after mid-century, in many areas these élites adopted Marxism, in most cases combining it with a revalorization of Andean culture that linked with the previous *indigenismo*. This is not the case, however, of Sendero Luminoso, whose official documents utterly ignore the ethnic dimension or directly reject the revalorization of Andean culture as "folk-lore" or bourgeois manipulation.

In the initial nucleus of Sendero Luminoso we thus find both continuity and rupture with an intellectual tradition. In this sense, the Senderistas offer the "coldest" version of Marxism to arise in Peru during the 1960s and 1970s. Nevertheless, their vision, while claiming to be absolutely scientific, became tremendously affective, and eventually turned its members into a discourse community, a "people of the book", grouped around the exegetic interpretation not only of Peruvian history but also of the universe. I cite a decisive phrase from one of Sendero's most import-ant documents, where communism is defined as:

The society of 'great harmony', the radical and definitive new society towards which 15 thousand million years of matter in motion, which is the part that we know of eternal matter, have necessarily and irrepress-ibly set out towards... . The unique new society, for which there is no substitute, without exploited or exploiters, without oppressed or oppres-sors, without classes, without state, without parties, without democracy, without arms, without wars.[19]

A society without movement, one should add. It is not strange that these people should long for this kind of nirvana, the society of great harmony, since they are the social classes that have been terribly beaten by the movement of history in Peru. Sendero Luminoso's nirvana, however, has the trappings of a cosmic epic. In order to bring about its climax, they must order it and plan it all, in accordance with the Book and with Marxism–Leninism–Maoism, these warrior-intellectuals in the service of that entirely exact science which regulates the universe like a boundless cosmic ballet, conquering or destroying all that stands in the way of its inescapable laws.[20]

Thus, four centuries later, a new Sacred Book has invaded Peru at another crucial moment in our history. And it turns out that according to the Book of Marxism–Leninism–Maoism, Peruvian society is "semi-feudal". Perhaps this Senderista thesis would not have generated the same violence in China in the 1930s. It seems to me that the level of violence Sendero develops is so tremendous because, among other reasons, the Senderistas find themselves forced to fit reality to their idea, and to do so they must not only stop time, they must turn it back until the page is once again blank and they can write the script for *their* Indians on it.

When I state that they want to adapt reality to their idea, I do not mean to say that there is no point of contact between the two. If that were the case, Sendero would not have found it possible to construct a social base. Seen from Ayacucho, or from the south-central highlands in general, Peru has much that is "semi-feudal". While the landowners have practically disappeared, the advance of peripheral capitalism has not helped the region progress. The intellectual élite that gave rise to Sendero emerged from that background of "semi-feudal" decadence and commercial weakness, and at the same time of exaggerated hopes for progress which were channelled through the pressure for education.

Sendero picked up and accentuated both features. First, via Marxism–Leninism–Maoism, it carried the longing for progress to its limit. But secondly, and at the same time, it took the authoritarianism of the old provincial *misti* élite to its limit, fighting against the predominant current in Peru, which aimed at the breakdown of *misti* power and the end of their "total domination".

In effect at least until the mid-1980s, Peru had one of the densest networks of independent popular organizations in Latin America. With this in mind, it becomes clear that if "total domination" (Portocarrero, 1993) or a "triangle without a base" were adequate descriptions of the traditional or semi-feudal relationship between *misti* and Indian, then Sendero in its practice constitutes a new kind of *misti*. A fundamental feature of their actions is the repudiation of popular organizations such as peasant organizations, labour unions, neighbourhood associations, etc., and their replacement with so-called "generated organizations", their "*own*" movements as organizations generated on different work fronts by the proletariat".[21] That is, generated by Sendero, by the party that "decides all" and which follows in the footsteps of all the *patrones* and local powers, by the party that has replaced the proletariat and the people, expropriating their very being and their capacity for decision-making.[22]

Like divine representatives of a belligerently monotheistic religion, the Senderistas admit no one else onto their Olympus; they alone must ordain in the rural world. But in contemporary Peru, unlike China in the 1930s and in spite of the growing weakness of the state and civil society in the present crisis, those spaces where the Senderistas wanted to be the solitary creator-gods are relatively crowded with peasant organizations, unions, leftist parties, the progressive Church, non-governmental organizations, etc. Senderista violence thus strikes not only against the state, but also against these other actors, because the PCP–SL has to be unique with relation to the masses in order, finally, to "educate them in the people's war".[23]

Sendero's main documents express the relationship between the party and the masses in terms such as: "the people's war is a political deed that goes pounding ideas into the minds of men with forceful action ...".[24] Let me cite Abimael Guzmán himself, known to his followers as "Presidente Gonzalo":

> ... the masses *must be taught with convincing facts.* You must *hammer home ideas* into them.... The masses in Peru need the direction of a Communist Party, we hope that with more revolutionary theory and practice, we may arrive at the very heart of the class and of the people, and really win them over. What for? To serve them, that is what we want ... (Guzmán, 1988, p. 36; *emphasis added*)

The language is one of astonishing violence against the masses, which in the same paragraph the party claims to love and to serve. This is why Sendero seems to be the third Aragon de Peralta brother, the synthesis of Don Fermin (modernization) and Don Bruno (the violent, tortured, authoritarian love of the superior for the inferior, of the teacher for his good but somewhat dull pupil who must be taught, as the Peruvian saying goes, "learning comes with blood").

But in order to pound and hammer the learnings in, the teachers needed a lesson, a (dis)course to dictate. They spent the 1970s preparing it, working in two directions.

First was the discourse itself. In 1975, Sendero published two important texts. In the first, "Let us Recover Mariategui and Rebuild His Party", they declare themselves the only and legitimate heirs of Mariategui. Officially, this text is the most important, and it appears in the anthology of Guzmán's writings published in Brussels in 1989 (Arce Borja, ed.). But the other is equally important: "Marxism, Mariátegui, and the Problem of Women". While the rest of the Peruvian left was concentrating on the peasant, worker, or student "problem", Sendero was the first Peruvian party to bring into discussion the problem of gender. Subordinating, of course, gender to class according to Marxist orthodoxy. But they could see what the others didn't: the role that women might play in their inversionary project. The results would be seen from 1980 on, when women held important positions in the party and in the so-called "People's Army". It has became tradition for women frequently to lead Senderista "annihilation squads", and to be tasked with the *coup de grâce* to the victims. There is no need to emphasize the inversionary nature of these deeds, or women Senderistas' ties with their forerunners – the women, children, and elderly combatants of 1969.[25]

The other direction in which Sendero moved was that of proselytism. But in contrast with the 1960s, when they emphasized winning influence over the social organizations, in the 1970s they concentrated on winning select cadres. This led to apparently paradoxical results. Sendero began to lose terrain on the social scene, which just then was growing more complex both at the regional and the national levels. The growth of the state apparatus during the decade brought Ayacucho government offices as well as banks and stores, thus expanding the employee and commercial sector. Migration from the highlands to the Apurimac Valley grew, and there, in the jungle region of the department, commercial crops proliferated and coca cultivation began to increase. With the growth of the university, students from more modern regions like the central highlands, the south-central coast, and even Lima came to Huamanga to study. Sendero did not know how to respond to the demands and expectations of these new sectors. In 1973 they lost control of the Federation of University Students, which they had controlled since the 1960s. In 1974, they were reduced to a minority in the union of university professors. Lastly, that same year they lost their hegemony in the Executive Council, the university's highest authority. Outside the university, the People's Defence Front, which they had tried to revive around 1972, continued to languish, and later in the decade they lost control of it. At the same time, new, more modern organizations in which Sendero lacked hegemony sprang up: a Departmental Federation of Workers linked to urban expansion and the growth of the bureaucracy; and a Peasant Federation in the Apurimac Valley, which in the early 1980s had more than 100 member unions (only to be caught and destroyed in the crossfire between Sendero and the Armed Forces).

But Sendero never lost control over the university's education department, nor over the departmental teachers' union. This control allowed them to build the next link in their chain: the rural teachers graduating from the university who scattered throughout the region's schools spreading Sendero's "good news". In this way, during the late 1970s, Sendero reproduced the earlier meeting between intellectuals and young people. But this time it was not professors and university students, but teachers and high school adolescents who came together. Having thus built the final link in the chain that through the so-called "generated organisms" tied the leader to the masses, they were ready to conquer social bases. They would do so while already at the war, and in an extremely authoritarian fashion.

In this way, though Sendero was reducing the scope of its social action and political alliances, it was gaining ideological density and organic cohesion. It became a sort of white dwarf (star), in which matter is compacted until there is almost no interatomic space and it attains a great weight far out of proportion to its size.

In a series of meetings held between 1977 and 1978, Sendero decided to begin the armed struggle. After mid-1977, dozens of cadres were sent to the countryside to fill the strategic needs of the people's war. Around the same time, Sendero began to send spores, specialists in student and military work, to other universities, and it spread via the teachers to Ayacucho's neighbouring departments, Huancavelica and Apurimac. Earlier in the decade, in 1974, Guzmán's psoriasis, which kept him from living at high altitudes, had forced him to leave Ayacucho (located 8,700 feet above sea level), and move to Lima. There he devoted himself to the formation of "study circles" with students from different universities, especially the National Educational University of La Cantuta.

VI

It should be recalled that Sendero planned to begin its adventure at a crucial moment in the history of Peru and of the international communist movement. On both fronts its wager was, as the saying says, "against all odds".

Peru was living through one of the high points of the social mobilization of the 1970s. These were the years of the massive national strikes of 1977 and 1978, which helped force the dictatorship to withdraw and in which Sendero played no part. On the contrary, since they were backed by the pro-Soviet PCP-*Unidad* and other leftist groups, Sendero considered the strikes "revisionist" and "at the service of Soviet social imperialism". These were also the years of the democratic transition, which allowed Peru's Marxist left to become, for the first time, an important political force.[26]

In the international communist movement, Mao had just died (in 1976). The Shanghai Group, led by his widow, had been defeated. The Cultural Revolution, which helped feed the *imaginaire* of much of the Peruvian left, had come to an end. The decade that followed would bring perestroika and the crumbling of the "real and existing socialism", and with it the crisis of totalizing explanations and of ideological parties.

During these years, the bulk of the Peruvian left came to accept, if at times partially and belatedly, what Nun has called the "choir's rebellion" – the idea that the "masses" have the capacity for political initiative. The left also admitted that no "guiding party" existed at the international level. But Sendero denied the new reality and instead proposed an alternative scenario. It rejected any protagonistic role for the masses: the party would decide all. It denied the superiority of politics over war: violence is the essence of revolution. And as its plans seemed unable to endure the passage of time, like Joshua it sought to hold back the sun, to hold back time. Peru by Sendero's definition continued to be a "semi-feudal" country, and the democratic transition meant nothing. The Constituent Assembly (1978–9) which preceded the transition was nothing more than "the third restructuring of the bureaucratic, corporative, landowning state". The civilian government elected in 1980 represented "fascist continuism".

Though Guzmán's "overcoming project" set itself above momentary vicissitudes in order to rise above the adverse conjuncture, Sendero found it necessary to advance towards a complete rupture. Crossing the desert or the Rubicon, burning its ships – no metaphor seems exaggerated.

The extent of this break can be gauged in four crucial texts, which Guzmán produced between 1979 and 1980. These are his hardest hitting texts, those of greatest symbolic density and "inversionary power". Their goal is to consolidate his following, which he himself calls "a handful of communists".

What first catches our ear in these texts is their abrupt change of tone. Until then Guzmán's writings, plagued with quotations from the Marxist pantheon, were dry and dull.[27] But suddenly Guzman passes from scholastic disquisition to prophetic discourse. The texts we shall discuss lack a "rational" structure, and are filled instead with parables, metaphors, and impassioned, reiterative calls. The change may be due to the fact that the aforementioned were mostly official texts, while these were speeches delivered in closed meetings with the circle of "apostles" on the verge of armed struggle. The imminence of combat gives a particularly epic tone to the speeches. But the greatest influence on their flavour seems to have been the bitter internal struggles Guzmán had to confront when he decided to launch the armed struggle.[28] Some sense of reality still cowered within the party. It was necessary to drive out of this Jerusalem in progress all the fearful and the vacillating, to eradicate any lingering fibres of doubt, to culminate the creation of a discourse community, an inner world armoured against a crushingly adverse reality (call it a correlation of forces).

The first text, "For the New Flag",[29] was written in June 1979, eleven months before the start of the war. It begins with a Biblical phrase: "Many are called but few are chosen". The echoes of the internal struggles resound in the phrase, as they do in others with equally deep Biblical roots, such as "The wind carries off the leaves, but the seed remains". It is interesting to see that in the party's decisive moments it is the Bible that appears as the great storehouse of symbols. But the God of Sendero's Book is Matter, advancing irresistibly towards the Light, communism.

In the speech, through a clever rhetorical twist, Guzmán and his followers appear embodying that movement of matter and thus become indestructible. As they gain cosmic strength, the opposition minority is reduced to "threads, spattered drops, dim voices, darkened sparks trying to deny the bonfire". For: "Can a spark rise up against the bonfire?" "How could the grains stop the millstone? They would be turned to dust." "Foolish it is to want to destroy matter." "Fifteen billion years it has taken Earth to bring forth communism.... Arrogant bubbles. Is that what we want to be? An infinitesimal fragment trying to rise up against fifteen billion years? What vanity, what putridness!"

The speech is wracked with what we might call positive fatalism: "Nothing can stop the revolution, that is the law, that is destiny."[30] We can thus understand a phrase repeated in slogans and proclamations and even in a poem written by a prisoner later murdered in the 1986 prison massacre: "We are condemned to win/What a beautiful sentence."

But in June 1979, it was not easy to raise the flag of optimism. Who better than Paul of Tarsus to inspire Guzmán's listeners? "What little faith some have, what little charity, what little hope.... We have taken the three theological virtues in order to interpret them. Paul said man of faith, hope, and charity." In other words, to yoke oneself to the cart of history, a total rupture, total belief, is needed. Like Lot leaving Sodom, one cannot look back, one must only look forward. Not even the possibility of rectification exists: "What's done is done, and cannot be restated."

Once again, the grandiloquent language barely hides the nastiness of a fierce internal struggle. Votes taken in previous events, accords that have brought the party to its current stand, possible manoeuverings, all are raised into cosmic deeds: "Are we to revoke what time has written, the deeds branded onto matter?" All that remains is to "rise into flight" and move ahead. And there, ahead, is the revolution, described with the verses of King Solomon himself, which the Catholic Church assigns to the honour of the Virgin Mary. "There is an old verse", says the cosmocrat, and goes on to recite the Magnificat: "Who is she that looketh forth as the morning, fair as the moon, clear as the sun, and terrible as an army with banners?"

The rupture Guzmán presents to his followers is collective, but it is also personal, internal. "Two flags [struggle] within the soul, one black and the other red. We are the left, let us make a holocaust of the black flag." To do so it is necessary to "cleanse our soul, cleanse it well. . . . Enough of putrid individual waters, of abandoned dung." All the militancy must share the cosmocrat's blazing intellectual battles, to emerge at last cleansed and born anew, like born-again Christians. Yet at the same time, "one is worth nothing, the mass is all… . Our love, our faith, our hope, are collective. They can be achieved, they are three in one flag." The soul can only purify itself within the discourse community, because "the Party is the salt of the earth, the living tree. The others are parasites."

According to Gorriti (1990, pp. 53–4), after this meeting one of Guzmán's lieutenants broke with him, accusing him of being "Hoxhista", and managed to form a dissident group from the Politburo and the Central Committee. "The group might have achieved a majority", Gorriti writes, "and thus changed the nation's history, but it lacked cohesion and was crushed by the reverential fear of Guzman." Defeated, the opposition leader abandoned the organization and left Peru.

The second text is titled "On Three Chapters of Our History".[31] The speech was given on Guzmán's birthday, 3 December 1979. Victorious in his internal battle and eager to link indissolvably his personal life with that of his political child, Guzmán took advantage of the date to give birth to the People's Army and to restate not only his own history but Peru's as well.

Here we find that Guzmán is very aware of his change in tone. He tells his audience: "There are moments when men turn to speaking in symbols, in metaphors, or in forms which are not so directly intellectual. Instead, we prefer that our group of communist beings speak for us, directly and fully."

As if through an oracle, the group of communists is to speak through his mouth although, oddly enough, they will express themselves in symbolic rather than scientific language. To fulfill his role as medium, the narrator uses a rhetorical device which we might call "the flash forward". He asks his listeners to "enter the field of revolutionary imagination" and put themselves in the second half of the twenty-first century. From there, they are to imagine history as written by future communists. After all, if victory is their destiny, nothing could be more natural than what Guzmán has them imagining. Guzmán tries in this way to abolish time and breathe faith in their triumph into his followers. The Goddess of History is on their side, and so is the Goddess of Matter, which is but another name for the same divinity. And so, having become a twenty-first century historian, the cosmocratic agent speaks: "There was a time when shadows prevailed… ."

Thousands of years of Peruvian history are condensed into three long chapters that lead us from darkness to light. The first, "On How the Shadows Prevailed", spans time from the arrival in the Andes of *homo sapiens* until the beginning of the twentieth century. If anything startles us here, it is the speaker's meagre attachment to the past and to the homeland. He is not trying here to reaffirm a parochial or primordial identity, nor to recover some paradise lost. In a country with Peru's historical richness, the text's coolness towards the great pre-Hispanic civilizations draws one's attention. Apparently, in Sendero's strictly classist vision, the ethnic has no place. What matters is the rise of the state, and of the classes, in the Wari period (the sixth to ninth centuries AD). The Conquest is but a changing of the guard among the exploiters. "As [the Inca empire] was a decayed system based on exploitation, it was buried in the clash with a superior order." There are no tears. The text deals more with projection than retrieval. Paradise lies in the future.

The second chapter's name is "On How Light Burst Forth and Steel was Forged." It begins between the late nineteenth and early twentieth centuries when, along with the new imperialist order, "a new class, the proletariat, dawned". At first, Mariategui and Peru's young working class play starring roles until, as in a cosmogony, out of the darkness: "There began to appear a purer light, a radiant light, that light which we carry within our breasts, within our souls. That light fused with the earth, and that clay turned to steel. Light, clay, steel, the PARTY emerged in 1928... ."

This is no longer only Biblical language. It is a Bible with its own proletarian Genesis – and, soon, a history of redemption with a classic trilogy of life, death, and resurrection, because Mariategui died at 36, just two years after he founded the party. Thus, "we had a possibility which came apart when the life of he who founded us ended". Nevertheless, "what could not be reality remained as Program and Plan", even though Mariategui's germinating legacy "was denied, ignored, hidden". This was, without a doubt, a time in hell. The Holy Grail – Programme and Plan – remained buried by the traitors and revisionists who seized the party. But it did not disappear, because "the class embodied it, it continued to beat within the combative class and people and within the communists". Until once again history speeds up to a dizzying speed. During the 1970s it reaches rapture because then:

Our people were enlightened by a more intense light, Marxism–Leninism–Mao Zedong Thought; at first we were blinded, at that first breaking of endless light, light and nothing more; little by little, our retinas began to embrace that light, we lowered our eyes and began to see our country, to see Mariategui and our reality, and we found our perspective: the Reconstitution of the Party.

Mount Tabor, Easter, and the Pentecost, condensed into a single sentence. Revived by a sort of God the Father who lives in China, those disciples, marginal and functionally superfluous, are ready to "speak in tongues" and be the protagonists in a third chapter that begins the very day on which the cosmocrat is giving his speech. Plan and Program me have been rebuilt. It is the day of resurrection, and hence this chapter title, "On How the Walls Came Tumbling Down and the Dawn Unfurled". The narrator returns to the twenty-first century and from there writes the history of the precise moment they are living.

It shall be said: our party, forged of the strongest light and the purest steel, faced a moment of decision and generated the National Plan of Construction, and the party, which was a piece of flag unfurled in the wind, grew until it illuminated our fatherland.... *The communists arose and the earth thundered, and as the earth thundered the comrades advanced.... The few communists there were convened from different places,* and at last they committed themselves and made a decision: to forge through deeds the First Company of the First Division of the People's Army. *And so, the shadows began to roll back for good, the walls trembled and were breached; with their fists dawn opened, darkness became light.... Their souls were joyful and their eyes shone with the light.*[32]

The third text is titled: "Let Us Begin to Tear Down the Walls and Unfurl the Dawn". It was given as a speech in a key meeting, the Second Plenary Session of the Central Committee,[33] which according to Gorriti (1990, p. 49) began on 17 March 1980 and lasted till the end of the month. It is worth specifying that in line with Guzmán's claustrophilia and preaching vocation, these meetings were generally long seclusions in which the leader was not only rhetorician, exegete, and prophet, but also strategist and organizer. They were long meetings, in which the master progressively overcame all of the disciples' resistance, moulding them in his own image. He worked more like a smith than a potter because, as he would repeat for years, with variations, about those who were neither disciples nor enemies:

It will not be easy for them to accept.... They will need overwhelming deeds ... that hammer their hard heads, that break their speculations into pieces, in order for the reality of this, our fatherland, to take root in their souls."We are the initiators". (Arce Borja, ed., 1989, p. 167)

This Second Session of the Central Committee was key because the internal opposition persisted, although leaderless since the Ninth Plenary held nine months earlier, as we explained above. The head of the opposition, who had fled the country, sent a document that was read "and defended" during this meeting. We can imagine the differences between the youths, dazzled by the cosmocrat's narratives and needing no hammer blows to open their souls to the "overcoming project", and their elders, older militants, battle hardened in the harsh struggles of the Peruvian left during the 1970s, who could moreover "see" the cresting wave of social movements and the great strides the rest of the left was making.[34] But we can only contemplate the degree of cynicism that must have existed in the narrator for him to use cosmology in order to resolve political problems.

In any case, Guzmán must once again fight an internal battle. If in the Ninth Expanded Session a fatherly tone predominated, this time he is the God of Rage, thundering and threatening from the unquestioned stronghold of Matter. Blood invades the stage. Not for nothing does the meeting read scraps of Macbeth, of Julius Caesar, and of Aeschylus' Prometheus (Gorriti, 1990, p. 57). "The blood of our people inflames us and boils within us." "We are blood, powerful and throbbing." Who is it that speaks through the mouths of the opposition? "The black gullets of oppression and exploitation, the black gullets, full of slime and blood. Do not forget that the reaction needs to spill blood in torrents to appease the people, that is their dream of fire and iron... ."

In "For the New Flag", echoes of Genesis sounded. The internal struggle separated darkness from light, day from night. Now the apocalypse has come. Fire replaces the light: "We have no choice but to burn the old idols, to burn what has decayed... ." The syntax at times turns frenetic: "Unacceptable, inadmissible: burn it, blow it up. " Before, the rupture implied cleansing the soul, and the opposition was silence, aged spume, an aged old sea rotted by time, waters black with decay. Now, as if in a fit of panic or hysteria, the cosmocrat demands:

Let us uproot the poisonous weeds. They are pure poison, cancerous to the bones, they will corrupt us; we cannot allow it, it is putrefaction and sinister pus; we cannot allow it, now less than ever ... Let us cast out those sinister vipers, those noxious vipers, we can allow neither cowardice nor betrayal, they are asps... . Let us begin to burn, to uproot that pus, that poison, it is urgent that we burn it. It exists, and it is not good, it is harmful, it is a slow death that could consume us... . Those who are in that situation must be the first to cauterize, uproot, burst their boils. Otherwise, the venom will spread. Poisons, purulence – they must be destroyed. The body is healthy, and if we don't destroy them it will lose its vigor.

It is impossible not to mention here the ills that forced Guzmán to leave Ayacucho in 1974. One, a disease of the blood, polysemia, which keeps him from living at high altitudes. The other, a disease of the skin, which causes open sores: psoriasis, a slow death.

And death, the great protagonist of the years to come, makes its appearance alongside blood. In order to decisively defeat the opposition, it is necessary:

That the armed actions confirm our preaching, that our blood merge with the blood of those who must spill it; we have no right for the other's blood to tremble alone, that its cold be cradled in the warmth of ours. Or we are not what we are.

To be in death. "If our blood and life are demanded, let us have a posture: to carry them in our hands to surrender them... ." Because "our death for the good cause would be the seal on our revolutionary action". To be for death. "Tomorrow, matter will gather us into its warlike peace, and there we will at last be able to rest."

Blood and death must be familiar to those who have decided to "convert the word into armed actions". The evangelical allusion to the Redeemer – "the word was made flesh" – is fully recognizable and not at all gratuitous. It announces Guzmán's and Sendero's attitude towards violence. She is the Redeemer. She is not the midwife, she is the Mother of History.

The fourth and final text, and the most important one, is titled "We are the Initiators". Given as a speech at the closing of Sendero's first Military School on 19 April 1980,[35] it preceded by only a month the commencement of armed actions. Once again, the narrator announces that he will speak "with his heart open, in the word of will and the reasoning of sentiment". But almost immediately, as if fearing that his apparently contradictory words might be misinterpreted by an audience accustomed to the "scientific" discourse of Marxism, he adds: "This, too, has a strict logic." He is not mistaken. To understand the degree of passion that Sendero Luminoso develops and unleashes, we would have to invert Pascal's phrase, "the heart has its reasons, whereof reason knows nothing", and understand that for Sendero's leadership core, "reason has passions of which the heart knows nothing".

Once purified and ready to interpret past, present, and future, the born-again Maoists can now move on to action. In doing so, they will shock the world. Because, according to Abimael Guzmán, the beginning of their armed struggle in the remote Peruvian Andes means that "we are entering the strategic offensive of the global revolution". The cosmocrat traces a thread which runs from the most ancient struggles of the masses, passing via the Paris Commune, the October Revolution, and the Chinese Revolution, until reaching that day. A day on which, "all those glorious actions across the centuries have become concrete here. The promise opens, the future is unfurled: ILA 80."

ILA are the Spanish initials for "initiating the armed struggle". Guzmán has the ability to condense into initials, like algebraic formulas, an enormous amount of symbolic capital. If in earlier texts he accumulated that capital by moving between physics and cosmology, he now tries to do so in the field of international political analysis. The text gives four reasons for why it can now speak of a "strategic offensive" in the global revolution: "the powerful international workers' movement; the rising waves of the movement for national liberation, the development of the communist parties, [and] the elevation of Marxism to the great summit of Mao Zedong Thought".

We may imagine that from Ayacucho, Peru, his listeners could not see the weaknesses of the international workers' movements and the cracks in the movement for national liberation, then in the midst of wars between Vietnam, China, and Cambodia, to mention just one example. But there is an inadmissible blind spot in the analysis of one who so closely followed the evolution of the Chinese Communist Party: the death of Mao and the defeat of the Group of Shanghai, the Gang of Four.

There is only one possible explanation. Higher than political correlation of forces the cosmocrat values symbolic capital. The Shangai Four have been defeated but before, Marxism has reached a new summit: Mao Zedong Thought. The Idea is there, floating over History, waiting for someone to become "incarnated" again. It is worth noting the boldness of Guzmán and his "handful of communists", who dare to grasp Mao's flags and proclaim, as they did shortly after on the walls of the city, "Ayacucho as the beacon of world revolution". Maybe hyperbole was the only way of instilling absolute faith in the disciples; and the optimist analysis over the possibilities of world revolution was born in the shadows between awareness and self-deceit. Although at first sight it may appear as a slow and patient effort, in fact Sendero's history from the 1970s onward can also be read as an ever more bloody escape forward. The construction of a discourse community as an impenetrable armour allowed them to ignore reality in the name of a dream and to ward off an overwhelming fact – they had arrived late on the stage of history. It is highly probable that Guzmán's decision to launch armed struggle was influenced by Velasco's reforms and the massive organization of the peasants, which did away with the peasant serfs who were the principal subject of his plans. Then came the 1978–80 democratic transition, which diluted a possible polarization between the "fascist" dictatorship and the revolution. The end of the Cultural Revolution in China wilted hopes for a triumphant worldwide Maoist revolution. What is remarkable is that Sendero achieved the density of a black hole, which allowed it to absorb all the blows and continue fleeing forward throughout the 1980s (in the context, it is true, of a crisis which multiplied the number of marginally superfluous youth in search of an overcoming project), and that from that immensely powerful "exegetical bonding", Guzmán molded his projections into deeds.

"We are the initiators" tries to sweep away every shadow of doubt and strengthen one conviction – the armed struggle is possible and necessary. The global situation is favourable and the national one justifies it. So-called structural violence lies at the basis of that justification:

> They in their old and bloody violence, in their peace of bayonets, in their accursed war which kills in the jails, in the schools, in the factories, in the fields, killing even children in their mothers' wombs.
> That sinister violence today has met its match.

If in earlier speeches he rose to the sublime, Guzmán now delves into the deepest structures in order to avoid "seeing" politics, and in order to ignore the immense majority in the country, which was living somewhere between the mythical "they" and Sendero Luminoso. Only the "revolution and the counter-revolution [which] prepares itself for violence" exist. In the centre is a vacuum. There are no people fighting *in some other way*.

These were the years of Peru's greatest social mobilization in this century, of labour, peasant, neighbourhood, regional movements, of the start of women's and political-electoral movements. The Marxist left won 28 per cent of the vote in the elections for the Constituent Assembly in 1978. They do not count. Every other form of struggle is denied and denigrated, and those who carry it out are accused of betrayal. This "blindness" would bring painful consequences in the years to follow, when Sendero became a true "social anti-movement" (Wieviorka, 1988), as it identified those who were not on the party's side with the mythical "they" of the state, the incarnation of absolute evil. These "others" thus became deserving of death, which Sendero took charge of lavishing ever more generously,[36] in the end pushing the survivors, in a self-fulfilling prophecy, towards a state which began to militarize and for a while seemed on the verge of resembling its Senderista definition.

We could say that when Guzmán remains somewhere between Genesis and the apocalypse, his analysis is less vulnerable. But it is discourse, and not political analysis of correlations of forces, that will channel into rage the grief of the functionally superfluous. Sendero thus becomes the handwriting on the wall in the middle of the banquet:

> The reaction has dreams of the blood of hyenas, disturbing dreams shake their dark nights. Their heart plots sinister hecatombs. They arm themselves to the teeth, but they shall not prevail. Their destiny is weighty and measured. The time has come to settle accounts.

ILA 80 marked the beginning of that settling of accounts. ILA is made possible by the strategic equilibrium at the global level. In the equilibrium:

> The people rear up, arm themselves, and rising up in rebellion slip a noose on the neck of imperialism and the reactionaries, they grab them by the throat, they bind them; and unavoidably they will strangle them, unavoidably. They will strip off the reactionary flesh, turn it into tatters, and will bury these black scraps in the mire. What remains will be burnt, and its ashes scattered to the winds of the earth so that nothing remains but a sinister memory of what must never return because it cannot and should not return.

The virulence of this language announces the coming violence, necessary to provoke the total inversion of the world:

> Their black hosts will move against us, they will mount powerful aggressions, great offensives. We will respond, we will pull them apart, we will divide them. Their offensive, we will convert into a multitude of our own small offensives, and the surrounders will be surrounded, and the would-be annihilators will be annihilated, and the would-be victors will be defeated and the beast at last will be trapped, and as we have been taught, the thunder of our armed voices will make them shake with horror and they will end, dead from fear, converted into a few black ashes.

If man is such stuff as dreams are made of, then there is no doubt that we here find ourselves facing the product of an unrestrained nightmare. What is important to understand is how Peru in the 1980s could generate an army of headhunters after whose passage it will never again be what it was.

After ILA 80, the discourse community was formed, the "overcoming project" vibrantly outlined. The party has been reconstituted and its militants turned into alchemists of light:

We are a growing torrent against which fire, stones and mud will be hurled; but our power is great, all will become our fire, the black fire we will make red and the red is light. This we are, this is the Reconstitution. Comrades, we are reconstituted.

Turned into supermen, anxious to start their long march to the promised land, the Levites of this new people of the Book then sign a pledge:

We, the communists of the first Military School of the Party, the closing seal of the time of peace and the commencement of the people's war, place ourself in combat readiness as its initiators; under the leadership of the Party and tied to the people, we take on the forging of the invincible iron legions of the Red Army of Peru. Glory to Marxism–Leninism–Mao Zedong Thought! Long live the Communist Party of Peru! By the way of comrade Gonzalo, let us initiate the armed struggle! (Gorriti, 1990, p. 67)

His work completed, the cosmocrat does not rest. He goes forward:

Comrades, we are entering the great rupture... . We must break many ties, for they tie us to the rotten old order and if we do not do so we cannot demolish it. Comrades, the hour is up, there is nothing to discuss, the debate has ended. It is time to act, it is the breaking point, and we will not do it in slow and belated meditation ... we will do it amidst the din of martial actions... .

The *jihad* was about to begin.

VII   THE CULTURE OF DEATH

During the 1980s the "exegetical bonding" that united the discourse community developed along three intertwined lines: the cult of death, the abolition of the self, and the exaltation of the leader.

The cult of death deepened in each new stage of the "people's war". In the Fourth Plenary Session of the Central Committee, in May 1981, Guzman pointed out the need to pay "the quota" of blood necessary for the revolution's triumph. From then on, the militants made a pledge, which among other points included "to struggle and give one's life for the world-wide revolution" (Gorriti, 1990, p. 67). The logic that upheld the cult of death is that "blood doesn't stop the revolution, it waters it". When Sendero decides to achieve "strategic equilibrium", Guzman begins to speak of a million deaths, and of the possible usefulness of a "genocide" in order to achieve that equilibrium (Guzmán, 1988). "The triumph of the revolution will cost a million lives", he repeated during his appearance on television on 24 September 1992, just days after his arrest.

To be consolidated, the cult demands the negation of the individual and, thus, of the value of human life in general and in particular that of the militants, who must "carry their lives in their fingertips". They must be willing to "pay the quota" and "cross the river of blood" necessary for the revolution's victory.

The devaluation of feelings, of love and of sex, flow naturally from this context. Thus Laura Zambrano, comrade Meche, one of the leaders captured with Guzmán, was able to state when she was asked about love in an interview some years ago, "love has a class character and is at the service of the people's war" (Zambrano, 1988, p. 9). Guzmán seems to have defined sex as a "physiological anxiety" (*Sí*, 24 September 1992). Certainly, a military cadre interviewed in *Sí* (2 November 1992) used these same terms. Deduction: the Deuteronomical, Pavlovian norms that seem to rule the sexual life of the combatants.

We have already seen, in the four texts covered, a rabid willingness to obliterate individuality, linked to the teleological vision that aids the "overcoming project". We saw how, in "For the New Flag", that will expressed itself in phrases with Biblical roots. In "Three Chapters of Our History", the imagined future takes on a touch of science fiction:

> Let us place ourselves in the second half of the next century. History will be written by us and those who follow are us, the future communists, because we are inexhaustible; others will come and then others, and those who come are us.

Time (and therefore death) have been abolished. Guzmán talks in a perpetual present where communists from the twentieth and twenty-first centuries intermingle. Moreover, the future is an all-encompassing *We*, more like the Catholic Church conceived as the mystical body of Christ, than communism.

At the same time, in that great *We*, some of us are more equal than others. This is a caudillo whose self is exalted through a personality cult never before seen in history.[37] Let us give some examples. In the "Bases for Discussion", written for the First Congress and published in *El Diario* in 1988, the chapters do not appear as the decisions of a collective (whether the Central Committee or the Politburo), but as the "teachings of Presidente Gonzalo". Since then, in Sendero leaders are not elected, they are *chosen*. "Presidente Gonzalo" takes charge of the selection. Strangest of all, since the early 1980s the militants must sign a "letter of submission", not to the party or to the "revolutionary line", but to "Presidente Gonzalo".[38] It is as if the militants stripped off their egos and siphoned them to the leader, whose own ego would grow proportionally. Already in "For the New Flag", Guzmán had given an indication of how this mechanism might function, using a musical work to explain it:

The Ninth Symphony [Beethoven] has a characteristic: a soft, growing murmur, a light being forged until it bursts into a musical explosion. The human voice enters, the voice of the choral mass. It is the earth, which is becoming the voice. Over a background of the choral mass, four individuals sing. The mass has generated those four voices that sing more loudly, but one voice must rise still higher. Never before could it be sung, by anyone, but in this century, after many attempts, what was once impossible was achieved.

Clearly, Guzmán identifies himself with that voice that manages to "rise still higher". In his obsessive pursuit of that dream, amidst a rising river of blood, the caudillo-teacher transforms into a teacher-messiah. Bit by bit, the references to Mariategui disappear. "Presidente Gonzalo" becomes "the greatest living Marxist–Leninist–Maoist", the "Fourth Sword of Marxism" after Marx, Lenin, and Mao. He is the soloist in the Ninth Symphony, who takes up there where Mao's voice failed and who will sound the note that will change the world.[39]

In a context of generalized crisis, throughout the 1980s those thrown out joined up with those denied entry. The *mestizo* provincial intellectuals whom the military government's reforms and the capitalist development of the 1970s had made superfluous managed to win over contingents of young provincial *mestizos*, generally with higher education. Youths who had fulfilled all of society's demands in order to receive its benefits, and who nevertheless found the doors to that promised land of "progress" slammed shut in their faces. They were not many. The continuing strength of the myth of progress, and the highly thanatic and bloody nature of the Senderista project dissuaded the majority, despite the generalized demoralization and the lack of expectations caused by economic crisis, inefficiency and corruption of governments and political parties. In a constant flight forward, these few held a gun to the state's head and nearly managed to strangle the country. Until the capture of the cosmocrat, too far from that Andean Yan'an where he had not ended but only begun his long march.

EPILOGUE: THE LAST TEMPTATION OF PRESIDENT GONZALO

For twelve years, to the average senderista Guzmán appeared to be truly capable of interpreting the laws of history and moulding it with the precision and the ease of a virtuoso. They had found the Fourth Sword! A will toward perfection that emanated from the apex of the pyramid spread throughout the party and intensified the zeal of its militants.

As part of this long march, Guzmán not only appeared as the interpreter of the laws of history but also as a military commander who could not be captured by the repressive forces of the "old state". He was both everywhere and nowhere. The media contributed to the figure of Guzmán taking on mythic proportions: he was never to be found.

Because of the elevated position he held and the aura that surrounded him, Guzmán's capture was a tremendous blow to the party. Sendero, however, possessed ideological resources that under the circumstances were used to combat demoralization in the party. They reminded that "for a revolutionary prison is a work accident". They highlighted the fact that what was important was the ideology and not the person. "Gonzalo thought is still free", they maintained. The fact that not one important Senderista leader surrendered to take advantage of the Repentance Law, passed in 1992, is proof that they avoided a collapse of the party.

In October 1993, however, from his prison cell Guzmán called on his followers to temporarily stop the popular war and enter into peace talks with the government. The astonishment of his followers (and the country as a whole) was palpable. While rejecting his call as a "baseless and ridiculous lie", they reaffirmed their recognition of:

> our dear, heroic and respected Presidente Gonzalo, the greatest living Marxist–Leninist–Maoist on earth ... [that] with his unwavering light, the all-powerful Gonzalo Thought ... has brought us to this point and will lead us to golden and splendorous communism with his firm and sure hand ...[40]

Later, however, there were more letters and Guzmán appeared on television surrounded by the rest of the Shining Path's high-ranking leaders who were in jail. Finally there was a long document in which the leader called for a new "great decision and great definition", as important as the decision made by the party in 1980: "fight for a peace accord" and move on to a new stage of "political war" (Guzmán, 1994).

The letters and the "new great decision" had a devastating effect on the Senderistas. Hundreds of militants took advantage of the Repentance Law.

Because what for Guzmán was, at least in part, an intellectual construction was assumed as a religious identity and was lived almost as a mystic rapture by his followers for thirteen years. In the end it was *faith* that moved Sendero's "war machine".

Within this framework, the fact that their leader was in jail did not mean the end. Various divinities and many mythical heroes had spent "time in hell". Being in jail was also a condition that could be reversed. The Sendero organized a brigade that was in charge of rescuing Gonzalo (*Sí*, 24 April 1993). Even his death would not have meant a definitive end. *Gonzalo, the Myth*[41] would have fed the imagination of the hard-line Senderista core long after his death. This is why so many people were astonished when the god of war decided to become human: a run-of-the-mill politician to be more precise.

Guzmán was able to "come down from the cross" because his role as prophet never overtook his role as a politician. Today, as he himself has stated, he has changed his discourse in order to preserve what remains of Sendero and, we would add, to continue to play a role in the party with the extremely remote hope of seeing it expand once again in the twenty-first century. The party, the one thing he had when he began and the only thing that he has left today.

Since his spectacular come back, Guzmán has had unequal success in convincing his followers to adhere to his "new direction". He has been most successful in convincing the party's militants who are in jail, not only because he has direct access to them himself or through his close followers who already have been convinced, but because Guzmán works best in enclosed spaces.[42] Guzmán was unbeatable in debates and party events in which only a small core of leaders participated, insurmountable in his handling of Stalinist rhetoric, non-tiring in "hammering" ideas into the minds of the militants until he had them completely drawn in with his circular arguments. Within the prisons it is also easier for the group to coerce the individual and it is also there where the leader exerts more control over the lower echelons of the hierarchy. Guzmán has been most successful with those who have the highest levels of education and are, therefore, the most "ideological". He has also been successful with Senderista's old guard, especially with those who came from the Stalinist PCP and Bandera Roja. This is the case not only because of the regional and even family solidarity – the old guard comes mainly from Ayacucho and because it is highly endogamic it is tightly knit by family ties – but also because of the ideological heritage of the communist parties of the Three International, accustomed, as it is known, to abrupt changes and surprising alliances. Finally, Guzmán's proposal has been accepted more readily by members of the party's apparatus than by those who form part of the military structures.

The dissidents, who have decided to carry on the war, have identified themselves as the Sendero Rojo. Within this faction are those who are still at large and who have not been demoralized; those who were not part of the old PCP, particularly those who joined Sendero after 1980; and those who form part of the Senderista army. For these sectors violence has been a fundamental part of their identity and even a way of life since the beginning. The Sendero Rojo is continuing the war in the most adverse conditions: hounded by the army; gripped by demoralization that is eating away at the periphery and even the militants who are still at large; overwhelmed by the weight Guzmán's figure carries after 13 years of deification. No one can fill this void because no one can become a cosmocrat and accumulate such an amount of symbolic capital in a short period. The Sendero Rojo militants can continue to fight but it is difficult because in their lifetimes they are not going to come across "the fifth sword of Marxism", be it in Peru or in any other part of the world.

NOTES

1. On the concept of revolutionary Platonism see David E. Apter and Tony Saich, *Revolutionary Discourse in Mao's Republic* (Cambridge, Mass.: Harvard University Press, 1994).
2. On the origins of SP, see Degregori (1990).
3. An explanation of the state's anti-subversive strategy goes beyond the limits of this study. Suffice it to say that the indiscriminate repression unleashed by the armed forces after 1983 merely blocked the spread of the contradictions which even then had begun to appear between the peasantry and Sendero. For many, at the time, the subversives seemed "the lesser evil". But when Sendero decided to move to the "strategic equilibrium", its demands upon the peasants grew. It recruited more youths, confiscated more foodstuffs, demanded more participation by the population as "mass" in military actions, and hardened Senderista discipline, which relied heavily on the death penalty. Precisely then, the armed forces had begun to modify the most repressive aspects of their counter-insurgent strategy and to adopt a more paternalistic attitude towards the rural populations. The result was an alliance of important sectors of the peasantry with the armed forces and a massive growth of the so-called "civil defence committees", which the army had been trying to build since 1984. The committees bogged Sendero down in a war of attrition in several highland zones, among them Ayacucho.

    In the cities, from the late 1980s onward the government stepped up intelligence work. Guzmán's capture was the work not of the armed forces, but of the police intelligence services, which for years had been carrying out a patient effort that slowly allowed them to draw near Sendero Luminoso's almost mythically unreachable leader. On state counter-insurgency see Degregori and Rivera (1993).

4. Keep in mind that even at its high point Sendero never did win the support of the majority of the population. In rural areas, its backing in 1992 was in open decline. In Lima, where conditions for its growth were optimal, 7 per cent of the population expressed a favourable opinion of Sendero in 1991, reaching 11 per cent in the poorest stratum (Balbi, 1991).

5. On the first years of war see Gorriti (1990). On Sendero and the peasantry see Berg (1992), Degregori (1991), Gonzáles (1992). On Sendero in the cities see Reyna (1991), Balbi (1991), Smith (1992). For a global vision of Peru and Sendero see Poole and Renique (1992). For a selection of articles in English see Palmer (1992).

6. Sendero's appearance brought forth a sort of fascination with millenarianism, in both foreign and Peruvian analysts, and among both radicals and conservatives. Since the connection between Sendero and Andean millenarianism does not rest on a solid empirical foundation, it is legitimate to conclude that the millenarian explanation rises at least in part from what Orin Starn (1991), paraphrasing Saïd, calls "Andeanism". On the millenarian interpretation of Sendero Luminoso see Degregori (1992a, 1992b).

7. The word *cholo* has a complex ethnic content. In general, it refers to populations of indigenous origin, especially the younger generations, which through geographical and occupational mobility adopt the lifestyles, dress, language, and customs traditionally reserved for *mestizos* or *criollos*. The *cholo* population has grown torrentially as the process of urbanization has advanced, to such an extent that some authors speak of Peru's "cholification". See Franco (1991), Nugent (1992), Quijano (1980).

8. In Peru's Andean regions, the name *mistis* is given to *mestizo* notables, members of the traditional local power structure. The term is similar to that of *ladino*, used in Guatemala and southern Mexico.

9. During the 1970s, Ayacucho had the second highest rate of net population expulsion in Peru (INE, 1987).

10. This educational growth did not evidence itself in the National Census, which between 1961 and 1972 showed Ayacucho's illiteracy rate in Ayacucho declining at only half the national rate. Only between 1972 and 1981 did the department reach the national average. Unless Gall's figures are wrong, the only possible explanation for this contradiction is migration, since various studies show that the most highly educated population tends to migrate.

11. All figures on the University of Huamanga are from Degregori (1990).

12. On the free education movement and its importance for understanding Sendero's emergence see Degregori (1990).

13. According to National Census data, the city of Ayacucho had 27,647 inhabitants in 1961, 48,100 inhabitants in 1972, and 74,551 inhabitants in 1981 (Degregori, 1986). Bloated with war refugees in the past decade, the city's population in 1992 was believed to exceed 120,000 inhabitants.

14. A "Peruvian meteor" according to Morse (1983), José Carlos Mariátegui (1884–1930) was the most important Marxist thinker in Latin America

during the 1920s. The different communists' and socialists' fractions claim Mariátegui as their founding father. Each emphasizing different aspects of his vast work. Sendero's Mariátegui was, of course, an orthodox Marxist–Leninist.

15. The set of courses in general studies taken by all first year students.

16. Here we limit ourselves to only a few characteristics of education in the Andes. We will not enlarge on its obvious ethnocidal aspects, nor on its use as a method of domination by new bourgeois classes. On this issue see Montoya (1980, pp. 310 onwards).

17. "Bases de discusión del PCP, Linea Militar, Sendero y el Ejército Guerrillero Popular, Bestrategia y táctica para la tome del poder", in *El Diario, suplemento especial*, Lima (8 January 1988).

18. There is a verse by Manuel Gonzalez Prada, a late nineteenth-century Peruvian poet who was anti-clerical, positivist, and eventually anarchist, which reads, "war on mean sentiment, divine cult to reason".

19. Partido Communista del Peru, *Desarrolar la guerra popular sirviendo a la revólucion mundial* (Lima, 1986), mimeographed and unpublished document.

20. In these pages we have been referring mainly to the contingent of intellectuals and young people formed in the 1960s and 1970s with which Sendero initiated their armed actions in 1980. Later, as Sendero incorporated new cadres and supporters, especially when it expanded into the coca-growing zone of the Upper Huallaga Valley and into Lima, the situation became more complicated. With respect to its ideology, we might depict the relationship between the established top-level cadres and the militants and sympathizers at the base as that which exists between theologians, village priests, and simple parishioners. The further we go from the leadership, the more the motivations and modes of action vary. I believe, nevertheless, that in a vertically structured party which defines itself as a "war machine" and forms a "discourse community", those whom we call the "theologians" continue to exert a decisive influence.

21. "Bases de discusion: el PCP llama a las masas a luchar por el poder, el pensmiento Gonzalo y los trabajadores", in *El Diario, suplemento especial*, Lima (4 January 1988).

22. The most notorious examples of Sendero's "deciding all" are the so-called "armed strikes", that occurred between 1987 and 1992 in different cities, strikes convoked not by trade unions or regional fronts, but by the party (Sendero Luminoso) or its "generated organizations".

23. PCP, 1988b, p. vii.

24. PCP, 1988b, p. iv.

25. The course this "inversion" followed is of course different and often in opposition to that of feminism. The Peruvian feminist movement denies that Senderismo is a project of "women's liberation", because the organization revolves around a great patriarch. In one of the buildings at San Marcos University in Lima, I recall seeing a large *dadzibao* of the Senderista Popular Women's Movement titled "We are daughters of Gonzalo".

26. In 1980, different leftist groups formed a front, United Left. Through the decade and until its division in 1989, United Left became the second electoral force of the country.

27. For example, "Against the Constitutional Illusions and for the State of New Democracy" (PCP, 1978), is sprinkled with statistical tables about land distribution and the evolution of the GDP. "Let us Develop the Growing Popular Protest" (PCP, 1979) tries to explain the weakness of the Peruvian state by citing Mao and turns to Lenin to prove the existence of a revolutionary situation. Both are mediocre in their statistical interpretations and utterly off-track in their political analysis.

28. In 1977 Sendero "crushed" an internal circle of "rightist" dissidents who proposed activities more like those of the rest of the left, emphasizing work with the labour and peasant unions, which were then booming. Later, between 1979 and 1980 they fought three "intense struggles" against those members of the party who opposed the beginning of the armed struggle (PCP, 1988a, p. vi). For a detailed description of the inner struggles during which these texts/speeches were produced see Gorriti (1990, ch. III).

29. The text was delivered as a speech on 7 June 1979 during the Ninth Expanded Session of the PCP Central Committee, on the occasion of the pledge to the party's flag. The flag, of course, is red; the day coincided with the Peruvian armed forces' annual pledge of fidelity to the Peruvian flag. (Arce Borja, ed., 1989, pp. 141–5).

30. Regarding this fatalistic acceptance of destiny, according to Gorriti (1990, ch. III), in a meeting held a few months later Guzmán gave one of those present a copy of one of his favourite books, *The Life of Mohammed*, by Washington Irving. If we keep in mind that just as Islam means submission, from the 1980s onward Senderista militants had to sign a "letter of submission" to Presidente Gonzalo, we might imagine that Guzmán embodied not only matter but also destiny.

31. The speech was given on 3 December 1979, in the National Expanded Conference of the PCP, on the occasion of the decision to "forge through deeds" the First Company of the First Division of the People's Army (Arce Borja, ed., 1989, pp. 145–50).

32. The highlighting is mine, to underscore the counterpoint between political acts and the symbology of resurrection and projection, mingling together in the same text.

33. Speech delivered on 28 March 1980 during the Second Plenary Session of the PCP Central Committee, in Arce Borja, ed. (1989) pp. 150–9.

34. According to Sendero's official history, the opposition recognized that the government had carried out an agrarian reform and proposed that the party "organize the peasants in the Peasant Confederation of Peru", in which different leftist groups coexisted. They also "developed workerism in the cities, focusing the class on trade unionism and opposing its fulfilling its leadership role". In other words, they proposed participation in the General Confederation of Workers of Peru (CGTP), which led the successful national strikes of 1977 and 1978 (see PCP, 1988a, p. v).

35. "We are the Initiators" (Arce Borja, ed., 1989, pp. 163–75).

36. Sendero's violence is exacerbated by their belief that practically everything that is not "generated" by the party is contaminated and is part of, or serves, the interest of some system: of the "old bureaucratic-landowning state", of bureaucratic capitalism, of imperialism, or of social imperialism (that is, of

the socialist bloc). This wholesale condemnation covers peasant communities, democratically elected mayors, non-governmental development organizations, and trade union and popular organizations, especially those influenced by other parties of the left.

37.   Remember that in Stalin's and Mao's cases, the cult broke loose *after* they took power.

38.   This letter is also a bureaucratic requisite that costs them. In such a secretive party, it might have been enough to swear within the cell or the immediately superior organism. Nevertheless, carefully registered letters of submission have been found in the party's central archives.

One of Sendero's strengths, the result of one of its flights forward, was to see itself from early on as a "new state", a "new republic under construction", and to therefore call their leader "Presidente Gonzalo". Sendero appeared as a more efficient state than the "old one", and the militants felt themselves much better supported than, for instance, the grassroots leaders that dared to oppose them. But at the same time the new state needed a bureaucracy, and a history. Perhaps that is the reason for the filming of two videos, with scenes in which Guzmán appeared, found by police in two Senderista safe houses in 1991 and 1992. The videos helped tighten the police circle around the cosmocrat. The videos were not for "us", nor for foreign propaganda. Nor were they the result of a fit of nostalgia. They were for History. The passion for history, so common in Peru (Adrianzen, 1990), brings their ruin. They needed history in both its dimensions. On the one hand, to strengthen the discourse community, and on the other, given the movement's solemnity and its leaders' need for recognition, the need to "take their place in history".

39.   In this process "Gonzalo Thought" begins to resemble a "Tibetan" version of Marxism, in which the revolutionary "idea" is incarnated in given individuals or "swords" – Marx, Lenin, Mao, Gonzalo – much the way the spirit of Buddha is reincarnated in each new Dalai Lama. Recall that the idea of Peru as the centre of the global revolution, and later of Gonzalo as the "Fourth Sword", begins to germinate shortly after Mao's *death*. Taken from Sendero's viewpoint, there has never been more than one living sword at any given time: Stalin assumed the role after Lenin's death and in a struggle against his rivals; Mao does so after Stalin's death and the "idea's" betrayal by Kruschev, who might otherwise have been the "natural" heir of the Georgian.

40.   See Roldán (1990).

41.   Title of a book written by an admirer.

42.   Throughout the 1980s, the country's prisons became the best place for the Shining Path to grow, where they created a Foucault-like reality, a "panoptical" situation within the cell blocks. The state was left only with the power to imprison (and not for very long because corruption and fear within the judicial branch and the Civil Guard had allowed the prisons to become sieves), while the party itself was in charge of "watching over and disciplining militants", organizing and running their lives 24-hours a day, and indoctrinating them, "pounding and hammering the ideas" through lectures, study groups, speeches, songs, plays and other forms of incessant activities.

REFERENCES

Adrianzèn, Alberto (1990) "Estado y sociedad: señores, masas y ciudadanos", in *Estado y sociedad: relaciones peligrosas* (Lima: DESCO) pp. 13–42.

Aguirre, Beltràn (1967) *Regiones de refugio*, Instituto Indigenista Interamericano, Mexico.

Ansiòn, Juan (1989) *La escuela en la comunidad campesina* (Lima: FAO).

Apter, David (1992) "Democracy, Violence and Emancipatory Movements: Notes for a Theory of Inversionary Discourse", UNRISD, Geneva, manuscript.

Arce Borja, Luis (1989) *Guerra popular en el Perù: El pensamiento Gonzalo* (Brussels).

Arguedas, Josè Maria (1964) *Todas las sangres* (Buenos Aires: Edit. Lozada).

Balbi, Carmen Rosa (1991) "Una inquietante encuesta de opiniòn", in *Quechacer no. 72* (Lima: DESCO) pp. 40–5.

Banco Central de Reserva del Peru (BCR) (1982) *Reseña Economica* (Lima, December).

Berg, Ronald (1992) "Peasant Responses to Shining Path in Andahuaylas", in *Shining Path of Peru*, ed. David S. Palmer, pp. 83–104.

Castillo, Aracelio (1972) *El movimiento popular de junio de 1969 (Huanta y Huamanga, Ayacucho)*, Programa de Ciencias Sociales, Universidad Nacional Mayor de San Marcos, Lima.

Cavarozzi, Marcelo (1991) *Beyond Transitions to Democracy in Latin America*.

Degregori, Carlos (1990) *El Surgimento de Sendero Leminoso* (Lima: Instituto de Estudios Peruanos).

Franco, Carlos (1991) *La otra modernidad: Imágenes de la sociedad peruana* (Lima: CEDEP).

Gall, Norman (1976) *La reforma educativa peruana*, ed. Mosca Azul (Lima).

Gonzales, Josè (1992) "Guerrillas and Coca in the Upper Huallaga Valley", in *Shining Path of Peru*, ed. David S. Palmer, pp. 105–26.

Gorriti, Gustavo (1990) *Sendero: Historia de la guerra milenaria en el Perù. Tomo I*, ed. Apoyo (Lima).

Gutiérrez, Miguel (1988) *La generaciòn del 50. Un mundo dividido* (Lima).

Guzmán, Abimael (1988) "Presidente Gonzala rompe el silencio, Entrevista en la clandestinidad", in *El Diario*, 24 July.

Guzmán, Abimael (1994) "I admired Stalin" (extracts from a recording of Guzmàn's conversations with his captors in the National Counterterrorism Directorate/DINCOTE in the second half of September 1992), in *Si*, no. 310 (Lima) 24–25 August.

Lynch, Nicolàs (1990) *Los jóvenes rojos de San Marcos: Radicalismo universitario de los años 70* (Lima).

Macera, Pablo (1986) "Sendero y Mama Huaco" (extracts from a paper given at the symposium on "Andean Mithology" at the Catholic University, June 1984); in *Cambio*, no. 20 (Lima) 28 August, pp. 9–10.

Marzal, Manuel (1979) "Functiones religiosas del mito en el mundo andino cuzqueño", in *Debates en Antropologia*, no. 4 (PUC, Lima).

McCormick, Gordon (1992) *From the Sierra to the Cities: The Urban Campaign of Shining Path* (New York: Ramd).

Montoya, Rodrigo (1980) *Capitalismo y no capitalismo en el Perù* (Lima, 8 January).

PCP (1988) "Bases de discusión del PCP. El presidente Gonzalo y la revolución democraticà. La guerra popular y el nuevo poder", in El Diario, Supplemento especial (Lima) 4 January.

PCP (1991) ¡Construir la conquista del poder en medio de la guerra popular! (mimeo).

Poole, Deborah and R. Gerardo, (1992) Peru: Time of Fear (London: Latin America Bureau).

Portocarrero, Gonzalo (1993) "La dominación total", in Racismo y mestizaje, (Lima: PUC), pp. 17–32.

Quijano, Anìbal (1980) Dominación y cultura, Lo cholo y el conflicto cultural en el Peru, Mosca Azul (Lima).

Reyna, Carlos (1991) "Gonzalo a la caza de Lima. El gran ensayo de Raucana", in Quehacer no. 73 (Lima: DESCO) September, pp. 30–4.

Senado de la República (1992) Violencia y pacificación en 1991, ed. Senado de la República (Lima).

Smith, Michael (1992) "Shining Path's Urban Strategy: Ate Vitarte", in Shining Path of Peru, ed. D. S. Palmer, pp. 127–48.

Starn, Orin (1991) "Missing the Revolution: Anthropologists and the War in Peru", in Cultural Athropology, 6 (1), February, pp. 63–91.

Urrutia, Jaime, Araujo, Antonio and Haydeè Joyo (1988) "Las commudades en la región de Huamanga, 1824–1968", in Perù, el problema agrario en debate, SEPIA II, ed. Fernando Eguren (Lima: UNSCH/SEPIA).

Universidad Nacional de San Cristòbal de Huamanga (UNSCH) (1977) Universidad Nacianal de San Crisòbal de Huamanga: Libro Jubilar en Homenaje al Tricentenario de su Fundaciòn (Ayacucho: UNSCH,).

Wieviorka, Michel (1988) Societè et Terrorism (Paris: Fayart).

Zambrano, Laura (1988) "Nuestra vida cotidiana es la guerra", interview in El Diario, 14 March, pp. 7–10.

3 Politics, Violence, Writing: The Rituals of "Armed Struggle" in Italy

DAVID MOSS

I   ITALIAN POLITICAL VIOLENCE IN CONTEXT

Where the Shining Path was an attempted revolutionary movement, its discourse disjunctive, its events terrifying, it is difficult to say how much support it received from those "peasants" who were its presumed beneficiaries. Certainly the insistence that Indians were peasants, and radical peasants at that, à la Mao, was hardly appreciated by those for whom the revolution was to be made. For if they were the principal beneficiaries of such a revolution they also paid the highest price.

The Italian case, involving radical terrorism, did not exact its casualties from among the proletariat – the class of preference in keeping with the Leninist tradition of the Red Brigades. Nevertheless there was plenty of political violence. It was inaugurated by a right-wing bomb massacre in 1969: it ended with the murder of a Christian Democrat intellectual by the residual members of the left-wing Red Brigades in 1988. The damage to people and property in those two decades – circa 400 murders, 5,000 injuries, and 12,500 attacks on property – was certainly substantial; yet it amounted to only half the number of deaths from political violence in Spain and barely one-sixth of the deaths in Northern Ireland over comparable periods (Hewitt, 1988).[1] Wider comparisons, too, will help to put the Italian case in perspective. In half the time and among a population little more than one-third of Italy's, left-wing and state violence in Peru produced 25,000 deaths and 22,000 attacks on property; and in Sri Lanka, over an even shorter period, ethnic and political strife caused between 70,000 and 90,000 deaths and the physical displacement of more than 10 per cent of the population.

These crude contrasts can tell us little directly about the social and political perceptions of violence in the different cases. But they do suggest a rather different degree of saturation of everyday life by violence. The chances of dangerous encounters, and the urgency of the need to choose openly to support, tolerate or oppose violence, vary greatly. Even allowing for territorial and temporal variations in the concentration of attacks, "living with violence" must have been different in Peru, where 25,000 insurgents were active among a population of 20 million, than it was in Italy, with no more than a few hundred people directly responsible for clandestine violence active at any one time and widely dispersed among 57 million people. These contrasts can be linked to two further differences. First, the greater or lesser density of violence is likely to have consequences for the force and stability of the meanings that violence carries. In Northern Ireland, for example, the concentration of violence on a miniaturized terrain supports the highly personalized theme of "victimhood" in a way that the dispersed, mostly experience-distant, violence in Italy could not. The Northern Irish conflict has produced a much more stable and elaborate set of conventions governing the meaning of violence than could ever be established in Italy. A second difference concerns the relative importance of particular channels of communication. The discourse community of participants, sympathizers and audiences in Italy was linked by ties that were relatively weak, indirect and impersonal. The meanings carried by violence have to be disseminated by writing rather than orally, exploiting to the full the rapid unregulated growth of print media in Italy in the 1970s. The writing of violence, and the sites and discursive terms in which accounts are produced and read, will therefore be a central theme for analysis.

Along the spectrum of possibilities for dissident violence identified by Apter in Chapter 1, the Italian case shows a progressive shift from the strategy of exchange towards a strategy of inversion. Initially embedded in the ritual projection of traditional forms and symbols for political conflict, clandestine violence, both on the Right and the Left, moved unevenly towards an inversionary rejection of state and society. That the shift stopped short of full inversion, which would have unified all users of violence in a common negative identity, is attributable not only to divisions within the community of armed struggle but also to the nature of the responses to violence, instrumental and interpretive, by the political élite and judiciary. I shall therefore begin by considering the management of the relations between politics and violence, identifying the essential communicative functions of writing and ritual. Then I shall describe the transformation of clandestine violence in the 1970s from the perspective of participants, both Left and Right. The evolution of extreme-Right violence has been largely ignored, even though its militants were responsible for more than half the attacks on people and property between 1969 and 1980;

and I shall suggest that the shift from exchange to inversion can only be properly understood by considering simultaneously the dynamics of the discourse communities on both wings of violence.[2] I shall conclude by examining the interpretive role of the political parties and the judiciary in fixing the public meanings of violence.

II POLITICS AND VIOLENCE

A comparison with Northern Ireland suggests a further distinctive feature of the Italian case. In advanced industrial societies attempts to promote clandestine social-revolutionary violence have to contend with a difficulty not encountered in cases of ethnic-nationalist violence. The activists of ethno-nationalist violence at least share a clear set of religious or ethnic characteristics with the populations on whose behalf they are fighting, as well as some straightforward political goals, even if the identification of exactly which hostile group stands between the population and its goals may be a matter of controversy. But the social-revolutionary users of violence in liberal-democratic societies such as Italy have to make violence not only an instrumental technique for damaging opponents but also the symbolic basis of the community of activists. Solidarities have to be built around availability for violence in order to attract sympathizers, encourage affiliates and identify enemies. Whatever support for social-revolutionary violence may be claimed from class identification, the dispersed social classes of present-day capitalist societies can only on very rare occasions provide the kind of direct explicit solidarity that ethnicity or religion confers. Creating a discourse community based on violence therefore requires, first, the organization of an intelligible relation between "politics" and "violence"; and, secondly, a structure for the relations between the groups or individuals who control the separate elements – material, symbolic and logistical – which have to be combined to make violence a vehicle of political communication.

The attempt to conjugate the terms "politics" and "violence" has to cope with the problem that, in the kind of liberal-democratic societies that political violence is intended to transform, the two terms indicate sharp discursive and practical contrasts. "Politics" marks the realm of rational persuasion through speech, representation by publicly visible and accountable figures, legitimate institutions organized according to public written rules, and decisions – reached by bargaining and compromise – which can always be revised or reversed. "Violence" is coercive, terminates the exchange of words, gains its effects through emotion, represents a zero-sum conflict between aggressors and victims, and has irreversible outcomes. Moreover, the kind of clandestine violence called "terrorism" marks the furthest reach of the contrast. Where "politics" is characterized by presence, symbolized by known representatives speaking directly to constituents at the hustings, to colleagues in Parliament or to the nation on television, "terrorism" is characterized by absence, the anonymity or pseudonymity of its authors, hidden behind stocking masks or symbolic "battle names", protected by clandestinity, and addressing their actions to an equally absent audience, the not-yet "revolutionary" working class. Those who intend their violence to have political outcomes have therefore to imagine and institutionalize relations between these opposed representations.

The sharpness of the contrast can, however, be weakened by considering the effects of what Derrida has called the logic of supplementarity – a pervasive feature of seemingly fundamental distinctions in which each term can be made to display the features of its opposite (Derrida, 1976; Culler, 1979). Deciding on the political role of violence, for example, immediately generates the question whether violence is to be seen as a supplement to, or as a surrogate of, ordinary politics. Is violence to be accepted as the necessary concluding step in a process which remains routinely political – the history-accelerating companion to pacific class struggle? In such circumstances, violence represents the means by which political commitment can be fully realized. Or is it, rather, a technique requiring adoption when the ordinary methods of political conflict are no longer possible or effective? In this case, violence signifies the exhaustion of politics, just as political orders can rely for legitimacy on the elimination of political violence from the social imagination. Disagreements on the supplementary or surrogate role for violence in politics necessarily emerge here among those who share a conviction that violence has become a necessary element in social transformation. Management of the instability in the nature of the distinction between "politics" and "violence" requires organizational mechanisms to support the decision to favour one, and suppress the other, possibility.

III WRITING AS MEDIATION

Although violence terminates the usual form of political communication, it is also paradoxically dependent on another. For acts of clandestine violence against people or property carry only a minimal load of intrinsic meaning: to reach their full effects, pedagogic or punitive, they must be explained by an accompanying written text: the documents which provide not only the reasons for a particular action (choice of a particular target, kind of violence used, intended consequence) but also the political analysis which justifies the recourse to violence at all. Writing therefore represents the terrain on which the opposing fields of politics and violence intersect; it is the medium in which attacks particularized by victim, place and time can be translated into symbolic actions invoking grand casts and great histories. Although the paradigm form of communication between those who are absent, writing is the only means by which the authors of clandestine violence can make themselves politically present, paradoxically in the very mode that emphasizes their absence. In the Italian case, written texts played essential roles in many contexts. They identified the authors of violence and permitted classification of their actions; their publication in the mass media was inevitably a source of controversy, revealing deep disagreements over the conventions that ought to govern this intermediary domain; the development of the most prolonged acts of violence (e.g. kidnappings) was entirely narrated through the victim's letters and his captors' communiqués; incrimination for involvement in violence often rested on the interpretation of texts, sometimes to the exclusion of other evidence; and – a probably unique sequel to violence – a vast corpus of first-person insider accounts, elicited in accordance with the laws rewarding truthful confessions, now awaits the sociological analyst of the *anni di piombo*. Once we cease to regard the functions of texts as simply supplying a transparent guide to the thoughts of their authors, their ubiquity and strategic use come clearly into focus, compelling us to pay close attention to the specific circumstances of their production, circulation and interpretation.

For clandestinely-authored political violence writing represents a supplement in so far as it is both denied as a communicative medium by violence, yet is the condition of its having any meaning at all. Because the document publicizing the meaning of a particular attack necessarily follows, rather than precedes, the action, the normal order between intention and action is inverted. Indeed, it is possible for authors to delay announcing the intended meaning of an action until after the responses to the act itself have appeared and the aim to provoke consequences that have already taken place can be proclaimed: this ploy was regularly used by the Turin column of the Red Brigades (using influential texts such as Giovanni Pesce's *Senza Tregua*). Indeed, left-wing groups in Italy explicitly rejected recourse to types of violence with minimal deferral of meaning, whether bomb massacres (whose meaning is displayed in their taking place at all and thus providing a self-exemplifying instance of the need for strong government to eliminate social insecurity) or *violenza giustizialista* (which assumes that the reasons for punishing the victim are notorious and require no elaborate textual explanation). The resulting deferral of meaning, therefore, allows for all the ambiguity of the act to be appreciated and exploited, setting off the hermeneutic conflicts to which all written texts are exposed. Furthermore, since the intentions revealed by the signatures of violence are retrospectively established and necessarily subject to later modification, the normal linear sequence of intention–action–consequence is upset, demanding explicit attention to the management of time: the time in which the act is set, the relation between successive acts of violence themselves, and the types of impact that they are designed to have on the normal flow of political time.

The interpretive space opened up by clandestine political violence between the acts and their meanings is necessarily filled up with action or refusal of action by its opponents. Whatever is chosen – silence, to show the impossibility of making violence a bearer of political communication, or indirect retaliation, to make the acts themselves more difficult to commit – cannot avoid conferring meaning on violence. In devising responses, the challenge is to ensure that opponents do not confirm the accusations about their identity made by the users of violence to legitimate their recourse to arms. Central to this task is the need to deflect any suggestion that the state itself is violent – that the hidden supplement to the political order itself, its condition of possibility, is the very violence that its rulers condemn in the insurgents. A parallel challenge appears in relation to the texts which supply the meanings for violence. Can journalists interview active participants in violence and print transcripts of their discussions? Does publication of communiqués by the authors of violence entail complicity? Should the accusations made in documents accompanying violence be directly addressed by opponents? Such questions are often most acute in the course of direct confrontations (sieges, hijacks, kidnappings), when the difficulty of answering them in ways acceptable to all opponents of violence is especially visible. Their task is a double one. First, they must prevent what seems like a merely supplementary task to the instrumental repression of violence being represented as the defining feature of the state itself: the authoritarian inability to tolerate dissenting opinion. Secondly, they must ensure that the contents of the texts accompanying violence remain entirely marginal to the acts of violence themselves. Violence must be prevented from appearing to take on the characteristics of writing, to be seen simply as a variant type of inscription which realizes the unmistakably political contents of texts.

IV   MEANING BY RITUAL

In representing the permanently unstable relations between politics, violence and writing, the users of violence are required to cope with the play of differentiation and deferral – the perpetual movement that Derrida (1972) describes as "differance". One, always precarious, resolution is to embed the use of violence itself in highly formalized rules and contexts by which the desired meanings can be made as unequivocal as possible. In single episodes, this tactic has prompted analysts to describe the action as a form of ritual (Moss, 1981; Wagner-Pacifici, 1986). But it is also possible to extend the description of clandestine political violence as a ritual to cover its entire trajectory.

Conventionally understood, ritual provides a framed context for the exploration and dissemination of basic values, permitting the meeting of visible and invisible entities, transforming identities, heightening emotional commitments among participants and spectators, and clarifying social and conceptual boundaries.[3] Typically, the vehicles for these activities are symbols, which unify different universes of meaning and allow for the distancing in which the private emotions of the participants can be separated from the public morality they are affirming (Tambiah, 1979, p. 124). Furthermore, the nature of the connections between the actions which take place within the ritual frame is often deliberately subversive of the everyday extra-ritual assumption of the simple linear flow of time. Ritual therefore produces a distinctive frame for action, establishing spatial and temporal co-ordinates for a new set of agents and generating a terrain on which normally separate universes of meaning and action can meet.

These features provide a description of clandestine political violence in Italy after 1969. The ritual frame itself was created and extended by acts of macro-violence. The right-wing bomb massacre of Piazza Fontana in December 1969 opened up a hitherto unthinkable field of political communication through violence. The boundary around the frame was subsequently moved outwards by further instances of macro-violence, each marking a rupture with the previous limits to the use of violence. The inauguration of kidnapping (1972), "kneecapping" (1975), deliberate murder (1976), and the murder of a kidnap hostage (1978) represented the realisation of hitherto merely latent possibilities. A similar shift was achieved by widening the categories of victim: the Red Brigades, for example, began with neo-Fascist targets in the factory, added Christian Democrat politicians (1975) and left-wing activists and sympathizers (1979), and finally included defectors from the group itself (1981). The shifting range of targets also signals that the creation and transformation of the boundaries among participants, and between participants and audiences, was a ubiquitous feature in ritual performance.

Action within the ritual frame was largely carried by acts of micro-violence. Although the most serious types of attack have naturally received the bulk of media and scholarly attention, some 95 per cent of political violence actually consisted of small-scale vandalism – the destruction of vehicles and minor damage to property. The group signatures ("Brigate rosse", "Prima Linea") claiming responsibility for these attacks populated the initially empty ritual field with agents: they acquired progressively more elaborate identities from their successive acts and texts and from the descriptions offered by outsiders. The number of ritual actors grew from two in 1969 to 269 in 1979, although few had a life-span of more than one year (Galleni, 1981, p. 176). As the number of signatures grew, the internal organization of the ritual field became more complicated, eventually becoming an issue of greater importance than the external relation between the ritual field itself and politics. Of course the signatures were written by flesh and blood activists (many different signatures by the same small set of physical authors); but it was only under those collective names that individuals had recognized access to the ritual terrain of violence. Sometimes supplemented by individual battle-names, the collective signatures also helped to provide individual participants with the self-estrangement claimed to be essential to any continuing involvement in wounding or murder. The distancing achieved by ritualization managed the inevitable tension between altruistic political motivations and readiness to inflict deliberate damage on individuals. For less serious actions, the acts themselves constituted interaction rituals, heightening the sense of membership in an "antagonistic community" for the protagonists (cf. Collins, 1981, pp. 276–81).

To provide a plausible context for violence, its ritual frame had to be given spatial and temporal co-ordinates, relative to the framework of routine politics. Its spatial boundary was marked by the cities and institutions where violent attacks were signed. Most clandestine violence was in fact concentrated in five of Italy's largest cities (Rome, Milan, Turin, Bologna and Genoa) and their hinterlands; and it was mostly directed at industrial, party and state institutions (Galleni, 1981). Placing violence in time was more complicated, requiring some specification of two relations: between the time of the ritual action and the real time of politics, and between successive acts within the ritual frame itself. As I shall show, the temporal co-ordinates for rites of violence were transformed in the course of the 1970s. Initially, the ritual frame was solidly grounded in the topos and symbols of the Resistance, offering an identity for participants and a means of splicing together their actions with a retrievable past and its political projects. However, the subsequent collapse of this reference-point pitched violence into a progressively more obvious timelessness which destroyed any consistent or intelligible relation to the political domain. Within the ritual frame, the kind of history written by the sequence of acts stood in contrast to the time-frame of routine politics. Some two-thirds of all signed violence, Left and Right, was characterized by its authors as "armed propaganda" (della Porta and Rossi, 1983, p. 28), a form of action that generates history-by-precedent: "examples of how things should or should not be done: incidents, events become examples of this and that rather than links in a chain of cause and effect" (Davis, 1992, p. 18). This contrast between the conceptualization of the flow of time in the ritual frame and the linear cause-and-effect time of ordinary politics created difficulties for the users of violence in representing the consequences of their ritual attacks for the political arena: their opponents worked to restrict any sense that ordinary time had been disrupted by violence.[4] Finally, ritual frames demand formal closure, a public conclusion to the disruptions of identity and time. The pressure to stage a reconciliatory ending was indeed visible after 1988, once the violence itself had ceased and the political transformations which the users of violence intended their rituals to accomplish had been averted. An essential element in determining the failure of armed struggle was the public clarification of the meanings of the major attacks, so that their potential to provoke further, potentially interminable conflicts was defused. Since the key clarifying role was played by the judiciary, the set of trials involving former participants in violence must be considered an integral part of the full ritual sequence. First, however, I shall track the main stages of the evolution, and eventual involution, of the rites of violence.

V   EXCHANGE AND RITUAL, 1969–74

(a)   Establishing the Frame for Violence

The right-wing bomb massacre of Piazza Fontana in Milan in December 1969 opened up the possibility of using violence in a new way: it served to "ungate" political imagination (Lewis, 1980, p. 31). Previously, most violence had occurred more or less openly in the course of the student and worker mobilizations, characterized by direct confrontations between extremists of the Right and Left and clashes with police in the course of mass demonstrations. Given the importance of the practice and discourse of violence in recent Italian history and the scale of mass mobilization and confrontations across all major institutions between 1967 and 1969, what is surprising about the first phase of clandestine violence is less its appearance than the reluctance to exploit it. Only two signatures of any significance appeared, the Red Brigades (BR) on the Left, the Squadre d'azione Mussolini (SAM) on the Right. Both were confined to Milan until 1973 when police pressure forced the local BR members to go underground and move to Turin. And both exploited the symbolic capital of the Resistance in creating a model for their actions and appealing for the support of the wider communities in which they claimed membership. As a result the violence which ensued fell rapidly into a predictable sequence of exchanges which reflected the dominant empirical and discursive opposition between Left and Right in post-war Italian politics.

The examples of macro-violence by the extreme Right and extreme Left revealed their different approaches to the distinction between politics and violence. The bomb massacres of the Right – four across Italy between 1969 and 1974 – were designed to create the sense that violence had become a pervasive element of everyday life. Making victims indiscriminately, the bombs demonstrated that violence was no longer a separate domain, remote from all but political extremists, but a potential threat to everyone. Trust in the governing parties to protect their electors and other citizens would be undermined. Similarly, by leaving their attacks unclaimed or trying to throw responsibility for them onto the Left, the extreme Right was also seeking to weaken the significance of the general distinction between Right and Left and the kinds of political strategy each was prepared to use. The disruption of these taken-for-granted distinctions was part of a general strategy to subvert the boundaries which had excluded the Right from full political legitimacy since the fall of Fascism. Those boundaries already appeared to be weakening in the early 1970s: the party of the extreme Right, the Movimento Sociale Italiano (MSI), made substantial electoral gains in 1972 and managed to get itself publicly aligned with the ruling Christian Democrat party in several political confrontations.[5] The repeated use of bombs exemplified the ritual work of upsetting category distinctions between participants as a necessary prelude to the transformation of relationships between them (Kapferer, 1979). Right-wing violence and politics moved in the same direction.[6]

A quite different relation between the fields of violence and politics was represented in the macro-violence of the extreme Left – the five bloodless kidnappings carried out by the Red Brigades between 1972 and 1974. They provided a carefully structured occasion for demonstrating the separate existence but mutual accessibility of the fields of open and clandestine politics by moving the victim across the boundary between them during his capture. His confessions – confirming the role of extreme Right violence in repressing working-class mobilization on the shop floor – were designed to transform the accusations of his captors into established knowledge for dissemination to the widest possible audience. Kidnappings – lasting up to several weeks – thus served as an elaborate mechanism for the production of knowledge about politics. In contrast to the incorporation of violence into everyday life and politics by the extreme Right, they represented a highly structured exterior site from which the reality of politics could be revealed.

Within the contrasting frames created by macro-violence, both Right and Left practised the micro-violence of attacks on opponents and their property. Right-wing militants attacked the activists of the extreme Left; members of the Left retaliated. Because the clandestine activists on both sides took themselves to be acting on behalf of wider constituencies, their violence can be described as a type of segmentary exchange.[7] The inventors of the BR, for example, saw themselves as a mere refraction of the Left as a whole: they repudiated the idea of creating a clearly distinctive political identity, refusing to "engage in sterile ideological conflict" with the Communist Party or the extra-parliamentary Left groups ("Lotta Continua", "Potere Operaio", and others) which had sprung up in the wake of the "Hot Autumn" and whose own distinctiveness with regard to the institutional Left was based on proclamations of the (eventual) need for revolutionary violence (Vettori, 1973; Bobbio, 1979). They also disclaimed exclusive ownership of their signature, declaring it available to anyone prepared to copy their attacks (Soccorso Rosso, 1976). The identity of the BR signature as one component of a larger unit was underlined by its authors' participation in grassroots politics, making violence just one element in their political repertoire and ensuring regular contact with members of the parliamentary and extra-parliamentary Left (Franceschini, 1988, pp. 78–82; Curcio, 1993, pp. 64–5). Their attacks were concentrated against neo-Fascist activists, accusing them of waging class war against the working class on the street and shopfloor, protected by the local representatives of an increasingly repressive state. To assess the results of their displays of "counter-power", they sought direct reports from factory floor or sympathizers from the extreme Left. Apart from their clandestine delivery and use of an accompanying signature, the activities by the BR and the SAM were virtually indistinguishable from the types and targets of the openly violent confrontations between Left and Right in factory, school and neighbourhood (della Porta and Tarrow, 1986).

Only in respect of their recent arrival in Milan were the founding-members of the Red Brigades perhaps distinctive from other left-wing activists. For Curcio, Franceschini, Moretti and their comrades had all been drawn to Milan after 1968 by the promise of direct participation in a revolutionary transformation. They therefore had no longstanding status in neighbourhood politics and no local political reputations to preserve. We can speculate that for militants with such fragile links to the community in which they were politically active, the slippage between open and clandestine politics was easier than for their comrades with deeper local roots and reputations. For the inventors of the Red Brigades, marginality of this kind made the incorporation of violence into their political repertoire a relatively unproblematic extension of their existential position in the city.

(b)   Retrieving the Resistance

Territorially anchored in Milan's local politics, the BR and SAM also shared the time-frame in which their actions were projected. In representing their identities, both extreme Right and extreme Left drew heavily on the rhetoric and symbols of the Resistance, the period of armed conflict between Fascists and partisans between 1943 and 1945. The retrieval of the Resistance condensed a set of powerful meanings. First, it signified the reality of violent confrontation between Left and Right, grounding the field of ritual violence after 1969 in a historical referent, which was of course interpreted differently on each side. For the extreme Right the signature "Squadre d'azione Mussolini" signalled the recovery of a continuity broken by the anti-Fascist provisions of the 1948 Constitution and the legal prohibition on reconstitution of the Fascist movement. The exclusions which followed the Resistance settlement encouraged the militants of the extreme Right to see themselves as victims, violated by the lies and discrimination of the victors (Fiasco, 1990, p. 159). For the extreme Left, the Resistance stood as the symbol of the possibility of social and political revolution, which had been aborted by the DC and PCI. Violence served, negatively, as the method for self-defence against resurgent Fascism; positively, as the means to overcome and redress the historical defeat of the Left's central ambitions.

The second source of discursive power in the Resistance lay in its unification of a set of overlapping but discrete conflicts. As Pavone (1991) has emphasized, the Resistance was a condensed symbol for three distinct antagonisms: a patriotic war against foreign occupation; a civil war against

Fascists; and a class war against the bourgeois supporters of Fascism to achieve a social revolution. Updated in its referents (the substitution of the imperialist United States for the occupying German forces of 1943–5), the Resistance could hold together the same mix of international, national and class oppositions. It could provide a genuine "world-view" linking conflicts all the way from the neighbourhood clashes with neo-Fascist thugs to the increasing role of the MSI in national politics to the armed resistance by the Vietcong against American imperialism. The Resistance represented the essential totalizing idiom for discourse involving violence, explaining the everyday experience of political militants at grassroots level as a local refraction of the master-narrative of conflict between Right and Left in post-war Italy and beyond. Its symbolic power to frame violence would no doubt have been weakened if the Red Brigades had attempted elaborate textual exegesis and thus exposed its necessarily discrepant meanings.

Finally, the Resistance was recent enough to be made available to the political militants of the early 1970s through the stories and anecdotes of former partisans and Fascists. Indeed, the oral histories and autobiographies transmitted directly to extra-parliamentary militants by survivors of the Resistance years helped to build the sense of a past for their future. The early members of the Red Brigades had extensive contacts with former partisans, who handed over their Resistance weapons, offered support and designated them as the heirs to complete their political and social tasks (Franceschini, 1988, pp. 3–11; Manconi, 1990; Curcio, 1993, pp. 18, 71). On the Right, too, many neo-Fascist activists came from families who had served in the short-lived Repubblica Sociale Italiana and been active, rather than nominal, Fascists (Ferraresi, 1988, p. 105). The symbolic capital retrievable from the accounts and artefacts of former partisans and Fascists thus gave a plausible historical place to the rites of violence: sometimes, too, the name of a known partisan supplied the battle-name which the members of the BR adopted to signal their shift into the frame of ritual violence (Curcio, 1993, p. 18).

Interpreting deliberate violence as the projection of a basic segmentary conflict between Right and Left ensured a measure of local tolerance for its users. But the accompanying reluctance to credit the signature with a clearly distinctive political identity also diminished its appeal. Semi-clandestine activities offered little substantial benefit over the more urgent task of resisting the same antagonists in open confrontations. Political militants who accepted violence as part of politics joined the defence squads ("servizi d'ordine") of an extra-parliamentary group, so that in the cities where the neighbourhood confrontations with neo-Fascism lasted longest, the recruitment to the left-wing armed groups was slowest (Moss, 1989, p. 54). In any case most left-wing activists accepted violence as a means of self-defence but not of deliberate attack. The Red Brigades therefore failed to recruit more than a handful of activists, even after the display of their ability to kidnap an unpopular magistrate in 1974. Their founding members were arrested later in the same year as a result of police infiltration; and the group's early attempts to establish new centres of support outside Milan had limited success in Turin and none in Rome, Genoa and the Veneto. Della Porta and Tarrow (1986) convincingly argue that the increase in clandestine violence had to await the decline in large-scale political and industrial mobilization.

VI   THE LOSS OF SEGMENTARY ORDER, 1974–6

(a)   The Disappearance of the "Other"

As long as violence was anchored in local politics and contained in the complementary opposition of Left and Right, the frame for its use remained stable. In the mid-1970s, however, the relatively stable organization of violence collapsed. First, the users of clandestine violence became detached from the wider community which they could lay claim to representing. Secondly, the ideological model for segmentary relations, the Resistance, was reappropriated by more powerful actors hostile to violence. The constraints, social and discursive, on clandestine violence were therefore relaxed, leading to a search for new contexts in which to provide meaning.

The scale of right-wing violence was directly affected by the general weakening of the Right in Italian politics after 1974. Its surrounding international platform of support disappeared with the changes of regime in Portugal, Greece and Spain; and the collaboration between DC and MSI was abandoned after their joint defeat in the 1974 divorce referendum, the return to a Centre-Left government, and the increasing attention to the possibility of a "Historic Compromise" between Catholics, Socialists and Communists. The MSI itself sustained a clear electoral rebuff in 1976, followed by a significant scission leading to further electoral decline (Caciagli, 1988). Furthermore, the party began to dissociate itself from the actions of its extra-parliamentary extremist groups, whose internal cohesion was undermined by the legal orders to dissolve "Ordine Nuovo" (1973) and "Avanguardia Nazionale" (1974) and by the deaths, arrests or self-exile of their leaders. Party discouragement of violence, and the withdrawal of protection by some branches of the state, ensured a fall in the levels of right-wing assaults. By 1976 the volume of right-wing violence had declined by two-thirds compared to 1971 (Galleni, 1981); and its clandestine forms were thereafter almost entirely confined to Rome, where 87 per cent of the 266 identified participants after 1977 were active (Ferraresi, 1988, p. 96, Table 2). Only three right-wing signatures ("Nuclei armati rivoluzionari", "Terza Posizione", and "Costruiamo l'Azione") claimed responsibility for more than ten acts of violence or made any claim to establishing a political identity. As the magistrature and police intensified their repression, so their most prominent local representatives became the direct target of right-wing violence. Antagonism towards the Left, associated with the failed strategy of the MSI in the early 1970s, was rejected as the primary symbolic referent of the extreme Right.

The decline in assaults from the extreme Right had repercussions on the strategy of the extreme Left. The reduced demand for "militant anti-Fascism" (*antifascismo militante*) left the members of the "defence squads" (*servizi d'ordine*), who had protected their extra-parliamentary groups against right-wing violence, without a clear role. At the same time the organizational framework in which the expertise in violence acquired by the squads' members had been held in check disintegrated. First, by the mid-1970s the larger groups had become almost self-contained communities for their more committed members. One of the leaders of "Avanguardia Operaia" noted that in Milan self-sufficient "ghettos" of the group's militants had emerged in which members could earn a living by selling second-hand clothes for the organization's benefit, get their news from the organization's newspaper and radio station, find their partners among fellow-members, live and relax in the organization's squats, enjoy themselves at Dario Fo's plays and at concerts of left-wing bands, and so on, leading gradually to "the all-but-complete ending of any contact with the rest of the world" (Corvisieri, 1979). Detachment from the world of ordinary politics was accentuated by a second factor: the collapse of the political framework of the extreme Left. In the determination to give the extra-parliamentary Left parliamentary representation, its leaders had begun to exchange fulltime "horizontal" bargaining with the leaders of other groups for "vertical" connections with the local professionals of violence in their own groups. But the unexpectedly poor showing of their cartel in the elections of 1975–6 caused many skilled and experienced activists to abandon politics altogether and provoked the virtual collapse of the organizational structure of the extreme Left. The political component accentuated its rejection of violence: the specialists in defensive violence developed its active use as the basis for their own political identity. As on the Right, the arena in which "politics" and "violence" were becoming less distinguishable was simultaneously moving further away from the world of non-violent politics. Combining the rites of violence and grassroots politics became more difficult.

(b)   The Exhaustion of the Resistance

More or less simultaneously, the legitimation of armed struggle by reference to the Resistance lost its power. In the first place, the primary bearers, the Red Brigades, had demonstrably failed. In the second place, the symbolic capital of the Resistance was rapidly displaced by the Communist Party's historiographic and ritual reappropriations of the years 1943–5 to legitimate its own "Historic Compromise" strategy. Party celebrations of the thirtieth anniversaries of the major events of the Resistance were designed less to emphasize either the continuing Fascist threat or the uncompleted social revolution than to remind Italians of the historically demonstrated value of an earlier collaboration between Catholics, Socialists and Communists.[8] Communist reassertion of control over the "true" meaning of the Resistance and its symbolic capital was accompanied by vastly increased levels of mobilization against the use of violence, especially in the cities in which left-wing coalitions had come to power in 1975. The PCI and trade unions came to conceptualize left-wing violence as a distinctive threat, reversing their earlier analyses that its actions were simply Fascist provocations; and they redoubled their commitment to organizing mass demonstrations to display the extent of their rejection of violence. Since the mobilizations, in the shape of marches, strikes and funeral attendance, were generally motivated by reference to the continuing importance of Resistance values, the opportunity for its much smaller political competitors on the extreme Left to make use of the Resistance as the diacritic of their own political identity or to legitimate violence was greatly reduced.

The loss of the Resistance as the primary source of the intelligibility of clandestine violence had several consequences. First, communication with the broad community which accepted Resistance values was undermined. Secondly, violence could no longer be presented as the necessary method of completing the political itinerary embarked on in 1943, the variant route to the realization of the same project that had helped to produce the Republic itself. Undermining the supplementary role of violence shifted attention towards its potential use as a surrogate, inversionary, activity. Thirdly, the power of Resistance discourse to unify separate conflicts was lost. In practice Resistance terminology had not only provided a morality and conventions for violence: its power to condense meanings at different levels had allowed low-level objectives to carry wide-ranging political meanings. The separation of violence from its symbolic moorings, so to speak, became possible. But the actualization of the potential for its dissemination required the set of "carriers" whom the Red Brigades had been unable to find. The mid-1970s supplied them from the ranks of the *servizi d'ordine* and the residual extreme Left movement of "Autonomia".

VII   ESCALATION, INVOLUTION, EXIT, 1976–88

(a)   Extension of the Ritual Frame

The murder of a Fascist provincial councillor by a new actor, "Prima Linea", and of a magistrate by the Red Brigades inaugurated a dramatic expansion of the ritual frame in 1976. New signatures appeared each year: twenty-eight in 1976, 269 in 1979, signing 40 per cent of all acts of violence attributed to left-wing groups over that period across all cities in Central and Northern Italy. New levels of clandestine violence were reached: four-fifths of all left-wing violence after 1969 was concentrated into the four years from 1976 to 1979, and a growing proportion of its actions – one in seven by 1979 – consisted of murders and deliberate woundings (Galleni, 1981). With the exception of the extreme Right's two further bomb massacres and actions more or less confined to Rome, the remaining years of clandestine political violence belonged to left-wing groups.[9]

In place of the territorially circumscribed egalitarian micro-community of the early years came a highly diverse array of users of violence, differentiated by city, signature, political experience, and marking a sharp break with the early years of clandestine violence when the tiny group of Red Brigades members had planned, executed and publicly defended their own attacks. Activists and exegetes of violence ceased to be the same people. Participants were spread out across many institutions, with different direct antagonists and occasions for conflict. Their variegation produced a discourse community stratified into the three milieux of intelligentsia, apparatchiks and locals, each maintaining control over one of the essential resources to manufacture intelligible violence and inserted into very different networks of social relations (Moss, 1989). The intelligentsia, active in left-wing politics before 1969, produced the public meanings for violence: its members were largely distributed between the prison and the courtroom (the founders of the Red Brigades) and the university (the leaders of "Autonomia"). The apparatchiks, initiated into politics in the "defence squads" of the extra-parliamentary Left, carried out and signed the attacks, protecting the association of particular signatures with specific types of violence. The locals, entering politics in the wake of the disintegration of the extra-parliamentary Left in the mid-1970s, supplied essential logistical help by providing lodgings, gathering information on potential targets and local conflicts, and distributing documents.[10]

Apart from belonging to different political generations, the three milieux were also stratified in terms of their levels of involvement in violence. For the intelligentsia, particularly after they had been brought together in one of the maximum security prisons, the composition of texts and the organization of conflict within the prison system was a full-time task. In the case of the Red Brigades' intelligentsia, members identified exclusively with the signature, to the extent of declaring their public support for the attacks it authored even when they strongly disagreed with their nature and direction. At the other extreme were the locals whose involvement in violence was part-time and limited. Two-thirds of participants in left-wing violence took no part in any attack on individuals, and two-fifths had no direct role in a violent act of any kind (della Porta, 1990, p. 167). The overwhelming majority expressed their commitment to armed struggle by providing intermittent support for a very small circle of more centrally-involved friends or acquaintances, combining their involvement in violence not only with open politics but with work and often family life (Novaro, 1990). They did not intend violence to be a rupture with these commitments or careers but wished to shape their particular levels of involvement in armed struggle around their other sources of identity.[11] Coming from many different cities and occupations (Moss, 1989, p. 43; della Porta, 1990, p. 144), the contexts in which they saw a use for violence were also very diverse. Since they often became involved for reasons of friendship or kinship, their attachments to any particular signature, as opposed to generic support for armed struggle, were very fragile. Moreover, at individual level, age and political experience divided them sharply from the intelligentsia: even when violence appeared to be enjoying its greatest appeal, the links between those who shared the attachment were extremely fragile.

Linking the milieux of intelligentsia and locals were the apparatchiks, the full-time clandestine activists of armed struggle who filled the various organizational roles in the separate groups and were responsible for the most serious attacks. The clandestine life was not, however, a product of choice but of the desire to escape arrest. The category was therefore always very small: in Rome, for example, the thirty-two murders and woundings by the Red Brigades over virtually the entire life of the local group between 1976 and 1982 were the responsibility of no more than twenty members. Most participants in armed struggle were clandestine only in the sense that they concealed their involvement in violence. The apparatchik milieu was therefore particularly unstable. Its members were deprived of a local context in which to display their political commitment openly; they were also divided between opposing attempts to make violence intelligible, elaborated by different segments of the intelligentsia and reflecting the contrasting existential positions of the intelligentsia and the locals.

(b)   The Attack on the State vs the Pursuit of Autonomy

Two contrasting political objectives for violence emerged, broadly distinguishable as the attack on the state and the pursuit of "autonomy". The attack on the state was directed by the Red Brigades, which made the strategy manifest by adding attacks on Christian Democrat politicians, magistrates and police to their long-standing targets at factory level. Identifying the state as the principal target, which provided the largest proportion of victims by the end of the 1970s (della Porta, 1990, pp. 245–50), met three objectives. First, since the intelligentsia were most directly in confrontation with the state in prison or during their trials, the state served to keep their own direct experiences in relation with the wider objectives. Prison riots and courtroom disruption provided the existential confirmation for the state as the most appropriate general target of violence. Secondly, the state – which was defined as including the major political parties – also provided a target which could unify the increasingly diverse users of the BR signature in different cities and institutional contexts. Since local conflicts were highly diverse in their intensity, personnel and scope, the identification of a clear trans-local target was a means of keeping the separate groups of users within a single discursive network. The state and its representatives were indeed everywhere and could therefore supply a general enemy for armed struggle. Thirdly, as represented by the police forces, the state provided a clear antagonist for the apparatchiks, especially after a special anti-terrorist unit was created in 1978.[12] For the apparatchiks, the texts by the BR intelligentsia offered a context to replace their declining local involvements and provided a political meaning for their otherwise merely defensive actions against the police.

In contrast to the state-referenced version of violence was the theme of autonomy. In the community of armed struggle, the goal of "autonomy" was associated particularly with "Prima Linea" and the overwhelming majority of the new, and usually short-lived signatures whose targets were people and property at local level. The term "autonomy" (*autonomia*), which has been described as "a touchstone of revolutionary politics" after 1968 (Lumley, 1990, p. 37), had appeared in the texts and talk of all the most significant extra-parliamentary groups after 1969, including the early productions of the Red Brigades. But "Autonomia Operaia" only became a widely adopted and loosely organised focus for political identity after 1975 with the formation of an intelligentsia ready to trace its genealogy through 1968–9 down to the university-based protests of 1977.[13] The principal theme uniting its many different formulations can be summarized as the deliberate negation of, and estrangement from, the political and economic institutions and methods of Italian democracy. In the same way that the identification of the state as a primary antagonist was tied to the contexts of intelligentsia and the apparatchiks, the emphasis on autonomy celebrated a parallel form of marginalization from politics.

With the decline of the mobilizations of 1969–73, the conflicts in the workplace and educational institutions became institutionalized. Once the goal of altering the frameworks for dispute had been abandoned, the issues tended to concern the implementation of the reforms that the mobilizations had generated.[14] Conflicts thus turned local and particularistic, managed by trade-union and political professionals who controlled access to the new systems of interest mediation. A similar process can be detected in the other stronghold of extra-parliamentary activity: neighbourhood politics. Conflicts over housing, transport and local services, which were the consequences, particularly in Milan, Turin and Rome, of the unregulated urban development and massive population movements of the preceding two decades, had been a major terrain for extra-parliamentary activism of the years 1968–73 (Lumley, 1990; Laganö et al., 1982; Corvisieri, 1979). After 1975, however, the opportunities for extra-parliamentary activism were progressively reduced. For the decentralization of administrative authority created neighbourhood councils, dominated by representatives of the major political parties, which took over responsibility for grassroots issues. The extension of party negotiation into neighbourhood-level politics was accelerated by the left-wing victories in the municipal elections of 1975 in Milan, Turin, Genoa, Rome and Naples in 1975: the left-wing parties had much closer grassroots links than the outgoing centrist parties. Their control over the new fora for representation served to marginalize the activities of the extreme Left groups and to reduce their opportunities for direct political intervention. What remained at neighbourhood level were two increasingly important issues which routine party and union politics was much less well-equipped to deal with – the decentralization of economic activity into the local sweat-shops of the black economy and the new forms taken by the drug trade (Arlacchi and Lewis, 1990). Regulation in both spheres was of course often extra-legal or illegal, involving intimidation and violence. For the militants of the extra-parliamentary Left who wanted to remain active in the shrinking political space at grassroots level, a readiness to respond to coercion with coercion and to add violence to their tactical repertoire was almost a necessary condition of political identity. Many of the transient *autonomia* groups of the second half of the 1970s were therefore situated on the fringes between legality and illegality. Unable or unwilling to take on institutionalized roles in social and political conflicts, some of their members promoted the use of violence as an expressive rite, performing the "antagonistic" identity otherwise denied them.

Moreover, the victories of the Left at the municipal elections in 1975 supplied the *autonomi* with immediate local antagonists, reinforcing their existing hostility to the reformist Left.[15] As the refusal of institutional commitments itself took semi-institutionalized shape, the activities of the collectives, squats, broadsheets and radio stations founded by "Autonomia" offered ample opportunity for direct confrontation with municipal authorities. In most large cities, therefore, the natural opponents of the *autonomi* were left-wing parties and trade unions, making the Red Brigades concern with the state and the DC too remote from the everyday experience of the contexts in which the *autonomi* were prepared to use or sympathize with violence. The result was to accentuate the existing differences among the supporters of armed struggle and to provoke severe disagreements about its proper targets. The rituals of generalized attacks on the state and of individualized performance of autonomy made up the endpoints on the spectrum of representations of violence, replacing the "opposed extremisms" of Right and Left in the early years of violence.

(c) Ritual Involution

The increasing scale and scope of the rites of violence forced opponents and participants to clarify their commitments publicly. Opposition to violence on the Left grew, making it much more difficult for the users of violence to combine armed struggle with grassroots politics. They could no longer claim that their attacks were simply supplements to existing conflicts and spontaneous violence: the frames for violence and politics grew further apart. At the same time, the clarification of action and identity within the ritual frame for violence produced inversionary shifts along its principal organizational and temporal co-ordinates.

As signatures multiplied, the concern to identify the differences between their authors became more urgent. Forms of violence could themselves mark some distinctions, and signatures could compete in staging dramatic attacks to display their power and increase their appeal to the dwindling number of potential recruits to armed struggle.[16] But the demand to elaborate the identity of the signatures offered a more significant exegetic role to the intelligentsia, who were best placed to define the new actors, show how particular attacks fitted into broader schemes, and explain their significance. The apparatchiks and locals required a context for their violence that could replace the declining immediate referents of shop floor and grassroots conflict. Moreover, the rising volume of violence made it more difficult to discern the impact of any particular attack: textual analysis could stand in here for the absent responses of local or state audiences. Where disagreements among the newly diverse users of single or different signatures occurred, the intelligentsia could also be called on to arbitrate their conflicts (Curcio, 1993, pp. 168–9). Hence, in 1978 at the time of the Moro kidnapping, the Red Brigades' intelligentsia decided for the first time to take on the role of "historic leaders" of the signature (Franceschini, 1988, p. 153). Guardianship of the Red Brigades' public identity, and the capacity to determine the meaning of its violence, was thus represented as passing under the control of those who were actually excluded from direct involvement in violence.[17] Their presence in court and absence from direct politics provided an ideal position from which to try to stabilize the paradoxical combination of presence and absence in clandestine armed struggle.

The privileged status of the intelligentsia also rested on their value as a source of knowledge for external audiences.[18] The identities and whereabouts of its members were known; and the virtually continuous presence in court of the Red Brigades' members of the intelligentsia in the later 1970s offered many opportunities to endorse their role as key interpreters of armed struggle. Neither apparatchiks nor locals could of course have access to so public a platform, nor did they have the personal contacts with journalists and politicians that the members of the intelligentsia could exploit to disseminate their versions of violence. Moreover, the circulation of the intelligentsia's texts enjoyed partial exemption from the normal strictures against direct contact with participants in violence as a source of news. Although no laws or self-regulatory codes to govern the reporting of violence were introduced, every case in which a journalist used interview or documentary materials from a clandestine meeting with a self-confessed user of political violence generated fierce controversy and often led to criminal charges. Use of texts and interviews authored by the imprisoned intelligentsia – who could not be the direct executors of the worst crimes – attracted far less opprobrium. Publication of such materials could be represented as a valuable contribution to an improved understanding of violence – a defence which assumed that the intelligentsia's texts were indeed a transparent guide to the truth about violence, not simply one among several competing versions.

The most dramatic event of the last phase – the kidnapping and murder of Moro in 1978 – displayed many of these features clearly.[19] The controversy over the "real authorship" of Moro's letters from his "people's prison" exhaustively rehearsed the interpretive difficulties of reading documents emanating from clandestine sources. The intentions of the BR remained uncertain: the document explaining the meaning of the attack was only distributed one year after the kidnapping and had been authored, not by those directly responsible, but by the intelligentsia. Notoriously, the "official" BR version of the attack failed to fix its meaning. Other interpretations have been in competition ever since, leaving open the extent to which the different, not necessarily incompatible, ambitions were significant: attack on the DC, deflection of the PCI from the path of the "Historic Compromise", or determination to provoke greater state repression and force the less-organized *autonomi* into the visibly more efficient Red Brigades for self-defence. Those uncertainties were coupled with ambiguities about the primary intentions of the Red Brigades' opponents: to secure Moro's release or to use the ritual to display their own identities. These interpretive conflicts lasted throughout the 1980s, aired extensively during the sequence of trials and resurfacing unpredictably in wider party-political disputes.[20] The prolonged interpretive sequel to the kidnapping has shown clearly their escape from determination by reference either to the intentions of the protagonists or the consequences of the events. Finally, whatever impact it may have had on its opponents, the kidnapping ritual revealed very clearly the divisions of various kinds within the community of armed struggle: between the *autonomi*, who refused the BR invitation to show support by increasing their attacks; between the BR apparatchiks, leading to the first public scission from the group, followed shortly by its definitive breakup into hostile factions; and between the BR apparatchiks and the intelligentsia, who had been in clandestine conflict for one year already.

As the public meanings for violence were longer deferred and were further removed from control by the direct participants, so the time frame for the rites of violence became uncertain. Represented as "armed propaganda", acts of violence claimed a direct linkage to concurrent politics, whose hidden features they were intended to reveal. From their origins in 1970 until 1978, the Red Brigades had characterized their attacks, including the kidnapping of Moro, in that way. By 1980, however, they concluded that the armed propaganda years were over but that the next phase – "civil war", in which their violence would have direct instrumental force – had not yet begun ("Brigate Rosse", 1980, p. 269). The placing of the current stage was left undefined. The collapse of any clear time-reference for the general strategy of violence thus accompanied the difficulty of representing plausibly any connection between the intention, action and consequence of single acts.

The conflicts publicly revealed by the murder of Moro also made clear an inversion of the function of the ritual of violence itself. Initially intended as a means of unmasking the strategies and identities of their political opponents, the rites of violence now served to display only the conflicts among their protagonists. The clarifying function of ritual was now turned on its agents, not on its victims or audiences. In 1981, for example, the four simultaneous kidnappings carried out under the Red Brigades' signature with victims from different occupational categories were designed primarily to publicize the differences between the strategies of the factions responsible. Violence had become primarily a means of communication internal to the world of armed struggle, to ensure the widest circulation of documents, define authors' identities and punish defectors.[21] Where the practice of armed struggle had once been merely supplemented by minimal documents, it now became a primary means of signalling agreement with the content of texts and of testing the accuracy of some of their claims. Awareness of these multiple confusions of intention, identity and time prompted some activists to start calling publicly for an end to armed struggle in 1979.

(d)   Out of the Ritual Frame: Repentance and Reconciliation

As an index of these perceptions, the annual incidence of violence fell very rapidly from 2,139 attacks in 1979 to 174 in 1982. The political impact of the most serious acts was also substantially reduced; and the subsequent right-wing massacres and left-wing murders, which continued sporadically until 1988, were made to appear all the more tragically futile by the disappearance both of any wider context for the attacks and by the intelligentsia's public dissociation from violence. Violence in fact vanished almost as quickly as it had escalated in the mid-1970s, at a speed and scale which only become comprehensible when the confessions of former participants revealed how fragile many of their commitments to armed struggle had really been.

The mechanism for individual exit from the rituals of armed struggle was provided by the "repentance legislation", the laws of 1980, 1982 and 1987 which offered substantially reduced sentences in return for various degrees of collaboration with the magistrature.[22] For full benefit, defectors had to sign a statement confirming their complete repudiation of, and dissociation from, armed struggle. Their descriptions of events and individual responsibilities had to be confirmed in open court where they could be questioned by the lawyers defending the fellow-members whom they had named. Interrogation also commonly took place in the presence of the close kin of their victims in their role as civil plaintiff. Defendants, self-confessed or not, were thus forced into direct confrontation with the public and private consequences of their actions. The courtroom offered an opportunity to shed the collective identity which they had assumed for action in the ritual frame of violence and to confirm reintegration into the legal political order. Between 1979 and 1984 the overwhelming majority of left-wing participants in violence passed through these rites; so that by the early 1990s only 127 of the 297 participants still in jail for the most serious attacks had refused to abjure their commitment to armed struggle (*La Repubblica*, 10 August 1991).

Not surprisingly, given their generational heterogeneity and different levels of involvement, the participants in political violence proceeded at various speeds through the distinctive stages of the exit process: renunciation of violence, dissociation from their armed group, admission of their own responsibilities, and full descriptions of everything and everyone connected with armed struggle. The broad pattern of defection does, however, shed further valuable light on the different types of affiliation and on the sources of identity. The earliest left-wing defectors (*pentiti*) were all from the apparatchik milieu, indicating the pressures on its members – especially on those who occupied marginal positions in their group organizations (Peci, Sandalo, Viscardi) or found themselves virtually without an organization at all (Barbone) – which the increasing distance from both the intelligentsia and the locals had created. These participants made the fullest confessions; their careers in armed struggle had gradually deprived them of the local social relations to inhibit them from providing details of their contacts, without permitting any compensatory solidarity in their own milieu. The second category of defectors, largely locals, adopted the strategy of "dissociation" (*dissociazione*), by which they repudiated violence but limited their confessions strictly to their own direct responsibilities. The rapidity with which the commitment to violence was jettisoned confirms how few locals had been convinced that violence was the only possible political strategy, rather than a supplementary technique of political intervention; neither the symbols nor the practice of violence had become the unambiguous core of their political or personal identities. The difficulties they encountered in declaring a clear break with their pasts and with their former comrades-in-arms were not prompted by ideological commitment but by the strength of the personal ties which had caused them to become entangled in the world of armed struggle at all.

Significantly, the participants who found it hardest to dissociate themselves from violence were the intelligentsia. Although the leading symbolic representatives of the Red Brigades, Curcio and Franceschini, had declared in 1984 that armed struggle was finished, Franceschini only formally affirmed his dissociation in 1987 (Franceschini, 1988, p. 223), and Curcio has continued to refuse to repudiate his past.[23] Likewise, the intelligentsia of "Autonomia", who denied any direct organizational or executive role in violence, maintained that they could therefore have no violent pasts from which to dissociate themselves. No doubt, the persistent refusal to recant was reinforced by the solidarity – and coerced by the mutual surveillance – of a shared prison life.[24] But the contrast between the stances of the apparatchiks and the intelligentsia suggests the effects of different connections between writing and violence. Until the confessions began to appear, the meanings which the apparatchiks and locals gave to violence had been very largely obscured by the attention paid to the meanings supplied by, and solicited from, the intelligentsia. A significant component of defection was therefore the opportunity to recount the details, motivations and meanings of acts of violence as they were understood by the actual participants, not as they had been interpreted for wider publics by the intelligentsia. The two levels of collaboration – "repentance" and "dissociation" – can be understood as the recovery of "voice" by, respectively, the apparatchiks against the intelligentsia, and the locals against the apparatchiks.

This suggestion gets some support from the much lower incidence of confessions among the extreme Right where no distinctive intelligentsia had emerged to monopolize public interpretations of the activists' attacks. Pressures to provide alternative accounts, recovering the local meanings of what activists saw themselves as trying to achieve by violence, were correspondingly weaker than on the Left: by 1991 only one in four right-wing prisoners, as against one in two from left-wing groups, had abjured their pasts (*La Repubblica*, 10 August 1991). In most cases the principal spur to collaboration was the felt need for dissociation from the strategy behind particular kinds of violence (the bomb massacres) rather than the repudiation of either violence itself or an activist past (De Lutiis, 1990, p. 189).

As the former participants repeated their stories in a range of public settings, they created a steadily more autobiographical version of armed struggle.[25] The passage to complete individualization was helped by the confrontation with their victims, or victims' family members, since it particularized the victim of each attack as well as the assailant. Although the voices of victims had been heard separately since the early 1980s, usually to condemn the application of the repentance legislation, the victims only acquired an effective public identity from mid-decade. The news of the meeting in prison between one of Moro's daughters and some of her father's kidnappers in 1984 prompted a very large number of similar encounters between the violent and their victims.[26] The contents of these private meetings were often made public, as assailant and victim explored the idiosyncratic meanings of particular attacks (Lenci, 1988; Bussu, 1988). By concentrating on direct consequences and individual responsibilities, former participants in violence were driven to confront explicitly the relations between the past self that they had often constructed in courtroom testimony and their present, not yet externally validated, self. The history of violence which had been written in collective, segmentary, mode, yielded to a history accounted for in the minutiae of individual biographies, allowing a generous place for coincidence and chance and divesting many attacks of the meanings ascribed to them at the time. The shift in the dominant public language for describing the years of violence helped in itself to reinforce their pastness.

VIII   WRITING VIOLENCE FROM THE OUTSIDE: THE POLITICAL ÉLITE

(a)   Problems of Response

Adherents of violence as a political technique need to show that violent acts can have political consequences. They must demonstrate that some kind of relation holds – or can be created – between act of violence and politics. The aim of the opponents of violence is exactly the reverse: to prevent any suggestion that a single political market exists in which some kind of calculable equivalence can be reached between violent and nonviolent actions. In maintaining the boundary between the two domains, governments need to tread a delicate line between showing that violence is powerless to acquire any kind of political exchange value and enacting the necessarily political responses which demonstrate their commitment to its repression. Those responses have to be given publicly and simultaneously to a wide range of audiences. The public needs to be reassured that the government is treating the threat to public order sufficiently seriously, yet preserving basic democratic rights; the police and judiciary are likely to insist on extra powers to ensure more successful repression; particular categories of target will want to see their own protection given a high priority; and the protagonists of violence have to be convinced that their actions are indeed powerless to influence the frameworks and content of ordinary political relations and can earn them no place or influence, open or surreptitious, in the democratic political community.

Co-ordinating political parties and public authorities to disseminate a consistent set of messages on violence is unlikely ever to be easy in a liberal-democratic state. When failure is especially blatant, the dissemination of clear and consistent messages about violence is frustrated and governments are permanently open to the accusation of irresponsible passivity. The visible gap between ambitious plans for response and their incomplete realization inevitably contributes to a persistent impression of uncertainty about the actual power of violence. Failure to fix the meaning of violence broadcasts the message that its political potential has not yet been fully explored and that the claims made by its supporters might indeed turn out not to be simple fantasies after all. On the other hand, the fragmentation of reactions also demonstrably undermines any claim that the targets of violence are merely components of a simple monolith whose power might be destroyed by a "Winter Palace" attack on an arbitrarily selected key institution or individual. In liberal democracies where debates over how to react to violence enter the rhetoric of wider party competition, therefore, the responses themselves contribute to the formation and plausibility of the meanings promoted by the users of violence. They confirm or undermine both the location of the ritual frame for violence and the identity of the actors within it. Among the many institutions, local and national, which made public responses to violence, the political élite and the judiciary dominated the interpretive field.[27]

(b)   Political Responses: Narratives of Violence

In representing the distance between politics and violence, the Italian political élite had to surmount a number of difficulties. In the first place, the Italian polity was, in various ways, rather closely linked to violence. Its founding charter, the Republican constitution of 1948, was a product of the successful anti-Fascist violence of the Resistance; Parliament itself contained substantial representation by parties (Communist, Neo-Fascist) which were widely perceived as tolerant of violence; and the regular recourse to firearms by the police at public demonstrations suggested that the political order might be essentially dependent on armed defence.[28] The suspicion that senior politicians had known in advance about the Piazza Fontana bombs or had helped to protect those responsible – which was voiced almost immediately after the massacre and has never been adequately resolved – offered further problems for the government. Secondly, the likelihood of clear and consistent messages about the nature and meaning of violence was small. Italy's ruling and opposition parties were too ideologically diverse to permit a consensual analysis of a very variegated violence. Moreover, during the years of violence between 1970 and 1984 Italy was governed by a sequence of eighteen different coalitions, made up of nine different combinations of parties. This hardly offered a promising context in which to pursue consistent policies against violence. The political responses to clandestine violence reflected both structural factors and strategic intent.

The first requirement of a co-ordinated response by opponents of violence is a shared understanding of its nature and goals. The ideological distance separating the major parties ensured that they held different interpretations of the origins of violence and thus different recipes for its elimination. In the early years of violence the interpretations of political violence by the Christian Democrat and Communist parties were far apart, their disagreements covering both evidence and substance.[29] The DC treated the declarations accompanying the clandestine violence of the extreme Left and extreme Right at face value: the problem of violence was a problem of equally threatening "opposed extremisms", each inevitably generated by the radical ideologies of Communism and Fascism and emphasising the importance of the DC's own "central" role in defending Italian democracy. The DC-led government's public stress on "opposed extremisms" thus reinforced the segmentary model of Left–Right violent exchanges. It did not, however, enjoy the support of its major coalition partners in the Centre–Left governments who were reluctant to grant the DC that central role. The major opposition party, the PCI, took a markedly different line, arguing that the texts over left-wing signatures should be ignored: what counted was the fact of indulging in violence at all, which could only be inspired by reactionary aims. "Left-wing" violence did not exist: the texts which indicated left-wing authorship were therefore forgeries, and the selection of any right-wing targets a mere "provocation".

These differences were attenuated as the parties moved towards the "National Solidarity" phase between 1976 and 1979. The PCI's early reading, protecting the institutional Left from charges of direct or indirect complicity, did not survive the escalation of violence after 1975. Indeed, it could hardly be sustained in the light of the known political origins and biographies of the second generation of activists, as well as the failure to unearth any evidence of their collusion with the extreme Right. The PCI therefore came to accept that the understanding of the nature and projects of left-wing armed struggle could indeed be derived from the growing number of texts authored by the intelligentsia of the Red Brigades and "Autonomia". Both the PCI and the DC were tempted by, but did not succumb to, the idea of direct organizational links between the two apparently distinct kinds of armed struggle. Nonetheless, although the major political parties agreed that the meanings of violence ought indeed to be read from its accompanying texts, they continued to disagree on what they found there concerning its aims and organization.

Because of those differences, and the consequent risk of exacerbating conflicts among their allies in resisting violence, the governments of the 1970s showed an extreme reluctance either to make any general pronouncements about the nature of the threat from which they intended to defend Italian democracy or to offer any clear public assessment of the motivations and causes of violence (Pasquino, 1990). The first attempt to produce a single extended public account based on the evidence of the 1970s was prompted by the Moro affair, which provoked the government in 1979 to set up a Parliamentary Commission of Enquiry not only to evaluate the state's performance during the kidnapping but also to provide a general analysis of "terrorism". After four years' work and persistent controversy, the Commission had finally to be content with producing six conflicting reports on the kidnapping: its attempt to write an overall account of violence was abandoned almost from the outset. A further Parliamentary Commission, dealing only with the most serious episodes of violence after 1968, was set up in 1984 but fared no better in its efforts to reach an agreed interpretation of the meanings and responsibilities of those acts.[30] These failures rested in part on the ideological differences between the authors from different parties. But they also reflected the changing political contexts in which the analyses had to be made. The Moro Commission was set up in the final phase of the "National Solidarity" period, after which the Christian Democrat, Communist and Socialist parties drifted increasingly apart. That drift, accompanied by the sharp fall in violence itself, reduced the pressures on the opponents of violence to generate a single consensual version of armed struggle. The reluctance to impose (and the failure to achieve) narrative closure during the years of violence itself helped to preserve the sense of a pluralistic polity, very unlike the descriptions of the monolithic state that figured in the texts of the armed groups.

(c)   Resisting Inversion

A similar picture can be derived from the legislative responses that, in addition to the discursive analyses of political violence, carried the major messages from the political opponents of violence. As far as the measures to repress violence adopted between 1974 and 1982 were concerned, the institutional responses were remarkably low-key and did very little to modify, even temporarily, Italy's wider political or legal processes. No new national rules were introduced to restrict freedoms of speech or opportunities for public protest; and no delegation of authority to defend public order was made to the army, whose eventual involvement would have provided evidence to support the Red Brigades' claim of a generalized civil war in the making. Decisions on what and how to publish were left to individual editors and media staff; and local police chiefs were empowered to determine what demonstrations to permit or ban. Most of the harsh sanctions to which the politically violent were subject derived from the application of measures introduced in the early 1970s to combat the rise in serious non-political crime. Although some elements of the so-called "emergency legislation" aroused controversy at the time of their introduction, the public support enjoyed by the major measures was shown by the substantial majorities in favour of their retention when they were submitted to referenda in 1981. Only a small minority of Italians (one in six) claimed that state responses to violence had actually curtailed democracy and individual freedoms (Moss, 1989, p. 139). Indeed, by comparison with initiatives taken in other European states – the introduction of the *berufsverbot* and legal restrictions in Germany or the nature of police enquiries and judicial direction in cases involving the IRA in Britain, and the drastic innovations in Northern Ireland itself – the Italian state's responses seem a model of restraint.

Alongside the protection of its own democratic credentials, the government also sought to prevent its responses offering a unifying identity to its armed opponents. A case in point is the use of the description "terrorist". First, both the government and senior police officers were notably reluctant to use the term "terrorism" to describe clandestine political violence, preferring the more generic term "subversion" (Pasquino, 1990, p. 103; Moss, 1989, p. 18). Secondly, although the term "terrorism" was formally introduced into the penal code in 1978, it was deliberately given no explicit definition: its interpretation was specifically delegated to local magistrates and courts whose decisions carried no general significance. Moreover, every law which made use of the term also introduced means to escape the penalties – a strategy which displayed the reversibility of the passage towards involvement in armed struggle and weakened the sense of definitive inversion. Official policy thus resisted measures that would be likely to encourage the users of violence to recognize themselves, or to perceive that their opponents recognized them, in a single identity. Calls to declare illegal the multitude of "autonomia"-oriented organizations, or the umbrella structure of "Autonomia Operaia" itself, were rejected, thereby avoiding any encouragement to all full-time and fringe users of violence to see themselves unified in a common outlaw status.[31]

On particular occasions the political parties were called on to display a more focused rejection of the rites of violence. In kidnapping cases, for example, the government was invited to recognize the kidnappers as direct political antagonists and, by negotiating for the release of the victim, accept the reality of the passage between the two frames. Negotiations also carried the clear message that activities in the two frames of politics and violence were symbolically and instrumentally linked. In the Moro kidnapping, where the strategy of preserving absolute inaccessibility between the two domains was under greatest strain, the government declared that Moro had shed his political status, and even his personal identity, once he had passed into the clandestine domain of the Red Brigades: his letters and specific appeals remained unanswered. At grassroots level, too, the Communist Party also worked to destroy the ritual framework for armed struggle. By organizing mass mobilizations to follow every serious act of violence, the party not only provided a public means to display the rejection of violence but also demolished the agent–enemy–audience relationship for "armed propaganda". Mass demonstrations conveyed the message that the category of "audience", containing merely neutral spectators to the conflict between armed groups and their designated enemies, did not exist.

In sum, the obstacles which the nature of the Italian political system and the substantive disagreements of its major parties placed in the way of an agreed macro-level interpretation of violence helped to prevent the translation of highly varied local meanings into a plausible narrative of a unified assault on the Italian state. It frustrated any opportunity for the users of violence to seize on a clear set of meanings to reinforce their own understandings of what they were doing and might achieve. Moreover, the low-key, particularized defence of the state also served to undermine the Red Brigades' identification of the monolithic state as the primary antagonist for armed struggle – an identification required for assailants to be able to claim "disarticulating" results for their actions. Disconfirmation thereby worked against the group's attempt to represent all users of violence. The instrumental and discursive pattern of state responses amounted to the rejection of an inversionary logic in combating violence, since the politico-legal responses provided little independent encouragement for the very heterogeneous armed community to unify itself around a clear identity as irretrievably "Other".

IX   WRITING VIOLENCE IN COURT: JUDICIAL ACCOUNTS

From 1980 onwards judicial readings of violence held centre stage in public debate. Political analyses had retreated behind the closed Parliamentary doors of the Moro enquiry and the commission into the right-wing massacres, so that the investigating magistrates and trial judges became the principal public interpreters of the *anni di piombo*. As the practice of violence declined, the judiciary began to write its history. Its members' privileged position as historians rested on initially exclusive access to the confessions made by former participants under the terms of the repentance legislation. The resulting judicial reconstructions necessarily went far beyond the routine institutional tasks of identifying individual criminal responsibilities. They offered the first detailed account of the evolution of armed struggle, snapshot histories of its various organizations, and a portrayal of the relationships among participants. These accounts were validated through the rituals of courtroom procedure and determined the hitherto-deferred meanings of the major rites of violence.

(a)   The Judicial Discourse Community: Organization and Interpretation

In composing their histories of political violence, magistrates worked under at least three sets of constraints: the organization of judicial enquiries, the categories of the penal code, and the nature of the evidence available for their enquiries. What impact did the exploitation, or evasion, of these constraints make on the nature of their accounts of an entire decade of armed struggle?

   The content of judicial interpretations must reflect the constraints on the extent of investigative powers. Unifying "national" interpretations will be encouraged in enquiries directed from a single investigative centre; local meanings will be favoured by decentralized, city-based enquiries. In the

Italian case, although support was occasionally voiced for the judicial handling of all political violence by one set of magistrates attached to a single court, no such formal proposal was ever seriously considered. A court of that kind was held to resemble too closely the special tribunals of the Fascist period and would therefore convey exactly the wrong message about the effects of violence on the democratic state. All judicial work was therefore carried out locally, according to the existing code of penal procedure.

After 1978, however, steps were taken to overcome the highly fragmented organization of Italian justice. Teams of magistrates were created in every major city to deal with all episodes of political violence. Their most knowledgeable members then arranged regular informal meetings to deal with urgent practical issues: to disseminate rapidly the information gained in particular enquiries; to reach agreement on the uniform application of the often unwieldy categories of a penal code whose relevant provisions had been devised for the quite differently organized anti-Fascist subversion half a century earlier; and to determine where the crimes authored by a group which had been active in several different parts of Italy should be brought to court. Collaboration among magistrates was also made easier from 1978 onwards by the relaxation of the rules of secrecy governing the materials of all criminal investigations; and the extensions of the limited terms of preventive custody for political crimes enabled magistrates to prolong the availability of suspects for interrogation. The deliberate construction of a judicial interpretive community, whose members could co-ordinate the content and justification of their decisions on awkward terminological and procedural issues, provided the essential organizational basis to establish the reading of armed struggle.

The favoured reading, constructed from the mass of information collected in separate enquiries, sealed the meanings of violence at city level. The magistrates' decision to deal with all episodes of violence authored by a particular signature through a single trial in the city where the acts occurred ensured that the local meanings would constitute the focus of attention; any accompanying supra-local meanings or aspirations were relegated to the background. Eventual similarities between the ideas and organization of distinct groups, or between the use of a single signature in different cities, were scarcely addressed, so that few opportunities arose to develop an inclusive interpretation of political violence as an overall co-ordinated attack on Italian democracy. Each episode of violence was accounted for in terms of its immediate local origins and intended meanings; and no obligation to examine the nature of relations between the affiliates of a single group in different cities was imposed.

A city-level, signature-focused reading of the organization and meanings of violence fitted neatly with the existential biographies of the primary sources for the magistrates' versions, the repentant apparatchiks. For most apparatchiks had operated in a single city and had based their participation in violence around affiliation to a single organization and control over use of its name. Moreover, their strongly organization-bound commitment to armed struggle – which distinguished them from the abstract internationalism of the intelligentsia and the generic community solidarities of the locals – provided the structuring theme in their accounts. Organizational loyalty was the best guide to their own experiences and to an explanation of the involvements of the affiliates with whom they had contact. In addition, the repentance legislation required explicit dissociation from both the practice and the organizations of armed struggle, encouraging would-be beneficiaries to (re)describe the loose network of their past relationships in strongly structural terms as a means of displaying their rupture with the past more sharply. Casual encounters were subtly transformed into purposive meetings among fellow militants; gestures of friendly support became commitments to a specific group's project; and support for a particular act of violence mutated into explicit consent to a decision made by the organizational hierarchy which the apparatchik represented. The emphasis common to those interpretations was also closely matched to the rigid formal criteria of membership that the penal code obliged magistrates to use for assessing individual responsibilities in collective violence.

Just as the apparatchiks had been spurred to offer their own versions of violence as a way of dissociating themselves from the publicly dominant accounts by the intelligentsia, so the locals became concerned to escape the new interpretive hegemony of the apparatchiks. The judicial and media endorsement given to courtroom accounts describing participation in terms of organizational roles not only threatened to saddle locals with criminal responsibilities far superior to their actual involvement but it also obscured the importance of their engagement in open political activity. In locals' own understandings and practice, violence represented a convenient additional tactic in their political repertoire: it did not constitute the central source of their identity in the way that the apparatchiks' versions suggested. As I suggested earlier (p. 000), locals thus found it necessary to offer progressively more complete versions of their own participation, as the judicial processing of their responsibilities moved from initial interrogations up to the court of appeal. Naturally, shifts in self-understanding marked many of the successive accounts. Both the locals and the apparatchiks frequently reworked the insights provided by collective discussions in prison and took advantage of appearances in open court to convey the transformation of their identities and their deepening appreciation of the nature and consequences of violence.

(b)   Deviant Accounts

The only significantly deviant readings of left-wing violence were produced by two magistrates in Padua and Rome who had not been central members of the interpretive community of magistrates and who largely rejected its informally agreed interpretive procedures. In both cases left-wing violence was credited with an organizational and strategic unity far transcending single cities, and evidence derived exclusively from the textual production of the 1970s was treated as conclusive. Texts were wrenched from their context of production and use, going back more than a decade, so that they could be attributed to a common author merely by virtue of the appearance of the same terms. The judicial outcome of this interpretive strategy was the very rare charge of "armed insurrection against the state", which led to large-scale trials in Rome, chosen as the appropriate site to decide on the existence of a single project to destroy Italian democracy. The magistrates' interpretations represented a concluding attempt to find a single overall pattern to armed struggle and to attribute at least a basic set of shared meanings to all participants. However, their fate showed clearly how the intelligentsia's macronarratives of violence had been superseded as plausible descriptions by city-level micro-versions based on the testimony of the apparatchiks and locals.

The first case involved the judicial evaluation of "Calogero's theorem", named for a Padua magistrate who claimed that left-wing violence was the product of a single co-ordinated attack by the Red Brigades and "Autonomia" (De Lutiis, 1982). Relying entirely on the allegedly identical meanings of the terms used in the intelligentsia's texts across more than a decade, and treating the contents of the texts as descriptions rather than aspirations, Calogero argued for the existence of a single "armed party". Apparent divergences or conflicts between its members were, he maintained, merely attempts to mask an organizational and strategic identity and throw investigators off the track. The failure of the repentant apparatchiks to provide the slightest confirmatory evidence was attributed to culpable reticence. An oddly, apparently symbolically, selected group of defendants was arrested in 1979, finally brought to trial in 1983, but acquitted on the armed insurrection charge. The second case concerned the Red Brigades alone. In 1982 the group's total membership, consisting of all 426 affiliates identified since 1970, was charged by a Rome magistrate with armed insurrection against the state and civil war. However, by the conclusion of the trial in late 1989, the public prosecutor himself acknowledged that, whatever the ambitions of some of their members, the Red Brigades had never constituted either the unitary assailant or the serious danger that would justify conviction. With the resulting failure to establish a single linear account of the only genuine candidate group, the courtroom manufacture of the history of armed struggle came to an end.[32]

X   POST-JUDICIAL CLOSURE: RESTORING THE FLOW OF POLITICAL TIME

The judicial rites had of course dealt with individuals, calibrating penalties according to responsibilities but modifying them greatly in the light of the repentance legislation. The resulting inequities – multiple, self-confessed killers spending little time in prison, reticent participants responsible for far less serious crimes receiving far heavier sentences – were felt to require redress. Still others – a reasonably substantial group – had escaped abroad, mainly to extradition-wary France, and had never been brought to book. Moreover, no collective rite of reconciliation had taken place to signal the mutual recognition by the former users and opponents of violence of their reconstructed identities. Political time, it was argued, could not fully recommence until some means to dismantle the ritual frame of clandestine violence, opened in 1969, had been found. The most active exponent of this view, the then President of the Republic, Cossiga, argued that the widely-demanded general reform of the Italian political system – indeed the inauguration of the Second Republic – could only take place once accounts with the *anni di piombo* had been settled.

The particular means that in 1991 Cossiga proposed – a politically-motivated presidential pardon for the human symbol of the Red Brigades, Curcio, who had then served less than half his forty-year prison term – failed, politicians and jurists raising insuperable objections of public acceptability and constitutional practice. But at least as inadmissible as the specific instrument of the pardon was the content of Cossiga's accompanying effort to write a narrative closure for the *anni di piombo*: "a more correct historical, political, ideological and social reading of this tragic phase of our national life".[33] His attribution of some of the responsibility for violence to the political parties and state institutions, which had failed to ensure that the post-1968 social conflicts were resolved on the terrain of ordinary politics, earned him the greatest hostility. For his determination to link the origins of political violence to the social inequalities and injustices produced by Italy's tumultuous development in the 1960s seemed to credit the Red Brigades and others retrospectively with exactly the status of quasi-representatives of disadvantaged social groups that the political parties had refused to grant them during the violence itself – even at the cost of refusing to enter into negotiations to save Moro from murder by his BR kidnappers in 1978. To many commentators, Cossiga's attempt at a definitive reading of armed struggle came too close to "Bitburg history" – the equation of perpetrators and victims of violence (Maier, 1988, p. 14).

With respect to the narratives that had been written in the courtroom, Cossiga's reading offered a set of final inversionary twists. In place of the radically individualized explanations of armed struggle, Cossiga offered a recollectivization of responsibilities; in place of criminal status for the participants, he recognized their political role; and in place of violence as a ritual rupture of real time, he acknowledged the linear continuity between political difficulties and the recourse to armed struggle. All these inversions produced an account of clandestine violence that tallied perfectly with the long-standing affirmations of armed organizations themselves (Curcio, 1993, pp. 216–20). The belated attempt to translate the discontinuous histories of violence into a single linear narrative was, however, no more successful than earlier efforts: by the intelligentsia of armed struggle, by the political élite, and by the magistrates in Padua and Rome. Further ventures to achieve narrative closure at macro-level now seem unlikely. The 1994 elections have swept from power the parties and politicians who managed the responses to violence, and their successors will not share the sense of issues still unresolved. Similarly, the release from prison of Curcio and many other protagonists of violence has stripped them of any residual representative status for those former users of violence who have renounced violence without benefiting from the repentance legislation. The discourse community within which armed struggle was produced, responded to and accounted for has disappeared.

The principal focus of this analysis has been on the changing and unstable relations between politics, violence and writing in the course of an extended ritual frame. I have treated the emergence of violence as the attempt to create a new frame for action, initially organized as a projection of existing political conflict, requiring little explication in the form of accompanying documents. As violence intensified in the second half of the 1970s, so texts took on increasing importance as elements supplying the increasingly fragile connection between the domains of politics and violence. A new role in disseminating the basic political meanings of armed struggle was thus created for its intelligentsia. Exegeses of violence from within the ritual frame became a more important component of the rituals themselves. The contents of the intelligentsia's versions, reflecting their own immediate context of production and the need to find common targets to unify the diversifying sites and signatures of armed struggle, drifted far from the meanings carried by the performative rites which local-level users of violence preferred. The progressive deferral of meaning for the most serious attacks, facilitated by the lack of a clear narrative account of violence from its political opponents, was terminated by the courtroom rituals which sealed the meanings of armed struggle at local and individual level. The productivity of the acts of violence – their enduring capacity to provoke conflicts among opponents – was finally removed. The failure of Cossiga's attempt to stage a national rite of political reconciliation which would celebrate this removal and formally close the frame for armed struggle opened in 1969 provided a concluding testimony to the power of violence both to compel and resist interpretation.

NOTES

Discussions at the UNRISD Workshops on Political Violence and Social Movements in November 1990 and May 1992 have greatly improved my understanding of political violence. I should like to acknowledge the very stimulating papers and comments of fellow-contributors to this volume and, in particular, of David Apter.

1. The relative weight of types of damage also varies. In Northern Ireland deaths and injuries outnumbered attacks on property by two to one; in Spain their incidence was approximately the same; but in Italy damage to property was twice as common as violence against people. For the most detailed statistics on Italian political violence see Galleni (1981), and della Porta and Rossi (1983).

2. Good reasons for the bias of analysts' attention towards left-wing violence exist. Data have often been scarce: magistrates and courts have been far less successful in identifying the responsibilities for the major episodes of right-wing violence; and only a few extreme Right former activists have turned state's evidence and revealed what they know. For recent contributions reducing the lack of knowledge about extreme Right violence see Borraccetti (1986); Weinberg and Eubank (1988); Ferraresi (1984; 1988); Clark (1988); Fiasco (1990); and Pisetta (1990).

3. The literature on ritual, theoretical and empirical, is vast. I have found Kapferer (1979) and Tambiah (1979) particularly stimulating for my purposes here.

4. Diego Novelli, mayor of Turin in its worst period of violence, held meetings with representatives of every organized group to persuade them to continue

with ordinary activities and thus avoid any impression that the ordinary flow of time had stopped (Novelli, 1980, p. 29). Perhaps the predilection among some sociologists in the 1970s for describing Italy as a "blocked society" was an indication of similar pressures.

5. The election of President Leone in 1972, the support for the Centre–Right coalition government in 1973, and the divorce referendum of 1974.

6. The return of Almirante to the leadership of the MSI signalled official party encouragement for the activities of the extra-parliamentary Right ("Avanguardia Nazionale", "Ordine Nuovo"). For details of the strategies of the MSI in this period see Caciagli (1988).

7. On the concept of "segmentation", see Dresch (1988) and Herzfeld (1990).

8. See Pridham (1981) for the revival of historical interest and local celebration of the Resistance by the PCI in Tuscany in the mid-1970s.

9. In view of the all but exclusive focus on the BR among left-wing groups, it is worth emphasizing that the signature was just one of the 526 recorded between 1969 and 1980, its members amounted to only one in seven left-wing activists, authoring fewer than one-quarter of all left-wing attacks. Just as left-wing violence after 1969 can only be understood in the context of right-wing violence, so grasping the dynamics of left-wing violence after 1976 must take into account the relations between signatures. For the experiences of users of violence who rejected the Red Brigades, see Novelli and Tranfaglia (1988) and Guicciardi (1988).

10. Only embryonic distinctions can be made between separate milieux in the world of right-wing armed struggle. Relations between the very few ideologues of violence and the activists appear to have been conflictual from the beginning (Fiasco, 1990). However, the disagreements between members of the extreme Right on the proper targets for their violence mirror the major disagreement on the Left described below (Ferraresi, 1988, pp. 97–103).

11. As the reference to work involvements implies, the evidence on participants in armed struggle does not support a direct connection between economic marginality and political violence. All surveys of left-wing and right-wing militants show that they were drawn from a wide range of blue-collar and white-collar occupations and that the number of activists from the Left or Right who were unemployed or sub-proletarians was less than 5 per cent (Moss, 1989, pp. 43–4; della Porta, 1990, pp. 143–4; Weinberg and Eubank, 1988, p. 539). Moreover, the overwhelming proportion of political violence in Italy actually took place in the wealthier areas of Central and North Italy, not in the poorer South.

12. Its head, General Dalla Chiesa, was frequently selected as their desired interlocutor by apparatchiks who wished to turn state's evidence, indicating how impersonal antagonism towards the state was transformed into personalized enmities.

13. "Autonomia's" most influential publications included *Rosso, Metropoli* and *Senza Tregua*; the most significant radio stations, Radio Onda Rossa in Rome and Radio Sherwood in Padua. Selections of illustrative documents can be found in Martignoni and Morandini (1977) and Castellano (1979). The arrest of its ideologues, principally Toni Negri and his colleagues from the Political Science faculty at the University of Padua in April 1979, followed by prolonged detention in the same maximum security jails as the

Red Brigades' intelligentsia, provided many opportunities for confrontation between the two versions of violence – especially since "Autonomia's" intelligentsia proclaimed themselves innocent of direct involvement.

14. Notably the Workers' Statute (1970) and the school reforms (1974).

15. Most of the post-1976 generation of participants in violence had begun their political socialization in the extra-parliamentary Left, which took the reformism of the Communist Party for granted. Only in very rare cases were activists from the institutional Left (Communist and Socialist parties, trade unions) recruited directly into violence: 3 per cent had been activists in the PCI and 6 per cent in trade unions prior to their involvement in armed struggle (della Porta, 1990). These figures imply that the ideological traditions, policy shifts and organizational experience in the institutional Left have a very limited explanatory role in accounting for the emergence or persistence of violence. Dissatisfaction with the Communist Party's retreat from revolution or with its adoption of the "Historic Compromise" policy can therefore be ruled out as a central motivation propelling people into violence.

16. For discussions of the impact of competition in the protest "market", see at national level (della Porta and Tarrow, 1986; Tarrow, 1989; della Porta, 1990; Tarrow, 1990) and for single cities (Moss, 1989, pp. 72–3).

17. Their views could, however, be solicited to decide the fate of kidnap victims, as in the D'Urso kidnapping of December 1980. Also, by creating a prison organization for arrested activists, the intelligentsia was able to turn to its own advantage in conflicts with apparatchiks the increasing success of police investigations after 1978.

18. Those audiences included investigators themselves. For organizational, cultural and interpretive reasons, neither police nor magistrature were able to build up an adequate picture of the general patterns and individual involvements in post-1976 violence until they obtained the first confessions in 1980 (Moss, 1989, pp. 173–82).

19. For details and analyses of the Moro kidnapping see Moss (1981) and Wagner-Pacifici (1986).

20. More than fifteen years later, in October 1993, the revelation of the identity of the BR member directly responsible for Moro' murder unleashed a further wave of speculations about the number, nature and objectives of the kidnappers (*La Repubblica*, 24–26 October 1993).

21. Actions came increasingly to be used to compel the circulation of texts themselves: a condition for the release of hostages in the BR kidnappings of 1980–1, for example, was publication of the group's documents in the mass media. The extreme point of this inversion was reached in 1982 when two security guards were murdered in Turin so that accusations of collaboration with police against a recently-arrested BR member could be broadcast as widely as possible. The leading founder-members of the BR attribute their definitive dissociation from the group to this action (Franceschini, 1988, p. 203; Curcio, 1993, pp. 194–5).

22. For full details and commentaries on the laws of 1980 and 1982, see G. Conso (ed.), *La Legislazione dell'Emergenza* (Giuffre: Varese, 1981–4), vols 8, 9, 12–15.

23. He finally left jail, on a day-release programme, in April 1993.

24.   The earliest repentant apparatchiks, whose exhaustive descriptions often made the denials of many others redundant, had not yet been transferred to prison, with its inescapable mutual surveillance, at the time of their confessions. Several participants who reached prison under suspicion of having collaborated were murdered or wounded.

25.   Courtrooms, television and press were the primary locations for these accounts; and several former Red Brigades members collaborated on extended versions of their pasts (Fenzi, 1982; Franceschini, 1988; Curcio, 1993). Although the rules, formal and informal, which shape descriptions given in different settings to different audiences were very varied, account-givers were under strong pressure to preserve a consistent core-story for all public occasions: if a new version suggested earlier reticence or falsity, the benefits of confession could be revoked by the courts.

26.   The publicity these initiatives received, and the pressures that some victims felt to forgive and forget too readily, stimulated the creation of an Association for the Victims of Terrorism in 1985. The Association became increasingly critical of the state's concession of benefits to former participants in violence as well as its failure to recognize, both morally and materially, the damage victims had sustained. Only in 1990 did the political élite grant the formal recognition and financial compensation which the Association sought.

27.   Space prevents me considering here the full range of relevant responses, which included work-force mobilization by trade unions and management of trials by judges (Moss, 1989, chs 3, 6). I shall also ignore the administrative and legal measures to facilitate police and judicial investigations.

28.   Two hundred and forty-six deaths of police and civilians had occurred in the course of demonstrations and protests between 1946 and 1977 (Viola, 1977).

29.   With occasional deviations, the smaller parties generally followed the interpretive line of one or other major party.

30.   Despite several prorogations, the Commission's work has not been completed, due in part to the political vicissitudes of 1992–4. Although it has dealt principally with right-wing violence, reports of its deliberations suggest that the parties disagreed equally strongly over right-wing and left-wing violence.

31.   See the testimony of Cossiga (Minister of the Interior during the period of most intense violence) to the Parliamentary Committee of Enquiry into the Moro kidnapping for a statement of the government's strategy.

32.   Some cases are nonetheless unresolved, notably the seven right-wing massacres between 1969 and 1984. In every case, the defendants initially found guilty have had their convictions overturned by superior courts: Borraccetti (1986) provides some reasons for the failure of the judicial process. As far as left-wing violence is concerned, only the murder of police-commissioner Calabresi in 1982 and the Moro kidnapping continue to generate confident affirmations that the real responsibilities remain to be uncovered (Ginzburg, 1991).

33.   See *La Repubblica*, 10 and 17 August 1991; *L'Espresso*, 1 September 1991, p. 116.

REFERENCES

Apter, David E., "Democracy and Emancipatory Movements: Notes for a Theory of Inversionary Discourse", in Jan Nederveen Pieterse (ed.), *Emancipations, Modern and Postmodern* (Newbury Park, Cal.: Sage, 1992), pp. 139–73.

Arlacchi, P., and Lewis, R., *Imprenditorialita illecita e droga* (Bologna: IC Mulino, 1990).

Associazione Italiana Vittime del terrorismo e dell'eversione contro l'Ordinamento Costituzionale dello Stato, *Atti del Convegno 'Lotta al Terrorismo: le ragioni e i diritti delle vittime* (Turin, 1986).

Bobbio, L., *Lotta Continua: Storia di una organizzazione rivoluzionaria* (Rome: Savelli, 1979).

Borraccetti, V. (ed.), *Eversione di destra, terrorismo, stragi* (Milan: Franco Angeli, 1986).

Brigate Rosse, "Le venti tesi finali", *Corrispondenza Internazionale*, vol. VI (1980), pp. 16/17, pp. 269–87.

Bussu, S., *Un prete e i terroristi* (Milan: Mursia, 1988).

Caciagli, M., "The Movimento Sociale Italiano-Destra Nazionale and Neo-Fascism in Italy", *West European Politics*, vol. 11, no. 2 (1988) pp. 19–33.

Castellano, L., *Aut. Op* (Rome: Savelli, 1979).

Clark, M., "Italian Squadrismo and Contemporary Vigilantism", *European History Quarterly*, vol. 18 (1988) pp. 33–49.

Collins, R., *Sociology Since Mid-Century* (New York: Academic Press, 1981).

Corvisieri, S., *Il mio viaggio nella sinistra* (Rome: Editoriale L'Espresso, 1979).

Culler, J., "Jacques Derrida", in J. Sturrock (ed.), *Structuralism and Since* (Oxford: Oxford University Press, 1979) pp. 154–80.

Curcio, R., *A viso aperto* (Milan: A. Mondadori, 1993).

Davis, J., "History and the People without Europe", in K. Hastrup (ed.), *Other Histories* (London: Routledge, 1992) pp. 14–28.

De Lutiis, G. (ed.), *Attacco allo Stato* (Rome: Napoleone, 1982).

De Lutiis, G., "Moventi e motivazioni della dissociazione", in R. Catanzaro (ed.), *La politica della violenza* (Bologna: Il Mulino, 1990).

della Porta, D., *Il terrorismo di sinistra* (Bologna: Il Mulino, 1990).

della Porta, D. and Rossi, M., "I terrorismi in Italia tra il 1969 e il 1982", *Cattaneo*, vol. III, no. 1 (1983) pp. 1–44.

della Porta, D. and Tarrow, S., "Unwanted Children: Political Violence and the Cycle of Protest in Italy, 1966–1973", *European Journal of Political Research*, vol. 14, no. 5–6 (1986) pp. 607–32.

Derrida, J., *Positions* (Paris: La Seuil, 1972).

Derrida, J., *Of Grammatology* (Baltimore, Md: Johns Hopkins University Press, 1976).

Diesch, P., "Segmentation: Its Roots in Arabia and Its Flowering Elsewhere", *Cultural Anthropology*, vol. 3 (1988) pp. 50–67.

Fenzi, Enrico, Memoriale, 27 September 1982, pp. 33–4.

Ferraresi, F. (ed.), *La destra radicale* (Milan: Feltrinelli, 1984).

Ferraresi, F., "The Radical Right in Postwar Italy", *Politics and Society*, vol. 16, no. 1 (1988) pp. 71–119.

Fiasco, M., "La simbiosi ambigua", in R. Catanzaro (ed.), *Ideologie, movimenti, terrorismi* (Bologna: Il Mulino, 1990).

126   The Legitimization of Violence

Franceschini, A., *Mara, Renato ed io* (Milan: A. Mondadori, 1988).

Galleni, M. (ed.), *Rapporto sul terrorismo* (Milan: Rizzoli, 1981).

Ginzburg, C., *Il giudice e lo storico* (Turin: Einaudi, 1991).

Guicciardi, L., *Il tempo del furore* (Milan: Rusconi, 1988).

Herzfeld, M., "Icons and Identity: Religious Orthodoxy and Social Practice in Rural Crete", *Anthropological Quarterly*, vol. 63, no. 3 (1990) pp. 109–21.

Hewitt, C., "The Costs of Terrorism: A Cross-National Study of Six Countries", *Terrorism*, vol. 11 (1988) pp. 169–80.

Kapferer, B., "Ritual Process and the Transformation of Context", *Social Analysis* vol. 1 (1979) pp. 3–19.

Laganö, G., Pianta, M. and Segre, A., "Urban Social Movements and Urban Restructuring in Turin, 1969–1976", *International Journal of Urban and Regional Research*, vol. 6, no. 2 (1982) pp. 223–45.

Lenci, S., *Colpo alla nuca* (Rome: Editori Riuniti, 1988).

Lewis, G., *Day of Shining Red: An Essay on Understanding Ritual* (Cambridge: Cambridge University Press, 1980).

Lumley, R., *States of Emergency* (London: Verso, 1990).

Maier, C., *The Unmasterable Past. History, Holocaust and German National Identity* (Cambridge, Mass.: Harvard University Press, 1988).

Manconi, L., "Il nemico assoluto. Antifascismo e contropotere nella fase aurorale del terrorismo di sinistra", in R. Catanzaro (ed.), *La politica della violenza* (Bologna: Il Mulino, 1990).

Martignoni, G. and Morandini, S., *Il diritto all'odio* (Verona: Bertani, 1977).

Moretti, M., *Brigate rosse: una storia italiana* (Milan: Anabasi, 1984).

Moss, D., "The Kidnapping and Murder of Aldo Moro", *Archives europeennes de sociologie*, vol. XXII, no. 2 (1981) pp. 265–95.

Moss, D., *The Politics of Leftwing Violence in Italy, 1969–1985* (London: Macmillan, 1989).

Novaro, C., "Reti di solidarietö e lotta armata", in R. Catanzaro (ed.), *Ideologie, movimenti, terrorismi* (Bologna: Il Mulino, 1990).

Novelli, D., *Vivere a Torino* (Rome: Editori Riuniti, 1980).

Novelli, D. and Tranfaglia, N. (eds), *Vite sospese* (Milan: Garzanti, 1988).

Pasquino, G., "I soliti ignoti: gli opposti terrorismi nelle analisi dei Presidenti del Consiglio (1969–1985)", in R. Catanzaro (ed.), *La politica della violenza* (Bologna: Il Mulino, 1990).

Pavone, C., *Una guerra civile: saggio sulla moralita della Resistenza* (Turin: Bollati Boringhieri, 1991).

Pisetta, E., "Militanza partitica e scelte eversive nei terroristi neofascisti", in R. Catanzaro (ed.), *Ideologie, movimenti, terrorismi* (Bologna: Il Mulino, 1990).

Pridham, G., *The Nature of the Italian Party System* (London: Croom Helm, 1981).

Soccorso Rosso, *Brigate Rosse* (Milan: Feltrinelli, 1976).

Tambiah, S., "A Performative Approach to Ritual", *Proceedings of the British Academy*, vol. LXV (1979) pp. 113–69.

Tarrow, S., *Democracy and Disorder: Protest and Politics in Italy 1965–1975* (Oxford: Oxford University Press, 1989).

Tarrow, S., "Violenza e istituzionalizzazione dopo il ciclo di protesta", in R. Catanzaro (ed.), *Ideologie, movimenti, terrorismi* (Bologna: Il Mulino, 1990).

Vettori, G., *La sinistra extraparlamentare in Italia* (Rome: Newton Compton, 1973).

Viola, G., *Polizia* (Verona: Bertani, 1977).

Wagner-Pacifici, R., *The Moro Morality Play* (Chicago, Ill.: Chicago University Press, 1986).

Weinberg, L. and Eubank, W., "Neo-Fascist and Far Left Terrorists in Italy: Some Biographical Observations", *British Journal of Political Science*, vol. 18, no. 4 (1988) pp. 531–49.

4 Violence as Memory and Desire: Neo-Nazism in Contemporary Germany

BRADDEN WEAVER

I INTRODUCTION

Whatever else it is or is not, the neo-Nazi movement is in part a new phenomenon and in part bound up inextricably with Germany's past. It can not escape, nor do its protagonists wish to escape, the dubious claim to representing Germany's *alter ego*. Indeed they would not have it any other way. In this it differs from Italian neo-Fascism which, at least for electoral reasons, pretends to disavow its past history. In Germany neo-Nazi groups constitute not only themselves and their current situation, but as well a sometimes visible sometimes invisible absent presence, one related causally to so many other absences, historically and figuratively speaking, which continue to haunt Germany. For most Germans such absences are preferably repressed. They constitute guilty knowledge, the erasure that leaves a stain. But even if the knowledge disappears – and generational amnesia is perhaps a national pastime – the guilt remains, the ghost in today's democracy.

It is perhaps for these and similar reasons that even a small but bold, and entirely unrepentant, neo-Nazi movement can produce such large reactions and fears. Despite the candlelight protests against xenophobic violence and the holding of memorial vigils in many German cities, the movement remains unabashedly defiant. Indeed, it celebrates and exploits what guilt there is as a previous expression of power even while denying the Holocaust itself. And because of its past, the movement can never be just a movement like any other. The more so since it claims to represent the continuity of, and nostalgia for, myths for a state which, once subservient to the will of the party, will be recreated by the latter's inheritors. It is through a violence of re-enactment – the strutting, the uniforms, insignia, and the discourse (including references to the legally forbidden *Mein Kampf*), punctuated by atrocities, walls smeared with hate slogans, immigrant hostels burned, individuals beaten – that the return of the Übermensch and the master race is signalled. In these ways violence retrieves principles while nostalgia evokes racial superiority, blood purity, military glory and conquest: the ingredients of an aesthetic of danger and death.

Not that most of those who number themselves among the ranks of neo-Nazi's are themselves aesthetic objects. Despite uniforms and boots, batons and whips, buckles and insignia, the goose-step and the straight-arm salute, not to speak of a preference for blond boys and maidens, a significant proportion of the neo-Nazi clientele hardly fit the picture of their Aryan ideal. Not least of all this is because the shared solidarities of hatred expressed in a convivial way by the prolonged and excessive consumption of beer tends to leave its mark on faces and bellies. The beer halls are still the venues for the party faithful, at least certain beer halls off-limits to outsiders and where many continue to meet and dream of the restoration of the Reich. So much so that if Nazism was once a tragedy its Second Coming is a farce.

But it is a farce which also produces tragedies. If absences, guilty knowledge, memory, and their inversion through the return of the Übermensch and the master race, belong to a larger history of Germany as Volk (as community), today it is not only directed against Jews and gypsies (who nevertheless remain pollutants) but other immigrants, from Turkey, Iran, Vietnam, Russia, Poland, and elsewhere in Eastern Europe. Although the authorities protest that the violence committed against them is unorganized, spontaneous, and localized – not programmatic – and difficult to connect directly to the secret meetings, the semi-secret celebrations, the furtive display of forbidden Nazi salutes, the wearing of uniforms and paraphernalia, the connection between purity, "spontaneous" violence is most certainly in part choreographed in order to create a a more general atmosphere of threat and danger. If the extermination of unwanted categories of immigrants appears unsystematic and unorganized – a product of chance encounters – looks may be deceiving.

Systematic or not, there is, as we shall see, plenty of violence. There is terror and the use of terror tactics. Nevertheless one would be hard put to call the movement "terrorist". Indeed, Nazism has always been one of those movements able to play off legalism and the use of institutions of state and society for violent ends.[1] Nor does any other movement combine designated actions aimed at disordering the bourgeois democratic state, and the form smashing that goes with it, with such a strong emphasis on order and discipline. Whatever their other differences, the old Nazism and the new have in common a preference for "disordering" as freedom and "ordering" as power and control.

Today's movement needs to be more careful because of legal proscriptions and public taboos. Hence there is something of the thrill of the "flasher" in being a neo-Nazi in Germany today: furtive, revelatory. Which would make it utterly trivial if it were not as well a fragment of a past which, if had its own kind of power (if not greatness), remains intriguing because "forbidden" to the Germans of today.

The presence of neo-Nazi groups in Germany also raises the question of whether or not Germany, and more particularly perhaps Austria, will retain their peculiar fascination for Nazism, and indeed the spectacles and drama that it entails. It also raises the uglier question which is how much neo-Nazism in both Germany and Austria represent attitudes quite widespread beneath the surface – attitudes which favour what Sternhell calls biological Fascism, which distinguishes the German variety sharply from Italian Fascism. It is in both Germany and Austria where one finds fairly widespread an aesthetic of repugnance against those traditionally regarded as polluting the race, an aesthetic which retrieves earlier themes including violation of sexual boundaries, the pure against the defiled, Christian against Jew, the myth of the Knight-Crusader and the Avenging Angel, with the Holocaust a trial by fire. The roots for these go deep, and not only in Germany but elsewhere: Holland, Flemish-speaking Belgium,[2] and of course France.[3]

One needs as well to distinguish between yesterday's forms and those of today. For example, there need be no intrinsic connection between neo-Nazism and modern corporatism. Most extreme rightist parties have successfully separated themselves from neo-Nazi doctrines. And, as between neo-Nazism and neo-Fascism it is the latter which appears to be looking for a new definition of itself, while the former tries to remain true to its past. Perhaps such blatancy is one reason for the recent repudiation of neo-Nazism in the recent German elections. Nevertheless, neo-Nazism is not likely to disappear, not least of all because it provides greater respectability to the "republican" forms of the extreme Right. This is happening in such diverse places today as France and Russia. Hence, even if relatively small, such movements are by no means powerless. Their significance is growing rather than declining. If this assumption is correct, neo-Nazism bears closer inspection – and in Germany where it originally took its most rigoristic form.

II INVERSIONARY MILLENARIANISM AND THE COMMUNITY OF THE LIKE-MINDED

Perhaps the first observation we can make about neo-National Socialism in today's Germany is that it is far from monolithic. The rightist extremist scene is divided into factions competing for a tiny pool of activists and sympathizers which the Federal Constitution Protection Agency has consistently estimated at between 1,500 and 2,000 persons.[4] Of this differentiated clientele, one organizational structure more than others has risen to a pre-eminent position and today dominates and influences the inchoate collection of rightist extremist organizations of which the "movement" is composed, the GdNF (*Gesinnungsgemeinschaft der Neuen Front*), literally, the "Community of the Like-minded of the New Front".

The growth of the GdNF's strength *vis-à-vis* other neo-Nazi organizations in the late 1980s can be attributed to a number of factors, of which memory and nostalgia, marginality in terms of prevailing economic and social hierarchies (a particular problem for those living in former East Germany) are obviously relevant. But the movement is peculiarly leader-oriented and the organizational and propaganda skills as well as the extremely effective personal leadership of the late Michael Kuehnen and his lieutenants, Christian Worch and Gottfried Kuessel cannot be discounted. These latter two have been primarily responsible for carrying forward Kuehnen's work since his death in 1991.

Kuehnen, despite serious setbacks dealt him by competitors within the neo-Nazi movement, was able to build a web of party and regional field organizations based upon a cult of personality and National Socialist dogma which far surpassed those of his competitors.

That said, however, organization-building, membership recruitment, and sympathizer mobilization presupposes a ready-made audience. And there was in Germany a significant proportion of the population already sympathetic to the community's message, and who accepted, as more correct, the interpretation of the central ideology offered by the GdNF than any of the other far Right communities. Among these were old, embittered, and hardened veterans of the SS who saw in a younger generation opportunities for restoration and revenge.

In order to explore how and why the GdNF was able to assume such a central role we must examine both the sub-text and the particular language of belief from which the GdNF derives its logic and coherency as a discourse community. We want to show how the GdNF grounds its claims to authority and authenticity, and how it is able to generate, reproduce and defend (in word and deed) its own form of symbolic capital, especially among the more marginalized sectors of the population and with repercussions beyond Germany itself.

We also want to discuss the particular place and role of violence in the movement. True to its tradition as heirs of the NSDAP, the GdNF is a creature of organized and violent spectacle. For the decade between 1977 and 1987, the Federal Constitution Protection Agency reported 1,500 crimes with rightist extremist motivations committed largely by members of neo-Nazi organizations. These crimes comprised vandalism, bodily injury against political opponents and foreign residents, and the distribution of propaganda.[5] The GdNF's use of such practices has escalated since German unification in 1990. In the autumn of 1991, GdNF members and Nazi "Skinheads" held numerous rallies in East German towns and were largely responsible for instigating attacks against asylum hostels in the towns of Hoyerswerda, Hunxa, Quedlinburg, Goerlitz and Rostock.[6]

The GdNF's reliance on violence raises a number of interesting questions. Are dramatic actions and violence integral to the life of the "community", and if so what purposes do they serve? How does the GdNF empower violence: that is, instill a violent act with meaning?

Our point of departure is to treat the GdNF as a discourse community. Its members participate in a unique conversation embellished by clandestinity. Discourse within the GdNF includes such themes as social and biological Darwinism, anti-semitism and anti-communism, all of which are bound into a master narrative. At the center of this narrative is the story of the Third Reich, a central myth on the basis of which the logic of neo-Nazism has been constructed.[7]

In itself the master narrative is not a theoretical treatise. If it had been no one would take it seriously. Rather it retrieves and incorporates events within living memory but beyond the horizon of experience for most people. It makes coherent the otherwise disjointed explanations of the causes of Nazism, the need for purification and revenge associated with Hitler's rise to power and the explanation of the demise of the Third Reich in terms which suggest its return. The master narrative contains within it the Germany myth of eternal return.

Specifically the master narrative of the GdNF combines a "long story" and a "short story". The point of departure of both is loss, grievance, and yearning. The "long story" presents the German nation's subjugation and loss of patrimony throughout history, culminating in Germany's post-war occupation and division. This "long story" can be thought of as a retelling – a rather poor one – and continuation of Adolf Hitler's *Mein Kampf*. Woven throughout this long narrative is a "short story" of the twenty-year struggle of the GdNF, namely its leader Michael Kuehnen, for political existence against a host of enemies.

The master narrative binds together both so that the problems raised by the long one constitute a rationale for the short. The first recounts Germany's helplessness and division while the "short story" focuses on the trials and triumphs of the GdNF and its leadership. Connecting historic events to the immediate experiences of the GdNF provides the community with a logic and legitimacy for its existence in today's world. But the GdNF places primary importance on the logic of the "short story" and its presentation of agency. The "short story" locates the mission, strategies, and the authority of its leaders *vis-à-vis* other would-be leaders and groups.[8]

We want to employ three concepts and two strategies by means of which in the GdNF's master narrative, legitimacy and authority are redefined and the GdNF leadership designated as principal agent. Events are organized around: (a) a historic negative pole of subjugation and grievance; (b) an unobtained positive pole of inversionary rupture; and (c) a logic of accomplishment as a derivation of the positive pole. Strategically the narrative signifies events by: (a) retrieving and linking parallel events of past and present, creating a mythic lineage of grievance; and (b) projecting the identified future from events.[9]

The negative pole around which the narrative orders many of its events is a depiction of the German nation in decay, a decline resulting from a conspiracy of oppression from without and subversion from within. Incarnating this pole is an evil "other", a set of historical "enemies". The "long story" of the narrative represents Germany as a nation long subjugated by foreign enemies – allied occupiers, communists and Jews – and their domestic proxies: federal authorities of all parties, socialists, and capitalists. Equally insidious are the ultra-conservative bourgeoisie, the "reactionaries" of the German People's Union (DVU) and the National Party of Germany (NPD).

Around this negative pole, the narrative creates a lineage of suffering which leads from the past to the present. Retrievals of these antecedents in Germany history provide symbolically dense metaphors of struggle, to assert German nationhood and to keep intact German integrity as a nation and a society as well as a state. Explanation of these antecedents requires the construction of a logic. Each event selected in the narrative is made metonymically significant. Recent events thus take their place in a continuous narrative which becomes the evidence for the logic which follows. Such events, formed into a pedigree by the narrative lead in one direction – the German people's age-old struggle for purification and self-determination against foreign, polluting forces. Within this narrative the GdNF becomes the agent of destiny.

In the "short story", the political suppression of the National Socialists in the Federal Republic is no different than the suffering of past national revolutionaries who have chosen to struggle against Germany's subjugation and those perpetuating it. In sum, the connecting and retrieving power of the narrative entwines past and current events with grand Germanic themes. By reinterpreting the past the GdNF justifies its missionary role.

The "long" and "short" stories of the GdNF's master narrative offer far more than an exposition of lineal grievance. By creating a context of palpable yearning, the GdNF has a platform from which to launch its project of overcoming, inversionary in purpose, rupturing in intent, and morally transformational.[10] The retrieval of past suffering establishes a point of departure which identifies a political project which is both overcoming and redeeming.

The second major concept around which the master narrative organizes events can be categorized as a positive pole of millenarian "inversionary chosenness".[11] Inversionary discourse can apply to communities as disparate as the early Christians, the Levellers and the Diggers, and the Bolsheviks, who have founded their legitimacy and authority on millennial and inversionary principles. Within their discourse are such common themes as predictions of impending upheaval of a kind which will bring ruin to the privileged few and herald a new, just order. In the long story of the GdNF narrative, inversion means an awakened Germany. The German nation would become ethnically self-conscious. Its people would rise up and protect vigorously its interests and purity, and throw out foreign influences. It would stop the moral decay brought about by capitalist materialism and its handmaiden, racial pollution. For followers of the movement there is no pleasure in the accomplishments of today's Germany. The Germany of tomorrow will be a corrective to both, a resurrection of a paradise lost not once but twice, i.e. the powerful Reich of the Wilhelmenian Germany and the Hitlerian "golden age".

As to the "short story", the inversion theme is clear enough. It narrates how a popular, national liberation revolution led by the GdNF will unify "movement" and "people". The streets become the venues for struggle, just as they were in the last days of Weimar Germany. Nazism is thus a form of street revolution, a creature of street theatre by means of which space is converted into meaning – a simulacrum complete with props, flags, music, volume controls and, of course, orality – oratory.

But it is necessary to prevent such theatre from becoming a theatre of the absurd. Hence the narrative needs to provide a logic of and for accomplishment. Between the two poles of story and text, the negative past and the future to be attained, the master narrative lays down the rules of the game – principles for action – which the community must follow to maintain its integrity and to realize its inversionary aspirations.[12] The logic of attainment calls for protest, struggle, and resistance, those polarizing the larger community. While the GdNF's narrative never explicitly urges violence *per se*, it encourages intransigence and non-compliance and implies that as the system breaks down, violent acts will further weaken constraints on the utilization of force. Movement toward compromise, power sharing, or working within the system are the mortal dangers to the integrity and character of the movement. In the logic of inversion, to be co-opted by the system is to lose all future reward – a position particularly directed against the accommodationist position taken by other rightist parties. Hence to "normalize" would be to lose the reason for existence.[13]

The narrative as constructed is a tale of rescue from failure. Its recounting shows that even major setbacks need not be total. Precursor events are by definition incomplete and imperfect. So GdNF narratives reinterpret defeats as instructional achievements, lessons for future reference.[14]

Whether one considers inversionary revolutions in terms of higher forces – God, destiny, race struggle – it is human agency which is the motor of history. In the GdNF master narrative the German people are destined to arise. Not anyone, however, can lead them to an inversionary restoration of the golden eras. Just as the chosen community represents the aggrieved majority so the events of a narrative must give witness to the privileged understanding and special insight which the movement and its leaders possess as the principal agents of historical change. In the "short story", the GdNF appears as a sole agent, a national avant-garde of the German people whose trials endow it with a clearer understanding of the "true nature" of things. They alone have the proper understanding of revolutionary strategy.[15]

These general remarks contextualize the neo-Nazi movement and show how intrinsically it aims to become a discourse community – one able to universalize itself within the German state in the same way its predecessor universalized itself in the Third Reich and beyond.

The GdNF narrates its discourse primarily through the circulation of two publications, its newspaper *NS-Kampfruf*, and Kuehnen's own autobiographical writings found in his book, *Die Zweite Revolution*. Both have circulated through the rightist extremist scene for the past decade and have surfaced at sites of xenophobic violence and in the apartments of GdNF activists.[16]

But it also "speaks" in events – especially those occurring over the last three years and which, incorporated into both stories connects the beginning to an end, the common thread of which is German unification. No theme has offered the GdNF more opportunities for transforming events into stories and stories into a logic which, if perverse, resonates in German philosophy as well as history.

Moreover, with unification, open borders and weakened police forces, not only have large immigrant populations increased, inspiring much public concern generally, but their congregation or clustering in asylum hostels have provided both the venues and occasions for rallies and attacks against foreigners. In turn these stimulate, mobilize and recruit followers. The illicit and choreographed spectacles of violence provide GdNF activists opportunities to act out the role of storm troopers. On the whole the police have been passive bystanders, not a few sharing the concerns of the protesters.

Bearing these general comments in mind we can now focus more sharply on more specific aspects of neo-Nazism as follows. First we will present the GdNF's pre-1990 history, its leaders, organizational structures and membership in order to anchor their narrative discourse in its historical and social context. Secondly, we want to examine the narrative formation of myths of legitimacy and authority prior to German unification using excerpts translated from GdNF publications. Particular attention will be given to how the narrative bestows upon the GdNF and its leadership pre-eminence *vis-à-vis* other rightist groups.[17] Thirdly, we will briefly discuss GdNF history since 1990 when the unification provided ample and explosive opportunities to extend the social text, and also discuss how the GdNF leadership represents a new wave of xenophobic violence reading into the events "signs" of "imminent attainment". Above all we want to stress the connection between neo-Nazism and inversionary movements generally in the sense that virtually all of them thrive on economic uncertainty, social turmoil, frustrated hopes and accumulated discriminatory grievance.[18] Their's is a politics of yearning; their currency: shame to be overcome, guilt to be exorcized, loss to be regained.

III   GdNF HISTORY, 1973–90

In 1985 a young, former officer of the Bundeswehr, Michael Kuehnen, founded the GdNF as a faction within a pre-existing neo-Nazi party, FAP (*Freie Arbeiter Partei*). By his own account, Kuehnen had become active with rightist extremists at the age of 14, but had floated from one radical organization to another. Kuehnen joined the ultra conservative National Party Germany (NPD) as a teenager during its high period in the later 1960s but became disillusioned with its decidedly non-revolutionary party line. After leaving the NPD, the 19-year-old Kuehnen left political activity and joined the army. But immediately after his discharge in the autumn of 1977, he founded the ANS/NA (*Aktionsfront Nationaler Sozialisten/Nationale Aktivisten*) which goal was to actively press for the legalization of the NSDAP through confrontational propaganda activities. Kuehnen's organizing activities came to an abrupt end in the summer of 1978 when he was arrested and sentenced to four years' imprisonment on conspiracy and weapons charges. After serving his sentence, Kuehnen immediately returned to ANS/NA leadership. When the federal government banned the ANS/NA in 1983, Kuehnen and 500 of his followers moved to the FAP, a previously insignificant party, and quickly organized themselves within its structure, making Kuehnen one of its most prominent members. Kuehnen cultivated his own myth by writing extensive treatises while in prison, as Hitler had done with *Mein Kampf,* and began to model his GdNF on the early SA *(Sturm Abteilung)* tradition of the NSDAP which emphasized the "socialist" and "revolutionary" side of Nazism.

Kuehnen's homosexuality and lengthy jail stays, however, made him vulnerable to his party rival Juergen Moesler who, in 1987, won the power struggle and drove Kuehnen and 150 loyal followers from the FAP. Kuehnen promptly founded the GdNF as an official movement of its own, and within two years of being ousted, Kuehnen's charisma and organizational skills had forged the GdNF into a strictly organized "cadre community" which exceeded FAP in numbers and public attention.[19] Kuehnen died of AIDS in April 1991 at the height of his power. Yet his death, while embarrassing to the movement, did little to disturb the GdNF. Long-time Kuehnen friends Gottfried Kuessel, Christian Worch, and Arnulf Priem took over the reigns in a troika leadership.

Today the GdNF represents a confusing array of front and parallel regional field organizations, purposefully set up to elude legal prosecution. A few of the most important are the political/recruiting parties: the Bremen-based DA *(Deutsche Alternative),* the Hamburg-based NL *(Nationale Liste),* and the Berlin-based NA *(National Alternative).* Another important GdNF front is the American-based NSDAP-AO *(NSDAP-Auslandsorganization)* headed by Kuehnen's long-time friend Gary "Gerhard" Lauck. Operating from Lincoln, Nebraska, the NSDAP-AO officially serves as the legal "party in exile". While not a member of GdNF hierarchy, Lauck serves as the movement's propagandist, producing the *NS-Kampfruf* and Kuehnen's writings in ten languages.[20]

Despite their willingness to use violence, the GdNF has never developed into a terrorist group *per se* like the Red Army Faction. As mentioned before, Kuehnen flirted with "armed struggle" against the state in the late 1970s, but abandoned these ideas after a subsequent jail sentence showed him the futility of such a course. Although its members practice paramilitary "war-sports" and stockpile weapons, the GdNF has never targeted state officials and facilities which could bring serious reprisals and force the community into the underground. Unlike the Red Army Fraction which has acted dramatically in broad daylight against key figures in German politics and finance, the GdNF aims its violence against minorities and the socially weak under the cover of night.[21]

IV THE MASTER NARRATIVE, 1984–90: TALES OF YEARNING, CHOSENNESS AND IMMANENCE

(a) Excerpts from the "Long Story"

The "long story" of the GdNF is essentially an epic. It starts with a negative pole defined in terms of both loss and yearning. Three themes are crucial to the story, loss of patrimony, in this case Germany's defeat, occupation and division; the alienation of the state from its Volk with the Federal Government the keeper of a corrupt state, itself a mere puppet of foreign domination; and finally the sick society destroying its own people. Post-1945 Germany appears as a shamed and defenceless nation, unable to withstand the perversions of capitalism, materialism, and racial integration forced upon it by the allied occupiers.

A March 1988 *NS-Kampfruf* article entitled, "Humiliation", provides a good example of all three themes. Although referring to the present it retrieves the past in terms of previous defeats, the shame of Weimar, and the destruction of the Third Reich:

> We stand a humiliated nation.... The root of this humiliation is in the Thirty Years' war, the treaty of Versailles and St Germain, 1919, to the last great war which entwined the best and most beautiful.... The humiliation of the German people were and are: the reparations to insatiable Israel. The traitorous "eastern treaties". Credit to communist Poland. The expulsion of Germans from the eastern territories.... The stationing of foreign missiles on German soil.... The refusal to conduct a peace treaty....
>
> What do the dark events of the post-war years have to do with our situation today. Yesterday points to today, today points to tomorrow. Never must we forget the monstrous humiliation through those who are responsible....[22]

This is fairly typical of the way historical grievances become endowed with power though narrative, i.e. by establishing a lineage for multiple grievance.[23] The narrative converts such disparate events in the life of the nation as the Treaty of Versailles, Willy Brandt's Ostpolitik and the NATO stationing of Pershing missiles into ordered episodes forming a chronological lineage in which each incident is loaded with images, faces, uniforms, broad avenues, marching armies – i.e. the symbolical density of Wilhelmine and Nazi Germany.

Against these previous two periods the contrast to the federal government is overwhelming. The latter is internationalist, a creature of the allied super powers and World Jewry. With the influx of asylees in the late 1980s this conspiracy theory receives a boost. The "foreigner" is part of a plot to weaken the German national body. A February 1991 *NS-Kampfruf* article, "The Struggle of the Jew against Germany", is indicative of this type of thinking:

> The flood against a defenceless Germany by foreigners and sham asylees of all races and breeds, which can only be described as targeted and controlled, leads us to ask the causes and the background of the political powers which push foreign races into Germany in a fight against the people....
>
> The primordial instincts of a people engaged in a fight for survival was and still is being suppressed in a surreptitious way. We are being robbed of this instinct, and now politically blind, are being forced without resistance into a multi-cultural society. And who stands to profit? – the Jewish-dominated capitalist and communist occupiers of Germany ... in a word, the eternal Jew.[24]

Here one can see the deployment of old, radical words and images, once reserved for Jews and communists, resurfacing in GdNF discourse. The end of *Mein Kampf* is, so to speak, "extended". Foreigners "flood" the country, posing threats to the economic, physical and cultural health of the German national body. They are "sham" or "pretend" asylees, just as Jews were labeled as "sham" citizen during the Third Reich, creating an insidiousness through the image of indetectability. In GdNF narratives, foreigners have come to serve as surrogates for long-standing grievance of lost patrimony. Germans must passively accept the newest "invasion" of the country. The asylee is the signifier of a nation robbed of its right to control its borders.[25] Hence the centerpiece of the "long story" is a Germany "robbed" of something far greater than its rights; Germany is being "robbed" of its very nature, its "primordial instincts" needed to survive, and thus, its very abilities of perception. Germany has been "blinded" and "weakened" in its degradation to the point that it can no longer see what is being done to it, a situation which positions the GdNF to be a savior.

Inversionary narratives tell more than "how it was or is"; they also hold out the hope of "how it must be", an imperative outcome. The positive pole of the GdNF master narrative is an inversionary vision of a resurrected, purified Aryan race-community in a Germany totally transformed and "nationally awakened" after years of foreign occupation and national degradation. But if this utopic end state lies in the future, it surely belongs to the past. What is wanted is not a modern Germany, but a return to an "authentic" one, clean and pure, and honourable. In the article "Humiliation", this Germany of the future is a return to a Reich of hardness and pride:

> We want to breath free, decide freely and live free. We want to throw off this humiliation. National Socialism has only one aim, the German Reich in its majesty and power. We want a Germany in the sense of the hardest, most glorious and totally unique German: Adolf Hitler. For every humiliation we will count the blow. This must be the confession of faith for the young Germans.[26]

An authentic Germany is not easily regained, for in the world of inversionary millenarian narratives, nothing precious is won without struggle. The marked quality of the positive pole is its millenarian promise. Hope of redemption will come through an inevitable cataclysm of popular revolution. In a particularly explicit article, "FRG Justice: The Whore of Politics", the coming inversionary upheaval will be undertaken by "the people":

> But you should know that a situation of rebellion and revolution will one day come. An uprising of the discontentment will one day sweep through the people. We know well of the attempts to disarm us spiritually as demanded by the enemy occupiers. But you should also know that there are always those natures which grow, which have courage and dare to resist the unjust system found on the soil of the German Reich.[27]

(b)   The "Short Story" of the GdNF

If the "long story" was essentially an epic the "short story" is a passion play of the community's history. With the "long story" establishing Germany's division and helplessness, the "short story" moves Kuehnen and his group to centre stage. If the loss of German greatness in the "long story" sets the standard for the redeeming project, then the "short story" shows how an oppressed community struggles to rectify this situation.[28]

The negative pole of the "short story" is represented by a host of enemies. An article, "The Fourth Reich" begins the dramatic enterprise by placing the National Socialist movement in a world of threat. Here, the heroism of the movement is underscored by the overwhelming obstacles which the community must overcome and the suffering it must endure:

> The National Socialist movement fights against a world of enemies: against liberal capitalism, Marxism, and reaction, against materialism, Zionism, and the dangers of a race war. Against us stand all established political forces in this country: from the communists to the NPD, and from capital to the unions.

> For us National Socialists, there is not friendly, harmless coexistence with this system. So many of our comrades through the world are humiliated without compare because of their beliefs. Beatings, tortures, and spiritual agency are inflicted against them. These are the agonies of suffering individuals.[29]

The "short story" presents events rooted in daily life, drawing from common experiences and converting them into higher principle.[30] Integral to the negative pole is Germany's Federal Government which the narrative gives responsibility for a host of social ills. In a February 1989 *NS-Kampfruf* article, "FRG-Justice: The Whore of Politics", the GdNF charges the government with harassment and cowardice.

> The FRG justice system is the whore of politics. They are cowards who will not deal once and for all with the drug dealers, the mafias, the sham asylees, the Autonomen in Hamburg and Berlin and now believe that they must show their strength.... We, as politically oppressed of this state which tries to criminalize our political expression, should not wonder that we receive only injustice in the trials which have been plotted against us.[31]

Juxtaposed to the negative pole of government harassment is the positive pole of inversionary revolution. For the GdNF, the long-awaited return to the national stage will begin with the lifting of the federal ban on the NSDAP. Such a day will come when the young join with the National Socialist avant-garde and march once again under the banner of the

swastika. Such a day will signal the awakening of Germany and the beginning of its revolution to regain national sovereignty and purity. This pole,
which provides events their ultimate meaning, is depicted in Kuehnen's
Die Zweite Revolution:

> Should I go again to prison, behind me and other leaders of the National
> Socialist fighting brigades would stand already hundreds of young com-
> rades, who are afraid of no challenge, who stand ready to sacrifice, their
> future, their youth and even their lives for their people. Once 18- and
> 20-year-olds came to us; now 14 to 60-year olds are ready to march
> under our flag. And daily more will come. Soon there will be thousands:
> The laws which ban the swastika and protect Jews will fall and the
> National Socialist Workers Party will once again hold the history of our
> people in its hands.[32]

In another *NS-Kampfruf* article entitled, "In the Spirit of the SA", the
vision of future Germany is cast in the spirit of the SA, hearkening back to
a time when the party was unencumbered by the burdens and corruption of
state power.

> Michael Kuehnen has shown us the way, the true path of the political
> soldier of the SA.... We stand at the beginning of a new peak and have
> the impression that the plutocracy is nearing its end. There is one path
> to victory. We must find our community and path in the spirit of the SA:
> sacrifice, fight, and stand by one another. A community of oath which
> will serve as the invincible pillars of the entire movement.... Then we
> will repeat the wonder: a new Volk community will be resurrected on
> the old values, and this community will bear the seal of the spirit of the
> SA.[33]

Here, Michael Kuehnen appears as "John the Baptist" pointing to the
"true path" of the SA and of "action" which will enable the GdNF to reap
the rewards of the coming inversionary revolution. Taking the path of the
SA will not only permit the GdNF to dominate the movement. It will make
them little less than human gods who can resurrect "the authentic" and
create a society in their own image.

The GdNF "short story" provides a logic of accomplishment – requirements and necessary actions – to overcome the community's predicament
and to achieve the utopic state. Although violence is never explicitly
called for, GdNF narratives make it clear that total non-compliance and
"struggle" are the only possible acts of transcendence possible. An excerpt

from "The Spirit of the SA", illustrates the banishment of speech and reason. "Action" subordinates and denigrates speech and "discussion" equals paralysis:

> We must be careful of the yammerers who can only talk about history but cannot make it. We must avoid those who always want to endlessly conduct discussions of "the basics". They lead to decay and paralysis where brave and certain stands are needed. There must be no more talk in Germany. For that time grows shorter and shorter. Here must be actions....[34]

The previously mentioned article "Humiliation", calls on readers to reject "reason", restraints, and tempered action as creatures of the exploiters and enemies of Germany. Since the moderation and accommodation are equated with submission and weakness, the door is open to banish them: "Are we a proud people? Are we not constantly submissive to the 'voice of reason' which offers only accommodation? Are we not constantly compromising in the name of 'survival is everything'? Yes! We stand a humiliated nation...."[35]

The GdNF is clearly located as a community where "principle" dominates "rational choice" and where "political gratification" in terms of co-operating with the system will be postponed for greater rewards. The narrative elevates their marginalized position and small numbers into one of superiority by holding out the hope of a coming crisis of the status quo. Enmity or hate is elevated as the strength of the community, for only in nihilistic rejection of the present order can the community hope to reap the greater awards of the future upheaval.

> But this should not shock us: It is this consequent rejection of all forces supporting or acknowledging this system that secures us the mass basis in the moment in which the system starts to shake and the people become dissatisfied. Our enmity with others brings us the support from those who – for whatever reasons – sense the system's emptiness, meaninglessness, and hypocrisy and want to demolish it.... We have to be the radical annihilation of the existing, the fundamental alternative....[36]

The inherent oppositional nature of the group is reconfirmed. The GdNF is placed inherently at odds with the bourgeois world. Their pride of accomplishment must come from frustrating the system by following a set of principles which few can understand, and by obeying a logic impervi ous to the market-place concerns of normal society. But this is a logic which gives nothing less than invincibility.

> The many others we don't want. The doubtful, the know-it-alls, the petty bourgeois! Those will come by themselves once the success is on our side. We don't give a damn about the scruples and fears of the bourgeois world, for as a sworn-in community, we are invincible.... Over us the party big whigs gnash their teeth. They do not understand us, therefore they are helpless. They think of well-being, calmness, economic growth.... "Engage yourself with the state, and no one will do anything to you." they say. No! We will never recognize this system.[37]

Since the option of working with other nationalist parties is rejected as "working with the system", only one option remains, that of struggle and resistance. In a final phrase, one can see that struggle is not only a means of attaining goals but the apotheosis of the meaning of existence.

> You cannot buy us in a time when everything seems up for sale. We spit on your respectability which is only a curtain to hide the unimaginably and spoiled in you. We do not give in to the coercion, not to bribery, and not your sweet ringing of words.... *The Struggle is the content of our life*.[38]

Struggle and suffering, though much bemoaned in the "short story", still are held forward as signs of legitimacy and authority. To have challenged the negative pole and emerged stronger signifies chosenness; purified by the trials of political persecution and public rejection, GdNF members are all the more leaders. Upon these acts of struggle the narrative retrieves the past and projects the future. Struggle and repressions place the community in the tradition of the early NSDAP. Just as the NSDAP struggled as a tiny party against state repression to become rulers of Germany, so every tiny action of the GdNF shares in this heritage and takes on greater significance. Events of struggle also bear signs of the coming inversion. By the logic of the first shall be last and the last shall be first, all struggle can be victory no matter how bad the loss. Should the hero fall or suffer a set back, to him belongs the wreath of martyrdom. Should the community be defeated, the narrative converts the setback into a time of testing in which the community grows.

Michael Kuehnen's memoirs published in *Die Zweite Revolution* and in the *NS-Kampfruf* are one of the most widely circulated sources of the "short story" of the GdNF community. Kuehnen's story exemplifies chosenness born of suffering. In his writings National Socialism appears as an oppressed, subjugated movement. Accounts begin with Kuehnen's own story of his conversion:

> I have been politically active since 1969 at 14 years old. It was a long and hard path to self-discovery and then to people who could introduce me to such a movement. In 1963, I received my first copy of the *NS-Kampfruf* but remained skeptical to the claim that there was an organized NS-underground.... But at that time, I believed in the reconcilability of nationalist thinking and a democratic system.... But when my party activity fell through, I was ripe! I was pulled to ever newer and more radical paths, which my repulsion for the ruling system only made more easy to follow. But the path is far from the good son of the bourgeoisie and loyal officer of the state to a national socialist revolutionary....[39]

This passage is indicative of much GdNF writing. Leaders such as Kuehnen are presented as pulled to a destined future. "Called" at a young age, Kuehnen's path of conversion appears as a mystic initiation into the National Socialist community, accompanied by ostracization and loneliness. Kuehnen stresses separateness as a sign of specialness and eventually utilizes the religious metaphor of the pilgrimage from the life of worldly comfort down the ascetic path of higher goals and service. Here one can well see the narrative's conversion of struggle to victory. Kuehnen's early confused wanderings led him to the true revolutionary path.

Another passage describes well Kuehnen's revelatory discovery of the greater National Socialist community:

> In March 1977, I drove with a young comrade from Hamburg to the NPD party convention in Hanover. On the night before, there was a rally with a torch light parade through the city. As we were about to take our places, a voice cried out from the darkness, "All NSDAP-AO people to the rear". Those of us from Hamburg only looked at ourselves and immediately moved to the end of the parade. But we were not alone. And suddenly we realized that almost a third of the comrades recognized themselves as members of the NSDAP-AO. We were not isolated madmen; the *NS-Kampruf* had not lied. Everywhere there were young activists. We were really a movement. Young comrades who come today to a known and organized movement will never really understand what that meant for us....[40]

This passage combines images of the NSDAP past and projection of the future inversion. Retrieving the past, the narrative shows the GdNF as a tiny party scorned even by conservative forces. But in this evening ritual, a voice "cries out in the darkness" making young National Socialists aware of their interconnectedness in a greater communion. The projection of the coming inversion is clear: though seemingly alone, fate will unify National Socialists Dismissal to the end of the parade line by the NPD, shows the discriminatory treatment of "revolutionaries" by bourgeois conservative forces. But the logic of inversionary discourse, dismissal to the last place is not disgrace but proves "electedness" and anticipates the future victory according to the axiom: the last shall be first, and the first shall be last.

In the narrative, "choseness" is eventually manifested in miraculousness. Kuehnen writes of the troubled founding of the ANS/NA which overcome many obstacles. Juxtaposing the ANS/NA's struggles with the NSDAP's early days – few people, no money, but eventual flourishing – Kuehnen projects the GdNF's successful future:

> As we began ten years ago, there was no openly organized NS movement, which could offer our ideas as a believable and real alternative in the general consciousness of our people. National Socialism appeared to be damned. But within a few months of the ANS/NA we were known beyond the borders of Germany. From our tiny troops of young sacrificing idealists without money, connections or organizational basis has developed a real National Socialist movement with hundreds of activists. We have become the most famous of these troops. For the first time our enemies were forced to recognize the existence of organized – and young – National Socialists. We are the leaders of the national freedom fighters, the political precursors of the Fourth Reich.... Our comrades are candidates in elections. Today we command headlines, the response of officials, and scientific studies. The existence of the National Socialist movement is a publicly acknowledged fact, whose bearer is nothing less than the German youth.[41]

Signs of choseness are also found with the connection to youth to signify virility of the party's mission which the old order and generation cannot understand. In the following passage of "The Fourth Reich", the chosenness of the group is once again affirmed by its youth and by its smallness.

> Two sorrows torture the young fighters of our movement, the great power of the enemy and the seemingly so small number of comrades. I

tell you, it is good that we are only so few! We form an élite. Our movement nurtures a generation of fighters to whom nothing will be impossible. To us, only those comrades find their way, who do not know any fear for their bourgeois existence. The ones who are decisive, in any case, ready to sacrifice their existence.[42]

When setbacks came, these could be incorporated into the narrative signs of chosenness. Trials are another form of preparation for the struggles of the future. One steels oneself in prison. Even a federal ban of the ANS/NA and arrests of its leaders become instructional victories in the "short story". Christian Worch writes in *Die Zweite Revolution* of the federal sanctions which lead to the demise of the ANS/NA:

The repression became stronger and many groups collapsed. But the spiritual climate, the readiness of our young men to stand for the old but eternally new ideas, became better. It was as if destiny was taking a breath, to wait for Michael Kuehnen's release. In 1982 it was time. And from there it went blow by blow. First came the public rallies which gained the attention of the foreign press. Then came the unification of all important national social forces to a closed organization.... All this despite a lack of printing machines, technical goods, meeting places and connections. Although we comprised no more than 270 members on 7 December 1983, we were banned. But for the first time in the history of the West German rump state an organizational ban was ineffective. Michael Kuehnen himself said on the day of the banning, "We are banned. Yes, and? Sieg Heil!" The community which had arisen through the years of fight and sacrifice, would not permit itself to simply be banned. Organizations can be dissolved but the people which fought for them remain. And the wonderful feeling, to have come together under a united leader for a common cause, also remains.[43]

Kuehnen, writing of the founding of the GdNF two years after the demise of the ANS/NA, provides another depiction of the strength and provenness born of suffering:

Ten years ago I founded with two other comrades the first cell of our present community of the GdNF. A decade of political battle for the refounding of the NSDAP and for Germany lies behind us. It was a hard decade of suffering and sacrifice, of defeats and beatings. I spent seven of these years as a prisoner of conscience and in exile. But this defeat has made us hard. We are raised on oppression. It is a part of our inner decisiveness. We are stronger than all other victims of the system. We are stronger because of this political oppression....[44]

This excerpt draws images of the past. Just as Hitler had served a prison sentence, so too has Kuehnen. The age-old metaphor is clear: who but the suffering exile can lead his country back to its true path. Struggle and travail are but tests of leadership ability which will be needed for the future struggle. Travail only confirms chosenness and authority. Thus, GdNF members are "chosen" above all rightist extremists.

The "short story" concludes with words of hope and encouragement:

It will be a long struggle and it is possible that our generation will not live to see a victory. Nobody can expect that only few decades after the complete defeat, the new victory stands before us. Therefore, our fighters are not driven by greed to the feeding stations of state power. Our movement lives from the love of the people and the faith to the idea.... But what are decades anyway in the eyes of history. The task of our generation – the 1950–1965 generation who are predominant in the movement – was to pick up the tradition and carry it on.... Yet on our side stands the logic of history....

Like the apostles of the Bible who would not live to see the Second Coming, so present day National Socialists accept that they are simply disciples preparing the way. Like a true saviour, the National Socialist makes this sacrifice in love of higher ideals, not earthly reward.

V HISTORY, 1990–2: EXTENDING THE NARRATIVE. IMMANENCE AND THE NARRATIVE CODING OF VIOLENCE

The collapse of the East German regime and the subsequent unification in 1990 offered the GdNF two unique xenophobic "opportunities" to attract attention and mobilize potential recruits. First, with the eradication of the East Bloc borders, economic and political refugees from the Balkans, East Asia and Africa arrived in Germany in overwhelming numbers to take advantage of its liberal asylum provisions.[45] Secondly, the radical move to the free market left many areas of East Germany in deep economic depression. The rationalization of moribund East German firms and their exposure to competition has condemned large segments of superfluous Eastern workers into seemingly permanent unemployment.[46] All of this has taken place in a setting of failed political promises to increase the standard of living and deep cynicism pervading German society about the state's ability to rectify the major social problems. As economic despair has grown, so has the potential for violence among young men who were not only extremely discontented with their social insecurity but were also convinced that foreigners competed for scarce public resources.[47]

For Kuehnen, xenophobia had long been viewed as a possible instrument of recruitment, and in the weeks after the opening of the Berlin Wall, GdNF activists moved quickly to exploit the untapped potential of xenophobic resentment.[48] Using the DA as the recruitment instrument of choice, Kuehnen convened the "Eastern Co-ordination Meeting" on 14 February 1990 with the participation of young neo-Nazis from Rostock, Frankfurt-on-Oder, Magdeburg, Dresden, Cottbus, and Berlin. The result was the "Eastern Working Plan". According to the Plan, DA activities concentrated first on erecting a regional party called *DA Mitteldeutschland* in East Berlin and then shifting the centre of operations to Dresden and Cottbus.

With the DA firmly in Berlin by mid-summer 1990, Kuehnen, Kuessel, and Worch devoted their full energies to Dresden, holding numerous rallies with explosive results. Not only did xenophobic violence flare up spontaneously wherever the GdNF activists agitated, but xenophobic agitation and violence soon became an instrument of mobilization and integration between DA members and the local burgeoning "Skinhead" scene. On 20 October, Dresden saw its first Nazi march since the Third Reich. In the immediate weeks afterwards, alternative cafés, leftist-occupied houses and asylum hostels were attacked and burned daily, and a young Angolan man became the first official casualty.[49] When Dresden party organizer Rainer Sonntag was gunned down in a confrontation with pimps, neo-Nazis used the occasion to terrorize foreigners on the streets for days. Since the GdNF began taking this violently confrontational stance, their membership has increased from 1,500 in 1989 to 2,100 in 1991. Additionally the Nazi faction of the "Skinhead" movement, or "Nazi-Skins", doubled in size to 4,500.[50]

In response to these outbreaks of violence, GdNF publications began to narrativize the acts as "symbolically drenched" episodes. This discursive reconstruction of the violence of the early 1990s occurred immediately. In 1991, after the attacks on asylee hostels in Hoyerswerda, Gottfried Kuessel wrote:

The patience of the German Volk was stretched to the breaking point. It was only a matter of time before there was an explosion.... Without being asked, the German Volk has finally taken to the streets ... and the slogans they chant are nationalistic slogans. With them in Western and Central Germany, National Socialist freedom fighters have taken to the streets to do battle with the anti-German, anti-white system.... The time – which we knew had to come – has finally come.

The world press have been reporting of the massive resistance in Germany against the foreign invasion.... This embarrassment has motivated the Bonn regime ... to "crackdown".... The race-treason, Jew-system unleashes every weapon in its vast arsenal including riot police and undercover agents in a desperate effort to destroy this popular all-white uprising. Fortunately this "crackdown" is doomed to utterly fail to crush the resistance movement![51]

Here, violence appears to have been inevitable, unstoppable: "The time – which we knew had to come – has finally come." "Our time is not coming, it is already here." "The crackdown is doomed to utterly fail...." It is inevitable because the law of racial conflict is a law of nature, and the policies of the Federal Government are thus doomed to culminate in inversionary revolution. Violence appears as an act of heroic, redemptive yearning within a saving moral order. Constituted into a narrative of struggle, violence may indeed be transformed into a semiotic structure, defining the moral moment between the forces of purity and those of corruption.

Once narrativized, violence represents the meaning of meaning radically altering the manner or mode of communicating within the movement. On the basis of violent identity there developed a discourse of violence. That is, violence becomes discourse with events of violence providing the movement with a "language" of its own including a coded manner of expressing legitimacy, oppression and dissent. When one looks at the GdNF, one must ask if violent struggle has become its own conversational framework through which communal ideals are explicated and conveyed.

VI CONCLUSION

We have examined how the interplay between the past and future, narrative and text, orality and the printed word, embodied in knowledgeable practices and events provide the GdNF with claims to legitimacy and authority. Playing on uncertainty, chaos, frustrated hopes and ambitions, the GdNF has converted a history of grievances, real and imagined, into new forms of truth, coding episodes into mythical narratives. The fictive truths of the GdNF are constructed from the events of a "long" and "short" story about the struggles of Germany and the GdNF against their oppressors. These stories of the master narrative define a negative pole to be transcended, a positive pole in the form of disjunctive, transformational end state, and a logic of attainment. Together these constitute a complete project, inversionary in object and transformational in consequence. These narratives use the power of retrieval portrayed as a mythic past to derive a logic of projection and a defined future.[52]

For those persons seeking totalizing solutions to personal plights projected onto the greater society, the neo-Nazism represents a peculiar millenarian movement which looks backward into the future, and offers both little and everything. Complete with myths of destiny, alternative truths, promises, a projective logic and unconventional speech and symbolic system, the movement speaks of the exceptionalism of its mission and its faith in the interrupted historical project of German greatness. It promises that by acting on truths as defined one can alter society and, implicitly, one's own condition.[53] For those who cannot find a place in society, the inversionary discourse offers new commitment over the ordinary, including affiliations of friends and family and moral absolutism triumphing over practical relativism.

So the "lost" in life can become found, the victim becoming the man (primarily) of action in a world divided and polarized between those who are inside the discourse community and the enemies at the gates. Hence, those who society brands as "losers" become a "chosen people". Each member can revel in his pariahdom, knowing that he has superior insights and a moral agenda which the average citizen cannot understand.

NOTES

1. Among the present goals of the NSDAP is a lifting of the federal ban and to become a legal party.
2. On the latter see Hugo Claus' novel *The Sorrow of Belgium* (London: Penguin Books, 1983).
3. See Zeev Sternhell, *Neither Right nor Left* (Berkeley, Calif.: University of California Press, 1986).
4. Heinrich Sippel, "Aktuelles Lagebild des Rechtsextremismus im vereinten Deutschland", in *Texte zur Inneren Sicherheit, Extremismus und Fremdenfeindlichkeit*, Band I (Bonn: Der Bundesminister des Innern, 1992) pp. 7, 9.

5.   Wolgang Benz (ed.), *Rechtsextremismus in der Bundesrepublik: Voraussetzungen, Zusammenhaenge, Wirkungen* (Frankfurt am Main: Fisher Verlag, 1992) p. 17.

6.   Heinrich Sippel, "Rechtsextremismus im Vereinten Deutschland unter besonderer Beruecksichtigung fremdenfeindlicher Gewalttaten", *Vortrag auf dem Seminar des Bundesministerium des Innern mit Leitern von Jugend und Sozialaemtern, Bad Lasphe, 10 November 1992* (Bonn: Bundesverfassungsschutz, Der Bundesminister des Innern, 1992) pp. 6, 9.

   See also *Bundesverfassungschutz, Verfassungschutzbericht* (Bonn: Der Bundesminister des Innern, 1991) pp. 74–88. In 1990 there were 1,578 non-violent, rightist-extremist offences. These include threats of violence, distribution of illegal propaganda and agitation, and harassment and insults. There were 270 acts of violence: 2 deaths, 47 cases of arson, 102 bodily assaults, and 119 cases of vandalism. Of the total 1,848 rightist crimes, acts of violence comprised only 10 per cent.

   In 1991 there were 2,401 non-violent rightist crimes and 1,483 acts of violence. Among those are 3 deaths, 384 arson attacks (354 of these arson attacks, or 93 per cent, were against foreigners), 449 bodily assaults, (336 or 74.8 per cent against foreigners), and 648 cases of vandalism (562 or 86.7 per cent against foreigners). Of the 3,884 rightist crimes, 2,598 or 66.8 per cent were xenophobic.

   In 1992, there were 2,285 rightist crimes, a 54 per cent increase over 1991. 1,760 of these were acts of violence: 11 deaths, 586 arson attacks (539 specifically against foreigners), 12 bombings and 600 critically injured victims. 1,566 of these were xenophobic. The ripple of effects of particularly well-publicized attacks were alarming. Crimes of rightist extremist motivations, measured at 461 during August, jumped to 1,163 in September after the infamous Rostock riots. 816 were reported in October, and 1,153 in November, eventually culminating in the Mölln fire bombings which killed three Turkish women.

   1993 has shown no signs of improvement. From January to 15 April 1993 there have been 529 acts of rightist violence as compared to the similar period in 1992 with 342 acts of violence. There have been in January and February of this year 936 criminal acts with xenophobic motives, almost a doubling of those in January and February of 1992. On 29 May, five turkish women were killed in an arson attack in Solingen, bringing the death toll of people murdered by rightist extremists to 26. In the first six months of 1993 there have been 971 acts of rightist violence of which 195 have been arson, 4 bombings, 261 cases of bodily injury and 364 cases of vandalism.

   See also Helmut Willems, Stefanie Wuertz and Roland Eckert, *Fremdenfeindlichen Gewalt: Eine Analyse von Taeternstrukturen and Eskalationsprozessen* (Bundesministerium fuer Frauen und Jugend, Jun 1993) p. 7. Between 1987 and 1990, the number of xenophobic crimes averaged 250 per year. In 1991 alone, the number rose almost ten times to 2427.

7.   The discourse analysis laid out in this paper is indebted to David Apter's work on revolutionary discourse in Maoist China. David E. Apter and Tony Saich, *Revolutionary Discourse in Mao's Republic* (Cambridge, Mass.: Harvard University Press, 1994).

8.   Apter and Saich, op. cit., p. 91.

9.   Ibid., p. 7.
10. Ibid., p. 88.
11. Maxwell Taylor, *The Fanatics* (New York: Brassey's, 1991) p. 121.
     Millenarian refers to the belief of an imminent and catastrophic upheaval.
     Inversionary chosenness is a timeless theme: the first shall be last, and the
     last shall be first. Taylor identifies five millenarian motifs as crucial for
     understanding the logic of groups like the GdNF:

     1. An analysis of the world in terms of an impending catastrophe.
     2. A revelation that explains a negative state of affairs and which offers
        salvation to redress these ills.
     3. As part of the revelation, the possession of special knowledge that the
        disastrous state of society is the result of malevolent subverting
        society. Through the possession of this special knowledge, the holder
        has a unique capacity to fight the corrupting forces.
     4. A sense of timeliness for action, in that the forces of corruption are
        nearing a self-destructive completion of their tasks. There is an imma-
        nency of the end.
     5. A conviction that the evil forces can be defeated because of the special
        insights, and that their defeat will result in the ushering in of a new
        and better world.

12. David E. Apter and Tony Saich, *Revolutionary Discourse in Mao's
     Republic* (Cambridge, Mass.: Harvard University Press, 1994).
13. Taylor, op. cit., pp. 155–6.
14. Apter and Saich, op. cit.
15. Taylor, op. cit., pp. 122–5
16. Special Edition, Anti-Defamation League of B'nai B'rith – Civil Rights
     Division (February 1993). At the end of 1991, German police tallied
     seventy-two criminal incidents involving Lauck's materials which bear his
     Nebraska post-office box. In 1992, the number of criminal incidents associ-
     ated with Lauck's inflammatory propaganda tripled.
17. Apter and Saich, op. cit., p. 6.
18. David E. Apter, "Yan'an and the Narrative Reconstruction of Reality", in
     Daedalus, vol. 22 (Spring 1993) pp. 207–32.
19. Amin Pfahl-Traughber, *Rechtsextremismus. Eine kritische Bestandsaufnahme
     nach der Wiedervereinigung* (Bonn: Bouvier Verlag, 1993) pp. 78–95.
20. Special Edition, Anti-Defamation League of B'nai B'rith – Civil Rights
     Division (February 1993). Lauck's work has not been without effect. At
     the end of 1991, German police tallied seventy-two criminal incidents
     where Lauck's materials had been found on site. In 1992, the number of
     criminal incidents associated with Lauck's inflammatory propaganda
     tripled.
21. Pfahl-Traughber, op. cit., p. 81.
22. *NS-Kampfruf* (March/April 1988) no. 70.
23. Apter and Saich, op. cit.
24. *NS-Kampfruf* (January/February 1991) no. 87.
25. The first references to foreigners appears in *NS-Kampfruf* (November/
     December 1987) no. 68. In this issue, the twenty-five-point programme of

the NSDAP is printed and commented on by Michael Kuehnen. Points 4 and 5 of the programme call for the strict regulation of who can obtain citizenship based upon German ancestry and for a special body of law for foreign "guests" living in Germany.

26. *NS-Kampfruf* (March/April 1988) no. 70.; *NS-Kampfruf* (January/February 1991) no. 87.
27. *NS-Kampfruf* (January/February 1989) no. 75.
28. Apter and Saich, *Revolutionary Discourse in Mao's Republic*, pp. 93–4.
29. Apter, "Yan'an and the Narrative Reconstruction of Reality", p. 221. See also David E. Apter, "A View From The Bogside", in H. Gilomee and J. Gagiano (eds), *The Elusive Search for Peace: South Africa, Israel, Northern Ireland* (Cape Town: Oxford University Press in association with IDASA, 1990). p. 2.; and
30. Apter, "Yan'an and the Narrative Reconstruction of Reality", p. 209..
31. *NS-Kampfruf* (January/February 1989) no. 79.
32. *Die Zweite Revolution*, p. 7.
33. *NS-Kampruf* (Summer 1986) no. 61.
34. *NS-Kampfruf* (March/April 1988) no. 70.
35. Ibid.
36. *NS-Kampfruf* (Winter 1984) no. 58.
37. Ibid.
38. Ibid.
39. *NS-Kampfruf* (Summer 1986) no. 60; *NS-Kampfruf* (July/August 1987) no. 66.
40. Ibid.
41. Ibid.
42. *NS-Kampfruf* (Winter 1984) no. 58.
43. *Die Zweiter Revolution*, p. 2.
44. *NS-Kampfruf* (Winter 1984) no. 58.
45. *PZ*, no. 69 (Bonn: Bundeszentral fuer politische Bildung, Juli 1992), p. 6. Since 1988 about 520,000 refugees have come to Germany, mainly from the former Yugoslavia. In 1992, 50,000 refugees came from Yugoslavia alone. Many cannot be repatriated until the civil war ends on political or humanitarian grounds. The greatest problem, however, is with those seeking political asylum. In 1988, 103,076 asylum seekers arrived. In 1989, the figure grew to 121,318, and in 1990, to almost 193,000. In 1991, the number was 256,112 and in 1992, nearly 450,000 sought refuge. In the first quarter of 1993 there have been 118,064 asylum seekers, a 21 per cent increase over the same time period last year. Amongst these hundreds of thousands, only the smallest percentage are political refugees. About 80 per cent originate from Rumania and Bulgaria, and 60 per cent of Rumanians are gypsies.
46. Roger Cohen, "Deceived and Sold, East Germans Weigh Down Europe", *International Herald-Tribune*, 9 March 1993, p. 1. Of the 9.8 million people employed in Eastern Germany in 1989, the Deutsche Bank estimates that about 5.4 million still have jobs in the eastern regions, In three years, 4.4 million jobs have been lost and industrial output has slumped by 70 per cent.
     See also *Die Welt*, 7 May 1993, p. 13. In the new states, 1,117,000 people are searching for work without success, an unemployment rate of approximately 15 per cent. If people in temporary work programmes are included,

unemployment has reached more than 30 per cent, and more than 45 per cent if early retirees and those obliged to work in the West are counted.

47.   Peter Koedderitzsch and Leo Mueller, *Rechtsextremismus in der DDR* (Goettingen: Lamuv Verlag, 1990) p. 20. Not only has the GDR's economic infrastructure collapsed, but so has its youth infrastructure. The desolate satellite communities like those of Marzahn and NeuKoeln, Berlin, or the Fritz-Heckert Gebiet in Chemnitz provide a larming examples. Constructed in the late 1970s for young couples starting families, these grey, monolithic, prefab high-rise apartments have an extremely high youth population. In the Fritz-Heckert complex, for example, there are 17,000 youth in a population of 85,000. Although there was always a shortage of recreational opportunities in these areas, the situation has only become worse. Gyms, movie house, libraries, once funded and administered by the GDR state, have been closed or drastically reduced due to budget cuts in the new federal states. Youth discotheques, camping trips, free vacations and athletic clubs have also been terminated with the disbanding of the Free German Youth and Young Pioneers. At most, rooms at an underfunded "recreational centre" are kept open as a coffee house.

See also Willaems, Wuertz and Eckert, op. cit., p. 38. The results have been the formation of loose-knit, xenophobic gangs which can be designated as "rightist radical" and estimated to comprise between 10,000 and 15,000 youth. Overwhelmingly comprised of young males under 21-years-old, these gangs have an extremely high potential for violence, "just for the fun of it". It is estimated that they are responsible for 93 per cent of all offences (the remaining 7 per cent are by lone assailants) and 80 per cent of the actual violence.

Also Pfahl-Traughber, op. cit., pp. 184–8. In 1992, the Freudenberg Foundation conducted a survey which yielded the following results:

- 49 per cent were of the opinion that in East German there were too many foreigners.
- 12 per cent agreed with the slogan, "Each foreigner is one too many".
- 55 per cent wanted to reduce the number of foreigners.
- 24 per cent agreed with the slogan "Foreigners out!"
- With the statement, "They take away our jobs", 50 per cent agreed fully or in part. Over 50 per cent of youth fully agreed.
- 2 per cent of male students and 4 per cent of male apprentices had hunted down and attacked foreigners and 9 per cent of male students and 15 per cent of apprentices would be willing to attack foreigners under certain circumstances.

Many journalistic monographs offer rich accounts of the marginalizing effects of unification on youth – especially East German youth – and their slide from GDR youth organizations such as the Free German Youth (FDJ) into rightist radical gangs (Heineman and Schubarth, 1992; Farin and Seidel-Pielen, 1992; Koedderitzsch and Mueller, 1990, Hirsch and Heim, 1991).

In the academic realm, political sociologist William Heitmeyer has been a pioneer in applying modernization theory to rightist youth violence, offering "frustration-aggression" or "relative deprivation" explanations for reactionary "orientations" and public sympathy "potentials" of rightist extremism in German society (Heitmeyer, 1987; Heitmeyer *et al.*, 1992). Others such as social-psychologist Hans-Joachim Maaz have examined the repressive political structures and totalitarian culture whose removal in 1990 led to violent social explosions.

48. *Antifaschistischen Autorenkollectivs Berlin, Drahtzieher im Braunen Netz. Der Wiederaufbau der NSDAP* (Berlin: Edition ID-Archive, 1992) p. 132.

49. Ibid., p. 94.

50. *Verfassungsschutzbericht*, pp. 72–4. The Federal Office of Constitutional Protection estimates that there are 60,000 rightist radicals in such "patriotic" parties as the DVU and the Republikaner. Considerably more militant are 40,000 rightist extremists who belong to seventy-six different organizations. About 6,400 can be called fanatical or "hard core". Of this number, approximately 2,100 belong to Hitlerite or "neo-Nazi" organizations such as FAP, DA, NO, and between 4,200 and 4,600 are "Nazi Skinheads" who also share membership in a variety of rightist extremist parties and gangs.

See also Willaems, Wuertz and Eckert, op. cit., p. 31. Of those accused of rightist crimes, 25.2 per cent belong to rightist extremist organizations and 37.9 per cent belong to "Skinhead" groups. Also *Verfassungsschutzbericht*, pp. 5–6, 91.

Although most attention is given to the "Nazi-Skins" and "Faschos", the "Skinhead" movement is quite diverse. In the West, the movement started in England as a counter-cultural group based on a stylized appearance, not Fascist politics. The "Oi-skins", known for their drunken rioting at public sporting events, are similar to the "Hooligans". Although they are nationalistic, they are distinctly non-Fascist and apolitical. Presently the "Oi-skins" are most numerous in the West. There are also the "Red-Skins" who are anti-Fascist and leftist and the "SHARPs", "Skins" who categorically reject racial prejudice. Before the reunification only 10 per cent of the "Skins" were politicized. Now 1,500 of the 3,500 "Skinheads" belong to the neo-Nazi splinter.

East German "Skins" are another case. East German groups, because they developed as protest to the GDR communistic apparatus, are much more politicized and their ties to Nazi ideology is much more formed than by their comrades in West Germany. Unpolitical and non-rightist extremist "Skins" are the exception in East Germany. In the East there are about 3,000 neo-Nazi activists. Almost all of the neo-Nazi violence potential in East Germany comes from "Skinheads" alone.

51. *The New Order* (March/April 1993) no. 103, p. 6.

52. Apter and Saich, op. cit.

53. Ibid. See also Michael Schmidt, *New Reich*. Schmidt offers insight into the personal problems of GdNF "prominents", and security offered by the community.

REFERENCES

Antifaschistischen Autorenkollektivs Berlin, *Drahtzieher im Braunen Netz: Der Wiederaufbau der NSDAP* (Berlin: Edition ID-Archive, 1992).

Apter, David and Saich, Tony, *Revolutionary Discourse in Mao's Republic* (Cambridge, Mass.: Harvard University Press, 1994).

Apter, David, "A View from the Bogside", in *The Elusive Search for Peace*, ed Herman Giliomee and Jannie Gagiano (Capetown: Oxford University Press, 1990, in association with IDASA).

Assheuer, Thomas and Sarkowicz, Hans, *Rechtsradikale in Deutschland: die Alte und die Neue Rechte* (Munich: C. H. Beck Verlag, 1992).

Backes, Uwe and Jesse, Eckhard, *Politischer Extremismus in der Bundesrepublik Deutschland*, vols 1–3 (Cologne: Verlag Wissenschaft und Politik, 1989).

Bahman, Nirumand (eds), *Angst vor den Deutschen* (Hamburg: Rotwohlt Taschenbuch Verlag, 1992).

Benz, Wolfgang (ed.), *Rechtsextremismus in der Bundesrepublik: Voraussetzungen, Zusammenhaenge, Wirkungen* (Frankfurt am Main: Fisher Verlag, 1992).

Bundesminister des Innern, *Extremismus und Fremdenfeindlichkeit*, vols 1–2 (Bonn: Der Bundesminister des Innern, 1992).

Bundesminister des Innern, *Verfassungsschutzbericht 1991* (Bonn: Der Bundesminister des Innern, 1992).

Butterwegge, Christoph and Horst, Isola (eds), *Rechtsextremismus im vereinten Deutschland* (Berlin: Ch. Links, 1991).

Dudek, Peter and Jaschke, Hans-Gerd, *Entstehung und Entwicklung des Rechtsextremismus in der Bundesrepublik*, vols 1 and 2 (Opladen: Westdeutscher Verlag, 1984).

Farin, Klaus and Seidel-Pielen, Eberhard, *Reschtsruck: Rassismus im Neuen Deutschland* (Berlin: Rotbuch Verlag, 1992).

Ford, Glyn (ed.), *Fascist Europe: The Rise of Racism and Xenophobia* (London: Pluto Press, 1992).

Gress, Franz, Jaschke, Hans-Gerd and Schoenekaes, Klaus, *Neue Rechte und Rechtsextremismus in Europa* (Opladen: Westdeutscher Verlag, 1990).

Hainsworth, Paul, *The Extreme Right in Europe and the USA* (London: Pinter Publishers, 1992).

Harris, Geoffrey, *The Dark Side of Europe Today* (Edinburgh: Edinburgh University Press, 1990).

Hartmann, Ulrich *et al.*, *Rechtsextremismus bei Jugenlichen* (Munich: Koesel Verlag, 1985).

Heinemann, Karl-Heinz and Schulbarth, Wilfried (eds), *Der antifaschistishe Staat entlaesst siene Kinder: Jugend und Rechtsextremismus in Ostdeutschland* (Cologne: PapyRossa Verlag, 1992).

Heitmeyer, Wilhelm, *Rechtsextremistiche Orientierungen bei Jugenlichen* (Munich: Juventa Verlag, 1987).

Heitmeyer, Wilhelm *et al.*, *Die Bielefelder Rechtsextremismus-Studie* (Munich: Juventa Verlag, 1992).

Helsinki Watch, *Foreigners Out: Xenophobia and Right-wing Violence in Germany* (New York: Human Rights Watch, October 1992).

Henle, Manfred, *Rauslaender Aus* (Cologne: PapyRossa Verlag 1993).

Hirsch, Kurt and Heim, Peter, *Von Links nach Rechts: Rechtsradikale Aktivitaeten in den neuen Bundeslaender* (Munich: Goldman Verlag, 1991).

Hockenos, Paul, *Free to Hate* (London: Routledge, 1993).

Horst, Richter, *Ein Rechtsradikale Jugendlicher Berichtet: Ich Heisse Gerald Wagener* (Munich: DVK-Verlag, 1981).

158   *The Legitimization of Violence*

Jugendwerk der Deutschen Shell, *Jugend 92: Gesamtdarstellung und Biografische Portraets*, vol. 1 (Opladen: Leske und Budrich, 1992).

Kleff, Sanem *et al.*, *BDR–DDR: Alte und Neue Rassismen im Zuge der deutsch-deutschen Einigung* (Frankfurt: Verlag fuer Interkulturelle Kommunikation, 1990).

Kloenne, Arno, "Modernisierungsschub und rechter Fundamentalismus", *Rechtsextremismus: Erscheinungsformen, Ursachen, Entwicklungen* (Landesinstitut fuer Schule und Weiterbildung Nordrhein-Westfalen, 1990).

Koedderitzsch, Peter and Mueller, Leo, *Rechtsextremismus in der DDR* (Goettingen: Lamuv Verlag, 1990).

Rosen, Klaus-Henning (eds), *Die zweite Vertreibung: Fremde in Deutschland* (Bonn: Dietz Verlag, 1992).

Schmidt, Michael, *The New Reich: Violent Extremism in the New Germany and Beyond* (New York: Patheon Books, 1993).

Stoess, Richard, *Die Extreme Rechte in Der Bundesrepublik: Entwicklungen, Ursach, Gegenmassnahmen* (Opladen: Westdeutsche Verlag, 1989).

5 Remythologizing Discourses: State and Insurrectionary Violence in Sri Lanka[1]

BRUCE KAPFERER

I   INTRODUCTION

With India and Burma, Sri Lanka, formerly Ceylon, a former British colony, inaugurated the great wave of decolonization which would not end until the colonial world was replaced by a world of independent nations. The transition to independence was peaceful and harmonious. Colombo was considered a possible site for the headquarters of the British Commonwealth. It seemed a model for peaceful pluralism. Today it is a country of angry widows. Two of them, daughter and mother, are as a result of recent elections respectively: "President", Mrs Chandrika Bandaranaike Kumaratunga, and "Prime Minister", Sirimavo Bandaranaike. The former's husband, Vijaya Kumaratunga, an actor and politician, was shot by leftist militants in 1988. The latter's husband, Solomon Bandaranaike, the president of the Sri Lanka Freedom Party which he founded, was assassinated by a Buddhist monk in 1959 (after which she became the world's first woman prime minister and Freedom Party leader). The opposition party candidate to Mrs Kumaratunga's People's Alliance was Srima Dissanayake, who stood for election for the United National Party in place of her husband who was blown up by a young woman who, positioning herself some ten feet from the rostrum where Mr Dissanayake was speaking, blew him up and herself with a bomb hidden under her shirt. This some eighteen months after a suicide bomber, riding a bicycle, sent by the Tamil Tigers had blown up the then President Ranashinghe Premadasa. A week before this event a political associate of Mr Dissanayake was also killed, on order it was widely rumoured of Mr Premadasa.

The most significant conflict is, of course, the eleven-year-old struggle between the mostly Hindu Tamil and mostly Buddhist Sinhalese, and the

Liberation Tigers of Tamil Eelam with its shadowy leader Vellupillai Prhbakaran widely regarded as a Tamil Sri-Lankan Pimpernel. It has resulted in some 34,000 deaths. The Tigers, who demand a separate state, make up about 3 million out of the country's 17- or 18-million population, the rest being Sinhalese.

At the same time there has been a bitter conflict between the governing parties and the extremist Sinhalese nationalist Janatha Vimukthi Peramuna which has resulted in the deaths of from 20,000 to 60,000 people between 1987 and 1990. Meanwhile, periodic elections continue to be held, the most recent on 9 November 1994, despite the continuation of random killings, gang warfare, the uprooting of communities, the use of terror squads by the government against opposition leaders, etc. Politically the situation can be described as democracy with little justice and a great deal of sheer chaos.

Trying to unravel the strands of so complex a situation is very difficult. There are too many events for the coding, too many discourses and projections, with both contending religious and secular texts, and conflict between political groups as well as between them and government. The best one can try to do is suggest some of the more salient features of the violence that has so tragically erupted. We will concentrate on those events mainly involving Sinhalese, focusing specifically on the 1988 and 1989 violence centring on the JVP insurrection. However, this insurrection cannot be understood outside of the wider context of the political violence between the Sri Lanka government and the Tamil guerrilla movement, i.e. the continuing fight for Tamil autonomy in the north and east of the island. Accordingly, we will in this chapter concentrate on state and anti-state nationalist discourses surrounding the violent insurrection by a revolutionary Sinhalese political organization to overthrow the Sri Lanka government in late 1989 and early 1990.

The dominant ethnic population of the island is Sinhalese and mainly Buddhist. It forms approximately 75 per cent of the island's population of some 16 million and occupies much of the western, central and southern regions of the island. Tamils are the other major ethnic category, comprising roughly 11 per cent of the total population, and are mainly distributed in the northern and eastern parts of the island. The 1989 revolt was organized from within the Sinhalese population by a political organization called the People's Liberation Front or Janatha Vimukthi Peramuna (subsequently referred to as the JVP).

The JVP originally manifested itself in Sri Lanka in 1970 and 1971 when its youthful cadres, under the leadership of Rohan Wijeweera, threatened to overthrow the government of Mrs Sirimavo Bandaranaike (Halliday, 1971; Alles, 1990; Moore, 1993). It was inspired by populist

Marxist views and had a substantial involvement of young intellectuals, some of bourgeois backgrounds. The insurrection, largely composed of Sinhalese youths in the west and south of the island, was ruthlessly crushed. Its surviving followers, including Wijeweera and other leaders, were pardoned with the coming to power in 1977 of the United National Party under the leadership of Junius Jayawardene. By the mid-1980s the JVP once again assumed a powerful political presence in the island but it had been significantly changed both in ideals and organization and, indeed, its character was strongly influenced by the overall political context of the war of Tamil separatism (see Chandraprema, 1991). The total situation of political violence engaging the Sri Lanka government and the Tamil guerrilla movement (the Tamil Tigers, or LTTE) is central to any discussion of the JVP insurrection of 1989/1990. I give a brief sketch of the events relating to the Sinhala–Tamil War in which an understanding of the insurrection should be placed.

II   BACKGROUND TO THE SINHALA–TAMIL WAR

The present situation of ethnic violence evolved steadily after Independence in 1947 (see Roberts, 1979; Tambiah, 1986, 1992; Kapferer, 1988, 1994). Violence took the form of periodic ethnic clashes (mainly between the Tamil Hindu and Sinhala Buddhist "communities") and intra-communal strife largely within the Sinhala population, especially approaching and during political elections. Mr S. W. R. D. Bandaranaike, the prime minister and leader of the Sri Lanka Freedom Party, was assassinated in 1959 by a Buddhist monk. Bandaranaike could be described as a Sinhala populist (although from the dominant English-speaking élite) who was killed by a representative of the forces of a Sinhala Buddhist chauvinism that he had encouraged. This killing was tragically symbolic of the close connection between an ethnic religious nationalism and political violence which has consumed Sri Lanka in recent years. The motion towards increasing political violence and ethnic tension was fuelled by other discourses rooted in class inequities, in caste antagonisms, and in regional allegiances. To a large extent these were refracted in the 1970/71 JVP insurrection, which in the government repression probably cost in the vicinity of 6,000 young Sinhalese lives. The JVP declared itself to be oriented in the direction of the communism of Mao Zedong and was deeply populist. The later resurfacing of a reorganized JVP, perhaps more oriented to Pol Pot, drew its impetus from the deep crisis of the Sri

Lanka state attendant on its full-scale war with the Tamils in the north and east of the island. This war had followed on the anti-Tamil riots of July 1983 in which around 2,000 Tamils (estimates vary greatly, from 300 – the government figure – upwards) in Sinhala-dominated areas were killed in little under a week. A further 300,000 were rendered homeless. The Tamil Tiger (LTTE) movement in the north of the island gathered steam from these events. In 1987 the Sri Lanka–India Accord was signed between President Jayawardene and Rajiv Gandhi. Sinhalese responded in violent rioting at what seemed to them to be a threat to Sri Lanka's national integrity. The JVP began a major campaign against Jayawardene, although he had pardoned their leaders in 1977 and allowed the JVP to reorganize and to enter mainstream politics. But Jayawardene falsely accused them of instigating the 1983 riots, deflecting attention away from clear suggestions of government involvement (see Wilson, 1988), and had them proscribed. Forced underground the JVP launched a wave of violent terror which reached its height between 1988 and 1990. It almost toppled the government of President Premadasa, Jayawardene's successor, who as already indicated was himself assassinated in 1993, in all probability by Tamil Tigers. The official figure of 30,000 persons who died in this conflict is perhaps too small. Numerous sources close to the events indicate far more. The crushing of this uprising in a manner quite unparalleled in Sri Lanka's history returned the government once more to its struggle against Tamils in the north and in the east.

The Sinhala–Tamil ethnic conflict, of course, constitutes the fundamental condition for violence throughout the island. Yet this cleavage is also a condition for growing political stability. The Sri Lanka government made some initial advances following the crushing of the JVP but then suffered some spectacular reverses. Recent information indicates that the Tigers have developed a governing infrastructure in the areas controlled by them and are engaging in programmes of social and economic reconstruction. Overall violence appears to be lessening, although there is evidence of further fragmentation along ethnic lines. For example, the small but economically significant Muslim minority have been pressing for greater autonomy and there is ethnic tension between Muslims and Buddhist Sinhalese.

III   THE PEACE IN THE FEUD?

The recent (August 1994) national election victory of the People's Alliance, under the leadership of Chandrika Kumaratunga and Kumaratunga's subsequent victory in the November presidential elections, promise a major change in political direction. The Tamil Tigers are indicating a preparedness to negotiate although, as may be expected, they continue to menace Sinhala populations possibly as part of a negotiating strategy. Various disaffected groups within the Sinhala-dominated population have an opportunity of greater participation in the democratic process than in the last few years. A resolution of the Sri Lanka government–Tamil Tiger War will, in the view of this author, not only reduce Sinhala–Tamil ethnic tensions but also reverse a tendency to further ethnic and regional fractionalization of a politically violent kind in the island.

The ethnic war exacerbated contradictions at the heart of the Sri Lanka state and in the political and social worlds of the Sinhala population. The JVP revolt of 1989/1990, and its furious suppression by government forces, was a violent expression of the forces, emergent in such contradiction and the engagement of violence as the key weapon of resolution. The JVP drew on the energies of increased class suffering, especially among the rural and urban poor intensified by the economic strains of the war. The timing of the revolt coincided with the apparent emptiness of the Sinhala nationalist rhetoric of the government (evidenced in the Sri Lanka–India Accord which occasioned serious mass rioting). The state appeared weak, too, in its confrontation with the Tigers' whose fighting capacity had reached legendary proportions among the Sinhalese population. In the representations among numerous Sinhalese, the Tigers are depicted as messianic in their commitment and, for many, present an aura of invulnerability. Prior to the JVP uprising rumour had circulated in Colombo that the Tigers were planning a surprise attack on the city and this had led to a small panic among the city's populace, some fleeing towards the countryside. There was wide belief that the ranks in the armed forces were highly sympathetic to the JVP and this undoubtedly encouraged the JVP leadership to embark on its final terror drive, in August 1989, to take over the government. It is generally understood that a JVP mistake (the enormity of which was almost unbelievable at the time and even more so in retrospect) in its discourse of violence at this time was responsible for its failure. The JVP leadership annnounced that it would attack the families of the armed forces if they did not disobey government directives to move against the JVP. This remarkable error is regarded as being instrumental in the turning of the tide against JVP fortunes and impelling a period of massive human destruction. This destruction often expressly took the form of "righteous" vengeance.[2]

The foregoing comments underline the power of rumour, rhetoric and the symbolic imagination in constituting worlds of violence. More generally, they demonstrate the role of discourses about the situations of experience – and the forces that impinge upon them – in creating the actualities of experience and, in the Sri Lanka context, actualities which are extremely violent. This is the overall theme of this chapter and compares with the work of other scholars elsewhere (e.g. see Taussig, 1987; Feldman, 1991). I start with a discussion of some of the ideological parameters of Sinhala nationalism, especially that version elaborated largely by ruling groups whose interests are pursued through the agents and agencies of the state. This extends into an analysis of the discourse of violence between the forces of the Sri Lanka government and those of the JVP. The ideology of what I refer to as Sinhala Buddhist nationalism, virtually the ideology of state power, constitutes, in my argument, the discursive context for the emergence and significance of much of the action surrounding the JVP revolt.

IV   CONSTITUTIVE DISCOURSE[3]

The key thesis that I pursue is that discursive practices are constitutive. That is, the actualities that in other analyses of a more conventional and rationalist kind interpret as producing ideological discourse are also created through the discourse itself. I outline some of the implications of this position for an understanding of nationalist processes in the Sri Lanka context and, specifically, for an interpretation of the violence of the JVP revolt.

A variety of conventional analyses of nationalisms and their ideologies or discourses correctly, in my view, identify them as the creations of the relatively recent and world-wide dominant political form, the sovereign nation-state. However, a problem with such approaches (see Kapferer, 1994) is that they tend to regard Western European and North American nationalisms (their ideologies and institutions) as the model or universal form. They neglect some of the distinct histories which gave rise to other nationalisms.[4] The fact that other nationalisms (e.g. those in Africa and in Asia) arose from within the depradations of colonial and imperial conquest and expansion suggests a basis for major distinction rather than a claim for nationalism and its ideologies as a generic export of the West, a common view. I (Kapferer, 1988) have argued for Sri Lanka that it is important to explore some of the arguments of nationalist discourse in order to better comprehend certain aspects of the violence, for instance, that has exploded in its wake (Kemper, 1994, has recently reiterated the same point).

The foregoing argument is extended in what follows through an exploration of Sinhala nationalist ideology as a remythologization. Broadly, this concept is used to underline nationalist discourse and its historical and other claims as simultaneously an "invention of tradition" or, better, a reinvention of legendary or mythic constructions of past events in the political and economic circumstances of the present. In this sense, a myth or a remythologization is a falsity regardless of the empirical evidence for some of the events it might record.(Although, as structuralists insist, mythological imagination may probe deeply into the dilemmas in thought and practice relating to the particular worlds of mythic production.) However, in so far as discourses of mythologization form the way people come to routinely grasp or comprehend aspects of their realities (and, thus, is thoroughly part of the materiality of these realities), then, to echo W. I. Thomas's famous dictum, the reality of the mythologization is real in its consequences.

What I stress is the power of discourse to constitute its reality and to have effect in the dynamics of the worlds in which it takes root. The issue is not so much the truth or falsity of nationalist rhetorics but the fact that they have effect: an effect which is a property of the discourse itself and not merely a function of the agencies and political and social relations through which it also gathers force. These agencies and relations do not stand independently of the discourses which they produce and support. Furthermore, in critical ways the discourses can in fact create the agents, agencies and relations which produce them and release possibilities of action not apparent hitherto. This is a major theme in this understanding of the largely state-engineered Sinhala Buddhist nationalism of contemporary Sri Lanka and the discourses of violence surrounding the JVP revolt.

The JVP achieved much of its impetus within the crisis of the Sri Lanka state constituted through a discourse of Sinhala Buddhist nationalism. Its violence operated through similar mythic metaphors but gave them different value or expanded possibilities implicit but relatively suppressed within official assertions. The JVP gave voice to the significance of other stories in the folk and textual sources of the nationalist imaginary. This was an aspect, following Apter, of the "inversionary discourse" of the JVP violence which strove to undermine the legitimacy of the government and the authority of its nationalist narrative.

I note that this discourse was not necessarily a complete negation, an absolute contradiction of state discourse, or an inverse in the sense of a reversal of the meaning of the terms of the "argument" of state ideological affirmations. The inversionary discourse of the JVP certainly strove to subvert state power by revealing the corruption, even decadence, of state power. But the JVP also took aspects of state-produced discourse off in new directions. These occasionally manifested a bringing-out of interpretational potential that was subdued or suppressed in state pronouncements.

The Buddhist nationalism of the state constrained some of the violent propensity of its discourse within a morality of Buddhism. The JVP was not so constrained. It became involved in the assassination of Buddhist priests, revealing perhaps the "bad conscience" of a state which hid its own violence behind a veil of Buddhist non-violent morality.[5]

One widely-observed objective of nationalist discourse is the creation of a sense of community unity in experience, both temporally and spatially (see Anderson, 1983; Gellner, 1983). This is motivated in actualities which manifest the obverse, so it is argued, of increasing individualization, alienation from power, and commoditization in contemporary capitalist processes. The contradiction of nationalism is that its ideologies are driven within these dynamics of global realities despite the traditionalism and reaffirmations of a "past" which are presented as remedies by the agents of such ideologies, for the disorientations or sufferings of the present. This was one aspect of the JVP discourse in relation to state forces.

Thus, the JVP violence explicitly drew attention to the impersonalization of the bureaucratic state and developed a discourse of violence centred around personal relations and the "restoration" of village and local community morality. Some of its violence took the paradoxical form of "making" relations and crossing the boundaries which limited the formation of ties and influence between persons of widely separate power and status in the state order. A routine JVP violent method was to deliver warnings to bureaucratic or politically powerful persons charging them with some favour or demanding that they desist from certain actions on threat of death, usually at the third warning. Such action, of course, generated the power of terror but it was also an example of the use of violence to create influence and relations where there were none. Its inversionary discourse was one of breaking through the hierarchial divisions of that society protected in the state.

I now want to examine the inversionary discourse of the violence surrounding the revolt in dialogical terms. What I refer to as the key actors, the state and the JVP, are not internally homogeneous but are a composite of a diversity of counter-vailing interests. This is a vital aspect to examine but is not my concern here. Rather I focus on the relation between the state and the JVP, which the protagonists in their discourse tended to see in unitary terms, even if this was far from the empirical case. The particular aspect that attracts my interest is how in the course of the violence the parties reveal the violent possibilities of the other and, in certain respects, come to manifest a transmutation of the other.

Deleuze and Guattari (1988) have written brilliantly of what they describe as the dynamics of the state and the "war-machine". Broadly, the state encloses a bounded space. It is concerned with the control of territory and with marking out an internally divided and striated social and political order. The war-machine (the nomad and the sorcerer are ideal examples), transcends territorial limitation, transgresses boundaries, and courses "rhizomically" from point-to-point and along the tendrils of social relations. Deleuze and Guattari focus on the way the dynamics of state/war-machine articulation leads to various kinds of transmutation: the state becoming war-machine and the war-machine becoming state. Such transmutation is a vital aspect of the violence which was integral to the inversionary discourse of violence involving the Sri Lanka government and the JVP. In many respects the transmutation of the state (the forces of the Sri Lanka government) into a war-machine in the sense described by Deleuze and Guattari expands an understanding of the inversionary discourse of violence that consumed the Sinhala population during the months of the JVP revolt (Kapferer, 1995).

V   DISCOURSES OF THE NATION-STATE: SINHALA BUDDHIST NATIONALISM

I have referred to Sinhala nationalism as a remythologization, whereby the myths and legends of the past are reinvented as an ideology of coherence in a world demythologized and fragmented in the processes of secular rationalism and the capitalist/technical transformations into contemporary society (Wyschogrod, 1983, pp. 27–9). The mark of the contemporary political state, possibly everywhere and certainly not Sri Lanka alone, is its legitimation, above all else, as a rational order which commands the bureaucratic and technical apparatuses necessary to the reproduction of the rationalist order of the state. Rationalist demythologization, impelled and effected in the historical circumstances of its generation, establishes a dominant discourse (also, a discourse of dominance) which at once is "literalist" and negates or suppresses the symbolic extensions, meanings and potentialities of those realities to which it refers. This is so in the interpretation of the significance of constructions about the "past" as, too, of the "present". Rationalist demythologizers tend to an impoverishment of the symbolic qualities of context. It is especially the case, as I will show, in the ideologies of contemporary state nationalism.

Global realities abound with examples of ideological rationalist demythologizations. Contemporary religious reformism and nationalism, the two frequently linked, provide rich illustration. In Sri Lanka, the phenomenon widely referred to as the Buddhist Revival is an instance. Buddhism, along with other civilizational religions like Christianity and Islam, have reformism, motivated in a search for authenticity or orthodoxy, as ideologically foundational and enduringly vital in their dynamic. To extend a little a continuing urge to "demythologize" is the name of their game. But this expansion obscures my usage of the term demythologization, which I see as occurring largely through schemes of meaning and interpretation alien or external to that cosmological or symbolic universe some of the key terms and statements of which are being asserted.

Buddhism in Sri Lanka (Gunawardena, 1990; Malalgoda, 1976), and elsewhere (Tambiah, 1976) has seen numerous "reformations" or periods of "revitalization", and well before the advent of colonialism and the incorporation of Sri Lanka within world-wide capitalist processes. The shifts and redirections in meaning and practice, which were integral to these revitalizations, were consistent with or possibilities of the wider field of symbolic discourse in which they were embedded. The Buddhist Revival to which I refer grew apace in the conditions of colonial penetration, and most especially in the nineteenth- and twentieth-century circumstances of British rule. The interpretations of Buddha doctrine, and the invention or reinvention of many Buddhist practices in the main period of the Revival, refracted the dominant rationalist bureaucratic/technological order of values that had now been established (Obeyesekere, 1979; Gombrich and Obeyesekere, 1989; Roberts, 1982; Kapferer, 1983). Ideologues of the Revival asserted the "scientific" validity of the Buddha's doctrine, attacked the "irrationalism" of Sinhala Buddhist practices like those centring on demons, and were concerned to establish personal habits and routines highly relevant to the new rationalist order. The demythologization of the Revival was not only a refraction of this order but also the Revival, through its inventions of practice and transformations of meaning, was vital in further-establishing the hegemony of rationalist value and the new bureaucratic/technical order. The Revival was an ideological process which *made* Buddhism rationalist in a contemporary sense and, conversely, made rationalism Buddhist.[6]

The process was one in which the circumstance and action of demythologization simultaneously provoked a remythologization. Such a dynamic could be fundamental in being human, intimately tied to the urgency in humanity as a whole both to establish meaning in experience and to totalize such meaning, to recognize a unity in self and other through the construction of shared frameworks of meaning.[7] Moreover, the engagement of a mythic consciousness, one which routinely resonates with the symbolic themes of Death, Rebirth, and, too, original unity, may be universal while it takes specific shape in certain moments of history. This is because the existential condition of being human must always be experientially diverse and fragmenting even as it reaches to overcome or to transcend such experience. In these senses, the remythologizations of the Revival, of political nationalists and contemporary ideologues of Buddhist state- and nation-mythologizations which include the restorations of ancient Buddhist rites, the popularization of festivals to mark major events in the life of the Buddha, the celebration of an essential cultural unity imagined to be present in art, belief and language, and the selection of specific myths of nation and historical events are particular, historically-conditioned and directed exfoliations of a universal human tension to mythic consciousness and thought.

I make this observation not in the interest of an ultimately trivial social scientific urgency to make some universally "true" statement about the nature of humanity. Rather, I wish to suggest that the general mythic consciousness of the remythologizations of contemporary nationalism in Sri Lanka are a dimension of nationalisms beyond Sri Lanka and are evident in numerous other human movements of self-affirmation which frequently involve violent passionate forces (e.g. millenarian movements, the European anti-witch craze, etc.). The often violent passions of nationalism in Sri Lanka are obviously widespread and demonstrate a more general phenomenon of human being and the part played by what I refer to as mythic consciousness and the human imaginary.

There is a religiosity to the violence in Sri Lanka which takes its form through certain "utopian" elements of the mythic consciousness. These elements are contained in its birth, death, rebirth or return to the glories of the past thematic, or projection towards a fantasied future. If there are ideological, even ontological universals, apparent in recent or current remythologizations in Sri Lanka, what I stress is the relevance of their distinct features in the present Sri Lanka crisis of violence: albeit features made relevant through recent historical and bureaucratic/technological processes.

I opened this discussion with some broad characterizations of the remythologizations of state power in Sri Lanka (see also Kapferer, 1988). What I noted was their infusion with dimensions of the demythologized structures and procedures against which their mythologies are in ostensible reaction. Thus the literalism of such mythology: the refusal by many of the mythologizers of the manifold symbolic significance of events drawn from within great cosmological themes, and their reduction to rationalist issues of the fact or fiction variety. In so doing they misconstrue or radically distort (reimagine the imaginary), dislocate mythic themes from their historical situations of relevance and employ them to support or to "mythicalize" the pragmatic and technical rationalities underpinning the modern state.

Thus, in the course of colonially-rooted transformations into the modern state, major festivals and rites – often the vehicles of cosmic myths relevant to ancient or medieval states in Sri Lanka – became vital in the ceremonial spectacle of the power of the contemporary bureaucratic sovereign nation-state. An example is the Kandy perahara, a festival of the revitalization of the king and cosmic state/social order in pre-colonial Sri Lanka (see Seneviratne, 1978). In the rupture of British colonial rule the perahara was co-opted by the colonial state into a celebration of the dominance of colonial power and the élites who depended upon it, in a manner similar to that described for British India by Cohn (1983). The post-colonial state manipulates the perahara along the same lines to represent the order of the divisions and striations internal to the contemporary bureaucratic state. In other words, the hierarchical logic of ritual flux and transformation whereby the king is re-created as a figure of ordering encompassment was made to legitimate a radically different and more rigid framework of power that the rite had little role in reproducing, save as an instrument of the hegemony of the colonial and post-colonial state. Some of the implications of this shift in the engagement of hierarchical logic are examined shortly, namely, the transmuted dynamic of cosmic hierarchical ideology in synergic relation with a contemporary centralized bureaucratic state.

A major feature of the nationalist remythologization or reinvention of the post-colonial state is the engagement of metaphors of cosmic hierarchy to a modern bureaucratic and class-based political economic order. In the construction of state-nationalist ideology myths and legends from the ancient and medieval chronicles (the "Dipavamsa" and "Mahavamsa") were engaged: myths still of relevance in the process of local and largely village-based ritual (see Kapferer, 1988, 1983). The fact that such myths are part of local traditions gives potency to nationalist reinventions. Moreover, the myths articulate an hierarchical logic, which in general terms is one of progressive incorporation and transformation. This is a totalizing process in the extreme which takes the fragmentation and reordering of the state as a continual dynamic process. The emergence of destructive forces within the state is a possibility of the hierarchical ordering of the state. This is so, for each level in the hierarchy subsumes and transforms dimensions of that beneath it and is in turn subsumed and transformed in the hierarchical level above.

Religious ideas and practices among Sinhalese Buddhists reflect such hierarchical notions. Thus powerful ordering gods such as those of Kataragama and Pattini incorporate lower dimensions of themselves and reduce to demonic forms at base. The object of much ritual is to achieve a transformation of such deities into ordering gods at the highest level of hierarchical organization, but also to engage their demonic properties.

These kinds of hierarchical notions transmuted via nationalist discourse into the political practice of the contemporary state intensifies, I suggest, the violent possibility of the contemporary state. The hierarchical ideology I describe was politically relevant to what Tambiah (1976, 1992) discusses as cosmic polities. These were highly unstable and the hierarchical ideologies of continual incorporation, breakdown and reformation was probably relevant to their constant crisis and instability features certainly apparent in the ancient and medieval chronicles of Sri Lanka. In other words they manifested a centralizing ideology directly proportional to their constantly decentralizing process. The application of such hierarchical ideology to a contemporary bureaucratic state with its powerful apparatuses of control can operate to intensify even more modern centralizing tendencies which can subvert even the democratizing assertions of such states, assertions certainly powerful at Sri Lanka's independence.

Hierarchical discourse explicitly links the capacity to order to destruction. Destructive power is the reduced aspect of the benign god but vital in the god's benevolence. Powerful, peace-loving kings have a demonic side which is critical to their transcendence of destruction. These are dimensions, it could be said, of all state systems and integral to the well-known Weberian definition of the state as the monopolization of the means to violence. In Western political philosophy this is stressed as essentially a peace-making move and the emphasis is on the ordering rather than the violent nature of the state: a representation, of course, belied by the strong ceremonial association of state authority and sovereignty with military might. Hierarchical ideology makes the violent nature of order more explicit and does not separate the two. The import of this observation is that where a contemporary bureaucratic state and its population operate hierarchical conceptions of the type I describe then there is likely to be a degree of tolerance for violent solutions and, moreover, violence against its own population.

This is so in a further sense. Hierarchical conceptions are sensitive to a reading of any kind of dissension as indicative of the weakening of order which necessitates strong and possibly demonically violent ordering reaction. Hierarchical discourse, especially in the sense of cosmic kingship that I describe, tends to a language of crisis and of strong control.

Many of the crises of Sri Lanka are common across nation-states world-wide. They are crises, as in numerous other democratic or ideal democracies[8] which revolve around such important human concerns as individual rights, the nature of citizenship, autonomy, etc. The way these issues are projected, and also the response to them, however, varies, I suggest, in accordance with the terms of the ideological arguments concerning the nature of "history", "culture", "identity", etc., through which human interests (democratic or not) are legitimated and pursued.

One area of ideological distinction in the hierarchical logic adapted from the chronicles into contemporary Sri Lanka nationalism of the Buddhist state relates to the role of "difference". Difference is made into a principle of unity through the hierarchializing force of power. Dumont (1980), in relation to caste in traditional India, has described such a system. However, the distinction for India is that the hierarchialization of difference is achieved through a separation of power from status whereby status (ritual status) determines power and is the encompassing and unifying principle. In pre-colonial Sri Lanka, power is more explicitly the hierarchializing force which forges an overall unity while sustaining difference. There are shades of the Indian system in the sense that successful hierarchializing power must be oriented towards the encompassing principles of the Buddha ideal. I underline the point that this conception of hierarchy, which is carried through into the discourse of state power via remythologizing reinventions, is not only a valuation of hierarchy and the ordering force of power but, in contrast to Western egalitarian ideologies, for instance, asserts the value of the highest power as being that which can establish a coherent organization of difference. Power is not a mediating force articulating differences but arranges them in hierarchical unity. In this sense, Sri Lankan state nationalist ideology contradicts the democratic and more egalitarian principles on which the modern state of Sri Lanka is ostensibly founded and which gives power a more mediating function, at least ideally if not in practice.[9] A discourse of hierarchy based in the stories of Cosmic Kingship is not oriented to mediating and negotiative strategies, rather towards the forceful incorporation of differentiating or separating groups or else their annihilation.

The press in hierarchical argument is to incorporate difference rather than to exclude, "assimilate", or homogenize it as in discourses of modern states, generally of the Western sort, expressive of what I have called ideas of egalitarian-individualism (Kapferer, 1988). Such discourse, played into a contemporary context of ethnic tension (promoted by the political and economic circumstances of dependency, among other factors, in the global situation of late capitalism), makes the capacity to hierarchically incorporate the ethnic "Other" vital both as a measure of the integrity of the state and of the Sinhala "community" with which the agents of the state in their nationalism seek to establish an identity. Should the agents of the state fail in their incorporative power, this simultaneously signs the fragmentation and loss of integrity of the dominant community or nation whose identity is defined in the unifying power of the state.

This process is, I extend, also potentially one of the "person". The integrity of the person is co-extensive with the state as it is mythologically imagined. A failure in the hierarchical incorporative power of the state, the incapacity to achieve Sinhala dominance, threatens the integrity of the person as it does the state. Living in such an imagined reality human beings may be motivated to reassert the power of the state through their own relatively independent political action. Such is the stuff of riots and more casual acts of violence against minorities which have become an aspect of life in Sri Lanka.

This potential identity of person and state has much in common with the hegemonic direction of most contemporary state nationalisms. The condition of the nation as a collectivity of individuals sharing the same identity is also the potential experience of each of the individuals who comprise the nation. The ideology is one which directs individuals to realize or to restore their own integrity through the power of the state.

But, I underline the distinction of nationalism constructed and mythologized through an ideology of Cosmic Kingship. The integrity of nation and of person is significantly linked to the hierarchical principle of encompassment or incorporation which conceives of the identities of the encompassed or the incorporated as vital elements, if subordinate elements, of those identities who define the totality of state and nation.

I stress that the mythic religious histories essay a particular approach to power which, I think, is radically distorted in the remythologizations of the contemporary state. The manner of this distortion, one which comes to value power as annihilation and which aligns the assertion of identity with annihilatory capacity, is a theme that I will shortly come to address.

VI   HIERARCHICAL DESTRUCTION AND VIOLENT INSCRIPTION

The events of ethnic conflict and destruction over recent years in Sri Lanka achieve a meaning for the participants, if not a necessary direction, through the contemporary logic of state nationalism and the Cosmic State that I have outlined. The myths of religious history provided a framework through which the import of events could be articulated and made to cohere meaningfully often by government leaders and frequently by the population at large. Contemporary political events could be said to have substantialized the constructions of imagined history.[10]

Thus, Tamil guerrilla attacks in the interests of ethnic autonomy sparked violent anti-Tamil rioting much of which received the support of agents of the state. The metaphors of the human destruction were occasionally those of powerful hierarchical reincorporation. Thus in the 1983 anti-Tamil riots, Tamil victims about to be slaughtered were made to bow in submission before their killers (Kapferer, 1989, 1994). While it may not have been intended as such, the action was mimetic of the final submission in death of Elara's general before the Sinhala King Dutugemunu as described in the chronicle of the "Mahavamsa". The violence of the riots created a deepening of ethnic division which gave the myths of ethnic identity greater relevance. Moreover, the riots generated the expansion of Tamil resistance. Sinhalese experienced territorial restriction which achieved conscious import: for example, through the well-known story of Prince Dutugemunu's experience of confinement through the subordination of his father's kingdom to that of the Tamil, Elara. That is, The weakness of the Sri Lanka state was made manifest in the India–Sri Lanka Accord of 1987 which involved an Indian military presence.

I noted earlier that Sinhalese rioted on this occasion in protest at the loss of their national integrity. There was a heightening of ethnic nationalist consciousness and a growth in internal civilian unrest among the Sinhalese population. Violence was directed against the state and was coordinated by the revolutionary JVP. Their orientation was no less nationalist than the state it opposed. A major direction of its violence was to restore the power and integrity of state and nation, to encompass where the state it opposed had failed. The metaphors of the JVP, as I will show, drew just as strongly from the cosmic myths as did those of the agents of the Sri Lanka government.

A general point is that contemporary events progressively deepened the apparent relevance of a nationalist mythic consciousness. Events, the product of a great diversity of historical forces and experienced very differently according to the way individuals were positioned in their daily realities, were made to conform to the simplicity of a nationalist mythic consciousness. In this process, a mythic consciousness and the logic of its imagined projections becomes more deeply ingrained as part of the everyday grasping of reality and its experience. The engagement of such a mythic consciousness in the interpretation of events expands and intensifies its imaginative hold. Its discourse, I suggest, becomes more and more motivational in the creation of political events. This is especially so if the agents of the state or its political opponents who command the institutions and organizations of power come to believe and to live the mythologizations of their creation. Prior to President Premadasa's assassination in 1993, it was widely reported that he officiated at meetings seated on the throne of the last King of Kandy whom the British had exiled upon their colonial conquest.

Power as Annihilation and the Distortion of Buddhist Value

The Sinhala Buddhist nationalism of the state, as with all modern nationalisms, is centrally concerned with affirming the power of the state. However, I have also indicated that its mythologization in terms of a discourse of Cosmic Kingship gives particular definition and import to the dynamic of state power. Moreover, in the current context of intra-ethnic and inter-ethnic violence officers of the state make intense appeals to the key Buddhist value of non-violence. Non-violence is a strong religious value but, I note, in this context, the subordination and use of the value in the interest of the maintenance of the power of the state. Further, there is, in the current situation, an implication that the state as constituted in reference to the Buddha ideal of non-violence is the supreme agent of Buddhist morality, a morality which is even present in the exercise by the state of extreme violence. It is a violence in the interest of the order of a Buddhist state.

In the legendary stories that the agents of the state engage to their discourse of legitimacy, the power of the king is separate from the ultimate Buddha ideal. Indeed, as with monks, the ideal king relinquishes his hold over secular power and removes himself from daily political affairs. When King Dutugemunu, a hero in the nationalist narratives of the state, realizes the destruction of his ordering violence in the conquest of the Tamil king, Elara, he moves outside the political and into a life of Buddhist virtue. Power is the guardian of Buddhism but the achievement of Buddhist virtue demands its transcendence. Ultimately, Buddhist virtue encompasses power and conditions and directs it.

This relation is reversed in the nationalist applications of the arguments of the myths to the current political situation of the state. Buddhist value is made conditional on the power of the state and is directed to the values the agents and agencies of the state come to enshrine. Religious value follows the order of the state. It is likely that this has always been the case but the point is that the present state political constructions invert the themes of those myths that are ideologically employed. Such remythologization intensifies the value that is placed on power as annihilation and subverts a morality of Buddhism that is antagonistic to violence and the engagement in action productive of suffering.

Power as annihilating force is contained in the myths of Cosmic Kingship in the concept of the demonic. But, this annihilating force is valued only in so far as it is ultimately constitutive of an hierarchical order conditioned within, and oriented to, ultimate Buddhist reason and value. Annihilating power in itself is not valued. It is valued only in its capacity to generate hierarchical order which, further, is possible only because it is oriented to the Buddha and his teaching as the ultimate encompassing principles. Thus the demon is distinguished from the demonic in the myths of history and also in present-day ritual practice: for example, in demon exorcisms and at urban sorcery shrines. Demons are an perfect annihilating power who cannot transcend their own destruction and violence and must remain outside the social order.

However, the demonic as a process (as distinct from the demon as a particular named kind of embodied being) is the power of annihilation which is also generative of its own transcendence. In my reading of the ancient myths it is a process of the inversion of the social order, a reduction of society outside itself, or an externalization of that dynamic from which the hierarchy of order is recreated. The Dutugemunu story outlines this process. Prior to his reconstitution of the Sinhala state, Prince Dutugemunu enters demonic space external to the political order and when he returns engages his demonic dynamic in the restoration and rebuilding of state power (Kapferer, 1988). The demonic, like the destructive power of Prince Dutugemunu or that curative force of an exorcist invoking the authority and teaching of the Buddha, rehierarchializes and reincorporates. In this process the demonic itself transforms into a Buddhist beneficence. This is also a feature of Sinhalese Buddhist deities who have demonic aspects which are an agency in their transformation into higher, reincorporating, totalizing and benign forms.

The argument of the great cosmic myths and much current ritual practice is one which devalues annihilating power in itself. Their message and their practice is the overcoming of such annihilating force. The demonic is the destructive energy of Non-Reason, of Ignorance, a space of horrible suffering and death, a void the direct antithesis of Buddhist non-existence (Kapferer, 1994). It is a death world, a world from which the Cosmic King, Dutugemunu in his Buddhist reasoning ultimately shrinks.

In the Buddhism of the contemporary state, power in itself is given value and, in its hierarchializing ordering capacity creates the conditions for the dominance of Buddhist value. Buddhism becomes the greater value because the state is powerful, not vice versa. The remythologization of the state opens the way for annihilating force and the capacity to exercise such force to be the major way in which the agents of the state can define and realize their power. This is an absolute inversion and perversion of Buddhist value whether the context of its meaning is ancient or modern. But such distortion is realized in practice through the structures of resistance established, in part, in reaction to the Buddhist nationalism of the state.

The radical resistance of Tamils to the authority of the power of the state, whose own struggle appears to define power as the capacity to annihilate, contributes to the intensification of the self-affirmation of the Sri Lanka state and its agents through a discourse of annihilatory violence. In so far as such discourse becomes a vital means for the definition and constitution of state power the possibility is open for it to be routinely engaged in any situation of resistance. I turn to aspects of the discourse of violence, one which engaged hierarchical value, waged by the agents of the Sri Lanka government in the context of the JVP insurrection.

VII   THE STATE AGAINST ITSELF

In August of 1989 a poster and graffiti war of words occurred involving the JVP and the agents of government. Placards appeared on hoardings throughout Colombo and the provinces. One, purportedly placed by the Sri Lanka army, depicted Rohan Wijeweera (the since-killed JVP leader) in demon guise, surrounded by death and skeletons. Wijeweera was presented as saying, in self-devouring demon terms: "Stalin, Mao and Marx did not kill their followers but I do for the sake of my Motherland." Another placard addressed to the JVP declared, "are you [*topi*] patriots? You hide in caves and destroy the property of the island." The opponents of the state are not simply "demonized", which is widespread in general rhetorics of violence, but their demon identity is given particular hierarchical meaning. The pronoun "you" (*topi*) is used in Sinhala to the lowest of beings and supports a rehierarchializing violence appropriate to the remythologizations of state power. Thus the same placard exhorted the general populace to kill the JVP when spotted and to inflict the punishment of the traditional kings upon them. One was suggested. It involved impaling (*ulatiyennava*) the victim on a stake driven through the anus.

Government destruction was reported as sometimes following the pattern dealt out by Sinhala kings. Thus I have one (unsubstantiated) account of a group of captured JVP youths being dismembered and their limbs hung from trees (see Knox, 1681 [1972], p. 61). This kind of fragmentation fits with the kind of fragmentation which demons threaten their human victims in traditional Sinhala exorcisms and which the order of hierarchy established in exorcism ultimately inflicts on demons.

The violent hierarchical and demonic rhetoric of the state was equal to the ferocity of its suppression of the JVP. This rhetoric did not *cause* the agents of the state to act violently. The dynamics for violence were part of a total situation of violence in which the agents and agencies of the state were already committed. What I do suggest is that a state discourse of hierarchy and demonically annihilating and reaffirming power gave direction and impetus to the process of state destruction. The discourse entered into the violent process and to a degree defined and legitimated appropriate violent objectives. Moreover, it supported the transmutation of the organs and principles of state control and social order, of bureaucracy and techno-rationality, into efficient weapons of human extermination.

A hierarchical discourse such as I have described asserts the legitimacy of a state in crisis becoming external to itself, becoming demonic. It facilitates and intensifies the emergence of the destructive face of order: in the context of the JVP, of the bureaucratic ordering of the state.

A general feature of what might be described as the bureaucratic/technical rationalism of contemporary state processes is a method of abstract taxonomic classification. The significant attributes of persons and populations, for example, are defined and manipulated largely independent of context. Such bureaucratic principles predict the nature of persons in terms of their category membership.

Thus, in the JVP suppression the military and para-military agents of the state recognized probable fields of resistance and political commitment through such abstract and crude indicators as youth, caste and village. This might be referred to as the bureaucratic imaginary whereby the "enemy" is constructed or fantasied into existence by those who are dedicated to operations of searching and destroying. An aspect of the bureaucratic imaginary is a tendency to take an individual instance as representative of a general class and to identify particular possibility on the basis of broad category membership. Thus, in government action, evidence of individual JVP activists in a village area occasionally became a pretext for action against the village as a whole. Government forces engaged in mass killings: "guilt" via category-membership and the grim evidence is now being revealed in public enquiries. The bureau-cratic/technical order of the state is not just the means or the instrument of state violence, it becomes itself generative of an expanding situation of violence.

The JVP were a major threat to the Sri Lanka state. However, their existence and who represented instances of the JVP threat were also a product of fantasy, a fantasy impelled in an ideology of power which affirms through the annihilation of resistance. Thus, innocent Sinhalese bearing the taxonomic indicators of resistance to the state are affirmed as resisters in their very destruction by the state.

A common technique of annihilation used by state forces was the burning of the bodies, usually in petrol-filled tyres. This was not merely a pragmatic destruction of evidence. Rather, this kind of action is, in itself, the very invention of evidence and an action of extraordinary symbolic potency. Whether JVP or not, victims in the mode of their destruction were created as violent enemy bodies, often the faceless bodies of a bureaucratic imaginary. The violence of the state was self-validating and, I suggest, was a factor in a voracious expansion of violence which could know few limits except those it created in its own violent dynamic. This was more especially so in the context of the JVP revolt, for a State of Emergency had been declared which suspended most civil restriction on the excesses of government agencies.

The power of the state is inscribed on the bodies of its victims, as Foucault and others have pointed out. The bodies of the "JVP" defined the state as the entity that confers identity and were so deployed as to mark the boundaries and space of state power. Such a discourse achieves further force in the context of a Cosmic State nationalism which aligns the integrity of personal identity with the encompassing hierarchical order of the state. External to the state persons have no place or integrity. The burning of corpses, in fact the destruction of outward signs of personal recognition, and their distribution at the roadside or in other places often marked in a cultural imagination as demonic and dangerous external space (a fact which additionally signed the bodies as objects of terror) expressed the constitutive/deconstitutive nature of state power and the boundaries of this power. The location of bodies was part of a process of state reterritorialization.

As the state affirmed and constituted itself through its violent discourse, so did the JVP. It assumed the form of the war-machine, in Deleuze and Guattari's sense, fundamentally deterritorializing and transgressing of the internal boundaries and striations of the state. The JVP's discourse of viol-ence elaborated these dynamics and gained its own ordering force through particular manipulations of cultural meaning and variant interpretations of broad nationalist historical themes.

VIII   THE JVP AS WAR-MACHINE

If a key hero of state discourse was Dutugemunu, perhaps King Vijayabahu was more central to the JVP. Vijayabahu was the *nom de guerre* of the leader of the JVP military wing. Vijayabahu is a medieval heroic Sinhala king whose story of conquest and unification of Sri Lanka is recounted in the extension of the "Mahavamsa", the "Culavamsa". His progress bears some important similarities with Dutugemunu but also critical differences. Both deny parental authority (a metaphor of the order of the state), refuse territorial limitation, and both are notorious slayers of Tamils. But Vijayabahu, more so than Dutugemunu, is through-and-through a warrior, a man capable of uncompromising violence. He is ruthless against Tamils and also against his own people who refuse his power. Vijayabahu captures the heads of his opponents and burns others at the stake. There is none of Dutugemunu's Buddhist quietude or ultimate commitment to Buddhist value as conditioning of the state. Vijayabahu is annihilating and conquering power incarnate, an heroic approximation, indeed, of the war-machine.

The JVP manifested dimensions of the war-machine in its own internal cellular organization, each locally based but articulated in a network of relations that linked together points across wide and diverse terrain. As such they could operate swiftly and with speed. Of course, this is typical of modern guerrilla organizations and is a mode of operation quite outside state principles of bureaucratic structuring and potentially completely disruptive of it. Furthermore, operating secretly and virtually invisible to the gaze of the state, the JVP through its network structure could breach the social and spatial boundaries of the state order. In 1989, the JVP was an alternative order to the state: a "war-machine-becoming-state". Its rule operated at night but in the months of August and September it began a series of daytime "hartals" whereby it matched the night-time curfews imposed by the government. The JVP declared all government and commercial business closed and for a short while achieved their objective and demonstrated their control.

Vital to the JVP was its network of relations and a capacity to expand its relational field. The JVP violence, its discourse of violence, was motivated in such a structure and was formational of it. At the start of this essay

I noted that JVP threats were a method for constituting and expanding their organization as much as for demonstrating or enforcing control. The JVP violence was generated in, and expressed this, dynamic.

Government violence tended to be oriented to the category. JVP violence was directed to the person in the fullness of their social and relational identity. Persons who occupied points in chains of political and social relations were targetted. Individuals who did not bend to the JVP will were eliminated and, to a degree, the relational sets of which they were a part. The JVP killed persons at their houses and in the midst of local neighbourhoods. Their relatives were not permitted the rights of burial, particularly shocking in this Buddhist cultural world where the beliefs are strong that the dead will not be re-born and will afflict their living relatives should the appropriate rites not be performed. Relatives were ordered to leave them where they were killed, occasionally at their own house entrance. Obviously a discourse of terror, such action had other ramifications. It effectively shamed[11] a set of persons connected to the dead and cut them out of a field of power that the JVP was constituting.

JVP violence asserted a "morality" of social relations. Its politics of capture promoted customary and local virtue by means of which the JVP could command the nodal points in the net of its power. People executed by the JVP were not only identified as government stooges, or as behaving in defiance of JVP authority, they were also presented as offending local moralities. The JVP executioners often presented themselves as exerting customary or rightful justice, as asserting the justice that the agents of the government had ignored or themselves had abused. People killed by the JVP included rapists, seducers, thieves, etc. The killing occasionally followed the course of long-standing village disputes and exhibited the passions of local enmities and the desire for revenge. The metaphors of execution occasionally inscribed on the body were those of the divine retribution of the Cosmic King exerting the power of his sword (*Kaduva*) of justice. I have one confirmed instance where a notorious seducer of village girls was cut ten times with a sword and his genitals removed, supposedly the traditional mutilations of the King's justice for such crimes.

Broadly, the violent discourse of the JVP engaged the dynamic of the war-machine. It expanded through social relations and to some extent became driven by the violence already integral within them. Thus, its energy of destruction joined with the enmities already present and often of a long-standing nature in local areas. The JVP violence became part of pre-existing structures of vengeance and a vehicle for the settling of old scores. The government's need to destroy the JVP and to attack it at base progressively involved government forces in similar processes of local vengeance which expanded the destruction as a whole.

IX   REMYTHOLOGIZATIONS AND THE REINVENTIONS OF VIOLENT FORMS

Sri Lanka in recent years has become dangerously poised on the brink of a death-world which Wyschogrod, referring to European experience of recent history, defines as "an attempt to make whole the broken cosmos by an imaginative act of radical negation, the destruction of the embedding matrix for all social forms, the life-world...." (1983, p. 28). In Sri Lanka this imaginative act is driven through particular remythologizations of power and identity. I have concentrated on the mythologizations of nationalism in Sri Lanka, of a "past" reinvented as a discourse of the contemporary agents and agencies of the state and those who oppose it.

These remythologizations have force in discourse. They can shape the way the circumstances of lived realities are grasped. In this sense they can play a role in the actual creation of the realities they imagine. The violent conflict between ethnic Tamils and Sinhalese has progressively assumed the shape of its nationalist imaginary. How the past is seen in terms of Tamil–Sinhala relations in the current discourse of nationalism has been instrumental in creating the ground of the conflict, the increasing separation of Tamils from areas where Sinhalas were dominant and vice versa. The actualities of society are in many senses always a projection of the imaginary and the remythologizations of nationalism in Sri Lanka and elsewhere are frequently a tragic demonstration.

However, I have focused on the logics of remythologizations of the past and their force within the organizational dynamics of violent political struggle. The metaphors of Cosmic Kingship and hierarchy which are dominantly present in the remythologizations contribute towards a shaping of the crisis of power in Sri Lanka. Their meaning is transmuted in the organizations or assemblages of power which appropriate them. Thus, the hierarchical logic of Divine Kingship becomes reattuned to the dynamics of a modern bureaucratic/rational state. Applied by the agents of the state to their political circumstance it intensifies the centralizing and totalizing possibility of contemporary state political institutions and participates in the subversion of its modernizing aims. Moreover, hierarchical discourse of the Cosmic variety can participate in contributing to the enormous destruction of which a contemporary bureaucratic/technical state is capable. The discourse of annihilation that is integral to the metaphors of hierarchializing power can, via the instrument of the bureaucratic/technical assemblages of the contemporary state, achieve grim realization.

I have characterized the violent struggle between the JVP and the Sri Lanka government in terms of Deleuze and Guattari's delineation of the state and war-machine. What Deleuze and Guattari describe as their dynamics are constantly repeated in space and in time but always in orig-inal and to a large extent discontinuous manifestations. The implication is that the kind of dynamics of violence I have been describing do not arise on the basis of pre-existing models but will emerge spontaneously in a diversity of different historical circumstances.

The JVP and the agents of the state drew on the mythologizations of past events, many of which manifest the kind of war-machine/state dynamics of Deleuze and Guattari's discussion. (Indeed, their work is strongly influenced by Asian materials.) I am stating that the mythologiza-tions of the past have potency in the present because they express a general dynamic force which is already a potential and a practice of the political processes to which they are applied. Their potency as metaphors and as elements in the constitutive discourse of which they are made a part is partly because of this fact. They operate to make the dynamic more evident in reflective consciousness and achieve impetus as a result. They also gather force, a hegemonic force, because aspects of their reference and import are also elements of routine social/cultural life, elements which are transmuted in the context of state nationalism and other political processes.

An understanding of the extraordinary discourse of violence of the JVP–government confrontation is extended through the notions of the war-machine and state. The one is not an inversion of the other or a con-tradiction of the other in a classic Hegelian dialectic. There is not a unity of opposition, the one being a dimension of the other, although as the conflict progressed there were more and more overlaps in practice. The JVP did not represent the negation or other side of a government positiv-ity, although this was a strong element of the government's propaganda. Rather the government forces manifested a distinct ordering dynamic from that of the JVP. They were mutually exclusive and eliminating. Their opposition might be likened to the clash of two positives, rather than of a positive and a negative, in which no resolution outside total extinction was possible.

The distinct dynamics of JVP and government violence expanded the dimensions of the violent context to create for a while a total situation of violence. This was all the more so because of what I have stressed continually as the nature of the violent discourses. As much as a struggle for controlling power, the violence was a vital element for constituting a social world in which a particular kind of dominating power was possible. Thus the Sinhalese population as a whole was increasingly drawn into the conflict and consumed in its fury.

NOTES

1. The research and writing of this essay has been assisted by a grant from the Harry Frank Guggenheim Foundation. I am grateful to Karen Colvard for her assistance and discussion.

2. In an analysis of the circumstances surrounding the riots of 1983 I (Kapferer, 1988) used the metaphors of exorcism and of sorcery to express the nature of their fury. This raised some scholarly eyebrows and one critic (Scott, 1990) in a attempt to correct my mistake asserted that I had it all wrong. He missed what could be called the revenge structure of exorcism and sorcery in Sri Lanka and their process of transformation whereby the destruction of attackers involves a reconstitution of victims. My metaphor of exorcism is appropriate to the riots. They followed after the Tamil Tiger killing of Sinhala soldiers. There was a revenge structure in their fury.

   This is also the case with the destruction of the JVP. The attack by the JVP on the families of state forces quite consciously brought forth the revenge structure of the "victim". The fury of human destruction expressed by victims at the shrines is, indeed, a relevant metaphor. A hero of the JVP destruction was Deputy Inspector General of Police Udugampola. Members of his close family were destroyed by a mine set by the JVP. He was depicted in the press at the time as a demonic figure of vengeance executing a righteous revenge.

3. The thesis I develop here extends earlier statements of mine (Kapferer, 1988, 1994). From the start it must be noted that I am not concerned with giving an explanation of the causes of the violence. The ethnic struggle, which has left few corners of Sri Lanka untouched, extends from a complex of historical processes. The critical ones for understanding the crisis have been widely debated already and debates will continue well into the foreseeable future (see, e.g., Committee for Rational Development, 1984; Tambiah, 1986, 1992; Wilson, 1988; Spencer, 1990). Among the forces to which I, and others in greater detail, have drawn attention are Sri Lanka's colonial history, the particular location of Sri Lanka within processes of capitalist globalization, the internal dynamics of class formation, uneven economic development, increasing poverty, and much else. My interest here is not with causation as such, which is always problematic, not least because of its linear, before and after perspective. Recent criticisms of so-called "modernist" theoretical perspectives, which tend towards explanations in terms of deterministic processes within closed systems or structures, has

asserted the openness of processes and their multidirectionality, in directions which are not necessarily tightly interconnected. This anti-modernist position is close to my own and fits with historical processes as they continue to work out. It is a position which underpins the present approach.

4. The dominant argument for Sri Lanka is that its ethnic conflict is a specific historical example of widespread processes of nationalism. Indeed, it is stated that modern nationalism, in which a heightened sense of ethnic identity is a marked feature, is a kind of European "export" (e.g. Spencer, 1990; Nissan, 1989; these follow the arguments of Gellner, 1983, and Kedourie, 1993). The particular force of Buddhist nationalism in Sri Lanka is driven within the familiar conditions of colonialism, class conflict, and so on.

In the context of discourse in Sri Lanka the argument is an important intervention. This is so, because it refuses the assertions of Sinhala and Tamil nationalists that they are playing out an age-old conflict: that the present situation is merely the reproduction of ancient events established in pre-colonial contexts. Recent scholarly arguments are still giving limited credence to the nationalist rhetoric (e.g. Roberts, 1993, who also presents an excellent survey of recent debates).

My own position is in agreement with the assertions that the current conflict is entirely the result of recent colonial and post-colonial circumstances. However, the historicist and materialist view has little place for ideology except as superstructural reflection or distortion. Nissan (1989) is quite explicit, citing approvingly the somewhat strange statement that: "Culture is less a reflection of society, than a reflection of history" (Peel, 1987, p. 112). The statement is odd, for I cannot see "culture" as something abstracted from history or, indeed, from society. While I do not reject out of hand the sentiment directing the position – ideology as distortion is a major theme of my discussion – the dualism of the approach reduces the force of ideology to the social and material circumstances of its production and existence. Ideology is left unexamined and its discursive (or in Benedict Anderson's terms its "style") unexplored. The perspective does not attend to hegemonic processes either. That is, on the way discourse achieves force through routine cultural practices in which the rhetorical references of politicians have place but an entirely distinct significance. This is the central argument of other work of mine (Kapferer, 1988).

5. This exposure was probably unintentional as the assassinations were linked to immediate and particular strategic ends which were to eliminate those priests supportive of the state.

6. The term "Buddhist Revival" imparts a far too coherent and monolithic sense to what were very diverse processes of a revaluation of Buddhist ideas that largely occurred in the context of colonial power. Scholars have presented the "Revival" as strongly influenced by Western and Christian ideas and practices. The Revival *made* such practices into Buddhist practices. This may have been the case until fairly recently. However, new directions in what I see as enduring "revitalization" processes are evident. Thus, there is a revaluation of "peasant" ritual practices (often labelled as "not Buddhist" by an earlier wave of urban bourgeois "revivalists") as, indeed, "authentic" Sinhala Buddhist practice. Such revaluation is related to the emergence into positions of power and status in the national arena of

Sinhalese of peasant or lower-class background previously excluded by the colonially-created and often English-speaking élites. Members of this "new class" were brought up in a milieu in which the rites they now value were common practice. Their revaluation has changed much of their erstwhile significance. Nevertheless, such revaluation by a new class which is politically powerful has been influential, I think, in the cultural directions and discourse of recent developments in Sinhala nationalism.

7.   The urgency of human beings to totalize, to achieve what they conceive as bounded and coherent universes of meaning and action, does not disagree with an observation that sees the worlds of lived experience and discourse as continually shifting, fragmenting, breaking boundaries, collapsing, etc. It could be said that the enduring tragedy of being human is born in an anxiety to totalize against the experience of its impossibility.

8.   Tambiah (1986) has documented the recent contraction or demise of democratic institutions and the rights of citizens in Sri Lanka. Much of this is to be attributed to the growth of national disturbance in response to growing Sinhala ethnic nationalism. The crisis of power generated has, in my view, given more and more space to a particular hierarchical imaginary of power which is contributing to a further erosion of democratic rights.

9.   Dumont (1980, 1986) argues that while Western political ideologies enshrine egalitarian values and displace hierarchical value, the latter, nonetheless, continues though in transformed significance within egalitarian value.

10. I have described what I call here the "logic of hierarchy", an ontology in earlier publications. I use the term ontology to distinguish it analytically from ideology. The former can be conceived as the orientational frame which articulates the contextual meaning of ideology. The ontological frame can, in my usage, organize a great diversity of ideological rhetoric. However, because these rhetorics share an ontology, the way is open for the meanings of nationalism to play, for example, into the ontological ground of village practices. Their ontological commonality establishes a metonymic exchange of meaning. A common ontology yields penetrative power to the ideology of nationalism, enables it to invade other contexts of meaning and to elicit their apparent support and to distort their import. Ontologies are never closed systems of meaning. Rather they are frames within which innumerable meanings, often highly innovative and original, can develop.

11. Obeyesekere (1981) states that Sinhalese cultural attitudes place great emphasis on notions of shame (*lajja*) and therefore on the public arenas of relationships and identity.

REFERENCES

Alles, A. C., *The JVP, 1969–1989* (Colombo: Lake House, 1990).

Anderson, Benedict, *Imagined Communities* (London: Verso, 1983).

Barth, Fredrik, *Ethnic Groups and Boundaries* (Bergen: Little, Brown, 1966).

Chandraprema, C. A., *Sri Lanka: The Years of Terror – The JVP Insurrection, 1987–1989* (Colombo: Lake House, 1991).

Cohn, B., "Representing Authority in Colonial India", in *The Invention of Tradition*, ed. Eric Hobsbawm and Terence Ranger (Cambridge: Cambridge University Press, 1983) pp. 165–209.

Committee for Rational Development, *Sri Lanka the Ethnic Conflict* (New Delhi: Navrang, 1984).

Deleuze, Gilles and Guattari, Felix, *A Thousand Plateaus* (London: Athlone Press, 1988).

——, *Essays on Individualism* (Chicago, Ill.: University of Chicago Press 1986).

Feldman, Alan, *Formations of Violence* (Chicago, Ill.: Chicago University Press, 1991).

Gellner, Ernest, *Nations and Nationalism* (Oxford: Blackwell, 1983).

Gombrich, R. and Gananath Obeyesekere, *Buddhism Transformed* (Princeton, N.J.: Princeton University Press, 1989).

Gunawardena, R. A. L. H., "The People of the Lion: Sinhalese Consciousness", in J. Spencer (ed.), *History in Sri Lanka: The Roots of Conflict* (London: Routledge, 1990).

Halliday, F., "The Ceylonese Insurrection", *New Left Review*, vol. 69 (1971), pp. 55–90.

Kapferer, B., *A Celebration of Demons* (Bloomington, Ind.: University of Indiana, 1983).

——, *Legends of People, Myths of State* (Washington: Smithsonian Institution Press, 1988).

——, "Nationalist Ideology and a Comparative Anthropology", *Ethnos*, vol. 54 (December 1989) pp. 161–99.

——, "Ethnic Nationalism and the Discourses of Violence in Sri Lanka", in B. Kapferer (ed.), *Nationalism and Violence* (Oxford: Oxford University Press, 1994).

——, *The Feast of Power: Sorcery, Sacrifice and Sociality in Sri Lanka* (1995).

Kedourie, E., *Nationalism* (Oxford: Blackwell, 1993).

Kemper, Steven, *The Presence of the Past: Chronicles, Politics, and Culture in Sinhala Nationalism* (Chicago, Ill.: Chicago University Press, 1994).

Knox, Robert, *An Historical Relation of Ceylon* [1681] (Colombo: Tisara Prakasakayo, 1972).

Malalagoda, K., *Buddhism in Sinhalese Society, 1750–1900: A Study of Religious Revival and Change* (Berkeley, Calif.: University of California Press, 1976).

Moore, Mick, "Thoroughly Modern Revolutionaries: The JVP in Sri Lanka", *Modern Asian Studies*, vol. 27, no. 3 (1993) pp. 593–642.

Nissan, E., "History in the Making: Anuradhapura and the Sinhala Buddhist Nation", *Social Analysis*, no. 25 (September 1989) pp. 64–77.

Obeyesekere, G., "The Vicissitudes of the Sinhala-Buddhist Identity Through Time and Change", in M. Roberts (ed.), *Collective Identities, Nationalisms and Protest in Modern Sri Lanka* (Colombo: Marga Institute, 1979) pp. 279–313.

——, *Medusa's Hair* (Chicago, Ill.: Chicago University Press, 1981).

Peel, J. D. Y., "History, Culture and the Comparative Method: A West African Puzzle" in L. Holy (ed.), *Comparative Anthropology* (Oxford: Blackwell, 1987) pp. 88–118.

Roberts, M. (ed.), *Collective Identities, Nationalism and Protest in Modern Sri Lanka* (Colombo: Marga Institute, 1979).

——, *Caste Conflict and Élite Formation: The Rise of the Karava Elite in Sri Lanka* (Cambridge: Cambridge University Press, 1982).
——, "Nationalism, the Past and the Present: The Case of Sri Lanka", *Ethnic and Racial Studies*, vol. 16, no. 1 (1993) pp. 133–66.
Scott, David, "The Demonology of Nationalism: On the Anthropology of Ethnicity and Violence in Sri Lanka", *Economy and Society*, vol. 19, no. 4 (1990) pp. 491–510.
Seneviratne, H. L., *Rituals of the Kandyan State* (London: Aldine Press, 1978).
Spencer, J. (ed.), *Sri Lanka: History and the Roots of Conflict* (London: Routledge, 1990).
Tambiah, S. J., *World Conqueror and World Renouncer* (Cambridge: Cambridge University Press, 1976).
——, *Sri Lanka: Ethnic Fracticide and the Dismantling of Democracy* (Chicago, Ill.: Chicago University Press, 1986).
——, *Buddhism Betrayed?* (Chicago, Ill.: University of Chicago Press, 1992).
Taussig, M., *Shamanism, Colonialism and the Wild Man* (Chicago, Ill.: Chicago University Press, 1987).
Wilson, Jeyaratnam A., *The Break-Up of Sri Lanka* (Honolulu: University of Hawaii Press, 1988).
Wyschogrod, Edith, *Spirit in Ashes: Hegel, Heidegger, and Manmade Mass Death* (New Haven, Conn.: Yale University Press, 1983).

6 The Lebanese Shi'a and Political Violence in Lebanon

ELIZABETH PICARD

I INTRODUCTION

Whatever else it is, and it is a complicated phenomenon, so-called "fundamentalism" is not only very different in different settings but rarely what it appears to be. Among its better-known characteristics are the reworking of retrievals from the past which evoke a nostalgia for a golden age – an age of devotional and doctrinal purity more mythic than could possibly be real, and narratives providing magical episodes as well as accounts of the fall from grace. By the same token, a projected and redeeming future can be grafted on to such retrievals so that the negative circumstances are overcome. In the process one finds clerics and ecclesiastics exorcizing enemies within, excoriating those without, redeeming the wretched of the earth, within a context which is millennial, salvational, and ecumenical. Among the faithful and the converted are those who, poring over sacred texts, bear witness to God's appreciation for sacrifice. These are some of the legitimizing ingredients for the mobilizing power of the sacred in secular life.

To see how this works requires attention to both the historical and analytical aspects of case materials. One needs to divide and set apart genuine from mythic historical antecedents. But it is the mythic ones which, if successfully coded, become a plunderable resource for the legitimization of political violence within a framework of "fundamentalism". Religion, ethnicity and political violence, as the analysis of Sri Lanka has indicated, suggest the analytical importance of the interior view. On the whole such a view has been lacking in the case of the Middle East, where terms have often been applied rough-shod, such as "fundamentalism" which scoops up vastly different phenomena and places them under the same rubric. Moreover, in this region, and especially in Lebanon, spectacular events – car bombings, the rash of abductions of Western citizens – have obscured the more underlying complexities which have led to political violence.

189

The present analysis focuses on the Lebanese Shi'i community and its efforts to obtain recognition and rights within Lebanon as a whole. The first part of the discussion considers the historical context of political mobilization and violence within the Shi'i community since the creation of the Lebanese state in 1920. The birth and acceleration of this violence are explained by demographic, sociological, economic, legal and constitutional, as well as strategic and military variables. The combination of these variables, the staggered nature of their respective evolutions, and their impact on the Shi'a, explain why members of the community, and organizations acting in its name, resorted to certain types of political violence. Three phenomena in particular are especially significant. First, the Lebanese Shi'a as a group was transformed in the space of forty years from an underdeveloped and submissive group to a community capable of rapid economic mobility and social mobilization. Secondly, the transformation from social mobilization to political mobilization was blocked, in part because the Lebanese communitarian system is itself governed by a set of rigid rules. Consequently, the Shi'a saw their identity reinforced, their borders establishing, and their mobilization as a "discourse community" strengthened. Thirdly, by using to their own advantage the failure of a new consensus within the Shi'i community and the impossibility of expanded political participation, outside forces intervened and propelled the discourse and practices of the Shi'a towards conflict and violence.

In the Middle East, indeed throughout the entire Arab–Muslim region stretching eastward from Morocco to the Gulf and from Caucasia down to Sudan, few countries offer a better example of political violence than Lebanon. Not even Algeria, which has suffered a large number of deaths in recent years. The only exception, it could be argued, is Iran. But the political violence in Iran, under Islamic rule since 1979, is quite specifically state-sponsored violence; whereas in Lebanon the example of the Shi'i community lends itself better to a general theoretical model of political violence. The Lebanese case seems to correspond even more precisely to such a model than a country such as Libya, with its role not only in the internal conflicts of neighbouring countries but in international terrorism as well. It seems to correspond to a model of political violence more precisely than Egypt or Syria, too. In the former country, the violent acts of Islamic militants – such as the assassination of Anwar el-Sadat – had long been a marginal phenomenon in a complex social order that was basically democratic, and in the latter, Islamic opposition forces led a violent civil war against the secularist military regime of Hafiz el-Assad between 1979 and 1982.

Indeed, the example of the Lebanese Shi'a offers a rich variety of characteristics and variables that enable us to construct a paradigm of political violence. Attempts to address political violence in the geo-politically important region of the Middle East have tended to approach the question from either a political economy perspective (though not strictly class-based) or a cultural perspective (though not exactly culturalist).[1] In this chapter, we shall go beyond these two perspectives in order to penetrate the internal logic of the actors involved in emancipatory movements: in order to understand a community's moral project and its confrontation with the state, we must interpret tumultuous events in their historic and metaphoric dimensions. First, however, it is indispensable, albeit oversimplified, to examine the variables and circumstances that can help us understand why "men rebel".[2]

A closer look at the Shi'a provides us with how such materials combine with political violence in ways paralleled by several other similar movements where political violence is used to return to the paradise which has been lost, especially to the "damnation" of Western secular modernism, and the millenarian gain brought down to earth in a context of social and cultural integration. By this means people become resistant to the negative consequences of both secularity and modernism.

With this aim in mind, and to provide sufficient perspective, the first part of this discussion will deal with the historical context of political mobilization and violence within the Lebanese Shi'i community since the creation of the Lebanese state in 1920. We will also discuss the Shi'i community's situation in the context of Lebanon's ultra-liberal economy, as well as the specific nature of the country's political system, and social structures will also be addressed: especially the rapid transformation the country has undergone since the Second World War. Regional conflicts – both the Arab–Israeli conflict and that between Israel and the Palestinians – have had tremendous repercussions within the Shi'i community, and will therefore also be considered. Finally, we will discuss the profound impact on the Shi'i community of the Iranian Revolution.

The second part of the discussion offers an analysis of the various acts of political violence in which the Shi'a have been implicated from 1974. It focuses on three particular types of violent acts: extra-institutional protest; revolutionary insurrection; and terrorist acts.[3] When discussing these three types, it is necessary to highlight how they are interco ordinated, how their actions can be scaled according to various stages, how they change according to time and place, and the nature of a possible inversion[4] as they make the necessary transitions through these various stages.

The third part of this paper focuses on the role of violence as a means of actualizing the past of the community, and of mobilizing its members, on a new basis and behind new boundaries. The interior dynamic of the Lebanese Shi'a as a community is examined. This approach, which can be called a "political culture" approach, serves to illustrate how political mobilization within the Shi'i community has in many ways been a mobilization of a collective repository of beliefs and values in relation to the local culture.[5] The ethnic basis of this political culture characterizes "Arab Mediterranean" societies divided into agonistic, clanic or tribal groupings where action within a code of honor is central. Violence functions as a sort of internal logic, even to the exclusion of social interaction. Our focus on the "militia" phenomenon will offer a contribution to the understanding of the specific form of political violence adopted by Lebanese communities in strife. In the Lebanese Civil War, the militia groups were the chief users of violence. Their violence was directed not only at the state, but also aimed at deepening the segmentation of society and thus reinforcing the identity of the group under their control.

The most important aspect of this political culture is the religious dimension – the topic of the fourth part of this paper – for it is essentially in this dimension that groups find the "mytho-logics" that structure its emancipatory discourse. It became critically important after the decline of Marxist and nationalist ideologies, both of which had long played leading roles in popular mobilization. In effect, religion became a new way of structuring and giving meaning to anti-state and anti-Western political violence. Despite its contradictions and weaknesses, religious discourse has become the foundation of a new Islamic political order, opposed to the international nation-state order. To analyse the process of popular mobilization, we shall specifically examine the annual *Ashûra* celebration, which for the Lebanese Shi'i community is a privileged moment of retrieval and projection. The *Ashûra* ritual, which serves as a *topos* for group fusion based on faith and an eschatological vision, has been turned into a political performance in which the community's founding traumas[6] are reversed in order to galvanize collective mobilization.

The fifth and final part of this paper concentrates on the evolution of the Shi'i emancipatory movement during the reconstruction of Lebanon. Since 1991, the Lebanese state has been attempting to regain control over its territory and populations. Confronted with a new national and international environment, the Shi'i movement faces a choice between compromise with the state or refusing totally the path of normalization through withdrawal back into the society. The choice between marginalization and future remobilization will ultimately depend to a large extent on the ability of the state to propose solutions for many serious problems such as war, unemployment, underdevelopment, criminality, emigration – the very problems that led to the creation of the Shi'i movement.

How, and to what extent, can we distinguish the events of the war from those which can be described as political violence? What logic and causality link these two phenomena? These questions are particularly crucial when one is examining the Lebanese Shi'i community, as it has been directly involved, for obvious geo-strategic reasons, in the violent confrontation with Israel. Lebanon – and especially southern Lebanon inhabited by the Shi'a – was drawn into an international conflict that gave birth to an armed resistance which was "Lebanese" if not "national". Should violent actions, such as hostage-taking or bomb attacks, be considered "acts of war" or "acts of terrorism", the ultimate expression of political violence? One encounters some difficulty when attempting to treat together the two adjoining questions of war and political violence, as each inevitably spills over into the other.

Contrary to the prejudices spread by Orientalists and supported by Islamists – there is nothing intrinsic to the Lebanese Shi'i community (or to Muslims generally) that leads to the conclusion that this social group is inclined towards political violence. Historical, spatial and economic contexts, as well as the constant cultural changes within the Shi'i community itself, have created a great variety of experiences which preclude any essentialist definition of the Shi'a. Moreover, studies of other ethnic and religious groups in the region,[7] as well as our own study of the mobilization of the Maronites by the Lebanese forces' militia within the context of the Lebanese War, suggest that analysis requires an examination of elements in the social structures and common cultural codes of Middle Eastern groups, notably in Lebanon, whatever the religious discourse. In other words, in examining the "political violence" of the Lebanese Maronites, for example, one should question the role of Christianism. A comparative study of Lebanon and Northern Ireland, conducted between 1990 and 1992, demonstrated the instrumentalization of violence both outside of and within each group in the invention of its identity and in its mobilization.[8]

II   VIOLENCE AS A POLITICAL MEANS

Irrespective of theoretical approach (political economy or culturalist), cultural origin, political beliefs, or personal distance to the Lebanese Shi'a, there is the unanimously held view, that the violence committed within the Shi'i community itself or outside the community, is mainly a *reactive* form of violence.[9] The birth and acceleration of this violence can be explained by demographic, sociological, economic, legal and constitutional, as well as strategic and military variables. Three phenomena in particular are especially significant. First, the Lebanese Shi'a, as a group, was transformed in the space of forty years from an under-developed and submissive group to a community capable of rapid economic mobility and social mobilization. Second, because the Lebanese communitarian system is governed by a set of rigid rules, there was no continuity in the Shi'i transition from *social* mobilization to *political* mobilization. Consequently, the Shi'a saw their identity reinforced, their borders established, and their mobilization as a "community" strengthened. Third, by using to their own advantage the failure of a new consensus within the Shi'i community and the impossibility of expanded political participation, outside forces – not only armed but "arming" – intervened and propelled the discourse and practices of the Shi'ah towards conflict and violence.

Since the early centuries of Islam, the Shi'a have been settled in the area which would become Lebanon. Successive waves of invasions, dominations, and massive migrations, some resulting in bloody massacres,[10] forced them to relocate on numerous occasions, shrinking their original Shi'i territory as they retreated into fortified, defensive positions until the middle of the nineteenth century.[11] When the state of Lebanon was born in 1920, only a small group of Shi'a were present on Mount Lebanon, in the high mountainous area overlooking the port of Jbayl. The vast majority of Shi'a were spread out over two regions: either the Jabal Amil in southern Lebanon or in Hermel and the Biqa' Valley near Baalbak. Not only were these two regions geographically peripheral, but neither had ever belonged to the autonomous Mount Lebanon as defined in its 1861 borders. The two regions were attached to Mount Lebanon by authorities under the French mandate. The Shi'i population supported the Arab nationalist movement and the independent Arab government of Damascus (October 1918–July 1920). The French conquest of these peripheral areas lasted until 1926. During the period, the Shi'i populations formed into armed bands, led revolts against the occupying forces and mounted attacks on neighbouring Christian villages.[12] The Christians were viewed as secular competitors of the Shi'a and, moreover, were quite favourable to the French presence in the area.

For a long time, the French occupation was so incomplete that, when the first official census was taken in Lebanon in 1932, it neglected a number of settlements in the two majority Shi'i regions.[13] At the time of independence in 1943, several thousand Shi'a in the Baalbak–Hermel region were still not registered as Lebanese, and many remain unregistered even today due to their nomadic way of life as shepherds, sometimes following their flocks outside the country for several months of the year. The Shi'a of Jabal Amil, on the contrary, felt their Lebanese identity reinforced since May 1948, when the creation of the state of Israel traced the border of South Lebanon.

The term "underdeveloped" is particularly apt to describe the situation of the Shi'a in these two regions. Prosperity in Lebanon – which should not be confused with development – was based chiefly on trade and financial activities in Beirut. Not only did Beirut, the oversized capital city of a small country, lure capital and wealth but at the same the city was attracting considerable human migrations from the peripheral regions.[14] The resulting disequilibrium between the capital and the rest of the country was strongly marked. In the decade from 1960 to 1970, Beirut showed all the exterior signs of a wealthy metropolis whose high standard of living, consumerist culture, and Western values sharply contrasted with the backward way of life in rural Lebanon.

Poverty was widespread in the rural areas, where about 85 per cent of the Shi'a[15] lived. Though 45 per cent of the Lebanese depended on agriculture, this activity produced only 15 per cent of the country's revenues.[16] Most of the Shi'a were cultivating soil that was rapidly losing its fertility, while water resources (the Orontes and the Litani) were under-utilized. Unlike the Maronite and Druze areas of Mount Lebanon, where a shift was made towards a one-crop export economy in the nineteeth century, in the Shi'i areas no such integration into a capitalist economy was made and no peasant uprisings took place. In the regions of Baalbak–Hermel and Jabal Amil, the traditional social and agrarian structures remained locked in place. For a whole century, large tracts of arable land remained in the hands of influential city merchants – the 'Usayrans from Sidon, the Khalils from Tyre, the Zayns from Nabatiyyah – and powerful tribes such as the As'ads from Tayyaba, the Husaynis and the Hamadas from Baalbak, who had prospered as tax agents working on behalf of the Ottoman ruler.[17]

The standard of living in the Shi'i rural areas was well below that of Beirut – in the 1950s, it was five times lower according to one Lebanese sociologist[18] – and there was very little in the way of economic and social infrastructures. According to a study by IRFED,[19] the Baalbak–Hermel and Jabal Amil regions were both badly in need of communication, medical, and education facilities. When political violence first broke out in 1975, some pointed to the city/country, wealthy/poor, and landowner/tenant-farmer contrasts, especially in the context of religious and class-struggle tensions, largely between middle-class Christian groups and under-privileged Muslim groups. In particular, the concept of "class community"[20] was applied to the Shi'a. This interpretation, which was widely accepted during the 1970s,[21] was based on one undeniable fact: by most measures of socio-economic status, the Shi'a fared poorly in comparison with the non-Shi'a.[22] But reality was in fact much more complex. Several other social groups in Lebanon, including the Maronites, had undergone painful economic mutations that had led to social transformations[23] and consequently to eruptions of violence.

The process of mobilization within the Shi'i community was the result of two external factors, the improvements brought by the Shihabist regime, and the upheaval in the social structures of the Shi'i community caused by merchant capitalism. Still other phenomena, intrinsic to the Shi'a themselves, must not be overlooked: their pattern of migration within and outside of the country, their cultural dynamics, and their class mobility.

The Lebanese government had become aware of the regional inequalities after the 1958 crisis.[24] A number of institutions such as the Social Development Agency and the "Green Plan" attempted to deal with social and economic underdevelopment. Within a decade, roads were built and electrical-power stations were constructed in the most remote areas, especially in South Lebanon and in the Biqa'. For the first time, people were able easily to gain access to the capital city by road, and the products and symbols of Beirut's urban prosperity were disseminated throughout Lebanon's rural areas. Rural populations also benefited from new educational facilities. Between 1958 and 1971, the number of Lebanese children in school almost quadrupled.[25] The Lebanese University, public and free, began admitting larger numbers of young Shi'a, who would form a new middle-class network ready to spearhead social and political mobilization. Also, the state increased its hiring of Shi'a, who until then had been under-represented in the civil service,[26] the army, and the security forces. Partly as a result of this closer contact with the centre, this dozen-year period was a time of major upheaval in the traditional life, culture and values of the rural Sh'i areas.

This policy of state outreach did not go without unforeseen side-effects, however. In the peripheral areas dominated by private landowners whose tracts of land took in several villages, the introduction of an export-based agro-capitalism[27] had an incalculable impact on the social and agricultural production systems of the Shi'i peasants, wiping out the tenant-farmer system. The only choice left for many was to migrate. Thus, in 1973, only 40 per cent of the Lebanese Shi'is in the two regions remained there. Some 50 per cent had moved to Beirut and its suburbs,[28] where they already made up 29 per cent of the population.[29]

Within a single generation, several hundred thousand Shi'ah had flooded into the Beirut area. While a small minority joined Beirut's salaried middle-class, the vast majority settled into shanty-towns and abandoned buildings on the city's edge. This strip of humanity formed an economic under-class, or a sort of quasi-proletariat in the late 1960s, when the Lebanese economy was flourishing. Instead of adapting to the commercially-oriented urban life of Beirut, most of new Shi'i migrants felt that their identity was threatened. They clung to their traditional ways once settled around Beirut, and indeed contributed to the "ruralization" of the city. Though transplanted, they managed to maintain strong links with their places of origin, which in most cases were never farther away than 100 kilometres or so. Family links were reinforced, including strict control over women,[30] and abandoned religious practices were embraced again in order to reaffirm the Shi'i collective identity.[31]

At the outset of the 1970s, the Shi'a showed all the signs of readiness for social mobilization. Their contact with other, more prosperous segments of Lebanese society made their unfavourable situation, and their lack of social mobility, all the more painfully obvious. Indeed, it did not result in a process of assimilation, but on the contrary one of rejection. Observers have described the situation of the uprooted Shi'a at this time as "revolutionary". The IRFED report, for example, was prescient when it noted that "the continuing acculturation of the Shi'a will not take long to make obvious the increasingly wide lifestyle disparities, which in turn will pave the way for regional revolts, anarchist social agitation by some groups, and the intervention by other groups in neighbouring areas".[32] This recipe for violence was even more potent because of the growing tension between the traditional Shi'i élite that had long controlled local villages and the community's new, educated élite centred in Beirut.

These economic and social transformations were certainly not unique to the Shi'i community. Indeed, other rural groups such as the Maronites underwent the same turbulence due to rapid economic modernization and urbanization. The tensions could have been resolved through "civil" forms of social actions, such as demonstrations, union negotiations, and national political battles, as one observes in other societies. But in Lebanon, the recourse to political violence was the result of a *blockage*, that is to say an incapacity on the part of the political process to deal with the social demands. The Lebanese political system was founded upon equilibrium and consensus among the different regional and cultural groups in the country. In keeping with the Ottoman system, which guaranteed the autonomy and political representation of each *millet* (religious community), the constitutional unity of the various social groups in Lebanon was built on their religious differences. Thus the Electoral Law of 1926 established parliamentary representation based on sectarian criteria, calculated *pro rata* according to the demographic weight of each of the fifteen, and later seventeen, communities in the country. This communitarian representation lacked flexibility, as its numerical calculations were based on the long-outdated census taken in 1932.[33] Nor had the census neglected to take into account peripheral populations, in particular among the Shi'ah, but subsequent differences in birth rates[34] meant that by the 1970s the Shi'ah had become the most numerous of all communities.[35] In a proportional electoral system still based on the 1932 census, the Shi'ah were consistently under-represented in parliament and in the government.

As a response to this problem, both the Constitution of 1926 and the Taif Constitutional Accord promise, in principle, the abandonment of the community-based system in favour of a majority system.[36] It is far from certain[37] that adoption of the demographic majority principle would lead the Lebanese polity to democratic practices and not to a (possibly religious-based) dictatorship of the majority. Thus, while waiting for a secular regime respecting the principle of "one man, one vote", political representation and power-sharing continue to be based on the principle of inter-community consensus[38] on important national issues.[39]

This principle proved remarkably resistant to change because it reflected the profound and lasting agreement among the conservative élites of *all* the Lebanese communities – including the Shi'i élites – on the question of shared powers and wealth. Indeed, contrary to the image of the Shi'i community as the victim of the other Lebanese communities, the Shi'i élites took full advantage of the community-based system and were reluctant to make social demands in parliament on behalf of the people they claim to represent. The main Shi'i leaders, members of important landowning families, augmented their economic power through other forms of legitimacy: either tribal, or inherited from the Ottoman empire with a *bey* title, or through membership in the *sayy*id-s – the descendants of the family of the Prophet. They used an uncommon form of corruption[40] to control entry into parliament and thus assured the exclusivity of access to the state through clientelist relations.[41] Whatever the nature of social change and popular pressure, this well-oiled system of political control tended to work smoothly in the elections of 1964, 1968 and 1972.

The 1974 by-election for the Shi'i seat of Nabatiyyah in which the engineer and *Amal* loyalist Rafiq Shahin defeated a member of the powerful As'ad family, was a watershed event in Lebanese politics. In one sense, it was only a symbolic victory, a sign of the social evolution that allowed new élites to take advantage of the various educational, migration and agricultural opportunities made possible by the failure of high-status families to adapt to changing social, economic and political circumstances.[42]

This election was a detonator for the political violence that would soon erupt: after their defeat, the traditional élites evidently resolved themselves, implicitly or explicitly, to block all further social change by shifting their rivalry with the new élites, and the masses from the political arena to the battlefield of armed struggle. In Lebanon, the reaction of the conservative élites, who dominated the state apparatus, proved decisive in the transition from political conflict to revolutionary insurrection.

The 1974 by-election was also the last example of a non-violent political transformation in Lebanon. After 1974, armed groups burst into the country's over-heated and fragile political arena, creating a climate of insecurity and illegality which was only exacerbated by the weakness, and then the utter collapse, of the regular Lebanese army. Moreover, various regional actors, as well as others outside the Middle East, promoted their own geo-strategical objectives through the intermediary of conflicting Lebanese groups, whom they armed and then incited to rise up in armed struggle.

One of the paradoxes of Lebanon's civil violence during the 1970s and 1980s was that the discourse of *all* the Lebanese groups squarely laid the blame for internal dissension on foreign elements: either the *ajnab* – the West, and particularly Israel – or the *gharîb*,[43] those who do not share Lebanese bloodlines. Not only was the notion of *gharîb* instrumental at de-emphasizing the internal cleavages in Lebanese society, but it also stirred up local passions against non-Lebanese and protracted the life of an indecisive political system that was mainly threatened by its own internal divisions. The belief in a foreign "plot" (American, Syrian, Saudi, etc.)[44] thus allowed the Lebanese to forge some semblance of a "national" consensus. Seeking to avoid mutual accusations and self-criticism, they preferred to deny the existence of an internal dimension to the violence in their country. But in doing so, they are rendered incapable of understanding the real causes and the function of this violence – which of course meant that they could not heal its causes.

What must be underscored is not so much the phenomenon of foreign interference itself, but rather the juncture between international conflict and internal violence. After 1975, it became difficult to distinguish, concretely and analytically, self-defensive violence, deliberate political violence, and violence resulting from international conflict. External and internal violence became inter-active. Arms supplies, whether sold or given outright, were falling into the hands of various Lebanese factions; and then, later, foreign governments were working out common strategies with these Lebanese factions, which had the effect of pitting Lebanese groups against one another, always to the benefit of the foreign state.[45]

Their intervention also had the effect of dramatically increasing the numbers involved in the conflict, improving their level of military training, and augmenting the level of the firepower of their ammunition. At this point the very nature of the Lebanese conflict was changed due to a break from traditional codes of civil violence. Respect of the dichotomy between public and private, for example, was violated when women joined the fight and civilians were among the victims. Temporal notions, too, were shattered with the constant violation of truces. And finally, the notion of territorial security was destroyed as the war became offensive instead of defensive.

III   FROM PROTEST TO REVOLUTION

The spectacular and widely viewed images of Shi'i political violence – of blown-up cars and the rash of abductions of Western citizens – should not divert attention from the most common aspects of the Shi'i violence that started in the 1970s. The transition was incremental, from a violence that was mainly symbolic and verbal in nature to a physical violence committed by armed militiamen, even against civilians, while fully 90 per cent of the Lebanese population remained outside of the armed struggle during the war and daily life continued, schoolchildren took exams, buildings were constructed, people went to the theatre, families spent the summer at the beach. While, in the successive stages of violence, the population furnished a reservoir for partisan mobilization, at the same time it constituted a force of civil resistance to the domination of the leaders promoting political violence.

Also a significant part of the population, albeit decreasing in numbers, remained loyal to their traditional leaders. A minority (like in other sects) was mobilized by secular political movements such as the Ba'th pan-Arab Party, the Social Syrian Nationalist Party, the Lebanese Communist Party, or the Communist Action Organization, for the first few years of the crisis, for the subsequent mounting of tensions, combined with the delegitimation of the Marxist model, provoked a gradual retreat back into community identities. As the war developed, the idea of "Shi'i mobilization" and "Shi'i violence" bore increasing resemblance to the reality and paralleled "Druze violence", "Maronite violence", and others as well, all mutually reinforcing one another.

The mobilization of the Shi'i community began several years before the outbreak of the Lebanese Civil War. It took the form of mass demonstrations and calls for radical reforms. For the first time in modern history, the Shi'a were pursuing their own autonomous strategy, but they were hardly a major political force, and even less a social movement. Contrary to leftist groups occupying the same political turf, the Shi'i movement was not an attempt by intellectuals to mobilize the grassroots, but rather an almost spontaneously formed movement of uprooted and impoverished Shi'i peasants, in the South or resettled in Beirut. Barricades set up by police failed to prevent the outbreak of clashes with security forces. Demonstrators occupied public buildings, notably the prefectures of Marjayoun (South Lebanon) and Baalbak. Petitions decrying the high cost of living and the growing insecurity were fired off to the parliament. During protest marches in southern Lebanon, as well as in the industrial suburbs of Beirut, workers held aloft huge black and green flags (black being the emblematic color of Shi'ism, green of Islam). In the pre-war period, the movement was still open to inter-community co-operation as well as to the influence of leftist parties. The strikes won the support of the General Council of Labour (UGTL), the country's central, inter-community trade union. Student and Palestinian organizations, too, joined the protest movement, calling for an armed struggle against Israel.

The first general Shi'i strike took place in the spring of 1970, just after a devastating Israeli bomb attack aimed at Palestinian *fidayin*, who had just set up their armed base among the villages of Jabal Amil. The strike, observed throughout southern Lebanon and the suburbs of Beirut (Shiyah, Ghobairy, and Borj al-Barajnah to the south; Nab'a and Borj Hammoud to the east), was called by the Supreme Islamic Shi'i Council (SISC).[46] Tens of thousands marched in front of the SISC seat. The SISC president, religious leader Musa Sadr,[47] threatened to send dozens of homeless from the South to occupy empty buildings or "palaces", as he called them, in the capital. The government took the threats and concrete demands seriously enough to set up, a few weeks later, a Council of the South, responsible for supporting development projects in the region. But it was too little, too late.

In March 1973, angry tobacco planters staged a sit-in in Nabatiyyah, the largest Shi'i city in Jabal Amil. Called both by the SISC and left-wing political parties, the sit-in degenerated into a violent clash with local security forces, leaving three tobacco planters dead. Mobilization efforts took a new turn when, in June 1973, Musa Sadr decided to give the movement a permanent structure and began organizing a series of mass rallies that drew tens of thousands of Shi'is, many of whom were armed, in the country's main Shi'i towns, Yatir in February 1974, Baalbak in March, Bidnayil in May, and Tyre in June of the same year.

The Shi'i movement was officially born during one of these meetings and baptised *Harakat al-mahrûmîn,* or the "Movement of the Deprived". In a society segmented into communitarian identities, the movement was, in the early stages, careful to appear as a patriotic and not a strictly ethnic organization, because it was competing with secular leftist parties. More importantly, the movement's patriotic aspect was necessary as its political demands were for reduced inequalities, a more equitable sharing of wealth, and readier access to participation in the government. Thus, the movement was open to all the Lebanese communities. Its founder, Musa Sadr, even undertook several co-operative charity efforts with Beirut's Greek Catholic bishop, Monsignor Gregoire Haddad. But the inter-community co-operation of the Movement of the Deprived soon began to show its limitations. Threatened by mobilized union members and by the class struggle led by leftist parties, the ruling élites actively sought to maintain the existing community-based cleavages in the political system through patronage networks. Consequently, the movement took on a community-based character under the aegis of the SISC, and specifically Musa Sadr himself.

The focus of Shi'i mobilization efforts remained the South, where levels of human misery were in stark contrast to the opulence of the city-state. This impoverished area was the chief victim of the war and also excluded from the power structure built on a compromise between Maronites and Sunnis. Thus, the choice of the South for political recruitment was part of the strategy of the Movement of the Deprived to make inroads into the countryside in order to create a new political space in which populations in the outer regions could participate. As opposed to the "modern" political practices in Beirut, the popular meetings organized by Musa Sadr were characterized by emotional outpourings. The effect of these mass rallies was to incite participants, whatever their original motivations for attending, into demonstrations of collective emotion: thousands of voices chanting; clusters of frenetic women shrieking out loud, and calling out for open rebellion by the *mu'ezzin.* In this turbulent atmosphere, rounds of machine-gun fire would be sprayed into the air. Random acts of vandalism and arson would be committed.

But during this early formative period of the Shi'i movement, most of the violence was maintained on a symbolic or verbal level. It was Musa Sadr who introduced change of tone in Shi'i demands. His discourse was not one of submission, but rather one of demands. One of his new slogans was: "Enough of patience, enough of humble petitions".[48] The time had come for open revolt, because "the patience of the people of the South has worn thin and civil disobedience and violence are not impossible".

Thawra, the word that was repeated over and over in public speeches signifies both "revolution" and "revolt", but it was more the second sense which the Shi'i protest intended to convey. That is clear in the following Shi'i call-to-arms:

> We do not want to clash with the regime, with those who neglect us. Today, we shout out loud the wrong against us, that a cloud of injustice has followed us since the beginning of our history. Starting from today, we will no longer complain or cry... . Our name is "men of refusal" [*râfidûn*], "men of vengeance", men who revolt against all tyranny, even though this costs us our blood and our lives.

Reference to the loss of human life was the second theme of the new community discourse: sacrifice to the point of martyrdom. Thus the tens of thousands of men who cheered Musa Sadr in Tyre and in Baalbak took an oath to "fight until the last drop of blood for the rights of the community". The third type of term employed in the discourse of violence was meant to put a high value on arms, often referred to as the "finery of man". However, during this phase of Shi'i mobilization, actual clashes with security forces were marginal, and were never deliberately provoked. In six years, during which numerous demonstrations attracted several tens of thousands of protestors, only about twenty people died in armed clashes. The symbolic violence employed by the movement's leaders seems to have served as a sort of catharsis, preventing the eruption of mob violence. However, increasingly, the movement's demonstrations degenerated into riots, protest against the state turned into insurrection. Clashes broke out between protesters and security forces in the South, now a military zone. Indeed, the beginning of the Lebanese Civil War can be put at 26 February 1975, when the member of parliament for Sidon, Ma'ruf Sa'd, was fatally wounded by a shot fired by security brigades as he was marching at the head of a popular protest of several thousand demonstrators.

Until the outbreak of the war, Shi'i violence was almost exclusively directed against the Lebanese state, although the main adversaries of the impoverished Shi'i peasants were the "feudal" landowners who siphoned off the wealth of southern Lebanon and who tightly controlled representation of the Shi'a within the state. Lebanon's clan-based social structure and segmented equilibrium meant that, in order to rebel against a "boss", a Shi'i group would have to form an alliance with the boss's rival, which would only perpetuate the existing clientelist relations. For example, it was through an alliance with the Zayn and 'Usayran clans that Musa Sadr's candidate in the 1974 legislative by-election was able to defeat the candidate of the parliamentary speaker, the powerful As'ad *bey* of Nabatiyyah.

The Lebanese state was thus the main target of Shi'i aggression, first verbal and then physical. The state was, after all, the object of the demands made by the Shi'i community, and as state influence penetrated the country's peripheral regions, demands intensified. Two documents – the Charter of the Movement of the Deprived in 1973[49] and that of its successor, *Amal*, in 1975[50] – expressed the demands of the Shi'i community. Both charters, which combined concrete demands (their utilitarian aspect) and incantatory slogans (their communication aspect) expressed the one essential goal of the Shi'i community: to share in the benefits of Beirut's prosperity. During that period, the patriotism of the Shi'i protest movement was never in question. Its willingness to co-operate with the Maronite establishment was obvious in 1982 when, in the wake of the Israeli invasion, the leader of *Amal* agreed, along with Bashir Gemayel, the champion of "political Maronitism" and presidential candidate, to take part in the Committee of Public Salvation. During this time, Shi'i violence was therefore far from revolutionary, but in fact rather legalist.

This "reformist" wing of the Shi'i movement, while losing influence, managed to survive well after 1982 and the transformations that saw the mainstream of the Shi'ah adopt new mobilization methods. A fringe of the movement succeeded, in the name of the whole community, in gaining access to the centre. The speaker of parliament, Husayn al-Husayni, and the cabinet minister Nabih Berri – both of whom were head of *Amal* – emerged as central figures in Lebanese political life. Berri became Minister of Justice and Minister for South Lebanon (a portfolio created especially for him) in all the governments after May 1984 and speaker of parliament since October 1992. The constitutional reform adopted at Taif in October 1989 was a victory for *Amal*, as it accorded more parliamentary seats and ministers to the Shi'i community[51] and reaffirmed the tradition of having a Shi'i in the speaker's chair, now with enlarged constitutional powers. The new élites who had gained access to the centre considered this change a victory, and proof that "consociational democracy" was the political system best suited to Lebanon. *Amal,* whose main platform was the abolition of political communalism to bring in a majority system, accepted "changes to the traditional order that amounted to little more than mere window-dressing".

From 1976 to 1982, while the state was in the process of dissolving, acts of political violence committed by and against the Lebanese Shi'a progressively changed both in character and in intensity. The symbolic and protest-oriented violence of the past became open warfare. At the outset of the war, when the Christian militia entered into armed conflict with Palestinian movements and their allies among leftist and Sunni militia, the Shi'i community was well behind in training to bear arms. These other groups, anticipating an explosion of violence, had been openly conducting armed training procedures for some ten years. *Amal* had been created in 1975, at which time only approximatively a hundred members had been armed and trained. This relative weakness, combined with the recent urban migration of a sizeable part of the community, explains why some 100,000 Shi'a fled in panic, without offering any resistance, when they came under attack by Christian militia in early 1976 in east Beirut, notably in the Karantina and Nab'a districts. The Shi'a closed themselves into three geographical clusters: in Baalbak–Hermel in the Biqa' region; in the Jabel Amil region and Tyre; and in the southern suburbs of Beirut, from the "green line" – the frontier between Christians and Muslims – to the beaches south of the international airport. From then on, armed force was used to protect community territory. During fifteen years of war, the rare attempts to go across the "green line" and win an armed conflict in enemy territory met with tragic defeat. The joint "Progressive Palestinian" offensive led by Kamal Jumblatt against the government and army of March–April 1976; Bashir Gemayel's abortive *coup de force* against Zahlah in 1981; the Lebanese forces' attempt in 1982 to penetrate in the Druze Shuf Mountain after the Israeli army or to conquer west Beirut between September 1983 and February 1984 all met with catastrophic results and resulted in more popular exodus in fear of reprisal. This explains why, most of the time, the militia of all denominations remained within their community territory; political violence developed within each of these newly defined sub-spaces, with their relatively fixed borders.

Armed violence was employed to become a dominant, instead of being a dominated, group. In order to impose their hegemony within the Muslim areas, Shi'i militiamen fought, sometimes simultaneously and sometimes successively, the Palestinian resistance who dominated the Beirut suburbs and southern Lebanon since the early 1970s, and the Druze and Sunni militia groups which controlled West Beirut *intra muros*. *Amal* 's central forces – *Jaysh Amal* – led a long siege, from December 1985 till February 1988, against the Palestinians in the refugee camps of Beirut as well as Tyre. Militarily, the Shi'a militia proved worse than mediocre, despite massive assistance from Syria, which supplied them with ammunition. It was only by starving civilians and refusing them access to hospitals, and due to the back-up of the Syrian heavy artillery, that they were able to emerge victorious. The guerrilla war they fought in Beirut against Druze,

Sunni and secular militia fighters from 1984 to 1987, a guerrilla referred to as the "green [Muslim] terror", was chiefly characterized by manhunts: searches and interrogations, arrests in the middle of the night, traps and several hundred assassinations.

Notwithstanding the international dimensions of the conflict, Shi'i violence during this period aimed at implementing objectives set out during the pre-war period but which could not be attained through symbolic violence alone. By 1983, for they had become the largest single community within Lebanon, the Shi'a decided to use the weight of their numbers to impose majority rule, although not through democratic processes. "I have a million soldiers behind me", proclaimed Nabih Berri in that year, alluding to the fact that the Shi'i community actually comprised nearly a third of Lebanon's population, much more than the official figure of 19 per cent. After exodus from the South provoked by the Israeli invasion of 1982, the Shi'a had become the majority not only in Beirut's southern suburbs but also in the western half of the capital, which for so long had been the fiefdom of two wealthy urban communities – the Sunnis and the Greek Orthodox – who held in contempt the "rustic" manners of the Shi'a. Thus, the reversing of the community equilibrium, which had not been possible through political and constitutional means nor through Shi'i protest, was being achieved through force. Moreover, after 1984, when Shi'i hegemony spread through the "Muslim part" of Lebanon, a unified Lebanese state had ceased to exist. The original source of the conflict had disappeared and had been replaced by hostilities between factions. After 1982, *Amal* had to respond to a challenge by *Hizbollah* and its many satellite organizations.[52] Control of the *dahiyya,* the southern suburbs of Beirut, became the stakes in the conflict. Here again, as with the hostilities between communities, the international dimension aggravated the competitive violence. Attacks and truces were often decided and negotiated in Teheran and Damascus; the truce of January 1989 resulted from the end of the first Gulf War, and the final accord of December 1990 marked the end of the fratricidal Shi'i War.

Besides the defensive and competitive community violence, a third form of violence, qualified as "terrorism", emerged during the revolutionary phase of the struggle. Bomb attacks aimed chiefly at spreading terror (such as the 1983 attacks against American and French army barracks of the Multinational Force in Beirut), hostage-taking (more than twenty Westerners were held in Lebanon between 1984 and 1990), and suicide missions were carried out (Israeli headquarters in Tyre were destroyed by an automobile packed with explosives in 1983). This form of violence, spectacular though marginal, raises four main questions.

First, at what point does one cross the line between "struggle for liberation" and "terrorism"? These acts of terrorism were acknowledged and interpreted by Shi'i militants, ideologues and tacticians as acts of war against an occupying power, Israel, and its allies, both local (the Christian militia in Lebanon) and international (the Western powers). The Shi'a, who constituted the majority of the population in South Lebanon, were the principal victims of the Israeli–Palestinian war after 1970 and the Israeli occupation after 1978. They were thus the first to adhere to the armed struggle against foreign enemies. Neither the Lebanese government nor the international community contested in principle their struggle for liberation. The issue was rather the use of violence against foreign civilians as part of the conflict, which raises the casuistical question of legitimacy as well as the existence of unequal forces between a local militia group and an over-armed state.

Second, putting terrorism in an international perspective, the relation between terrorist groups and the foreign states that sponsor them must be examined. Both the study of the Fu'ad Ali Saleh's "Shi'i" terrorist network in France[53] and the process of liberation of the last hostages in 1991 following the end of the the Gulf War show that most of these groups are financed by those states, including Iran and Syria, which opted in favour of a terrorist strategy in the second half of the 1980s. When, at the outset of the 1990s, they abandoned this strategy due to a changed international situation, they quickly and with almost total success imposed a return to international legality.

Third, the instrumental use of terrorist groups by foreign states raises the question of the relation between the Shi'i social movement and such groups. Here, the problem is not so much the organizational aspect of this relationship. On one hand, the testimony of liberated hostages[54] and the biographical information on certain of the authors of anti-Israeli attacks in South Lebanon[55] indicate a definite social, even psychological, alienation on the part of extremist militants, as well as their doctrinaire rigidity. They show the characteristics that can be found among similar groups in Europe (Red Brigades, Action Directe>), whose implacable logic led to their self-destruction. But on the other hand, the hagiographic literature,[56] and the number and strength of popular demonstrations commemorating the memory of the martyrs, indicate that the action of terrorists, even if criticized by those in the Shi'i population who are victimized by reprisals, was in line with a majority political vision, all the more so that this action fit into a culture of violence. In this sense, "terrorism" does not involve an inversion of the social movement but rather the extreme accomplishment of its aims.

Finally, we must question the relationship between terrorism and Islam. This link has been denounced by rightists in the West for whom the confrontation with Islam, and above all with Shi'i Islam as embodied by the Islamic Republic of Iran, has replaced the struggle against communism. Shi'i publications such as *al-Ahd* and *al-Badîl* and the sermons and writings of religious authorities, show the contradiction between, on one hand, a doctrine committed to the respect for life (by condemning suicide, for example) and the realization of earthly happiness and, on the other hand, the casuistry invented in the context of *jihâd* in order to justify terrorist actions, including martyrdom.[57]

IV   THE CULTURE OF VIOLENCE

To understand political violence, examination of its external mechanisms, logical links, causal relations, and successive forms is of limited use. It is necessary to go straight to the heart of society in order to identify the cultural resources in which the authors of violence find inspiration for their acts and to determine the mechanisms which enable political violence to take place at the centre of the system of signification for the social groups involved in armed conflict.

Looking for the cultural elements in the Lebanese Shi'i community that provided fertile ground for political violence, implies the understanding of current communication codes and social interaction, which together animate the group structure.[58] Little need to refer to the history of the Shi'i community, or to the Shi'i interpretation of the history of Lebanon and the Middle East. Notwithstanding its polysemic, controversial and manifestly "imagined"[59] character, the past has tended to be systematically distorted and over-interpreted[60] in Lebanon since the outset of the war, indeed to a point where "history itself was at war".[61]

Furthermore, the reference to Lebanese Shi'i culture should not be confused with the special kind of psychology that developed within the society in the context of war. The length of the confrontations, the intermingling of objectives, the fragmentation of the players involved as well as the levels of the conflict, the rapid and almost wholesale substitution of illegal violence for more "regular" forms of violence, and the confusion of ethical values and ideals were all factors that no doubt contributed to a collective sense of alienation which spared virtually none of the actors, from pacifist civilians to the soldiers of the foreign armies stationed in the country.[62] Indeed, involvement in battle served to merge individual and group aspirations.[63] It brought the fighters a kind of personal liberation from a frustrated life by pretending to give them control of their own identity and it sometimes offered participation in a paramilitary organization which was seen as fulfilling the fundamental aspiration of their native group.

Beyond these behavioural responses to the war, and beyond the instrumentalization of history, the phenomenon of political violence can be understood, and its importance for the structuring of the society analysed, through two dominant aspects of Lebanese political culture: the institutionalization of oppression and the durability of agonistic segmentation.

During the 1960s and 1970s, anthropological studies on Lebanon demonstrated that, to a significant extent, local groups continued to be dominated by a single individual (*bey,* or *za'îm*) assisted by his strongmen (the '*abadayat*). Far from vanishing with the mandatory regime, this system was perpetuated and modernized, and became a set pattern with the new political institutions. It stretched back to the Ottoman rule (and even earlier). It was founded on the armed defence of a territory, the control of agricultural production, and the raising of tax revenues in the name of the Sultan, on behalf of whom the military exercised its power. Economic domination was exercised in a context of severe competition for land and other scarce resources, and rested on the use and abuse of open violence.[64] On the symbolic level, the domination of the local landlord was made all the more complete with his exclusive appropriation of honours (thanks to his genealogy) and of the shared memory of the community (limited to the history of his family). Mild violence (imposition of etiquette, customs, the maintenance of patriarchal traditions) was combined with more open forms of violence (threats against opponents, chasing labourers off the land, attacks by strongmen, feuds, kidnappings and elopements). These forms of violence were enhanced by what Michael Gilsenan calls the "sanctification of violence",[65] either through the re-enactment of dramatic events of the past, or the reiterative narration of violent acts and situations lived and relived by the local community as a whole. Thus the social order was structured by a network of unequal exchanges which operated less on a clientelist basis than through the exercise of physical and symbolic violence.

The birth of a republican and parliamentary political system in Lebanon in 1920 changed the outward form of this domination. It moved from a "feudal" system to one with an public administration and elected officials, particularly mayors and members of parliament. However, the Lebanese elected official acted as a mediator. As the representative of his community, he was able to short-circuit the relation between the community and the state. Locally, he could use his position in parliament to impose his patronage; in the eyes of the people, elected officials were, virtually by definition, the holders of power. What changed in the new system of "republican" domination was that the landlord himself had become an elected official and could thus exercise extended powers within the state. Moreover, he acquired part of his political power from the reciprocal relations he developed with the members of the new urban middle classes.

To be sure, this clientelist system is less inequitable than an outright feudal arrangement; but in rural areas and with the new industrial proletariat, coercion remained the chief arm of control by the social élites. Johnson's study of political engineering in the Sunni areas of Beirut,[66] gives evidence of the degree to which domination by an individual is accepted and absorbed by the community. Ajami offers an astounding description of the young Kamel (*bey*) el-As'ad returning home, in a splendid automobile, to his paternal mansion at Tayyaba after university studies in France. Back to Lebanon in order to succeed his father as the local strongman and member of parliament for Nabatiyyah, and speaker of parliament, he stipulated arrogantly that any local village people wanting an audience with him wear a suit and tie.[67]

In the decades following independence, the exercise of violence was modernized through the use of efficient technology, with the complicity of state institutions. Access to the judicial system, far from being democratized, became more difficult for the dominated segments of the population, not only for financial reasons (due above all to the corruption of magistrates) but also because of the sophistication of the arcana of the judicial process. The civil service was unable to bypass the community bosses in order to provide ordinary citizens with a genuine means of access to the state.

What changed is not so much the nature of the system – which evolved from "feudal" to "democratic" status – but the quality of the instruments of coercion which the dominant class had at its disposal. Before the war, local strongmen were armed with hunting rifles or revolvers, while most families had a weapon stashed away in a bedroom cupboard. This changed drastically within a few months of the beginning of the war, with the training of paramilitaries and the importing of Kalashnikov machine guns and Czech rifles, followed by heavy weaponry including armoured vehicles, tanks and various kinds of missiles. With the disappearance of state-based legality, oppression by and of private individuals took on the dimensions of a full-scale war: between 20,000 and 30,000 people were abducted and detained in private prisons, and group assassinations became common.

But the escalation of violence in Lebanon was not the result solely of the institutionalization and the modernization of the unequal relationship between dominant and dominated. It has been at the core of the divisions and segmented antagonisms that structure societies in the Middle East as a whole, even in Israel, although varying forms of government in modern times have tended to hide this shared heritage. The segmentation of Lebanese society into religious communities makes it a paradigmatic example of the pattern of social relations familiar today throughout the Arab world. This pattern is characterized by the juxtaposition of equal agnatic groups, relations between which are not hierarchical but based on the constant search for equilibrium. In this segmented system, which preceded the state order and is still perpetuated beyond its control, the maintenance of external security involves a pattern of aggression and reprisals against neighbouring groups. Once started, "each reciprocation being thought of as a justified response to the preceding injury, grievances never end and balance is never restored".[68] Violence is deemed necessary not only as the intrinsic consequence of segmented divisions, but also as their point of articulation. It tends to feed upon itself and creates still wider divisions between communities. The internal solidarity within each group involves the use of coercion on its members through submission to the group's code of honour. Clans struggle to maintain social and material order and, even more so, to defend their symbolic capital:[69] the group identity, the values to which its members are attached, and the rights which they consider to be inalienable.

Recent studies have shown subtlety and produced rich results by applying to war-torn Lebanon the concepts and categories forged by the fourteenth-century philosopher Ibn Khaldun to describe the cycles of violence that were common in the Maghreb societies of that era. The *'asabiyya*, or blood solidarity, pitted clans against one another in competition for the *mulk* (urban power and its rewards) in the name of a *da'wa* (a politico-religious prediction whose message changed according to opportunities).[70] Such analysis emphasizes the role of violence in the structuring the cohesion and dynamic of a social group. For example, between 1982 (the assassination of Bashir Gemayel) and 1986 (the triumph of Samir Ja'ja' over the other lieutenants of Bashir), the Lebanese forces were jolted by a series of *intifâdhât*, or insurrections, which were above all factional conflicts for the control of the Maronite community. In the case of the Shi'a, the same phenomenon could be observed between 1986 and 1989, when clashes broke out between local warlords in the Tyre region and between several clans in the Baalbak region. At the same time, local factions switched from the secular discourse of *Amal* to the Islamist discourse of *Hizbollah*. Further conflicts erupted between *Amal* and *Hizbollah* for the control of Beirut's southern suburbs, of the strategic region of Iqlim el-Tuffah, and more generally for the domination and exclusive representation of the entire Shi'i community.

Nevertheless, oppression and segmentation varied in time. Indeed, the fifteen years of war witnessed a great richness and flexibility of social innovation in order to avoid the rigidity of the agonistic *face-à-face*. On many occasions, the shift from physical violence to verbal forms of violence, such as lies and the political art of cunning, led to a certain de-escalation and appeasement. Traditional customs such as hospitality were also a precious warrant against the spread of violence.[71] They were used, for example, in the complex game of alliance and opposition between lieutenants (incidentally, cousins and brothers-in-law) of Bashir Gemayel. This same casuistical tactic allowed, in November 1991, the takers of American hostages to suddenly proclaim "useless" acts of hostage taking, in order to call for the release of Lebanese prisoners in Israel. But all in all, the collapse of the state after the first two years of the war gave a new dimension to the phenomena of oppression and segmentation. Violence regulated by the state was replaced with inter-community violence organized and perpetrated by the militia groups. The community-based organization of civil society was replaced with a new, much more divisive and oppressive, social order, in which warlords reigned over their own turf.

Although the new militia rule was largely unpredictable, to qualify it as anarchical would be excessive, for it did succeed in establishing order at the local level, a sort of "societal" order. A process of "democratization of the instruments of violence"[72] went hand-in-hand with the society's growing obsession with security. A private market for arms developed and within a few years, a Kalashnikov could be had for $ 40 U.S. Only a few years after the founding of *Hizbollah*, its members were equipped with M-113 armed personnel carriers, Sagger anti-tank weapons, GRAD rockets, and towed artillery pieces. In this environment, lacking any public order, every armed group was tempted to dispense its own justice or turn to predatory acts.

The militia groups organized community defence on a territorial basis, by tracing with a line of fire the frontier demarcations. Individuals from other communities were expelled *manu militari*, members of a community outside home territory were forced to return and forbidden from leaving their home area. In short, the border was drawn between "us" and "them". The remarkable stability of the borders within Lebanon reveals the defensive nature of the strategies of communitarian groups, each loyal to its militia and each communicating with other groups through a combination of threats and negotiations. Closed in by a devastated "no man's land" overgrown with weeds, fortified by the charred carcasses of burnt automobiles, sandbags, and makeshift barricades, the militia territories could be entered only through check-points, where men armed with machine-guns conducted searches and interrogations. Militiamen hid in abandoned buildings along the line of demarcation, the existence of which they reinforced by blindly shooting rounds of ammunition at anyone they spotted on the "other side". Their shooting sprees punished by death any violation of newly defined borders.[73] Rule was further enforced by the omnipresent sight of summary executions of captured enemies: naked corpses strewed street corners, others were dragged behind automobiles, and in newspapers one could see the photos of the victims of kidnappings or summary executions.

In this new territorially-based "order", the figure of the armed militia-man was central, replacing in the hierarchy the political bosses and the economic entrepreneurs who had dominated Lebanon's social landscape before the war. The number of militiamen involved in the armed conflicts throughout the war approximated 50,000 (of which 15,000 for *Amal* in February 1984, and 5,000 for *Hizbollah*); barely one man for every ten old enough to bear arms. Certain battles on both sides of the line of demar-cation were waged by a few hundred men at most. Some were ill-trained "voluntary" militiamen, who were ready to take up arms in a local crisis, and others "combatants", who were salaried and permanent militiamen. Through the war, these salaried combatants began to be recruited at younger ages and increasingly among rural populations, notably those which had been displaced because of the war. These non-urban militia-men, who made up most of *Amal* and the Lebanese forces, were on the whole outsiders and unfamiliar with the urban populations on whom they were imposing order.

The local ringleaders incarnated the triumph of the militia order. Their numerous outward display of dominance – paramilitary outfits, deploy-ment of arms and armed vehicles, ostentatious show of their new wealth, their arrogant behaviour in public, unpredictable and limitless demands – made them the putative successors of the traditional *qabadayât*. In every district, the leader of each local group, charged with security, owed his authority to his strategic and redistributive capacities, though his legit-imacy was still based on tradition, lineage, property ownership, religion and other such ascribed attributes. This chief was quite often a young man. He organized the actions of his own sector, and it was at his house that arms were stocked.[74] At this local level, objectives were not political, but tactical: the goal was to achieve a hegemonic position and to defend it, entailing a form of violence not unlike that practised by street gangs. Each group tried to dominate, intimidate, remove, or co-opt a rival or neighbouring group through a subtle game of protection and alliance. In each district, the militia headquarters became the seat of a mini-government ruling over the local population under its control. It was a rule untempered by a judiciary, a religious authority, or the media, as all three were under direct militia control. Inside each district, one could observe the omnipresent and exclusive signs of the locally hegemonic group, the intimidation and physical aggression against deviants (for example, in regions controlled by *Hizbollah*, against those who drank alcohol, or women not wearing a *hijâb*. At the blockades that closed off access to the district and at check-points, arbitrary decision was the rule. Militia inflicted threats, humiliations and physical brutality on the very civilians they were supposed to be protecting.

From the very first few months of the war, militia groups waged urban battles over the economic activity on which Lebanon's prosperity had been based: the banking industry at the heart of Beirut, the customs' inspection at the city's port and airport, the electric-power stations, the telephone system, the oil refineries, the main communication routes, as well as the new industrial zones surrounding the capital. After twenty years, the ravages of wilful destruction totalled more than $20 billion US.,[75] the militia groups were able to guarantee themselves huge financial windfalls, which were fattened even more through the arms trade and widespread trafficking of drugs from the Biqa' and elsewhere. This predatory system was based on a co-operative/competitive relation among the different militia – not unlike that between Mafia "families" – as well as on their shared opposition to everything that promised to bring back a legal system.

Militia money was partly used to build a clientelist network by the means of social redistribution, with the regular remuneration of the militiamen as a top priority. Though the pay was meagre at the outset of the war, militia salaries were still an important motive for many sign-ups. After the collapse of Lebanon's financial system in 1986, militia pay in hard currency became a major source of income for tens of thousand of families from all Lebanese communities. A hundred dollars a month – twice as much in the *Hizbollah* militia, which benefited from a monthly allocation from Iran of roughly $7 million US.[76] – represented a salary much higher than the Lebanese state was paying teachers, or even members of its own army. Also, all the major militia groups set up medical, social and educational assistance schemes in the areas under their control as a way of winning over the local populations. This included the taxation, at higher level than state taxes before the war, of the people and economic activities.[77] Provision of essential infrastructures and activities were taken over by the militia. The result after fifteen years was that the population was doubly alienated from the state: not only had people become accustomed to *not* relying on state services, but they had transferred their loyalty, or their submission, to an illegally armed force.

Militia order was much more than a newly-installed security, social and economic order. It also implied, on a given territory, the forging of a new identity structured by the exercise of physical and symbolic violence. In Lebanon, the protective sealing off of community territory was strengthened within each region by a monopoly over the media, by the instrumental use of religion, and by taking charge of the youth. As far as the means of communication were concerned, the militia did not limit themselves to the killing of journalists, the banning of certain newspapers, and the destruction of archives and printing materials. They each quickly developed a "communications" sector, using state-of-the-art audiovisual technology, in order to to wage a fierce propaganda war throughout Lebanon and beyond its borders to the outside world.

This was all the more true given that one of the main strengths of the Lebanese militia groups was their ability to attract intellectuals and professors, who contributed their knowledge (of history, psychology, etc.) to the militants' cause. In the various religious groups one could also readily find clerics willing to dress up the militia's culture of discord in the garb of theological discourse, thus legitimating it from the top of the religious hierarchy. Some clerics, to be sure, did so out of profound conviction, guided by a strategy aimed at strengthening community identities and hence reinforcing their own socio-political authority. Many religious figures and intellectuals failed to resist the pressures of a violence that had become hegemonic within each community space.

V   RITUAL AS MEANING

The shift from Shi'i protest to revolutionary insurrection, and the radicalization of the culture of violence through the phenomenon of the militia was brought about by the gradual extension of anomy to the society at large and its penetration into the very core of social relations. In other words, Lebanese society, especially Shi'i society, suffered a brutal loss of direction. It lost its spatial compass and its familiar environment as a result of the sudden transplantation from villages to the capital. Society also lost its economic bearings: the new urban majority was on a path not of social promotion but rather one of descent into a proletarian poverty. The relation of protection/submission that once tied it to the traditional élites was now broken. And if the new city dwellers enjoyed more freedom, they were also more vulnerable. This destabilization occurred in a context of double undoing of traditional beliefs and values. Students and intellectuals in Beirut were jolted by the student protests all over the world in May 1968. And the ravages of the war, and the daily sight of death, had the effect of alienating people from the ordinary rules of behaviour.[78]

In order to reverse the relations of exclusion and reconnect the broken links between society and its own past and future, the Shi'i movement reconstructed a collective identity through a discourse of both rupture and totality: rupture with the "others" – that is, the other communities – as a way of strengthening the internal cohesion of the group; and rupture with traditional politics and with the community-based state.

Breaking with the Marxist and nationalist tone of Lebanese pre-war emancipatory movements, the Shi'i mobilization showed a clear preference for religious discourse, directly understandable among the protestors of the disenfranchised regions of Baalbak–Hermel, South Lebanon and the southern suburbs of Beirut. For these populations, Islamism – that is to say, the mobilization of the Islam for political aims – offered two advantages which explained its success as a cement for community cohesion and as the best means of liberation at a time of crisis. First of all, Islam, if not as a faith at least as a culture, provides a code of mobilization directly accessible to Muslim societies. Islamism, contrary to secular ideologies that borrow categories from an alien culture, takes its symbols and its vision of the world from a religious universe familiar to all members of the Muslim community, even those who have put some distance between themselves and the Muslim faith and its authorities.

Islamism also portrays itself as an universalism, rival of the dominant universalism associated with democracy, the market and the rule of law. The ambition of Islamism, eminently political in nature, is the domination of both the state and society through the denunciation of past failures of regimes in Muslim countries. This tactic is aimed at depriving politics of an autonomous space separate from private life and religion. Rejecting the contingent and cynical nature of politics, Islamism instead offers a religious alternative which is both immanent and moral. With little regard for historical and theological thinking, radical Islamism affirms that there can be no separation of religion and politics in Islam, no pluralism, and no public debate open to contradictory views. It thus escapes the contradictions of modernity and the tensions between the state and civil society through a holist conception of the *umma* (Muslim community) based on transcendental certitudes that serve as guiding principles for political governance.

The immediacy and globality of this system of belief have rendered incomparably effective the emancipatory movements' mythic and metaphysical discourse. A number of social and historical variables explain the role of dramatic, and often violent, religious ritual in the collective experience of the Lebanese Shi'a during the war: the blocked community-based political system, the devaluing of secular ideologies, the centuries of persecution inflicted on the Shi'ah by the dominant Sunnis, their marginalization under the French mandate and after independence. More important was the Iranian Revolution in 1979, when the new Islamic Republic sponsored a propaganda and mobilization campaign directed at the Lebanese Shi'i community, which is, along with the Shi'a in Iraq, one of the largest Shi'i communities in the Arab world.

Other factors are more closely related to the social organization and practices of Shi'ism. The distinction between Shi'ism and the majority Sunni Islam, which appeared during the very first decades of Islam, has little to do with religious doctrine. What distinguishes the Shi'ah from the Sunnis is mainly the question of the legitimacy of political power. The Shi'ah recognize the legitimacy only of members of the prophet's family, and hence consider as usurpers the political leaders since the death of the last of the prophet's direct descendants. This power vacuum that has transferred authority to Shi'i divines (*mollah*-s and *mujtahid*-s), leading to the emergence of a clerical class which puts a great deal of emphasis on ritual. Indeed, the symbolic power and material resources of these religious figures depend on their ability effectively to organize and supervise religious ritual.[79]

It was therefore around very specific religious rites that the recomposition of the Shi'i community's identity and its political mobilization crystallized. Among these rites, the *Ashûra* ritual constituted the *topos* of the Shi'a's collective experience: the commemoration of saints and heroes (Ali, the first *imâm*; Fatima, his wife and the daughter of Muhammad, etc.), and the great dates of Shi'ism. *Ashûra* mourning (*ta'ziyya*) and the ritual commemorating the murder of Husayn, the second son of Ali, by the cavalry of the Omayyad caliph Yazid at Kerbala on the tenth day of the month of *muharrâm* of the year 61 (A.D. 680), was introduced (or reintroduced) in the city of Nabatiyyah in Jabal Amil by Iranian immigrants as recently as the late nineteenth century. The ritual was not widely practiced in the region until after 1936, with the drafting of a corpus in Arabic.[80] It later spread following the dispersion of the Shi'i community.[81]

The *Ashûra* ritual gathers members of the community in assemblies of lamentation (*majlis ta'ziyya*), either in private houses or in meeting halls (*husayniyya*) where they hear narrative tales of the battle of Kerbala. The events are even represented on a stage. Each meeting is followed by a religious harangue. On the tenth day of the ceremony, a procession of self-flagellants garbed in white march through the streets. There are scenes of self-inflicted violence in which penitents, their heads shaved and wearing headbands inscribed with verses of the Koran, beat themselves about the head with daggers and swords to the point of drawing blood from wounds that occasionally prove fatal.[82] The ritual features a mixture of practices linked to Shi'i Islam in Lebanon and pre-Islamic funerary rites also practiced by Christians in the region.[83]

Although an "invented tradition",[84] this meta-history of the events of the battle of Kerbala offered to contemporary Shi'i society non-temporal themes, particularly that of corruption and oppression of the power, which triumphs over the true believers. It has constituted ever since an inexhaustible well-spring of rhetorical devices that could be interpreted variously according to the context.[85] The collective Shi'i conscience has forged its own interpretation: while marching towards death, Husayn was choosing martyrdom over injustice and the usurpation of his power. At the same time, he was exposing the treason of his own community, *shî'at Ali* – the 'party of Ali' – which had abandoned him at the decisive moment of the battle.

During the 1930s, the ritual was an instrument of religious legitimation of the domination by the local élites. It was all the more instrumental given the fact that it transmitted from one generation to the next the guilt-inducing message contained in the story of a community that had betrayed its leader. This guilt complex was reinforced by the patriarchal social structures and by the frustrations engendered by sexual repression.[86] Confronted at the same time by interdictions and adversity, the Shi'ah turned on themselves and, through this self-punishing rite, neutralized any potential aggressivity. The function of the ritual was therefore to "appease intestinal violence and to prevent conflicts from breaking out".[87]

When the Movement of the Deprived emerged as an organized force, the *Ashûra* ceremony underwent a transformation in its geographical dissemination and in the way in which it was interpreted. In its transformed version, the climax of the ceremony occurs when the penitential cortège circulates befind huge black and green banners through the village or urban district while the crowd, accompanying the self-flagellants, chants "*Allah akbar*" as well as the names of the great Shi'i *imâm*-s. The cortège becomes a demonstration of power, not only by the number of participants but also because the procession traces and sets the ever-expanding limits of Shi'i territory: in the past fifteen years, the performance has gone from taking in seven places to more than twenty-five,[88] through the new districts "squatted" by the Shi'a, such as Bir el-Abed and Khaldeh in the southern suburbs of Beirut. In 1985, the ceremony flooded into the very centre of the city around the Zuqaq el-Blât mosque; *Ashûra* had become a central event in Lebanese society.

The new interpretation of the ritual – its actualization and inversion – constituted an even more dramatic change as of 1974. In the particularly tense atmosphere of social mobilization the *Ashûra* celebrations were transformed from a penitent rite to a revolutionary one, from a chorus of lamentations to one of imprecations, from an act of submission to one of rebellion. In Yater (Jabal Amil), Musa Sadr presided over the ceremonies that year, exhorting the overcharged crowd – which was chanting "evolution, revolution, oh *imâm* !" – "not to consider the tears and the participation at a funeral as a substitute for action, or as a way of avoiding anger and vengeance, or an excuse for not taking more constructive actions".[89] It was not only a cathartic discourse or a merely symbolic call to arms, but an unequivocal battle cry *hic et nunc*. The following day, Sadr even participated in the creation of a committee "against the high cost of living" at Nabatiyyah, and on 6 February marched at the head of a huge demonstration in Sidon. For the Shi'i community, the days of civil strife that followed throughout the South were nothing less than the extension of the *Ashûra* ceremony, without a hiatus or change in tone. Social ritual had thus been transformed into political mobilization. "Through the enactment of an important event of the past, the 'now' of a religious community [had been] extended back into the past and forward into the future."[90]

Rid of its quietist interpretation, the ritual furnished a new paradigm of Shi'i mobilization during the war – the "paradigm of Kerbala". The community, as a response to the non-temporal violence of which it was a victim, sanctified its own violence. Throughout the annual religious cycles, other less significant commemorations were added to the *Ashûra* ritual, such as that of Zayn el-Abidin (the son of Husayn), the day of Jerusalem (the third sacred city of Islam), or the anniversary of Musa Sadr's disappearance in 1978. The ritual was also embellished by techniques borrowed from the Iranian tradition, such as the presence of a limousine cloaked in black, the wearing of shrouds by demonstrators, and skirmishes on the fringes of the cortège. From that point on, the annual *Ashûra* ritual marked the most intense moment in community mobilization.

For the Shi'i community, the *Ashûra* ritual penetrated the very core of daily existence. Through the actualization of the past, the ceremony breathed a new dynamic into the community spirit. Each of the episodes of aggression, destruction, exodus, attack, and armed reprisal that successively occurred during the war became the actualization of the misfortune, suffering, and oppression of the followers of Ali. It is not that history is repeating itself. It is rather that time was abolished. Thus, in the testimony of the local village people of Jabal Amil who witnessed battles between Palestinians and Israelis, and later between the Lebanese resistance and the Israelis on their territory, recollections of punitive acts, bombardments, imprisonment and forced exodus are precise, but mixed with evocations of mythic tales stretching back to the birth of Shi'ism.[91] When, for example, the wife of sheikh Raghib Harb, who was assassinated in 1983, recounts that she was pregnant when being beaten by Israeli soldiers, she is also reproducing a traditional tale of the wife of the *imâm* who was beaten by the enemies of Shi'ism.[92] The tale of this traumatic event becomes even more authentic in the telling. Transgressions both physical (the searches and destruction of houses) and bodily (the beating of a pregnant woman, the murder of a sheikh) acquire an immediate symbolic density through their non-temporality.

Shi'i experience was not only that of victimhood. It was also a sacrificial violence in the name of the community's salvation. The combatant who died in a skirmish or during a terrorist attack was not a victim, and even less so a "scapegoat" – to use René Girard's term.[93] He was rather a *shahîd*, a martyr as well as a witness. The exemplary and religious nature of such acts has been documented in letters and diaries kept by young men killed in combat and reprinted or cited by the militant press,[94] or in confessions recorded on video and aired on television. The aim of the *shahîd* is not so much military success, but rather the exemplary effect of his violent experience and the mystic fusion of the community with the heroes of the past. With this heavy emphasis on the theme of sacrifice, the fabric of Shi'i community life became a web of unifying, interwoven symbols[95] which enveloped political action. These symbols were carried at first by the clerics whose sermons served to contextualize violence for adherents, in a fiery mixture of Koranic language and Third World rhetoric.

Also a part of this ritualization of violence was the popular invention of body movements, music, decoration, and spatial organization – all of which helped enrich the new community gospel. Added to the explicit religious symbols (a globe, the Koran, and a rifle for *Hizbollah*), the omnipresent portraits of the leaders and martyrs, the posters and banderols, and the well-planned, militia-organized processions, other gestures proved equally inventive: the renaming of streets, the erection of luminous religious symbols at night, the installation of loudspeakers from which bellowed the sermon from the previous Friday, and invocations in, of all languages, Persian. The identification with one's community group also encouraged people to wear an "Islamic" costume (the *jellabah*), albeit a modern jacket-like version, and an Iranian-style beard. Women, for their part, had to hide their body beneath an *'abaya*, which was a symbol of a rejection of Western values.[96]

The Shi'i Islamic discourse did not work as a discourse of interpretation, but one of comprehension. Ritual dressed up every community action in symbolic attire, expressed people's social dependence, deepened the divide separating the Shi'ah from other communities and thus gave meaning to communitarian violence. Ritual not only abolished temporal differences, linking past to present and future by abrogating history and time, but also overcame individual differences through the dramatization of collective emotions.[97]

VI   BACK TO POLITICS: ÉLITE COMPETITION WITHIN THE STATE

Barely three years after this wave of revolutionary fervour, the Shi'i movement began to normalize its practices and re-emphasize the legitimacy of its aims in the Lebanese political framework. *Amal* readily accepted the constitutional Taif Accord in 1989, including the dissolution of the militia groups and the incorporation in the spring of 1991 of some of its members in the restructured Lebanese army. Within a few months the Western hostages held by groups linked to *Hizbollah* were freed, and the spiritual guide of the radical Shi'a commented that "violence [was] no longer paying off for those who generated it".[98] But the most tangible sign of normalization was the participation of the revolutionary movement in the legislative elections of August and September 1992–not just *Amal* but also *Hizbollah*, which won eight of the twenty-seven seats reserved for the Shi'a.

The weakening of the communitarian movements during the years 1989–92 allows us to reflect *a posteriori* on the Shi'i entanglement with political violence and the factors contributing to the appeasement of this violence. Three elements help explain this change: the competition between élites of the community, the role of external influences and, last but not least, the restoration of the Lebanese state.

While most communitarian movements of Lebanon resulted from wide popular mobilization, competing interests were still present and active behind the scenes. Indeed, the main weakness of these movements was to allow the agents of violence to put their conflicts of interest before their collective goals: for fifteen years the Sunni urban élites remained paralysed by the rivalries of their political bosses and the Maronite warlords dragged their followers into a series of fratricidal wars. As for the revolutionary Shi'a of *Amal* and *Hizbollah*, each was inspired by the same ambition of supplanting the traditional "feudal" élites as well as the secular political parties in order to become the exclusive representative of their community.[99] Personal interests and leadership rivalries were competing with the revolutionary ideal, and the logic of bargaining prevailed over the discourse of revolution.

Sometimes referred to as the new intellectuals of Islam,[100] the leaders of *Amal* and *Hizbollah* represented a new generation of revolutionary cadres bound to replace the traditional community élites and their scions. Their differences in age, geographical and social origin and education help to explain the divisions and open conflict inside the Shi'i movement. *Amal* was controlled by the new crop of university-educated Shi'a who had risen above their rural origins through schooling. Among its leading figures, more were from modest origins (Dawud Dawud, Ayyub Humayyed) than from major Shi'i clans (Husayn Husayni; Muhammad Beydun). Those originating from southern Lebanon outnumbered by ten those from the Biqa'. Some of the cadres chose the route of the civil service – and even the army (Aqif Haydar). Others took advantage of the economic growth, notably in commerce and real estate in western Africa and in the Persian Gulf. They established relations with the business and banking bourgeoisie of other Lebanese communities. The most emblematic profession of the *Amal* new managerial class was the law: several members of the *Amal* politburo were lawyers, beginning with its Secretary General since 1982, Nabih Berri. By contrast, religious figures were constantly in a minority position within the movement's politburo of twenty members.

On the whole, the leaders of *Amal* had ambitions extending in accord with the clan-based and communitarian. Among the top officials there was a growing temptation to make deals with the leaders of other sects in order to gain access to positions of power – whether as a minister, in the bureaucracy, or an MP seat – or even as a way of entering the lucrative business world. Thus the participation of *Amal* in "the national reconciliation" governments after 1984 allowed an entire generation of ambitious cadres to occupy positions in public administration, and to reap the benefits from these positions. The Higher Council of the South, for example, which manages millions of dollars intended for reconstruction projects, was controlled by *Amal* since 1984. This is why, fifteen years after its creation, the movement was rigged with "incompetence, corruption, and arrogance".[101]

Against the looseness of *Amal,* one could set the ideological virulence – both doctrinaire and moral – and the organization of *Hizbollah.* Even if, since 1989, *Hizbollah* tended to take on the structures of a "Leninist" party by electing politburo members as well as a Secretary General,[102] the movement was almost exclusively dominated by high-ranking religious figures.[103] With a single exception the twelve (eight after 1991) members of the *majlis al-shûra* (Consultative Council) which governed *Hizbollah* in Lebanon were sheikhs born around 1950, most of them in the regions of Baalbak and Zahlah.[104] They had studied in Qom in Iran, and in Najaf in Iraq at the time Khomeyni lived there in exile. They shared the belief that secular political power was illegitimate and accepted Khomeyni's proclamation of the *vilâyat al-faqîh* – the devolution of political power towards the "just jurisconsult". Such ideological positions established a vision of power prone to totalitarianism. *Hizbollah* leaders were demanding the control of the earthly city, both in the public sphere and in the private lives of Muslims. Indeed, the reinforcement of their legitimacy in the Shi'i community at the expense of *Amal* depended on their refusal to make political compromises, and on the sanctification of violence, including violence against civilians, perpetrated in the name of an Islamic "imperative".[105]

Rapidly, however, the competition between *Amal* and *Hizbollah* became less a conflict between a revolutionary project and a religious programme and more a contest for control over the Shi'i community. From 1985 to 1989, the confrontation between both movements took the shape of an unrelenting territorial advance from *Hizbollah* at the expense of *Amal.* To emerge victorious, *Hizbollah* took advantage of the fact that *Amal* was still suffering from its calamitous battle against the Palestinians. Also, *Hizbollah* cleverly lured away *Amal* militiamen by offering them between $150 and $200 a month. Finally, *Hizbollah* succeeded in unifying the southern Shi'i suburbs of Beirut. Several hundred combatants were killed on both sides before Berri, admitting defeat, proclaimed the dissolution of *Amal* in the *dahiyya* in June 1988.[106] The following phase of the conflict unravelled in the south where *Hizbollah* became the principal force against the Israeli army when many *Amal* militants chose to give up the armed struggle and accepted the demobilization set out in the Taif Accord.

The competition between *Amal* and *Hizbollah* had the ultimate effect of directing the emancipatory movement back to the realm of conventional political rationality. First, it had repeatedly exposed the fragility of the discourse community, particularly among localist groups capable of shifting their loyalty from one movement to the other when their interests or their security were at stake. Secondly, in order to use victory to its advantage, *Hizbollah* had to exchange its eschatological aims for concrete objectives, or at least promote the latter and relegate the former to a distant and improbable future. Faced with this necessity, the leaders of the *majlis as-shûra*, utilized their unexpected doctrinal flexibility and negotiating talents as doctors of theology and Islamic law. They showed that they were as capable as the *Amal* cadres of taking part in the subtleties of the Lebanese power game. Finally, the most spectacular effect of the confrontation within the Shi'i camp was the shift from its hostile discourse of inversion to one of participation on the forefront of the Lebanese political debate.

Regional normalization had a decisive influence on the reversal of the Shi'i movement, all the more so because its universalist discourse and its entrenchment in the conflict zone of South Lebanon implicated it directly in the key problems of the Middle East. Although the end of the Cold War and the Gulf War had no direct impact on the Shi'i movement itself, it accelerated the return of Syria to the international "order" and forced its leader to renounce altogether both Syria's quest for "strategic parity" with Israel and its claim to support and control the various subversive organizations of the Near East.[107] For Lebanon this meant that with the tacit agreement of the United States and Saudi Arabia, Damascus would take charge of the Lebanese crisis and try to keep it under control, particularly avoiding serious confrontation on the frontier with Israel. The "new regional order" reorganized under American leadership during the Gulf War confirmed this inclination so that in the autumn of 1990, Syria succeeded both in crushing General Michel Aoun's rebellion and in imposing a cease-fire accord between *Amal* and *Hizbollah*. Since then, all the political and military forces of Lebanon have submitted to the domination of Damascus, confirmed by the Syrian–Lebanese Friendship Treaty of May 1991. Having put an end to the Lebanese Civil War, Syria has imposed all the militia to surrender their arms and dissolve themselves or transform themselves into political parties.

The Gulf War had also the effect of accelerating the transformation of the Islamic Republic of Iran after its defeat by Iraq in 1988 and the death of Khomeyni in 1989. Teheran had distanced itself somewhat from the Shi'i movements in Lebanon. Not only did its subsidies diminish, but the ruling circles of *Amal* and *Hizbollah* resented Teheran's hesitations and the conflict between its moderates and radicals. This tendency has been confirmed since the end of the Gulf War, with the Arabian Peninsula and Central Asia being Iran's foremost concerns, ahead of the Arab–Israeli conflict and the problem of southern Lebanon. From that time on the waning of Iranian influence on the Lebanese Shi'a movements was reflected through the rapid denouement of the Western hostage crisis and

President Rafsanjani's statements supporting peace in Lebanon and the observance of the Taif Accord.

The progressive transformation of the Near East from war to peace affects deeply the nature and signification of the struggle of the Islamic resistance (the fighting forces of *Hizbollah*) against the IDF and the South Lebanon army. On the one hand, the struggle is still fierce – "we will fight as long as one square metre of Lebanon remain occupied", said the movement's Secretary General[108] – and the level of armament high: air shelling by Israel and use of Grad rockets of Iranian origin by *Hizbollah* in July 1993 and July 1994. But on the other hand, the Islamic resistance proves nearly ineffective on the ground. Rather than a liberation force, it has become a card played by Syria and Israel in the complex game of negotiation involving the Golan and South Lebanon altogether, with Iran in the back and Lebanon as the main stake. At the same time, on the Lebanese scene, its remains a major source of armed mobilization, for in the name of the "liberation struggle" *Hizbollah* was the only militia group spared by demobilization; and a source of emotional mobilization, for armed struggle was a kernel of collective identity.

The reorientation of the Sh'i movement towards political negotiation depends ultimately on the nature of the newly revived Lebanese state, and the future status of the armed movements which dominated the country for the last fifteen years. However justified the criticisms of the legality and constitutionality of the Second Lebanese Republic may be, they are secondary to the necessity of bringing back the state and formulating a new social pact. The trauma of the civil war helped shape in the minds of the Lebanese an idealist image of the state, different from the ultra-liberal state of the 1950s and 1960s. This image was the opposite of what the Lebanese had suffered under the domination of the militia groups. The state is "the boundary which secures all boundaries":[109] it defines domestic law and order, brings security to the borders, encourages economic prosperity and supervises social redistribution of wealth; its interlocutors are the élites of civil society, not the power-brokers of the communitarian hierarchies. In disarming the militia and recovering its legitimate monopoly on force it protects society against the two dangers, fragmentation and domination, which have historically threatened it. This image of the state is shared by the majority of civilians in all regions and all communities, including those who remained silent under the militia terror.

In contrast to the state of 1943, modelled on a segmented society and so tolerant of diversity as to border on anarchy, the new state which is being put in place in Lebanon conforms to the model of a unifying and authoritarian state, dominated by security concerns. Since its setting in Lebanon, daily life has been normalized, criminal activity linked to the proliferation of armed local groups has diminished drastically, all militia groups (with the exception of *Hizbollah*) have been disarmed and disbanded, and law is applied equally in all regions of the country (except for the occupied South). For the relative security of the community group, the state has substituted unconditional collective security imposed by the modernized and reinforced security apparatuses of the police and the army. The communitarian discourses of religion, exclusivist despite their pretensions to universalism, have been replaced with the discourse of an unified nation.

An important issue to the future of the democratic system in Lebanon is the question of the transformation of militia apparatuses into political organizations and their integration into the political process, and, more specifically, of the ability of the warlords to become civilian participants in a parliamentary system. The incorporation of the members of the dismantled militia into the Lebanese army or their demobilization occurred rapidly in 1991. Much could be said on the ease with which men who used the anonymity of a militiaman's role to terrorize and plunder have been able to resume civilian life or slip into the regular army, trading for example the meager salary of an *Amal* militiaman for the pay of an army infantryman. At the highest level – that of ministers, deputies, and high-level administrators – the political system is filled with warlords.[110] These men traded their camouflage uniforms for suits and ties, their "kalashes" for minister's portfolios, and their Koran for a profession of faith in the state's institutions. The relationship between the new state and the militia political class, and between that class and the Lebanese population which it claims to represent, has little to do with the negotiation of interest groups or the construction of a social pact. As before the war, it remains a clientelist relation in which violence, instead of having been expelled to the margins of the system, has been introduced as a dynamic principle into its very core. While the hostilities have been suspended (an appreciable relief for the population) it is not at all certain that either the state or the militia chiefs who run it have the inclination or the means to guarantee a return to civility.

Hizbollah also took part in the process. From an armed resistance organization it turned into a powerful social and political movement, owing to the end of the war, by combining charity with modern educational activities in spite of its archaic discourse: religious circles, martial art academies, radios and TVs, newspapers, libraries and vocational schools, and, overall, hospitals and care centre which the Sh'i regions lacked so cruelly. An institution like *Jihâd al-bina'* ("reconstruction endeavour") is a tentacular apparatus linked to the Martyrs Foundation which depends directly from Iran. Its committees are in charge of building, water and electricity adduction as well as consumers co-operatives.[111]

No wonder if many in Lebanon suspect, behind *Hizbollah*'s demand for abolishment of the communitarian system and the adoption of the majority rule, a new strategy aiming at enforcing its Islamic vision and law to the Lebanese society. Since its victory over *Amal*, and its success in the legislative elections of 1992,[112] *Hizbollah* has become the largest legal opposition force in the Second Lebanese Republic. By virtue of the number, it might claim the leadership in the future majority system which should once replace the communitarian system, according to the Taif Accord.

The question remains, of this pretention of *Hizbollah* to represent the whole of the Sh'i community. Adding to the process of rapid modernization and urbanization, the upheaval of the war has accelerated the shattering of traditional social structures and enhanced individualistic aspirations and behaviours – among the Shi'a, even more than in other communities – thus reinforcing the trend toward secularism. But, simultaneously, violence against and inside the community stimulated a dynamics of "invention" of collective identity and strengthened Shi'i internal cohesion. *Hizbollah* has been the main benefitor of the process. The Shi'i emancipatory movement, legalized at the end of the war, legitimated by its struggle for "national liberation", legalist in its new contest for the Lebanese government, is still on an upward trajectory. Moreover, it is strengthened by the re-islamization process all over the Middle East.

NOTES

1. J. Leca, "L'économie contre la culture dans l'explication des dynamiques politiques", *Bulletin du CEDEJ*, no. 23 (1988).
2. T. Gurr, *Why Men Rebel* (Princeton, N.J.: Princeton University Press, 1970).
3. David E. Apter, Preface, p. viii of this volume.
4. M. Wieviorka, *Sociétés et terrorisme* (Paris: Fayard, 1988) ch. VI "L'inversion".
5. C. Geertz, *The Interpretation of Cultures* (New York: Basic Book, 1973).
6. R. Girard, *La violence et le sacré* (Paris: Grasset, 1972).
7. E. Sivan and M. Friedman, *Religious Radicalism and Politics in the Middle East* (Albany, N.Y.: State University of New York Press, 1990).
8. "Milices libanaises et paramilitaries nord-irlandais: de la mobilisation du groupe à la construction de son identité", in D. C. Martin (ed.), *Comment dit-on "nous" en politique?* (Paris: Presses de la FNSP, 1994).

9. M. Amil (Hasan Hamdan), *Al-Nazâriyya fil-mumârasa l-siyâsiya* (Beirut: Dar al-Farâbî, 1979). See also M. Chiha (one of the best known theoreticians of the "Phoenician identity"), *Politique intérieure* (Beirut: Le Trident, 1964).

10. Especially the "devastation of Kisrawân" in the fourteenth century, whose main victims were the Shi'ah. See A. Beydoun, "Les morts du Kisrawân", *Identité confessionnelle et temps social chez les historiens libanais contemporains* (Beirut: Librairie orientale, 1984) p. 102 *et seq.*

11. D. Chevallier, *La société du Mont Liban à l'époque de la révolution industrielle en Europe* (Paris: Geuthner, 1971) p. 91.

12. M. Jaber, *Pouvoir et société au Jabal Amel de 1749 à 1920 dans la conscience des chroniques chiites et dans un essai d'interprétation* (Paris IV: Thèse, 1978).

13. According to the census of 1932, Lebanon counted 155,000 Shi'ah, that is to say 19.6 per cent of its population. See P. Rondot, *Les institutions politiques du Liban, des communautés traditionnelles à l'État moderne* (Paris: Institut d'étude de l'Orient contemporain, 1947) pp. 28–9.

14. A. Kher, "Polarisation au Liban", *Développement et civilisation*, no. 5 (1961) p. 52.

15. S. Nasr, "La transition des Chiites vers Beyrouth: mutations sociales et mobilisation communautaire à la veille de 1975", in CERMOC (ed.), *Mouvements communautaires et espaces urbains au Machreq* (Beyrouth: Cermoc, 1985) pp. 85–116. They were 70–85 per cent of the residents in the Jabal Amil and Baalbak–Hermel, and only 3.5 per cent of the population of Beirut in 1948.

16. Kher, op. cit.

17. A. R. Norton, *Amal and the Shi'a: Struggle for the Soul of Lebanon* (Austin: University of Texas Press, 1987) p. 15 *et seq.*

18. A. Khalîl, "Junûb Lubnân bayna l-dawla wal-thawra", *Dirâsât 'arabiyya*, no. 4 (1975) pp. 53–75.

19. Institut de recherche et de formation en vue du développement (IRFED), *Besoins et possibilités de développement au Liban* (Beirut, 1960).

20. Under the influence of Muhsin Ibrahim, the General Secretary of the Organization for Communist Action in Lebanon (OACL). See E. Picard, "Political Identities and Communal Identities: Shifting Mobilization Among the Lebanese Shî'a through Ten Years of War", in D. Ronen and D. Thompson (eds), *Ethnicity, Politics and Development* (Boulder, Col.: Lynne Rienner Publishers, 1986).

21. G. Twaynî, "The Shî'a are the proletarians of the earth, apparently the most submissive class, but the most revolutionary at the bottom", *al-Nahâr* (18 March 1974) p. 1.

22. J. Chamié, "Lebanese Civil War: An Investigation into the Causes", *World Affairs*, no. 113 (1977) p. 179; M. Hudson, *The Precarious Republic: Political Modernization in Lebanon* (New York: Random House, 1968) p. 79; G. Haddad, "Primum vivere", *L'Orient-le Jour* (15 July 1975) p. 1.

23. G. Corm, *Géopolitique du conflit libanais* (Paris: La Découverte, 1986). Especially "l'affaiblissement de la communauté maronite", pp. 172–4.

24. The crisis of 1958, as a mixture of Christian–Muslim and pro-Western–Arabist antagonism, was a harbinger to the 1975 Civil War.

25. According to a survey made by the Family Planning Association in 1971, 31 per cent of the men and 70 per cent of the women were illiterate among the Shi'ah, compared to 13 per cent and 20 per cent respectively among the Greek Orthodox. *Les fiches du monde arabe*, no. I-L17a (Nicosia, 1980).

26. General Shihab imposed a quota of 50 per cent for Muslims in the civil service. While this measure aimed at balancing communal representation, it played against individual competences. Still, it was often difficult to find first-grade civil servants among the Shi'ah.

27. Its part fell to 8 per cent of the GDP in the early 1970s. See Lebanese Communist Party, *Al-qadhiyya l-zirâ'iyya fî Lubnân* (Beirut, 1973) pp. 108–9.

28. Y. Schemeil, *Sociologie du système politique libanais, Université des Sciences Sociales* (Grenoble, 1976) p. 71.

29. A. Faour, "Migration from South Lebanon with a Field Study of Forced Mass Migration", *Ecwa Population Bulletin*, no. 21 (1981).

30. Everywhere in the Muslim world, city women are more prone to be veiled than country women.

31. F. Khuri, *From Village to Suburb: Order and Change in Greater Beirut* (Chicago, Ill.: University of Chicago Press, 1975).

32. Ibid.

33. P. Rondot, op. cit. Until the Taif Accord of 1989 and the Second Republic, this proportion was strictly respected. See E. Picard, *Liban, État de discorde* (Paris: Flammarion, 1988).

Community	Per cent in the 1932 Census
Maronites	28
Sunnis	22
Shi'is	20
Orthodox	10
Other Christians	12
Druze	7
Alawis	1

34. This data is directly linked to social and economic conditions as well as to educational and professional facilities for women. According to the survey quoted in note 31, Shi'i women have 58 per cent more children than Christian women.

35. The controversy about the figures is very heated, thus reflecting the political stakes. Y. Courbage and Ph. Fargues, *La situation démographique au Liban* (Beirut: Éditions libanaises, 1974) put the Shi'ah at 27 per cent of the total Lebanese population, the Supreme Islamic Shi'i Council (SISC) puts them at 32 per cent (February 1976), and the (Christian) Lebanese Front places it at 20 per cent, according to *Les fiches du monde arabe*, no. I-L17a (Nicosia, 1980).

36. The Constitution of 1926 stipulates (art. 95) that the community allotment is adopted on a provisional basis. The national document signed at Taif in 1989 states (I-I-G) that the abolition of political communalism is "an essential national objective".

37. Theodore Hanf and Antoine Messara are the leaders of this analysis which favours *consociatio*. See T. Hanf *et al.*, *La société de concordance, approche comparative* (Beirut: Université libanaise, 1986).

38. Though on an equal basis between Christian and Muslim representation in parliament. J. Maïla, "Le document d'entente nationale, un commentaire", *Les cahiers de l'Orient*, nos 16–17 (1989–90).

39. The government agreement known as the National Pact was adopted at the time of independence (1943) by the Maronite President and the Sunni Prime Minister. It stressed symmetrical independence with respect to the surrounding Arab world and Western influence.

40. F. Ajami, *The Vanished Imam* (London: I. B. Tauris, 1986) pp. 63–72.

41. S. Khalaf, *Lebanon's Predicament* (New York: Columbia University Press, 1987) pp. 126–35.

42. E. L. Peters, "Shifts of Power in a Lebanese Village", in R. Antoun and I. Harik (eds), *Rural Politics and Social Change in the Middle East* (Bloomington, Ind.: Indiana University Press, 1972).

43. M. Abou Chedid Nasr, "Le gharîb (étranger) ou la difficulté d'être dans le discours libanais sur la guerre civile", *Mots*, no. 17 (1988).

44. The plot theory was very fashionable among Lebanese intellectuals. See G. Tuéni, *Une guerre pour les autres* (Paris: Lattès, 1985).

45. E. Picard, "La politique de la Syrie au Liban: les développements incontrôlables d'une stratégie ambitieuse", *Maghreb-Machrek*, no. 116 (1987).

46. The SISC was created by Law 72/67 (1967), which recognizes the Shi'i community in Lebanon as distinct from the Sunni. The SISC is the state's interlocutor for the community and exerts moral and legal authority on its members.

47. An Iranian of Lebanese ascendancy, Musa Sadr became a *mujtahid*, a doctor in theology and law after studying in Teheran, Najaf (Iraq) and Qom (Iran). He became *mufti* of Tyre in 1959 and was granted Lebanese nationality in 1961. He was elected president of the SISC for life in 1969.

48. The discourses of Musa Sadr quoted here were translated from the Arabic by Thomas Sicking and Shereen Khairallah in "The Shi'a Awakening in Lebanon: A Search for Radical Change in a Traditional Way", *Cemam Report 1974* (Beirut: Dar el-Mashreq, 1975).

49. *Al-Hayat* (12 February 1974) p. 2.

50. *Mithâq harakat Amal* (Beirut, 1975). See also *Al-Nahâr*, "A Political, Social and Economic Reform" (in arabic, 28 November 1975). The militia, *Afwaj al-muqaw ama al-lubnaniyya* (Lebanese Resistance Detachments), known by its acronym *Amal* (Hope), was formed sometime around June 1975 under the leadership of Musa Sadr.

51. The electoral law of June 1992 granted the Shi'ah 27 seats (out of 128) instead of 19 (out of 99).

52. *Amal Islami* was created in the summer of 1982 by Husayn Musawi after he had been expelled from *Amal* because he criticized the collusion between the movement's leadership and the Israeli Defence Forces (IDF) in South Lebanon. *Hizbollah* ("God's party"), founded in 1978, became active at the same time in the Baalbak–Hermel region. The following groups can be considered as being linked to *Hizbollah*: Islamic Jihad, al-Fajr al-Islami, Islamic Liberation Organization, Muslim Martyrs, al-Haqq, al-Jihad, Junud Allah, and The Young Muslim Mujahidun.

53. D. Bigo, "Les attentats de 1986 en France: un cas de violence transnationale et ses implications", *Cultures et conflits*, no. 4 (1992).
54. Especially Terry Waite's various interviews, and R. Auque, *Un otage à Beyrouth* (Paris: Filipacchi, 1988).
55. M. Kramer, "Sacrifice and Fratricide in Shiite Lebanon", *Terrorism and political violence*, vol. 3, no. 3 (1991).
56. In the periodical press, in leaflets and in books such as *Al-tahaddi wal-tasaddi*, vol. 2, "Al-shuhada al-arab al-lubnaniyyun fi junub lubnan, 1982–1987" (Damascus: Dar Tlas, 1988).
57. M. Kramer, "The Moral Logic of Hizballah", in W. Reich (ed.), *Origins of Terrorism, Psychologies, Ideologies, Theologies, States of Mind*, (Cambridge: Cambridge University Press, 1990).
58. See P. Brass, "Ethnic Groups and the State" in P. Brass (ed.), *Ethnic Groups and the State* (London: Croom Helm, 1985).
59. B. Anderson, *Imagined Communities: Reflections on the Origin and Spread of Nationalism* (London: Verso, 1983).
60. K. Salibi, *A House of Many Mansions. The History of Lebanon Reconsidered* (London: I. B. Tauris, 1988).
61. Beydoun, op. cit.
62. J. Malakey, "Notes on the Psychology of War in Lebanon", in H. Barakat (ed.), *Toward a Viable Lebanon* (London: Croom Helm, 1988).
63. J. McDougals, "La génération de la kalachnikov", in E. Fernea (ed.), *Women and the Family in the Middle East* (Austin: University of Texas Press, 1985).
64. D. Chevallier, *La société du Mont Liban à l'époque de la révolution industrielle en Europe* (Paris: Geuthner, 1971).
65. M. Gilsenan, "Domination as Social Practice. Patrimonialism in North Lebanon: Arbitrary Power, Desecration, and the Aesthetics of Violence", *Critique of Anthropology*, vol. 6, no. 1 (1986).
66. M. Johnson, *Class and Client in Beirut: the Sunni Lebanese Community and the Lebanese State, 1840–1985* (London: Ithaca Press, 1986).
67. Ajami, op. cit., p. 69.
68. David Riches (ed.), *The Anthropology of Violence* (Oxford: Basil Blackwell, 1986).
69. Pierre Bourdieu, *Esguisse d'une theorie de la pratique* (Paris: Librarie Droz, 1972).
70. A. al-Azmeh, *Ibn Khaldun, an Essay in Reinterpretation* (London: Frank Cass, 1981).
71. J. Hannoyer, "L'hospitalité, économie de la violence", *Maghreb-Machrek*, no. 123 (1989).
72. Norton, op. cit., p. 127.
73. P. Meney, *Même les tueurs ont une mére* (Paris: La Table ronde, 1986) pp. 160–1. H. al-Sheikh, *The Story of Zahra* (London: Quartet Books, 1986).
74. G. Delafon, *Beyrouth. Les soldats de l'islam* (Paris: Stock, 1989) p. 154.
75. G. Corm, "Hégémonie milicienne et problème du rétablissement de l'État", *Liban: les guerres de l'Europe et de l'Orient, 1840–1992* (Paris: Gallimard, 1992) pp. 25–57.
76. *Al-Dustûr* (14 October 1985). Estimations of the resources of the movement stood around US$10 million per month at the time Iranian and *Hizbollah*

was financing its Lebanese counterpart. After 1988, the Iranian government took direct charge of the movement and the sum decreased sharply.

77. E. Picard, "Le rôle du Front Libanais dans la guerre civile", *Maghreb-Machrek*, no. 90 (1980).
78. This has been strongly expressed in novels such as *Al-mustabidd* ("the tyrant") by Rachid al-Daif (Beirut: dar Ibn Rushd, 1983).
79. F. Khuri, "Secularization and 'ulama' Networks Among Sunni and Shi'i Religious Officials", in H. Barakat (ed.), *Toward a Viable Lebanon* (London: Croom Helm, 1988), p. 92.
80. F. Maatouk, *La représentation de la mort de l'imam Hussein* (Beirut: Institute des sciences sociales, 1974).
81. F. Khuri, *From Village*, p. 182 *et seq.*
82. See the yearly (every twelfth lunar month) report in *al-Hayât* from 4 February 1974 to 20 October 1983.
83. H. Kassatly, "Local Traditions and Islamic Traditions: The Dynamics of a Conflict Seen Through the Study of Specific Case: Funeral Rites in a Shi'ite Village in South Lebanon", *Islam and Christian–Muslim relations*, vol. 2, no. 1 (1991).
84. As suggested in E. Hobsbawm (ed.), *The Invention of Tradition* (Cambridge: Cambridge University Press, 1983).
85. M. Fischer, *Iran: From Religious Dispute to Revolution* (Cambridge, Mass.: Harvard University Press, 1980).
86. R. Rizkallah, "Contribution à une approche psycho-sociologique d'un rite chez les Chi'ites du Liban Sud", doctoral dissertation, University of Paris VII (1977).
87. Girard, op. cit., p. 30.
88. The number of *ta'ziyya* decreased in 1978–82. During these years, the Lebanese Shi'a were troubled by the disappearance of Musa Sadr in Libya in 1978 and the replacement of Husayn al-Husayni by Nabih Berri as the Secretary General of *Amal* in 1980.
89. J. Aucagne, "L'imam Moussa Sadr et la communauté chiite", *Travaux et Jours*, no. 53 (1974).
90. M. Ayoub, *Redemptive Suffering in Islam* (La Haye: Mouton, 1978), especially ch. 5.2, pp. 148–58, "the *ta'zîyah* celebration: its growth and general characteristics".
91. Muhammad Ghanim, *Al-mantiqat l-junûbiyya l-muhtalla. Qadhiyyat sha'b wa-ardh* (Beirut: dar al-Nasr, 1991).
92. *Pasdar e-Islam*, "Report from South Lebanon" (August–September 1984) pp. 56–9. Article translated from Persian into English by Rexane Dehdashti (Frei Universität, Berlin).
93. Ibid., p. 122.
94. Such as *al-'Ahd* or *al-Shirâ'*. See also M. Shams, *Al-harakat al-islamiyya fî Lubnân* (Beirut, 1991). And P. Vieille and F. Khosrovar, *Le discours populaire de la révolution iranienne* (Paris: Contemporaneité, 1990) vol. 2, "Entretiens".
95. C. Geertz, "Centers, Kings and Charisma: Reflections on the Symbolics of Power", in J. Ben-David and T. Clark (eds), *Culture and its Creators* (Chicago, Ill.: University of Chicago Press, 1977) p. 168.

96. N. Beyhum, "Espaces éclatés, espaces dominés: étude de la recomposition des espaces publics centraux de Beyrouth de 1975 à 1990", doctoral dissertation, University of Lyon II (1991) pp. 425–7.

97. D. Kertzer, *Ritual, Politics and Power* (New Haven, Conn.: Yale University Press, 1988) pp. 48, 65–8, 182 *et seq.*

98. Interview of Sheikh Muhammad Husayn Fadlallah to *Arabies* (September 1992) p. 14.

99. Notwithstanding that in the late 1980s, 45 per cent of the Shi'ah would rather declare traditional or secular allegiances, according to H. Kashan, "Antiwestern Perceptions Among Lebanese Shii College Students", PhD dissertation" American University of Beirut (1987).

100. O. Roy, "Les nouveaux intellectuels islamistes: essai d'approche philosophique", in G. Kepel and Y. Richard (eds), *Intellectuels et militants de l'islam contemporain* (Paris: le Seuil, 1990) p. 281 *et seq.*

101. R. Norton, "Lebanon: The Internal Conflict and the Iranian Connection", in J. Esposito (ed.), *The Iranian Revolution* (Miami: Florida International University Press, 1990).

102. A. Abul Khalil, "Ideology and Practice of Hizballah in Lebanon: Islamization of Leninist Organization Principles", *Middle Eastern Studies*, vol. 27, no. 3 (1991).

103. F. Khuri, "Secularization and 'ulama' networks among Sunni and Shi'i religious officials", in H. Barakat (ed.), *Toward a Viable Lebanon* (London: Croom Helm, 1988).

104. The composition of the *majlis al-shûra* is kept secret. See S. al-Husayni, "Hizbollah: haraka 'askariyya am siyasiyya am diniyya?", *al-Shirâ'* (15 March 1986) pp. 14–21.

105. See M. Kramer, "The moral logic ...", op. cit.

106. Interviews with Nabih Berri and Muhammad Husayn Fadlallah, *Al-Nahâr al-'arabi l-duwali*, no. 609 (9–15 January 1989) pp. 8–12.

107. E. Picard, "Le Moyen-Orient après la guerre froide et la guerre du Golfe", in Z. Laïdi (ed.), *Sens et puissance après la Guerre froide* (Paris: Presses de la FNSP, 1992).

108. Sheikh Hasan Nasrallah to *AFP* (3 October 1993).

109. David E. Apter, "Democracy, Violence and Emancipatory Movements: Notes for a Theory of Inversionary Discourse" (draft, June 1992).

110. Through nominations of 40 new MPs in June 1991 and the legislative elections of August 1992. The Parliament of 1992 is made up of 64 Christians: 34 Maronites, 14 Greek Orthodox, 8 Greek Catholics, 6 Armenians, 2 others; and 64 Muslims: 27 Sunnis, 27 Shi'is, 8 Druzes and 2 Alawites. A number of seats was "reserved" for each large or small militia group. See F. al-Khazen and P. Salem (eds), *Al-Intikhabât al-ûla fî Lubnân ma ba'd al-harb* ("The First Elections in Lebanon After the War") (Beirut: Dar al-Nahâr, 1993).

111. A. N. Hamzeh, "Lebanon's Hizbullah: from Islamic Revolution to Parliamentary Accommodation", *Third World Quarterly*, vol. 14, no. 2 (1993) p. 322 *et seq.*

112. With eight deputies, *Hizbollah* is the largest political group represented in the parliament.

7 "Reading" Violence: Ireland

PAUL ARTHUR

History is only one way of being significant. Memory gives the unofficial sense of history, effects an order not sequential but agglutinative. That is why we never ask our memories to line up rationally or sequentially, like soldiers on parade: they obey our orders, but not always or in the form we prescribe.

(Donoghue, 1991, p. 124).

It is possible that there is no other memory than the memory of wounds.

Czesaw Miosz

I INTRODUCTION

In terms of discourse theory what stands out very sharply is just how long the IRA is on retrievals and how short on projections. The uses of history as memory, not only to keep the past alive but sustain a sense of loss, deprivation, marginalization, not to speak of the affronts, discrimination, prejudice, and the like has sustained the tensed boundaries of the Irish working-class community extremely well and not only in places like Derry or West Belfast. Everywhere in the Six Counties there is evidence of the past. Handed out generationally, the stories of the fall, victimization, colonialization, pariahization, etc., are almost as deeply relevant as were myths of the eternal return among the Jews. Such memory was important not only within Northern Ireland but the Republic and the diaspora as well. For it fed the clienteles. To be sure, to keep alive, and use memory to intensify yearning, fresh events are required. And where the IRA was not the perpetrator, the various Protestant paramilitary organizations obliged. Between both sides, and of course under the watchful eyes of the British army, there were political events galore.

Indeed, observers of political violence in Ireland are confronted with two stark facts which complement each other: the longevity of the conflict

234

and the price which has been inflicted on the civilian community. In the present campaign there have been almost 3,400 deaths within a remarkably tiny land mass. In the period between 1969 and 1989 there have been 296 fatal casualties among republican paramilitaries (10.62 per cent of the total), 73 loyalist paramilitaries (2.62 per cent), 902 Catholic civilians (32.38 per cent), 575 Protestants (20.64 per cent) with the remainder being either unidentified or security forces. Republicans have been responsible for 1,608 (57.72 per cent) of these fatalities and loyalists for 705 (25.31 per cent) (Bruce, 1992, p. 294). What the figures bear out is that this has not been simply a low-intensity "war" but also a campaign of attrition visited primarily on civilian communities conducted often by their *soi-disant* defenders (and often with the complicity of the community). But they also mask the degree to which the violence is "controlled" as if it operated under strict rules of the game – unlike Lebanon from the 1970s or former Yugoslavia where ethnic conflict had been kept under artificial wraps for a generation or more and then exploded with an intense ferocity. The purpose of this chapter is to begin to understand the culture under which violence of this magnitude operated.

That culture wil be examined through the activities and the ideology of the Irish Republican Army (IRA) and its political wing, Sinn Fein. It will lay particular emphasis on the hunger strikes of 1980–1 because that enables us to establish the environment in which violence flourishes as well as retrieve from a past rich in symbols and in activity. We shall use Geertz's definition (1975, p. 89) of culture as denoting "an historically transmitted pattern of meanings embodied in symbols, a system of inherited conceptions expressed in symbolic forms by means of which men communicate, perpetuate and develop their knowledge about and attitudes towards life ...", while accepting that cultures "are systems of restraint upon mimetic rivalry. Without culture, mimesis can expand without limit" (Wright, 1987, p. 21). We shall examine the degree to which the Irish experience represents a revolutionary archetype through structural roots which can be traced back to the French Revolution (at least) and through the vast realm of strategies and tactics which have been deployed by Irish republicanism over the last two centuries. We shall be looking at the way "history" has been fashioned as a weapon for present purposes; and we shall consider that what has evolved in Ireland and in the diaspora "is not simply a movement or a secret army with a train of supporters but an Irish Republican world, fully Irish and so sharing all the nation's culture but also a world special, covert, accessible only to believers" (Bell, 1990, p. 8).

That last statement stresses the *sui generis* nature of the Irish experience. Add to that its incapacity for projection and its many layers of ambiguity.

The former can be found in Sean O'Faolain's quote: "the policy of Sinn Fein has always been, since its foundation, that simple formula: Freedom first; other things after" (cited in Patterson, 1989, p. 12). And the latter was enunciated by William O'Brien, an Irish nationalist MP, in the late nineteenth century when he spoke of violence as "the only way of securing a hearing for moderation". Moreover it is an ambiguity reflected in the two Irish traditions of loyalism and republicanism: in two of the great texts which reflect these traditions in the twentieth century – the 1912 Solemn League and Covenant (which proclaimed "Ulster's" loyalty to the United Kingdom) and the First Dáil's Declaration of Independence the same sentiments ("all means necessary" and "by every means at our command") – and appear as an intent of their commitment to resistance. So the practitioners of violence read it as a different kind of discourse rather than the antithesis of discourse: one that served the ends of freedom and equality by establishing an equality of influence – in one case Irish unity or, in the other, Ulster autonomy. In this sense Irish republicanism saw itself as an emancipatory movement. We will explore this claim by examining it as a discourse community whereby violence has been utilized as a particular way of creating power – some would say the only way.

Equally we need to be conscious of the relationship between violence-prone movements and the state, of the dynamic which is created and of the unpredictability caused by the sheer momentum of violence. By placing our emphasis on an examination of the present tense of Irish violence from the community level upwards we can begin to probe the problem from an "interior" as well as exterior perspective and the degree to which exterior pressure and insensitivity creates a rationale for interior "resistance":

> we want to examine, in many-sided terms, how violence evolves … we want to show how the most marginal people in a society bring up the most central issues – a circumstance which makes a democratic government less, rather than more, responsive, because it cannot allow its policies to be determined by minorities utterly lacking in political power or economic significance…. Our emphasis is on the people who do things in a context which is part of their own making. They are not mere surrogates for larger forces. Nor do they consider what they do to be separate from what goes on in the rest of society or the world. (Apter and Sawa, 1984, pp. 13–14).

This will enable us to make comparisons with emancipatory movements elsewhere as well as place Irish political violence in the context of a climate of violence generally in the twentieth century. One analysis of the latter traces the evolution of contemporary man-made mass death, the "death event", in opposition to the "authenticity paradigm" which accepts life and death as a unity in which dying acceptably

> is only possible if death has become ingredient in life itself. Life in turn can be lived in integrity only if death is already accepted as inseparable from it. Death is the wound life bears in itself: to know and accept this frees us from the pursuit of rational contemplation, integration into the cosmic whole, or more intense participation in the here-and-now, depending upon the pattern that organizes experience (Wyschogrod, 1985, pp. 2–3)

In short the paradigm is a "durable point of view, which posits a reciprocal relation between the manner in which death is appropriated and a person's moral situation" (Wyschogrod, 1985, pp. 2–3). The "death event", on the other hand, " 'lights up' the horizon from which death can be interpreted so that the death of the individual due to the natural hazards of existence seems insignificant when contrasted with ending one's life in an event of mass extermination" (Wyschogrod, 1985, p. 13).

> It is the death event and the death world which dominates the twentieth-century: ... the death event has undermined the schema of interpretation governing the meaning of death in Western culture, particularly the authenticity paradigm. The Socratic version of the paradigm presumes that the style of one's dying will reflect the character of one's life: the good man dies well.... The postmodern version of the authenticity paradigm ... places a priority on the quality of experience, on the actualization of the present as an eternal now so that the miracle of consciousness, of sheer existence, is affirmed.... But neither the older nor the newer version of the paradigm can any longer provide meaning for death in a world in which the death event, contemporary man-made mass death, has come into being, and in which a death-world, a sphere of life in which the living are forced to exist as if already dead, has been created. The death-world reflects the attempt of technological society, which is alienated from the life-world, the embedding matrix of all praxes, to repair the broken cosmos by an act of radically negative remythologizing: death becomes the ultimate meaning of totality. (Wyschogrod, 1985, p. 34)

The death-world manifests itself in the slaughter of the Great War in which nearly ten million people died, six thousand each day for fifteen hundred days creating a postmodern culture of mass death, a culture of necropolis, of impersonality, of the slave labour and concentration camps, of the "Red Guards in the Cultural Revolution [who] set out to destroy the four olds: old ideas, old culture, old customs and old habits". (Wyschogrod, 1985, p. 139 and passim)

The violence of the emancipatory movement becomes more comprehensible in this context. It allows for "the politics of the moral moment [where] the defects of society are interpreted as failures of the State" and where discourse is examined as a "combination of narratives and texts, in the context of transcending projects. They take on an independent life of their own whether from above, in the form of the discourse of the state, or below in an anti-discourse directed against the state" an anti-discourse which undermines ordered jurisdictions and stable networks by downgrading "conventional knowledge while claiming superior moral insight". The point of departure for contemporary emancipatory movement's "is not equality but *victimhood*. This is what distinguishes them from 'old' social movements which fought for equality or greater participation. Today it is the 'negativized other' which takes the moral measure of the whole ..." (Apter, 1992, p. 20; my emphasis).

The IRA fits into this model in that they are an inversionary protest movement which is

confrontational and violence-prone and relatively uninterested in rectifying this or that economic, social, or political ill, or providing greater political access to those deprived by reason of religion, gender, ethnicity, race, language, class, role, or other affiliations. Such affiliations are interesting only as provocations requiring the violation of standing jurisdictions. (Apter, 1992, pp. 22–3)

From the state's perspective the IRA's ongoing campaign is immoral and counter-productive. It was always thus; during the nineteenth century Britain introduced no less than seventy-three separate statutes of a coercive character for Ireland and habeas corpus was imposed on four different occasions for a total of eleven years. In 1829 Sir Robert Peel launched a model police service for metropolitan London rather than a "continental" gendarmerie. The introduction of emergency powers and the deployment of troops for domestic purposes was morally repugnant. Nor was it necessary. A modern society could handle these matters in a more enlightened way. But Ireland did not fit into that version of modernity; and the British state perceived her task there as sisyphean. Ireland could serve as an ideal laboratory for testing the role of policing in crisis politics – hence the creation of an Irish "gendarmerie" in 1836 which marked off Ireland as "different". The debate between local and centralized forces was resolved in favour of the latter. Law was to function as an expression of the impulse to order, especially since Ireland was being governed "in answer to a British strategic imperative rather than an imagined duty to the people" (Townshend, 1983, p. 102). Hence Britain's contribution to that relationship was her perception of a civilizing mission.

Consequently, if the "enforcement of the law provoked disorder, as it appeared to do in Ireland, the fault lay in English eyes not with the law but with the people" (Townshend, 1983, p. 102). One could argue that nineteenth-century Ireland was a good example of the difficulties encountered in the transition from an order to a choice model of democracy. As part of the United Kingdom it was to inherit liberal-democratic institutions but it was ruled by a rigid sense of order and it was not to benefit from economic growth elsewhere in the Kingdom: indeed, it may serve as a useful case study of internal colonialism (cf. Hechter, 1975, *passim*).

Viewed from below – and Ireland is essentially a bottom-up society with a demotic culture – in place of civilization and progress people read conquest and dispossesion and a loss of patrimony and a historic sense of grievance. Theirs was not

a world of choice from which some have been excluded but a universe of meaning in which insight is inspired by victimhood and confrontation [where] inversionary discourse is a means of altering prevailing boundaries and jurisdictions on the ground and in the mind. If they reject ordinary claims and demands and remain aloof from negotiation and the bargaining that accompanies democracy the intent is to create moral and symbolic capital in opposition to economic capital. (Apter, 1992, p. 23)

There is in Ireland a whole literary tradition devoted to the creation of moral and symbolic capital. It can be found in some of the poetry of the seventeenth century onwards, i.e. after the Elizabethan conquest had been assured with the defeat of the Irish forces at Kinsale in 1601 when the old Irish aristocratic order disappeared and 85 per cent of Irish land was transferred into the hands of new English colonists all of which affirmed the dispossesion of an entire caste (cf. O'Tuama and Kinsella, 1981, *passim*).

Ireland reverted to the strategem of wrapping itself in ambiguity because, as J. J. Lee (1989, p. 375) comments, it would be "unnatural for any society enduring the traumas of nineteenth-century Ireland, including not only colonization, but famine, depopulation, language loss and religious revival, not to have developed protective layers of ambiguity".

Another feature of Irish violence is its comparative lack of great texts and a meta-narrative, and the absence of a cosmocratic agent. It is not that there have not been "great men" in Irish history – Wolfe Tone and Padraig Pearse spring most readily to mind – but in a demotic culture the cult of personality plays second fiddle to the concept of the "risen people" engaged in an eternal campaign of resistance whereby "there is no place in Irish political culture for greatness outside the 'heroic' model. Greatness is defined in terms of defiance of the external enemy" (Lee, 1989, p. 406). In any case why a cosmocratic agent when the Almighty could be invoked? Rather than great texts and meta-narratives it was a visual culture of aurality and orality and, above all, a selective reading of "History".

II   HISTORY AS MEMORY

The preamble to the present Constitution of Ireland, Bunreacht na hEireann (1937), reads:

> In the Name of the Most Holy Trinity, from Whom is all authority and to Whom, as our final end, all actions both of men and States must be referred,
>
> We, the people of Eire Humbly acknowledging all our obligations to our Divine Lord, Jesus Christ, Who sustained our fathers through centuries of trial,
>
> Gratefully remembering their heroic and unremitting struggle to regain the rightful independence of our Nation,
>
> And seeking to promote the common good, with due observance of Prudence, Justice and Charity, so that the dignity and freedom of the individual may be assured, true social order attained, the unity of our country restored, and concord established with other nations,
>
> Do hereby adopt, enact, and give to ourselves this Constitution.

There you have a political culture laid out in one simple statement: a profound sense of piety, a deep sense of history and of grievance, and an essential sense of the contemporaneousness of the past. It is a narrative of dispossession overlaid by a fundamental religiosity secularized by a doctrine of manifest destiny. It is what has sustained Irish nationalism through centuries of failure.

The same message, shorn of its decorative verbiage and presented more graphically, appears in the 1916 Proclamation: "Irishmen and Irishwomen: In the name of God and of the dead generations from which she receives her old tradition of nationhood Ireland, through us, summons her children to the flag and strikes for her freedom." Both documents share the same profound beliefs but there the similarity ends. The distance between them is more than a question of time. Those who took control of the (twenty-six-county) Irish Free State after 1921 allowed it to develop "in a way that was a negation of the national revolution.... The leadership of the republican struggle passed effectively into the hands of non-republicans.... The new state had all the symbols of freedom but little of the substance of freedom" (Adams, 1986, p. 39).

Whereas the inheritors of modern Ireland shared this common loss of patrimony their "memory" moved in different directions as they attempted to establish a small independent state born in less than propitious circumstances. The Irish Free State was born with its national ideal unfulfilled, an embittered and armed minority within its boundaries, a humiliating economic reliance on its traditional enemy, the United Kingdom, and an economy which supported too many unproductive people. And yet it endured. Its very endurance was an affront to those who believed that the 1916 rising had been betrayed. They believed that the new political establishment indulged in what the Japanese call *mokusatsu*, that is killing with silence.

The mission of contemporary republicanism is no less than to restore that "memory", to rediscover Ireland's soul. And that entails tackling all those vested interests who have recreated modern Ireland. It means moving beyond the status of double marginality – the loss of patrimony in the past and the removal of "voice" in the present. It is an historic task in the heroic mould and it means returning to first principles. It works on the assumption of splendid failure within a characteristic Irish time-frame which

inclines Irishmen to a repetitive view of history and that such a view inclines them – perhaps in defensive wariness and from fear of failure – to prize the moral as against the actual, and the bearing of witness as against success. The *locus classicus* of this cast of mind is the Proclamation of the Republic on Easter Monday 1916. (MacDonagh, 1983, p. 13)

We shall see that there are constraints on that mission, that it should not simply be an "active remembering which reinterprets the suppressed voices of tradition" but that that reinterpretation has to be in a critical relation to modernity. This "entails the development of an *anticipatory memory* capable of projecting future images of liberation drawn from the past" (Kearney, 1988, p. 270).

(a)   1916

This recurring sense of timelessness reinforced by "the Christian view of God as standing outside time entirely", this "sense of timeless justice spreads in all directions in Ireland, north as well as south, to fundamental law as well as natural rights" (MacDonagh, 1983, pp. 6–7), enables Irish revolutionaries to elide time, to choose from the past to validate or invalidate actions of the present. There is no shortage of material from which to choose. In this century the 1916 Rising is the crucial event which explains all others. The President of Sinn Fein, Gerry Adams, has no doubts as to its significance and relevance to today's struggles:

> Oglaigh na hEireann (the IRA) today takes its historical and organizational origins from the forces which engaged in the Easter Rising of 1916, though one can trace its ancestry much further back if one wishes. But the circumstances which shaped the support for the IRA are above all the experience of the barricade days from 1969–72. These days are of continuing importance not just in terms of the IRA but because they saw the development of tremendous communal solidarity, more than a memory of which remains today'.   (Adams, 1986, p. 52)

"Memory" again and that umbilical link between 1916 and the barricade days of the 1970s!

The problem with 1916 is that the "philosophers and political thinkers of the 1916 Rising did not survive it, and this set the stage for counter-revolution. What we have done is that we have taken a step towards reversing the effects of the counter-revolution" (Adams, 1986, p. 160). There is an obvious tactical advantage in taking such a step. It removes republicanism from its conspiratorial ethos onto centre-stage as a mass movement built on communal solidarity. It combines the heroic failure of 1916 with the self-reliance and mutual solidarity created in the mobilization spaces of West Belfast, Free Derry and elsewhere. It has a wider *political* meaning:

We are not engaged in any new departure. We are committed absolutely to the objective of Irish independence.... In the past the republican movement was a separatist movement with radical tendencies. In its current embodiment the radical tendency is for the first time in control. (Adams, 1986, p. 162)

In this reading political violence should not be read as some sort of aberration. It has a motivation and a purpose, one of which is to bring order out of disorder. And if you take the long view – and the Irish tend to do so – you can begin to discern the outlines of order, first within the republican strongholds and then in the wider society.

In that respect the rising does not stand on its own. The Proclamation acknowledges as much when it alludes to the fact that in the past three centuries Irish independence had been asserted by force of arms on six separate occasions. This, the seventh, vindicated the honour of the current generation; and when Adams makes the connection between 1916 and the barricade days after 1969 he is "blooding" his own generation and placing the IRA at the forefront of emancipatory movements:

When organized confrontation connects generalized moral specific goals and moral moments are generated, they serve as historical punctuation marks. Although emancipatory movements rarely succeed on their own terms, when they are successful they leave more than a trace, or better, a deposit which at least for a time may alter thought, provoke new knowledge and challenge predispositions, providing authenticity to the next round of confrontational action. One might call this a politics of the high moral ground. (Apter, 1992, p. 29)

1916 was a significant historical punctuation mark, an exercise in calculated martyrdom whereby the blood of the fallen would irrigate the barren soil and create the climate for a new generation to continue with the struggle. It was another step along the road to national liberation begun by Wolfe Tone in 1798 and continued by the Fenians in the nineteenth century. It was part of a *narrative* – "the universal desire to make sense of history by retelling the story to ourselves". Narrative can serve to release new, and hitherto concealed possibilities, of understanding one's history ... the contemporary act of rereading (i.e. retelling) tradition can actually disclose uncompleted narratives which opens up new possibilities of understanding. That was what the 1916 Rising was about: "to examine one's culture, consequently, is also to examine one's conscience – in the sense of critically discriminating between rival interpretations" (Kearney,

1988, p. 272). And, it might be added, to impose one interpretation over another: those who gave their lives in 1916 were eschewing the constitutionalism of those MPs who believed that Britain could be trusted to deliver Home Rule after the Great War.

It was not for nothing that it was known as the poets' rising and that Yeats composed "The Rose Tree" as an imaginary dialogue between Pearse and Connolly using the Rose, the central Fenian symbol of Ireland, as a motif. They lament the withering of the Rose Tree of Ireland and its need to be rewatered if it is to blossom again. The last verse, as Kearney (1988, p. 218) reminds us, "provides us with one of the most succinct expressions of the whole mythic cult of sacrifice":

> *But where can we draw water*
> *Said Pearse to Connolly*
> *When all the walls are parched away?*
> *O plain as plain can be*
> *There's nothing but our own red blood*
> *Can make a right Rose Tree.*

It belongs to the evolution of an ideology of violence developing in five stages from the eighteenth-century agrarian societies to Padraig Pearse's *religion* of revolutionary nationalism of 1916 (MacDonagh, 1983, pp. 71–90). The latter was religious in that Pearse cast himself and his comrades "in various biblical roles, as witness-martyr, as scapegoat, as suffering servant, as redeemer ... of bearing testimony, even at the ultimate price, the laying down of life". Ireland's cause was a holy war:

> We pursue her [England] like a sleuth-hound; we lie in wait for her like a thief in the night; and some day we will overwhelm her with the wrath of God.... It is not that we are apostles of hate. Who like us has carried Christ's word of charity about the earth?   (Pearse, quoted in Edwards, 1977, p. 191)

And finally Pearse "merged orthodox Catholicism and Irish insurrectionism to form virtually a new faith" (MacDonagh, 1983, p. 87). Pearse has been held up as the role model of the late twentieth-century insurrectionists; and 1916 as part of the accretion of political violence.

But in two important respects the 1916 Rising marked Irish violence off as being "different". Lenin, no less, described it as having "a hundred times more political significance than a blow of equal weight would have in Asia or Africa", but went on to say tellingly that the Irish misfortune was that they "rose prematurely, when the European revolt of the proletariat had not yet matured". Secondly there "is nothing abnormal about violence as a means of expressing grievances in pre-political societies. What is abnormal is the use of violence as a means of political communication in a modern society." Not so in Ireland – there "violence continued to be used as an auxiliary to, or even a substitute for, modern political dialogue" (Townshend, 1983, pp. 14, 47). Other European examples later in the twentieth century call into question this sweeping assertion but it does highlight the degree to which violence in Ireland persisted, indeed its very normality.

(b) Wolfe Tone and the Diffusion of Texts

Irish republicanism is not replete with great texts. The 1916 Proclamation is held up as one. Some of the speeches and writings of Theobald Wolfe Tone (1763–98) are suggested as another. In both cases they are stronger on rhetoric than on logical projections, they are part of a language of resistance. Tone was a member of the Protestant élite involved in Irish radical politics and hailed as the Father of Irish Republicanism. He was the founder of the Society of United Irishmen in Belfast in October 1791 and the leader of a French invasion force to Ireland in 1798. The invasion went wrong and he was captured (but committed suicide before his execution). Although the '98 was a military disaster it continues to serve as a powerful myth. Twentieth-century republicans hold it as a central tenet of their belief that a non-sectarian working-class alliance is not only possible but inevitable as soon as Protestant workers divest themselves of those political leaders who have duped them for selfish economic reasons – a belief expressed as late as March 1988 when, in a party document, Towards a Strategy for Peace, Sinn Fein stated that the

> establishment of a society free from British interference, with the Union at an end, will see sectarianism shrivel and with the emergence of class politics a re-alignment of political forces along left and right lines. The Irish democracy thus created will usher in the conditions for a permanent peace, a demilitarization of the situation, and the creation of a just society.

This belief is sustained by paying homage to that small body of Protestants who identified with Irish nationalism down the centuries.

The most memorable of Tone's utterances first appeared in his published *Life* edited by his wife and son:

To subvert the tyranny of our execrable government, to break the connection with England, the never-failing source of all our political evils,
and to assert the independence of my country – these were my objects.
To unite the whole people of Ireland, to abolish the memory of all past
dissensions, and to substitute the common name of Irishman in place of
the denominations of Protestant, Catholic and Dissenter – these were
my means.

The distinction between "means" and "objects" was to become (conveniently) confused by some of his latter-day disciples but his service to
Irish revolutionaries was two-fold: he had identified the enemy as the connection with England; and he had launched a rhetorical non-sectarian
republicanism which continues to give succour to the present generation.
His *Life* was

> the first nationalist reading of Irish history, a reading that was to
> become the gospel of Irish republicanism. The elements of that gospel,
> stripped of its American and French terminology, are that the Catholics
> are the Irish nation proper; Protestant power is based on 'massacre and
> plunder' and penalization of the Catholics, reducing them to the slavish-
> ness which the Catholic Committee finally broke in 1792.   (Elliott,
> 1989, p. 310)

That message had a certain seductive charm in republican Belfast and
Derry in the 1970s.

Two further quotations from Tone deserve repetition. The first categor-
izes the agent to achieve freedom: "Our independence must be had at all
hazards. If the men of property will not support us, they must fall: we can
support ourselves by the aid of that respectable and numerous class of the
community, the Men of no property." And the second is as significant for
its location as its content. It is his speech from the dock during his trial for
treason in Dublin on 10 November 1798 when he asserted that the great
object of his life "has been the independence of my country.... For a fair
and open war I was prepared; if that has degenerated into a system of
assassination, massacre and plunder I do ... most sincerely lament it."
Here was heroic failure *and* magnanimity which added to the lustre of
Tone.

Indeed a cult developed around Tone after his death. The Young
Irelanders, a group imbued with the romantic nationalism which was
sweeping Europe at the time, set about venerating his name in the 1840s.
They made his final resting place, Bodenstown, a place for national pil-

grimage and erected a gravestone in his memory in 1844. To this day Bodenstown remains a holy place in Irish republican martyrology and attracts annual commemorations from all republicans including the Fianna Fáil Party, the largest party in the state. Through their newspaper *The Nation* they popularized details of his life, and they produced a booklet, *The Spirit of the Nation*, full of poems and ballads and aimed at a popular market. (Significantly Charles Haughey, Fianna Fáil leader and Taoiseach during the 1980s, chose the same title for a book of *his* speeches in 1986.)

The use of the popular handbook was to be a feature of nineteenth-century republicanism. A twopenny pamphlet, *Speeches from the Dock*, was published in 1867 and had reached its thirty-ninth edition by 1887. (An edition appeared as late as 1968 by which time it had gone through a curious metamorphosis when Tone's death was recorded as "murdered" by an "agent of England" rather than suicide.) As the title suggests the pamphlet was replete with traditions of noble failure and republican martyrdom. Different generations of school children were to learn by rote passages of some such speeches. Textuality and orality were prominent features in the propaganda arm of republicanism.

Republicanism, of course, was also about "armed struggle" and Tone's legacy may not have been so benign. In one respect he was the perfect archetype. He had no real sense of projection. His message was "almost empty of positive content. Breaking the connection with England, and the eradication of English influence in Ireland, were the obsessive concerns. What would succeed independence was hazy indeed, especially in social and economic terms" (MacDonagh, 1983, p. 75). As well as being a failure the '98 was in part sectarian in character. Besides his obsessive concerns he also "contributed the notion of the Republic (especially as epitomized by its Army, the repository of civic virtue and authority) and in general favoured the movement's totalitarian strain" (MacDonah, 1983, p. 89).

That strain can be detected in some of the Young Irelanders who mounted a hopeless revolt in 1848. One such was the Ulster Presbyterian, John Mitchell, whose new weekly *The United Irishman* inspired a succession of young intellectuals from the Fenians onwards. The Fenians, or the Irish Republican Brotherhood formed in 1858, tried during decades of conspiracy and intrigue everything from dynamite terror through a formal invasion of Canada from the United States and a rising in Ireland. One of their contributions was the opening up of a "second front" against the British in the United States: this organizational capacity of the Irish diaspora was to be a feature of the present campaign. Their successors (the Irish Volunteer movement) launched the heroic failure of 1916 which in turn inspired a guerrilla resistance. But the most noted disciple was Pearse who described Bodenstown as the "holiest place in Ireland; holier to us even than the place where [St] Patrick sleeps in Down. *Patrick brought us life but this man died for us ... the greatest of all that have died for Ireland* (Elliott, 1989, p. 416, my italics). According to Pearse, Tone bequeathed a gospel of Irish nationalism which "armed his generation in defence of it" as was apparent in Easter 1916.

(c) Independent Ireland: The Dynamics of Difference

In his study of Italian political violence David Moss (1992, p. 10) concerns himself with "ways in which 'politics' and 'violence' have been or might be bound together". Many contemporary democracies have arisen either through revolutionary violence or have been refined by political violence or the threat of such. They tend to fall back on political prudery and forget the role that violence played in their development. No one could deny the role of violence in the creation of independent Ireland nor the fuzzy dividing line between politics and violence. The bare facts are the following. When the leaders of the 1916 Rising were executed the Irish electorate abandoned the more moderate constitutional nationalists and identified with Sinn Fein. In the meantime an Anglo-Irish War raged until 1921 while negotiations went on with the British concluding with a Treaty in December 1921 which led to Irish partition and a horrendous civil war in which a much greater number were killed in fratricide then in the five years of revolutionary struggle against British forces.

The political system which developed in the Irish Free State did well to survive. It may well be that adversity has been the mother of invention and that one of its outstanding assets has been a richness in integrative resources. It became a truly homogenous political entity with Catholicism as the badge of Irish national identity. It was an identity which transcended the social and economic rigours of its beginnings and allowed the nation to adopt the mode of thought which saw Ireland as having a peculiar destiny in human affairs. It was de Valera in 1933 who expressed this internationalism when he urged his listeners to undertake the new mission "of helping to save Western civilization" from the scourge of materialism – in place of an empire of nations, a spiritual empire.

The fledgling state could not rely solely on the heroic ideal as a metaphor of political hope. It had developed as well a

dependency culture which had wormed its way into the Irish psyche during the long centuries of foreign dominance.... The Irish mind was enveloped in, and to some extent suffocated by, the English mental embrace. This was quite natural. A small occupied country, with an alien ruling class, culturally penetrated by the language and many of the thought processes of the colonizer, was bound in large measure to imitate the example of the powerful and the prosperous. (Lee, 1989, p. 627)

It was not that surprising that independent Ireland displayed many of the traits of dependency. Its parliamentary and administrative system had been closely modelled on the British. The existence of an entrenched minority unhappy with an unresolved border dispute inevitably led to a crisis in authority. Although the police service, the Garda Siochana, broke with Anglo-Irish practice and were unarmed, coercive measures continued to be used in Ireland after the British departure. They were part of what Mulloy (1986, passim) calls "dynasties of coercion". Besides the problem of the "unfinished business" of Northern Ireland continuing dependency had to be placed against a general backcloth of relative economic underdevelopment and the perennial problem of emigration whose influence was malign and paradoxical: "Emigration was the enemy of economic change, the solvent of economic conflict. More than any other single force it was responsible for the immobility of Ireland – the politics of constitutional forms apart – in the opening decades of the present century" (MacDonagh, 1977, p. 125). The consequence?: "a certain air of impermanence pervaded Irish society: so much of it was provisional, preparatory" (MacDonagh, 1977, p. 137). A similar pattern was to be found in independent Ireland; for example, more than 500,000 emigrated from the Republic between 1945 and 1961.

In addition to denting potential at home emigration helped to construct a sense of grievance among the Irish diaspora. One historian asserts that "as the central experience of post-famine life, emigration demanded interpretation in political and religious contexts". Central to this interpretation was "emigration as exile, as *in*voluntary expatriation, which was [made obligatory] by forces beyond individual choice and communal control: sometimes by fate or destiny, but usually by the political and economic consequences of 'British misgovernment', 'Protestant ascendancy', and 'landlord tyranny'". This "misperception of emigration as political banishment was integral to Catholic Irishmen's sense of individual and collective identity" (Miller, 1990, pp. 92, 96). In the United States it took the form of an "accentuated anti-Britishness" and of using that territory as a second front in the nineteenth century such as the Fenian raids on Canada. But while that grievance has been exploited during the present campaign of violence it would be foolish to assume that the Irish diaspora speaks with one voice (Arthur, 1991, pp. 143–63).

Partition was cited as the scapegoat for much of Ireland's ills including emigration. The ending of partition would deliver nirvana. Some politicians wanted to avoid the despotism of fact by eschewing the political. Garvin (1981, p. 193) unveils a political culture in which politicians "were puritanical, idealistic and austere and were adherents of the politics of national redemption rather than the politics of compromise, bargaining and pay-offs". There were those impatient pragmatic politicians, however, who were more concerned with the business of state-building. Sean Lemass, Fianna Fáil leader and Taoiseach, epitomized them: he "was an abrasive critic of those in Sinn Fein whose idealist insistence on the 'de jure' republic of 1919 prevented then from acknowledging current realities": "There are some who would have us sit by the roadside and debate abstruse points about 'de jure' this and 'de facto' that, but the reality we want is away in the distance and we cannot get there unless we move" (Patterson, 1989, p. 27).

Because Fianna Fáil had grown out of Sinn Fein (in 1926) and presented itself as the party of national redemption – its full title is "Fianna Fáil: The Republican Party" and its two core values are the unity of Ireland and the restoration of the Irish language – there is a certain degree of ambiguity about its brand of republicanism. After all some senior Fianna Fáil members were allegedly involved in gun-running for the beleagured northern minority in 1969, an activity which led to the acquittal of two ministers for trying to import arms into the country illegally. That may be one reason why Gerry Adams (1986, p. 46) writes of the "survival of instinctive republicanism amongst supporters of every party [in the Republic]". He could also have mentioned a study of the Irish political élite (Cohan, 1972, pp. 37–8) which illustrates that 45 per cent of that group had revolutionary experience and 18 per cent had participated in the 1916 Rising including two who became Taoiseach (de Valera and Lemass) and two who became President (Kelly and de Valera).

It is because independent Ireland is/was a failed political entity that the IRA (like the Red Brigades) "must base their claim to a political identity on difference: their distinction from the world of ordinary non-violent politics". But we shall see that as Sinn Fein began to confront the world of conventional politics that the dynamics of difference created its own tensions and contradictions because

they must be sensitive to the tensions provoked by the double necessity to address internal and external audiences in each single action and to transmit messages which simultaneously affirm a symbolic identity and show that violence is an effective – the only effective – method for reaching shared political goals. (Moss, 1992, pp. 10–11)

(d) Northern Ireland: The Politics of Community

By thrusting the Anglo-Irish problem into one tiny territory partition highlighted the religious and territorial dimensions to the conflict, bestowing on it an exceptionally high degree of intimacy. The role of religion cannot be ignored in Anglo-Irish relations. Garvin (1981, p. 36) comments that when England became embroiled in Ireland its concern was political and strategic rather than economic:

Even the emphasis on religious issues apparent in British policy drew much of its force from a fear of Catholicism as an international political organization actually or potentially hostile to the English post-revolutionary political settlement. It was evident that religion was central to Anglo-Irish relations because religion was central to the basis of *English* national political integration in the seventeenth century: Catholics in seventeenth-century Britain or Ireland were politically unassimilable because the British constitution was profoundly sectarian.... The confessional basis of Irish ethnic identity was unwittingly derived from the religious basis of the English national revolution....

Ireland became a country in which the religion of the people was not the religion of the state. This was without parallel in post-Reformation Europe so that religion was an additional Irish grievance against the English. The (Catholic) Church was the religion of around 75 per cent of the Irish people with a practice rate of about 80 per cent in the 1980s; as an instrument of cultural defence (particularly after the Irish language had been abandoned by the mass of the people in favour of English); as a body which asserted a distinctive national identity – for all these reasons it developed a certain heteronomous relationship with politics. Its Anglophobia rested on its self-image as the Church of the Penal Laws; and, after 1921, an exiled community separated from its co-religionists by an artificial and arbitrary boundary. In these circumstances it displayed the same traits as its flock. MacDonagh (1983, pp. 97–101) has analysed the systematic political ambivalence of the Irish Church in the last century and concludes with a commonplace which is profound: "The priests were but the populace writ large." He traces a triple ambiguity – the "recessional", the "gestural" and the "humanitarian" – which enabled the Church to maintain its position when the revolutionary secret society was rising in Ireland.

Religion, of course, is only one dimension of a sense of identity. One study (Burton, 1978, pp. 10, 125) of a Belfast Catholic working-class community stresses identity based on "kin, class, religion and territory" which has enabled the community to withstand virtually any depredation. Like Apter's Bogside (1990, p. 164) it remains "a community, not a war zone":

> Precisely because the community manages to contain and disperse the troubles into its institutional framework, its normative structure and its symbolic universes, it manages to prevent the dominance of external social control. In turn, the community retains enough of its solidarity to allow the militant activist to continue the politics of violence.... The possibility of an IRA campaign is dependent in this respect on the social structure of its community being able to withstand the deleterious consequences that urban guerrilla activity creates.

One of the social consequences has been "the suspension of due process [which has] seriously damaged the legitimacy of the law in the Catholic districts.... Into this void of legitimacy the IRA have injected their own quest for moral acceptability. The political struggle in the community is precisely the attempt to gain authority for their own law and order" (Apter, 1990, p. 164). Within this framework we can see why many people do not see political violence as aberrant.

Territoriality is another manifestation of the lack of harmony reflected in the sporadic outbursts of intercommunal hostility from the 1800s. In a particularly apt phrase Wright (1987, p. xiii) comments that in place of what "metropolitans call peace" Northern Ireland enjoyed at best "a tranquillity of communal deterrence". His research is complemented by an analysis of political violence in the north of Ireland since the 1800s. It depicts a polity which has operated under an intimidatory culture in which

> the power of intimidation springs from its essentially defensive nature. Local minorities were driven by violence and fear to move to other communities in which they could become part of a majority. They were often willing to encourage the expulsion of ethnic opponents from their new community.

The study argues that 'Northern Ireland's conflict is remarkable for the limitations on its violence rather than for the violence itself' (Darby, 1986, pp. viii–ix, 10). Darby's is an important study because it brings out several critical factors. One is the "normality" of Irish violence which has gone on for so long operating under a generally agreed code. A second is its insolubility which allows for "no resolution because the violence has not been intolerable". A third is that it is not blanket violence as such but violence visited on certain communities from time to time. This enhances the significance of community (and the lack of contact between communities).

Besides the historically encoded restraints on violence partition stressed the marginality of republicanism. In critical periods it could play a crucial role as defender of the Catholic community but that was not sustained and, in any case, it was in competition with independent Ireland with its alternative reality.

Within Northern Ireland it had to contend with constitutional nationalism and, until the 1980s Sinn Fein made no significant electoral impact – with the exception of the British general election of 1955 when it won two of the twelve Westminster seats and took the largest anti-partition vote since the foundation of the state. Republicans interpreted that as a vote of confidence in their methods and on 12 December 1956 the IRA launched "Operation Harvest", a disastrous border campaign which led to needless loss of life and a diminution of support for Sinn Fein. It was abandoned in February 1962: "Foremost among the factors motivating this course of action has been the attitude of the general public whose minds have been deliberately distracted from the supreme issue facing the Irish people – the unity and freedom of Ireland."

The dismal experience of Operation Harvest led to a rethink among republicans. Among those who engaged in this was Gerry Adams. His manifesto, *The Politics of Irish Freedom*, recognizes that since the 1930s there had been no real effort to map out "what type of a republic was aimed at…. We could not free the Irish people. We could only, with their support, create the conditions in which they would free themselves" (p. 8). Instead the movement had been controlled by a southern-dominated, deeply conservative and pietistic leadership. The failure of the 1956–62 campaign led to the beginnings of their removal but, even when the radicals took control, they moved with great caution. By 1967 the Ard-Fheis defined its aims as the establishment of a Socialist Republic "in accordance with the Democratic Programme of the First Dail. A year later Sinn Fein President, Tomas MacGiolla, assured the delegates that 'socialism has nothing to do with Atheism and Totalitarianism as is evident from a superficial reading of Connolly. Neither is it a philosophy which must be imported. It is part of the Republican tradition since the founding of the United Irishmen'" (Patterson, 1989, p. 104). Yet again the elision of history and the creation of an iconography! The movement had some way to go yet before it addressed the cartography of the new republic.

III CONTEXT

When protracted violence re-erupted in Northern Ireland in 1969 republicanism was unprepared partially because it had been engaged in its own internal debate. It lacked the resources to defend its community but, paradoxically, that meant a stronger sense of communal solidarity because often it was the ordinary citizen rather than a revolutionary élite which organized the barricades to defend the areas of Catholic west Belfast against an onslaught launched by protestant mobs with RUC complicity. It was in this milieu that the new generation began to assert themselves.

They started with several assets the most crucial being that "the whole process was so *natural* as to be beyond comment". Attitudes were more important than weapons, and that was to be the key to republican strategy: "Nothing had to be imported, nothing fashioned by ideologues, nothing sold to the people, nothing secretly arranged because of events. All that was needed was to exploit the existing reality" (Bell, 1990, p. 41). That reality was based on a memory of past oppressions and the nature of an intimidatory culture with the emphasis on territoriality and the need for vigilance. Settler vigilance, whether in the form of loyalist mobs or locally recruited militias (offical and unofficial), "taught the natives that power and self-assertion were the property of those who could successfully inflict violence" (Wright, 1987, p. 130). The result was a circularity of violence whereby "vigilance of power perpetually generates the symptoms of rebellion it purportedly guards against; while rebellion on the principle of collective responsibility validates the anxieties of the dominant" (Wright, 1987, p. 124).

It was a circularity which predated the establishment of Northern Ireland – indeed it was at the heart of the essential weakness of British rule in Ireland. As early as 1644 Ulster Protestants were engaged in contractarian social practice which had evolved through "the centuries of weak central government in the kingdom" by which the nobility and gentry "had developed a tradition of entering into 'bands' for mutual protection". This tradition of "public banding" was a manifestation of settler vigilance whereby protestant Ulster settlers sought their own security throughout the centuries (Miller, 1978, pp. 12, 25). It was a practice which asserted itself during the final Home Rule crisis (1912–14) with the creation of the Ulster

Volunteer Force (UVF) and the establishment of a Provisional Ulster Government under the leadership of Sir Edward Carson and Sir James Craig. Hence their reading of the 1920–1 settlement was that a "band had been entered into, its adherents had stood on their guard against the enemy, and in the end the sovereign authority seemed to have contracted with the banded community to exercise its sovereignty in the territory in question: to hold the pass against the king's enemies and their own" (Miller, 1978, p. 132). In more recent times sections of protestant Ulster perceived the civil rights' campaign as a challenge to their very existence and entered into a form of public banding because they believed that state power could not monopolize coercive relationships. In that situation "the whole system is one of threatened violence in which the state is a feeble pivot between its ostensible supporters ... and the natives" (Wright, 1987, p. 122). The state's over-reaction to the civil rights' challenge raised the question of how institutional democracy deals in structural terms with an emancipatory movement which created "a discourse community at variance root and branch with the state itself". One way to approach this is to examine the power of discourse as a "mytho-logics [whereby the] creation of myth out of events in the telling provides symbolic logic" (Apter, 1992, p. 15).

The problem of constructing a "mytho-logics" is that there "is no unitary master narrative of Irish cultural history, but a plurality of transitions between different perspectives" (Kearney, 1988, p. 16). In this case "where the text of imagination interweaves with the context of history" (Kearney, 1988, p. 10), Irish discourse was ready to invoke history but reluctant to come to terms with it. Kearney sees the tension in Irish discourse between the revivalist and the traditionalist in which the modernist tendency is characterized by "a determination to *demythologize* the orthodox heritage of tradition in so far as it lays constraints upon the openness and plurality of experience"; and he cites Ricoeur on the paradox of "how to become modern and return to sources; how to respect an old dormant civilization and take part in universal civilisation" (Kearney, 1988, pp. 13, 16).

That was the predicament which confronted republicanism from 1969 onwards. They were able to present politics as a narrative of oppression. They found no difficulty in revealing the state's hegemony in incidents like the introduction of internment in August 1971 when only republicans were lifted. They demonstrated their capability to resist compromise when the Northern Ireland government and parliament were prorogued in March 1972. Rather than accept that as a "victory" they followed the predictable pattern of emancipatory movements "to move from immediate ends to ultimate values and to define their objects in terms of the widest moral imperative". But by standing outside the normal framework of politics "using doctrine, ideology and theory to challenge the *doxa*" (Kearney, 1988, p. 59) they confront the problem that adherents "of violence as a political technique need to show that violent acts can have political consequences. They must demonstrate that some kind of exchange relation holds – or can be created – between the worlds of violence and politics." Equally governments "need to tread a delicate line between showing that violence is powerless to acquire any kind of political exchange value and formulating the political responses which demonstrate their commitment to its repression" (Moss, 1992, p. 12). Irish republicans relied on two components: repression and the elevation of the symbolic side of political life.

IV   THE "MYTHO-LOGICS" OF CONTEMPORARY REPUBLICANISM

> Man depends upon symbols and symbol systems with a dependence so great as to be decisive for his creatural viability and, as a result, his sensitivity to even the remotest indication that they may prove unable to cope with one or another aspect of experience raises within him the gravest sort of anxiety.   (Geertz, 1963, p. 99)

It might be argued that Irish political violence of the past twenty years has moved from the extra-institutional protest of the civil rights' movement through a politics of oppression to a politics of sacrifice in search of a logical project.

Interestingly, it was symbolism as much as anything else which brought Gerry Adams into politics. During a British general election in October 1964 Sinn Fein displayed a tricolour in the windows of their election offices contrary to the Flags and Emblems Act (1954). When the RUC removed it forcefully two days of intense rioting broke out with fifty civilians and twenty-one RUC injured: "I was in school at the time but the Divis Street events concentrated my mind on politics. I already possessed a vague sense of discontent and the naked display of state violence against the people of the Falls made me feel I did not want merely to stand by looking on" (Adams, 1986, p. 2). The movement he joined was badly split – following the debacle in Belfast in August 1969 – over whether the IRA should enter into a "National Liberation Front" in close co-operation with organizations of the "radical left". There were other issues such as whether the republican movement should recognize the legitimacy of Westminster and Leinster House; military policy; the maintenance of internal discipline; and whether to campaign for the abolition or retention of Stormont. But the "primary problem" according to Adams (1986, p. 35) "was lack of politics, a shortcoming which was to remain even after guns had become plentiful". The Dublin leadership was rejected in Belfast where "the various defence groups, created in the barricaded Catholic ghettoes in the aftermath of the violence, were often led by republicans who had resisted the new direction or had dropped out in disgust" (Patterson, 1989, p. 120). It is important to note that the rejection of Dublin leadership was based not so much on geography as on an appreciation as to what was acceptable in the Catholic ghettoes – and Marxism was not.

Henceforth there were two organizations, the Marxist Officials and the more traditional Provisionals. The latter title "rang a bell in the memory of the Irish people. The men of 1916 had signed the Proclamation as the provisional Government of the Irish Republic" (MacStiofain, 1975, p. 142). That advantage was countered by the fact that the organization remained in the hands of the Officials – in the meantime. In the longer term it was the Provisionals with their combination of extra-institutional protest and terrorism who were able to claim the mantle of contemporary republicanism.

In January of 1970 the seven-man Army Council met to plan strategy without an organization, without any money and without any arms. Earlier a reorganized Republican Publicity Bureau had issued the Provisional Council's first public statement (on 28 December 1969) which summed up (in part) its ideology:

We declare our allegiance to the 32-county Irish Republic proclaimed at Easter 1916, established by the First Dail Eireann in 1919, overthrown by force of arms in 1922 and suppressed to this day by the existing British-imposed six-county and twenty-six county partition states.

Add to that a statement issued by the Provisional IRA in January 1970 and one begins to see how the movement was appropriating the entire tradition of Irish republicanism. The latter, *Where Sinn Fein Stands*, was an exclusivist statement: "Ours is a socialism based on the *native Irish tradition* of Comhar na gComharsan, which is founded on ... our Irish and Christian values." To which they added, "we take our inspiration and experience from the past". There you have a claim of continuity to the republican pantheon. It was a movement embedded in Mother Ireland, neither alien nor unfamiliar.

It was this very familiarity and intimacy which sustained the movement while it began to put in place a durable structure. Familiarity and intimacy took many forms but above all there was/is a sense of victimhood. The Provisionals represented the Catholics of West Belfast who had endured the pogroms of August 1969. And they represented the minority in Northern Ireland which had been abandoned while the Irish government stood idly by. Familiarity and intimacy were central to a demotic culture, to generational continuity and the aurality and visuality of the streets. Gerry Adams, who was to be interned for his republican activities and was to rise to be President of Sinn Fein (as well as MP for West Belfast), personified all of it.

He came from a family of republican "aristocrats". Both his parents came from highly respected (because activist) republican families who could trace their lineage in the struggle back to, at least, 1918, and his father had been imprisoned in the 1940s for his involvement in the movement. Indeed at one stage, in the early 1970s, his father, brother, two cousins and an uncle were all in the Maze prison (c. Keena, 1990, pp. 16–23). This passing of the baton could be found in both communities even among those who were not so politically committed. One of the conclusions of a social anthropological study of a rural community was that it "seemed that even the adults' attitude to children and adolescents were made more friendly by the strength of the recognition that it was on them that adults had to count for their fulfilment of their political hopes, and for this if for no other everyone was anxious to involve the young in community life" (Harris, 1972, p. 199). Curiously this reinforces the degree to which this particular emancipatory movement is deeply conservative.

Familiarity was to be found in a long tradition of using song as an instrument of political propaganda. As early as 1775 and 1776 a series of booklets known as *Paddy's Resource* or *The Harps of Erin* were published with song and broadside. Young Ireland followed the trend self-consciously when it announced in *The Nation* (11 March 1843) – "We furnish political songs to stimulate flagging zeal, or create it where it does not exist." And it was James Connolly, the socialist leader in the Easter Rising, who stated unequivocally the power of the political song: "No revolutionary movement is complete without its poetical expression. If such a movement has caught hold of the imagination of the masses, they will seek a vent in song for their aspirations." When combined with resistance the power of the ballad can take the struggle beyond mere conspiratorial activity. Its role should not be underestimated. Much of the balladry of the present campaign lacks the subtlety of "poetical expression" – such as the childrens' chant, "If you hate the British army clap your hands" – but its very directness makes it amenable to a vastly wider audience.

It was there already, of course: indeed, the sense of community helps to explain the intensity of the conflict. Many of Belfast's nineteenth-century riots centred around a form of competitive localism. As a result people felt safer living among "their own". In Belfast in 1968 two-thirds of all families lived in streets in which 91 per cent of the households were of the same religion. Often the degree of denominational interaction was minimal. Rural areas conformed to the same pattern. In a typical area there was a fairly clear segregation with Catholics owning 75 per cent of the (poorer) hill farms and protestants 65 per cent of the lowland farms. The sale of land:

> was more often directed to its symbolic worth than its monetary value. Ownership of a farm meant the symbolic occupation of an area. The transfer of a farm from a Protestant to a Catholic, or vice versa, was an issue that was emotionally more important if the townland in which the farm was situated had previously been owned entirely by the members of one faith. (Harris, 1972, p. 168)

This can be understood in the context of Catholic loss of patrimony dating back to Tudor times. Confiscation took on a more systematic turn with the Plantation of Ulster beginning in 1607 which entailed the building of twenty-three new towns to protect the new settlers. By 1703 Catholics owned less than 14 per cent of the land.

So territorial integrity was keenly felt, and riots often occurred as a result of encroachment by the enemy: "shatter zones", a kind of neutral battle area, were established. Even in what became known as the battle of the Bogside in August 1969 the fighting was always at boundaries represented by mainly mixed streets, or on the borders of separate Catholic and Protestant streets. It sometimes looked as if both sides had agreed on certain battlegrounds and stuck to them. But in Belfast the rules of the game were breached with the street-burnings of August 1969. And that was not forgotten. In an anonymous letter to the *Irish News* (12 March 1992) one correspondent gave three reasons as to why he voted Sinn Fein:

> The past. I have vivid memories of Dover Street and Percy Street burning, of petrol bombs raining down on Bombay Street and Coates Street. And I have vivid memories of the men and women prepared to put their lives on the line to defend these and other areas. I know where these men and women stand today.

The present. Members of Sinn Fein are always present to help with any and all complaints. Their constituency work is undoubtedly by far the best there is available. Given the constant harassment and attacks on Sinn Fein members, the provision of this service is remarkable.

The future. The British Government never had and never can have any right to be in Ireland. How can I, who does not support the armed struggle of the IRA, put pressure in a peaceful, lawful fashion on the British Government to leave Ireland? By casting my vote for Sinn Fein.

It is against that backcloth that we see the particularism of Free Belfast and Free Derry and other insular communities. As the troubles deepened so did the need to cling on to the familiar, and that often meant a life of fear and monotony and the development of certain skills.

One was the concept of "telling":

the pattern of signs and cues by which religious ascription is arrived at in the everyday interaction of Protestants and Catholics.... Telling is based on the social significance attached to name, face and dress, area of residence, school attended, linguistic and possibly phonetic use, colour and symbolism. It is not based on undisputed fact but, as an ideological representation, is a mixture of "myth" and "reality".   (Burton, 1978, p. 37)

Telling is part of the warp and woof of everyday social life in Northern Ireland. The community has developed its own highly sensitive antennae whereby "one of the other side" or a "stranger" can be identified immediately. It is is like a sixth-sense covering everything from the rhythm of speech to the distance between one's eyes.

Telling is reinforced by a staple diet of self-imposed censorship. Three provincial dailies, supplemented by forty-three local newspapers, tend to reflect their readers' political outlook; and, historically, the Catholic community had little faith in the BBC (cf. Cathcart, 1984, *passim*). So the troubles created their own outgrowth of community newspapers and political pamphlets as if the usual sources of information were tainted. Some localities turned to pirate radio. Radio Free Derry was the first to broadcast in January 1969. It was followed by Radio Free Belfast from the Falls Road area in August 1969, which proclaimed in its first broadcast: "We have not erected barricades to keep Catholic and Protestant apart. We have erected barricades because the people of the barricaded districts are terrified and must be protected against a possible repetition of the savagery of the 14th and 15th of August. We are not going to ever again risk the murder of children and innocent people" (Arthur, 1974, p. 131). The message encapsulates the fears of a whole community which believed (with some cause) that a pogrom would be visited upon them. The (Protestant) Shankill Road responded with Radio Orange.

In these circumstances it was hardly surprising that communities drew their boundaries to include those, and only those, who subscribed to their traditional and customary practices. A visitor to Northern Ireland is struck by the physical apartness of the two communities. Their territorial boundaries were marked by distinctive symbols: the Union Jack or the Irish Tricolour or Connolly's Starry Plough; wall murals celebrating William III or Mother Ireland, or acting as warning signals to the other side; graffiti; kerb stones in some areas displaying party colours. It was a visual culture. But it was not a culture which had to be invented by the troubles. Those who founded the Provisional IRA had a ready-made audience and an ideal setting. The wall murals, for example, were part of a tradition which went back to the turn of the century in the loyalist community and was visible in party banners for as long as the Orange Order and the Ancient Order of Hibernians marched on their traditional parades. They were part of a folk tradition, a "people's art", brought up to date to allow for present realities. They were seen as a defensive celebration of one's heritage rather than an offensive symbol of hatred (cf. Loftus, 1990, *passim*). Bowyer Bell (1991, p. 34) read them as a "sign that communication has occurred, that commitment exists, that the makers have faith. The faithful may be thereby encouraged, the wavering influenced and the opposition defied. The central dynamics of republican murals in Belfast is an act of faith, producing not good works but reinforcement and renewal."

The standard veered from the crude to the ornate but all had a message to convey ranging from *"Provos Rule – Ireland for the Irish"*; to the hortatory *"The Great only Appear Great because We Are on Our Knees: Let Us Rise"*; to the enigmatic – *"For Those Who Believe No Explanation is Necessary. For Those Who Don't Believe No Explanation is Possible"*. Many were highly professional and drew on resistance struggles elsewhere with references to the ANC and PLO. All of this represents what Moss (1983, p. 92) has entitled "the production and diffusion of texts" which

> may vary in length and complexity from single-sentence claims of responsibility for actions to analyses of specific actions or organizations to full-scale political tracts.... Texts acknowledging responsibility for actions over the Red Brigades' signature convert otherwise unrelated episodes of violence into the elements of a political strategy, so that

their production and diffusion must be a necessary part of constructing an identity....

Moss identifies a crucial component of republican endurance – violence and suffering are not random but can be explained by the desire to move beyond marginality in which the individual reinforces the collective in search of the ideal: "Commitment is defined as obligation of self to an emergent society, a society-in-becoming, with no anticipated faults or visible imperfections, a utopic community which both the truth and the form it takes politically, constitute an appropriate next stage of the human condition" (Apter, 1992, p. 28). Such a project can have a significant religious dimension.

Translated into the realities of Northern Ireland in 1970 the Provisional movement appropriated the religion of nationalism – with its emphasis on redemption and sacrifice – enunciated by Pearse. 1970 was an extension of the genealogical invocation of 1916, which was in its turn an extension of: we can go back to the beginning of time. It is precisely this use of "myth" as expressing "the absolute truth because it narrates a sacred history; that is a trans-human revelation which took place at the dawn of the Great Time, in the holy time of the beginning ... by *imitating* the exemplary acts of the mythic dieties and heroes man detaches himself from profane time and magically re-enters the Great Time, the Sacred Time" (Eliade, cited in Kearney, 1988, p. 212) which gives the present campaign its great powers of endurance. Because "sacrifice obeys the laws of myth not politics [it can] operate on the assumption that victory can only spring from defeat, and total rejuvenation of the community from the oblation of a chosen hero or heroic elite". Kearney (1988, p. 213) goes on to consider myth as both seeking to transcend the logic of pragmatic political action *and* influencing the political consciousness of a people in a significant manner. We will see that the hunger strikes serves as a paradigm of both. And we will need to consider whether there is any tension between transcending pragmatic politics while influencing the wider body politic.

V   BEYOND EXTRA-INSTITUTIONAL PROTEST

It was as well that the republican movement could rely on ready-made assets because the speed and nature of events in August 1969 took everyone by surprise. The IRA had very little weaponry in Belfast (the scene of the most intense fighting) and too few volunteers on the ground. A local republican was responsible for forming the Central Citizens' Defence Committee, a co-ordinating body for the defence of the area, which elected ninety-five delegates to represent 75,000 people in the mobilization space known as Free Belfast while the infant movement attempted to build up resources in terms of weaponry, infrastructure and intellectual content. The first two could be attained relatively easily by relying on the ready-made assets such as over-reaction by the state apparatus and the emotional commitment of sections of the diaspora. The last was to present greater problems perhaps because, as a "clear distinction between 'military' and 'political' wings of any armed organization [it was] merely the extreme resolution of a general problem: how the powers to establish the identity of groups, by violence or by texts, are actually distributed in any group claiming distinctiveness". In this organizational division of labour within an armed group concerned with "the syntax and semantics of violence itself", where the producers of violence may be separated from "the producers of meaning", they may reproduce "in the world of armed struggle itself the cleavage between armed struggle and its opponents" (Moss, 1992, p. 11). It was not an issue which confronted the Provisional movement at the outset. They saw their role as acting as defenders of their community and as appropriating the mantle of true republicanism. In that respect they needed to demonstrate their distinctiveness from any other like-minded group and insert themselves as the heirs to the men of 1916. Here they were establishing the dynamics of difference.

The first to be challenged was the Official IRA. After all it controlled the organizational key to contemporary Irish republicanism, an organization which had been superior in the production of texts although deficient in the production of violence. Marxist vaporizing was of little use to those who desperately sought the defence of their communities. Their removal was aided and abetted when they made themselves redundant in May 1972, after they declared a ceasefire because they believed continuing violence thwarted their socialist objective of a non-sectarian working-class solidarity. In any case they had other problems. They suffered a setback with the formation of the Irish Republican Socialist Party (IRSP) in December 1974. The IRSP claimed to be Marxist and militarist, and soon spawned the Irish National Liberation Army (INLA) after a feud with the Officials. The outcome was the violent deaths of some prominent republicans and a further diminution of the Official IRA. INLA (and later splinter groups such as the Irish People's Liberation Organization [IPLO]) occupied the wilder shores of the physical force tradition but never had mass appeal. Thus the Provisionals *appear* to have met its first political objective of holding the moral high ground in contemporary Irish republicanism.

But that, as we shall see, would be to ignore the general problem of producers of text and producers of violence in the more inclusive world of pragmatic political action.

In some respects the republican movement was shaped by events external to itself. The Catholic community had lost what little faith it had in the system following August 1969. The police were not to be trusted; the army had turned from protectors into aggressors – "You're giving them tea now; I wonder what you'll be giving them in six months' time" was the rhetorical (and prophetic) question of one radical when the troops came in to relieve a bedraggled RUC – especially after a Conservative government came into office in June 1970. Neither the British nor the Irish nor the Stormont government could hope to win the confidence of the Catholic community. London's reform programme led to a revolution in rising expectations which it could not hope to meet after more than fifty years of benign neglect. In any case the Conservatives turned from reform to a security response. Dublin had stood idly by when Belfast was burning in 1969, other than set up a few field hospitals around the border. Stormont remained the citadel of unreconstructed unionism as the introduction of internment was to demonstrate.

The consequence of all this was that street rioting increased significantly and became more sophisticated. The death of the first soldier on the streets in February 1971 convinced Unionists that the IRA had declared war. The IRA, according to Gerry Adams, had recruited at such a rapid rate that it was able to carry out 125 bombings in June and July 1971 alone. The Northern Ireland Prime Minister, Brian Faulkner, persuaded the British authorities that he could halt the troubles at a stroke with a massive internment swoop of all known republican activists. It had been a security measure which had been tried (moderately) successfully in 1921–4, 1938–45 and 1956–62. It was tried again on 9 August 1971 with the arrest of over 300. It lasted until 5 December 1975 by which time 2,158 "graduates" had passed through the internment camps. In 1978 the RUC Chief Constable was to describe it as a "disaster" in political and security terms. Internment "had a major effect in making people conscious participants in the struggle. Those who were already politicized were not surprised, but there were many Catholics who did not believe that such a thing could happen, and to them internment came as a crucial indication that the road to reform was blocked off" (Adams, 1986, p. 56).

It failed miserably to control the violence; of the 172 who died violently in 1971 only twenty-eight were killed before the introduction of internment. The whole operation was perceived by Catholics as yet another attack on their community. The Catholic middle class withdrew from all publicly appointed bodies and 30,000 Catholic households went on a rent and rate strike in protest. Internment also led to the arraignment of the British government before the European Court of Human Rights at Strasbourg on a charge of torturing fourteen men in army barracks in Northern Ireland between August and October 1971. Final judgement, in January 1978, found against the U.K. for degrading and inhuman treatment. Furthermore, no punishments had been meted out, and no promotions – in either the army or the police – had been affected of those guilty of using the technique.

The incident which had an immediate and devastating effect on the relationship between the army and Catholics was Bloody Sunday, 30 January 1972, when an illegal anti-internment march resulted in the statutory skirmish between the army and a small section of the march and escalated into the deaths of fourteen male civilians. An offical tribunal consisting of the Lord Chief Justice, Lord Widgery, failed to prove that any of the victims had been carrying weapons and the authorities felt it necessary to make "out of court settlements" to their relatives. Bloody Sunday had a profound effect on Ulster Catholics and on the Heath government. The former totally and irrevocably withdrew their consent from the Unionist regime, and the latter imposed direct rule on 24 March 1972:

> ... it was a time of complete and utter jubilation ... a feeling that so quickly after the events of 1968/69, something that was hated, something that was symbolic of all that was wrong in the state had been removed. And probably most people who were anti-Unionist felt quite rightly that they had played a part in the removal of Stormont. The IRA was seen as acting on their behalf. (Adams, 1986, p. 56).

VI ESTABLISHING A COMMUNICATIVE FRAMEWORK

The nature of Irish political violence has resonances elsewhere, for to:

> focus on the communicative dimensions of violence is to take seriously the Red Brigades' reiterated claim that their actions are intended as "armed propaganda" designed to illustrate new possibilities of political action, secure some form of political recognition for the group and provoke effects among opponents which will contribute to their own projects. By the systematic use of violence conveying the rejection of the current rules the Red Brigades establish a frame for communication

between themselves and the political defenders of that order, whose actions and inactions cannot avoid interpretation as responses, direct or indirect, to the [sequence of] acts of violence.   (Moss, 1983, p. 85)

The fall of Stormont was indeed perceived as a victory of heroic proportions. Direct rule held out real possibilities if only violence was seen as being more than reactive and random. Armed struggle had to become armed propaganda and the morality of armed struggle had to withstand the most intense scrutiny; and the Catholic community needed to be assured that if armed struggle "did not exist there would be no hope of getting change". They would have to believe that "IRA volunteers are actually civilians, political people who decide for short periods in their lives to take part in armed action.... The reality is of people who have consciously decided that armed struggle is a political necessity ..." (Adams, 1986, pp. 64–5). The tacit support of the community was essential. In this the IRA was assisted by the growth of loyalist paramilitarism some of whose activities, Catholics believed, were condoned by the authorities. It was only after the British government had imposed direct rule that the first loyalists were interned; and in March 1973 the Prime Minister went so far as to dub them "disloyalists".

But security-force incursions were a more pronounced irritant. Burton's observer-participation in one self-contained Catholic ghetto in Belfast, Anro, confirms a sense of anomie where dozens of people had been killed and many more seriously wounded within its streets: "The area has been saturated by troops and is under constant surveillance. Hundreds of the district's inhabitants have been interned or detained or sentenced to prison. Such a violent affront upon the conventional activities of the community might well have resulted in anomic breakdown" (1978, p. 9). He sets out to explain why anomie – "a condition in which our existing knowledge and beliefs are no longer able to cope with a radical new situation. A resulting struggle takes place to reconstruct both mental and moral worlds" – has been contained "whereby the existing culture of Anro stretches to accommodate the unknowable and unthinkable, reinterpreting events to sustain a sense of reality and striving to maintain coherence in the face of massive disturbance" (Burton, 1978, p. 19).

In these conditions and in these communities it was not altogether surprising that there was a fundamental distrust of pragmatic political action. Those who stood for Sinn Fein did not fit the normal conventions of electoral politics: of their fourteen candidates in the British general election (1992) nine "had spent time in prison. Some had been interned. One was currently out on bail. One was the daughter of a Sinn Fein councillor who had been shot dead by loyalists. The father of another had been seriously injured in a loyalist attack. Several reported losing close friends and colleagues, and several had been the subjects of assassination attempts and threats" (*The Irish Times*, 19 March 1992).

With that type of profile it is not surprising that the campaign has demanded commitment and a steady stream of willing volunteers. And as befits a movement which takes its inspiration from 1916 with Thomas MacDonagh's description of the revival of the national spirit as "the supreme song of victory on the dying lips of martyrs" (Kearney, 1988, p. 214) it has been noted for the calibre of its personnel. O'Malley's survey (1983, p. 271) of the political prisoners notes that the rate of recidivism among those convicted under the emergency laws is very low: "... the educational level prior to incarceration is relatively high, and a majority of the prisoners pursue and achieve a higher educational level while inside. Two thirds of those serving long-term sentences were under fifteen when the conflict erupted in 1969 and one third were under nine."

A more surprising endorsement of the IRA's calibre comes from a British army report, "Northern Ireland: Future Terrorist Trends", written by a Brigader Glover in 1979, which fell into the hands of the IRA. It alludes to the calibre of "the rank and file terrorists [which] does not support the view that they are merely mindless hooligans drawn from the unemployed and unemployable.... PIRA is essentially a working-class organization based in the ghetto areas of the cities and in the poor rural areas." The report was written after the IRA had abandoned its leaky neighbourhood structure in favour of a much tighter cellular structure (in 1977). Yet they could continue to rely on communal support and maintain a disproportionate level of violence (O'Malley, 1983, pp. 262–3). Glover concluded gloomily that he saw no prospect in the political or military terrain of defeat of the IRA over the next five years – and that was a report written in 1979.

Some explanation for such endurance and calibre comes from the mytho-logics of the mobilization space. Kearney (1988, pp. 222–3), following Sartre, argues that mythical consciousness is not some lawless disorder but "an ordered pattern of means directed towards an end", that is myth enables us to seek to negate a real world that has grown intolerable in order to transform it into an imaginary world which we can tolerate: "By altering our *attitude* to the world, myth provides imaginary solutions to real conflicts. Hence the enormous appeal of mythological paradigms of belief for the consciousness of an oppressed or colonized people." In the context of Northern Ireland since 1970 Kearney (1988, p. 211) raises the crucial question of a lack of projection in the mythical-nucleus latent in the symbols of the 1916 Proclamation itself:

Is it possible that the guiding motivation of militant Republicanism was, and still is to some extent, less the appropriation of the socio-economic means of production, than an exigency of sacrifice to a mythological Ireland: an ancestral diety which would respond to the martyrdom of her sons by rising from her ancient slumber to avenge them?

Such an attitude was to be found among those 1916 insurgents like Pearse and MacDonagh who preserved their sacrifice in song and poetry and who fulfilled the roles of producers of violence *and* of meaning. The attitude is presented more prosaically by the insurgents in Boland's Mill who, when called on to surrender, pronounced that they had come to die and not to win. And it was reproduced by the purveyors of meaning immediately following 1916 when posters appeared around Dublin with the caption *"All is Changed* – depicting the martyred Pearse in a *pieta* position supported by the mythic figure Mother Erin brandishing a tricolour. Precisely the same images and symbols were to re-appear sixty-five years later in the aftermath of the hunger strikes.

While it would appear that more than six decades later the same assumptions held we shall see that the "long war" was not simply about tactics and targets and strategies changing to suit the military terrain and political landscape. The dimensions seemed limitless: "In any act of violence the basic vehicles of meaning are the identity of the victim or the target, and the timing, location and form of the act" (Moss, 1983, p. 91). In the beginning more thought was given to the quality and acquisition of weapons than to targets. The latter fell into a crude category of "economic" – property, bricks and mortar, anything that cost the British Exchequer dearly – and "Brits" (because they were the oppressors). With the passage of time a more sophisticated analysis of tactical aspects was undertaken. Targets could be people or resources. The latter could be the destruction of property or bank robberies – one example will suffice. During 1992 the IRA caused £800 million worth of damage to property in London, one blast in April alone causing £700 million. Each category was to contain its own (burgeoning) sub-categories.

Individuals as targets might be chosen for their category (military personnel or informers, for example). The death of an informer carried a distinct message. One source estimates that between 1976 and 1987 "around fifty active Provisionals have been informers.... This represents a very significant level of penetration – perhaps one-in-thirty or one-in-forty of the organization's frontline membership during these years. Their deaths were about maintaining the very existence of the movement. Individual targets could carry even greater value as symbols – the assassinations of Christopher Ewart-Biggs, the British Ambassador to Ireland, in July 1976, and Lord Mountbatten in August 1979. The latter's death represented the IRA's first "success" against a member of the royal family and coincided with the murder of eighteen British soldiers on the same day. The locations of these deaths was significant – Mountbatten had been murdered in the Irish Republic and the soldiers were killed not far from the international border. The result was that two states, Britain and Ireland, were involved. Indeed *The Economist* (1 September 1979) also implicated the United States because, it asserted, the killers were partly financed by U.S. citizens and it went on to call for the need for "unrestricted police cooperation across frontiers". All of this raised the status of the IRA as a body in the mainstream of international terrorism.

Perhaps the IRA's greatest propaganda coup was the attempted assassination of the British Cabinet in October 1984 when five people, including a Conservative MP, were killed in an IRA explosion. The IRA statement of admission was simplicity itself:

The IRA claims responsibility for the detonation of 100 lb of gelignite in Brighton against the British Cabinet and Tory warmongers. Mrs Thatcher will now realise that Britain cannot occupy our country and torture our prisoners and shoot our people on their own streets and get away with it. Today we were unlucky, but remember we only have to be lucky once – you will have to be lucky always. Give Ireland peace and there will be no war.

It is difficult to underestimate the success of the Brighton bomb. It highlighted the IRA's ingenuity in planting a bomb in a maximum security area. It targetted the one individual for whom republicans felt the greatest contempt, the Prime Minister, especially because of her role in the hunger strikes. As the statement implied it meant that the British authorities had to be on constant alert with the concomitant expectation that repressive measures would be imposed on the Irish diaspora in Britain. It gave the IRA maximum publicity across the world.

The statistics on violence *per se* were not important, a fact acknowledged by a member of the IRA Army Council in an interview in September 1980 when he accepted that they had not been as active that year as in previous ones; but he warned that the "British are sliding into their 1977 mistake of predicting our defeat. They're fighting a statistical war. We're not. We're fighting a political war" (cited in Kearney, 1988, p. 313). The conflict has long since become self-regulatory.

The point was not so much how much damage the IRA could inflict but the fact that they had established the communicative dimension of political violence. Their "opponents had no exit, no opportunity simply to refuse to notice acts of violence and thus to escape the communicative frame" (Moss, 1983, p. 86). In that respect they had gone beyond *endurance*. Their real challenge was to demonstrate that they had made the link which proved that violent acts could have *substantial* political consequences. We shall examine this challenge through their use of the hunger strikes, a paradigm of the IRA as an emancipatory movement operating under inversionary discourse.

VII THE "HUNGER STRIKES": THE "EGOISM OF VICTIMIZATION"

In politics ... the strategy which post-modernism advances is one which gives up on the idea of consensus. The establishment of consensus depends upon a kind of imperialism, under which divergent and discordant acts of reflective judgement are themselves judged according to an imposed overarching determinant judgement; again, the possibility of a post-modern justice is eradicated under the aetheticization/"modernization" of the political. There can be no consensus without a corollary imperialism. In the face of this, post-modernism proposes an elaboration and complexification of dissensus, dissent, irreconcilable *differends*. An exponential production of and assertion of difference becomes the riposte to demands for "identity" or any form of totalitarian "unity". The passage to thought, and to ethical and political justice, is thereby opened up.   (Docherty, in Kearney (ed.), 1988, p. 275)

Apter (1992, p. 24) may well have had the hunger strikes in mind when he wrote that endowing "confrontational events with political symbolism is itself a strategy which changes the political process from accountability and consensus to a politics of spectacle, theater, violence, drama ...". Here was a confrontational event imbued with political symbolism which challenged the *doxa* in a highly theatrical manner. While the republican campaign had been launched against the prevailing accountability and consensus no one single incident or event invested as much spectacle as did the hunger strikes. They raise fundamental questions about the place of the IRA in a typology of violence-prone movements; about the extent to which it is an archetype of emancipatory movements; about whether we can "read" the strikes as a version of the authenticity paradigm which challenges the impersonality of man-made mass deaths and, as such, as an inversion of the death-world; and finally, once again, whether contemporary republicanism has a logical project.

If any one episode explains the resilience of republicanism it is the hunger strikes of 1980–1. The background is simple: since the introduction of internment in 1971 a battle has been waged between the prisoners and the authorities over the question of political status inside the prisons. Republicans considered they were not criminals. Adams (1986, pp. 67–8) cites the Glover report and a study by lawyers of defendants appearing before the Diplock (non-jury) courts on "scheduled" offences. He insists that the importance of political prisoner status "has nothing to do with any contempt for the 'ordinary criminals' who are so often the victims of social inequality and injustice. From Thomas Ashe to Bobby Sands the concern has always been to assert the political nature of the struggle in which the IRA has been engaged" (p. 71). Generally the Catholic community shared Adams's belief that the profile of the prisoners was not that of a criminal class. The emotional reaction by the Cardinal (O'Fiach) after a visit to protesting republican prisoners in 1978 was a precursor of things to come: "... they prefer to face death rather than submit to be classed as criminals ... anyone with the least knowledge of Irish history knows how deeply rooted this attitude is in our country's past" (O'Malley, 1983, p. 272).

By putting it in this historical perspective the Cardinal was drawing attention to the fact that before 1980 no less than twelve republicans had starved to death for their beliefs in this century. It was a practice which flourished in pre-Christian times in Ireland and derives from the ancient Irish (Brehon) Laws which recognized and strove to regulate the rite of "fasting against a person of exalted state in order to enforce a claim against him" in order to embarrass the debtor to pay up. The alternatives for the exalted person were three-fold: the first was to concede the claim; the second to start a counter-fast; and the third was to let the hunger-striker starve himself to death. None of them, as the British authorities were to realize, were congenial. And it was a practice which "disappears only as a stream that vanishes underground only to resurface elsewhere" (O'Faolain, 1981). When it resurfaced it carried an overtly political message. Sean MacBride, former IRA Chief of Staff and Nobel Peace Prize winner in 1974, argued that "it was not some isolated political happening of our time but a deep symptom of a historically recurring persecution: 'a fall-out resulting from the cruel interference by Britain in the affairs of the Irish nation'" (Kearney, 1988, p. 227).

More importantly the prisons' campaign made the distinction between a *sacrificial* ideology and the *revolutionary* ideology of the military campaign. It linked them more closely to the Pearsean mode than any of their ersatz challengers. Like the rebels in Boland's Mill in 1916 they had gone there not to win but to die. And it was seeped in martyrology and religious symbolism: Sinn Feins's plea for a vote to save Sands's life; the grafitto in West Belfast of a dying hunger striker being comforted by the Virgin Mary with the message, "Blessed are those who hunger for justice"; the prisoners using their bodies as social texts "in the act of refusal, i.e. refusing to eat, wash, smearing body and cell with human excrement, acts which not only violate conventional notions of cleanliness and dirt, but are shockingly redolent of the purification by putrefaction of the flesh, as with the early Christian anchorites [which one might add is embodied in the texts and discourse of Irish Catholicism]" (Apter, 1992, p. 75); their supporters sense of theatre with the hunger strikers portrayed in crucified postures with the barbed wire of the prisons being transferred into the crown of thorns and the H-Block blanket (their only piece of "clothing") into a burial shroud; Sands's prison testimony as an inversionary text "as a 'tale of faith' and 'triumph of endurance' which became a 'morale booster' for a cause that depended 'more on integrity and courage than on what politicians and lawyers term reason and common sense'" (Kearney, 1988, p. 226); and, above all, the place of religion with the Mass as a "real sacrifice" and source of comfort and strength to the prisoners. And at the heart of the Mass is the Eucharistic prayer with the memorial acclamation of the people, a version of which reads: "Lord, by your cross and resurrection/ you have set us free./You are the Saviour of the world." Kearney (1988, p. 226) notes that once they were deprived of political status they fell back on the Catholic religion and Gaelic as "symbols of primary significance.... In prison to be Gaelic and Catholic was almost synonymous with being nationalist; for all three categories of identification served to remind the Republican inmates of their forefathers' long history of persecution."

In 1972 they were granted special category status because the authorities thought that that might wean them away from violence. In effect the prisoners had run their own regime and had strengthened the organization inside the prisons and their respectability outside. In 1976 the NIO reverted to a policy of "criminalisation" in its place. They did not realize how deeply they were striking at the republican psyche. They did not appreciate the extent to which they were merging context and community

– kin, class, territory and religion – in republicanism. Bobby Sands, the first to die in the hunger strikes, expresses their abhorrence of criminalization in one of his poems

> *We do not wear the guilty stare*
> *Of those who bear a crime,*
> *Nor do we don that badge of wrong*
> *To tramp the penal line.*
> *So men endure a pit of sewer*
> *For freedom of the mind.*

It clashed also with their concept of social republicanism whereby *they* appropriated the role of guardians of the law. Burton (1978, p. 106) recognizes that besides the clearly instrumental motives for policing an area "is the awareness of the symbolic importance of appearing as community police ... the IRA flouted any moral authority possessed by the State" as well as usurping the "moral authority of all other contenders within the community". They could not be both criminals and upholders of law and order. When they lost their special category status in 1976 the prisoners embarked on a blanket and no-wash protest whereby they refused to wear prison clothing and clean out their cells. It was only when all else failed that they resorted to the ultimate protest – the hunger strike. They were supported by Relatives' Action Committees (RACs) which were distributed across Northern Ireland and were often independent of the republican leadership.

One of the features of the RACs was the role played by women – indeed it was a feature of the whole "war" and of Irish nationalism/Catholicism generally. Maryology had always been strong in Irish devotional practice. It also formed part of the mytho-nucleus of the Irish nation: "the more spiritually idealized the collective memory of the nation becomes the more it assumes the form of a death cult erected upon the dual fetishisation of the Past (the golden age of Celtic myth) and the Motherland (Caitlin ni Houlihan and the sacrificial Rosaleen)". One who nearly went to her death for Ireland was Countess Markiecivicz of Anglo-Irish stock and a foreign title by marriage, who was sentenced to death for her part in the 1916 Rising. She was reprieved because of her sex. Markiecivicz's role indicated a small but strong feminist movement in Ireland. "Inghinidhe na hEireann" (or the "Daughters of Ireland") was founded in 1900 and was open to women of Irish birth or descent who were dedicated to "complete independence". Its first President, Maud Gonne MacBride, was the mother of Sean MacBride who was to become Chief of Staff of the IRA in the

1930s. Another organization, Cumann na mBhan, was founded in 1913 to act as radical auxiliaries of the Irish Volunteers, the IRA's forerunners.

Women were to continue playing a prominent role in the armed struggle after 1969. Maire Drumm, who was vice-president of Sinn Fein, was assassinated by loyalists in her hospital bed in 1976. And from the younger generation Mairead Farrell, gunned down in the Gibraltar shootings in 1988, and Sheena Campbell, a former Sinn Fein parliamentary candidate, killed by loyalists in 1992. Both of them were undergraduates and Farrell, as the commanding officer of the IRA protesting prisoners in Armagh Women's Prison, had taken part in the first hunger strike in December 1980. They were representative of a more radical feminist voice inside the republican movement. Independent groups, such as Women Against Imperialism, had begun to make the link between national independence and women's liberation. The issue could not be ignored and Sinn Fein established a Department of Women's Affairs to ensure "a unity of struggle which will guarantee women's freedom in a free Ireland".

But it was the wives and mothers of the hunger strikers who personified republican resistance, a fact recognized in the graveside oration to Bobby Sands: "Someone once said it is hard to be a hero's mother and nobody knows that better than Mrs Sands who watched her son being daily crucified for sixty-six long days and eventually killed. Mrs Sands epitomises Irish mothers who in every generation watched their children go out and fight and die for freedom." One study (Fairweather, *et al.*, 1984, p. 49) calculates an estimated 60,000 mothers, wives and children "currently affected by the imprisonment of a near relative". These "wire widows" – i.e. the wives of the prisoners "behind the wire" – had to bear the emotional and social brunt of raising families in what was in any case recessionary times.

The RACs developed into a mass movement offering an alternative to a pointless military campaign. There is evidence of republican incomprehension of this nuisance that was distracting attention away from the "war". Gerry Adams (1986, p. 75) concedes as much: "we were temperamentally and organizationally disinclined to engage in any form of action with elements outside the movement itself". It forced Sinn Fein to organize a conference involving the whole membership in detailed consideration of the prisons' question. This was when Sinn Fein moved out of its conspiratorial mode and began to embrace the political process. In the local government elections of May 1981 (following Sands's death) candidates identifying with the hunger strikes with 51,000 first preference votes and thirty-six seats could have become the fifth largest political party if they had all joined together in one group. Clearly there was a constituency to be nurtured.

The first hunger strike began on 27 October 1980 with a statement from the prisoners:

> For the past four years we have endured brutality in deplorable conditions – we have been stripped naked and robbed of our individuality, yet we refuse to be broken ... we wish to make it clear that every channel has been exhausted and, not wishing to break faith with those from whom we have inherited our principles, we now commit ourselves to hunger-strike.

The second began on 1 March 1981. In both instances seven volunteers were selected initially. The timing and the numbers were significant. The first was to culminate at Christmas (except that it was called off on 18 December because the prisoners believed [wrongly] that they had extracted the necessary concessions) and the second at Easter – both great Christian celebrations. The seven corresponded with the number of signatories to the 1916 Proclamation. Their self-image was one of a revolutionary vanguard and of the sacred keeper of the nation's history. The hunger strikes contain all the ingredients of a successful myth in the making. It is a contemporary and contentious issue which reaches back into the recesses of history for justification. It is used to create a *sacred history*: "... through myth man stands outside [ex-stasis] the futile flow of history which no longer seems to offer any possibility of rational reform or progress. He takes recourse in the mythic law of "eternal recurrence of the same", i.e. the recurrence of the same ancestral heroes, of the same paradigms of destruction and renewal, of the same time of the Holy Begin-ning" (Kearney, 1988, p. 222).

The first to volunteer was Bobby Sands, O.C. of the Provisionals inside the prison. He was a victim of an intimidatory culture: his family had been driven out of their homes twice in loyalist estates and he had been forced out of work where he had been apprenticed as a coach-builder. Given this background he was an obvious recruit for the IRA (which he joined in 1972). His self-perception is evident in a poem he wrote after he had been sentenced to fourteen years in prison:

> *The beady eyes they peered at me*
> *The time had come to be,*
> *To walk the lonely road*
> *Like that of Calvary.*

And take up the cross of Irishmen
Who've carried liberty.

His biographer, indeed hagiographer, describes this prison sentence as the beginning of his *"Via Dolorosa"*; and his funeral "as if the Republican Movement had reached its Calvary with no Resurrection in sight ..." (Feehan, 1983, pp. 20, 99). He could expect to be dead by Easter – both a secular celebration of destruction and renewal, as well as of a Holy Beginning – if his demands were not met. His inspiration extended back to Christ: "No greater love hath a man than to lay down his life for his friends." The imagery and the symbolism were politico-religious in character. Speaking of Bobby Sands a republican critic, Fr Denis Faul, said that all intercessions were of no avail: "He saw himself as the Messiah, Christlike, and he was determined to go ahead" (O'Malley, 1990, p. 64). The words of another hunger striker, the Lord Mayor of Cork, Terence McSwiney, in 1920 – "It is not those who inflict the most but those who suffer the most who will conquer" – returned as the "theology of mystical Republicanism, the philosophy of non-violence of physical force separatism, the embodiment of the warrior without weapons, the fighting man as the apostle of passive resistance" (O'Malley, 1990, pp. 26–7).

The whole campaign had become suffused in politics *and* religion and had challenged the authority of the Church. It was not that the Catholic hierarchy had endorsed the hunger strike. Indeed the Bishop of Down and Connor argued that the contemporary "armed struggle" failed the test of the "just war" tradition on the grounds of "competent authority" and "just means". But individual clergy identified with the cause and senior church-men went to considerable lengths to persuade the strikers to call off the protest. The Church *as an institution* was only too aware of the capacity of religion to anchor our symbolic resources for formulating analytic ideas *and* for expressing emotions:

> For those able to embrace them, and for as long as they are able to embrace them, religious symbols provide a cosmic guarantee not only for their ability to comprehend the world but also, comprehending it, to give a precision to their feeling, a definition to their emotions, which enables them, morosely or joyfully, grimly or cavalierly, to *endure* it. (Geertz, 1963, p. 104; my italics)

In fulfilling their pastoral role the clergy were conscious that they were engaged in a battle with republicans about the nature of the religion of nationalism – and as the prisoners' statement after the collapse of the hunger strike confirmed the battle between the institutional Church and that (growing) section of its flock was conducted in deadly earnest. The hierarchy was conscious of the growing popularity of the cause – although only 4,000 had greeted his hunger strike decision 70,000 had turned out for his funeral procession. If "religious belief involves ... a prior acceptance of authority which transforms that [everyday] experience ..." (Geertz, 1963, p. 109) the question arose, where did the authority reside: with the Church or the hunger strikers? Yet again we have an example of the disordering and reordering, of the shattering of the conventional boundaries of political language and discourse, which is at the heart of inversionary discourse.

It raised fundamental questions:

A death-way then? Or a life-way? In the imagery of the Sermon on the Mount, the broad way that leadeth to destruction? Or the narrow way that leadeth unto life? Or since living and dying imply one another, a way of asserting values, personal, racial, national, even philosophical, common to both living and dying.   (O'Faolain, 1981)

It led to questions about the nature of their deaths: suicide or self-starvation? The families of the dead hunger strikers had protested at the original pathologist's report which recorded "self-imposed starvation". The medical certificates were then amended to record the cause of death as "starvation"; and the coroner found the cause of death to be "starvation, self imposed". In a deeply religious community it led to a debate about the Thomist tradition and whether "intention" was the crucial factor: "To intend to terminate one's life – that is the distinguishing mark of the act of suicide. To bring about the termination of one's life by so arranging the circumstances that one dies but with the intention of bringing about some other state of affairs, is not suicide" (O'Keeffe, 1984, p. 355).

Bobby Sands died on 5 May 1981. Another nine were to die before the remaining six ended their protest on 3 October. The Catholic ghetto had no trouble identifying with the very ordinariness of the striking prisoners. None had third-level education and only three had finished high school. Except for two on the run all lived at home in ordinary jobs or were unemployed. All had come of age during the civil rights campaign. Two were very religious and seven came from staunchly republican families or areas with a history of resistance: "The three who didn't compensated for their lack of Republican credentials with a commitment which even the ardent might have found excessive at times" (O'Malley, 1990, pp. 102–3).

As soon as the hunger strike was called off the prisoners issued a very long statement (published in *The Irish Times* on 5 October 1981 – incidentally the anniverary of what is considered to be the beginning of the civil rights campaign in 1968) which is a classic example of the diffusion of a core text: "Texts acknowledging responsibility for actions ... convert otherwise unrelated episodes of violence into the elements of a political strategy, so that their production and diffusion must be a necessary part of constructing an identity" (Moss, 1983, p. 92). The language of the statement is in the heroic mode, the appeal is to the *whole* nationalist community – with outright condemnation of the role of the SDLP, the Dublin political parties and the Catholic hierarchy – and the sentiments are religious. Two reasons are given for the hunger strike. The first is cast in the language of "victimhood", what Robert Elias calls "a political economy of helplessness" with Northern Ireland as "a victim-bonded society in which memories of past injustice and humiliation are so firmly entrenched in both communities ..." (O'Malley, 1990, pp. 8–9). The prisoners believed they had no other choice and no "other means of securing a principled solution to the four-year protest".

But the second reason was about a republican mode of political discourse. The hunger strike was "of fundamental importance ... to advance the Irish people's right for liberty. We believe that the age-old struggle for Irish self-determination and freedom has been immeasurably advanced by this hunger strike and therefore we claim a massive political victory." So the purpose of the diatribe was not solely moral outrage. It was an attempt to gain the high ground of undisputed anti-partitionist leadership: "The logical conclusion of this analysis is that nationalist pacifism in the Northern Ireland context dooms the nationalist population to subserviency, perpetuates partition and thwarts the quest for a just and lasting peace in Ireland." If Sinn Fein was to take over it could do so only by "the primitive force of a symbolic act" and by breaking "the relation between politics and discourse":

The IRA can hardly hope to achieve its aim by force of argument, definition and reason. They must transcend the terms of any such discourse. The only way to do that is by taking some morally intimidating course of action, something that requires courage, passion and selflessness. Discourse can only be transcended by action; inside a prison action can only take a symbolic form, all the more potent for being irrational and in every respect exorbitant. There is no gesture more compelling than the hunger strike, and ideally the hunger strike to death. (Donoghue, 1981, p. 227).

The mythopoeic at the heart of the hunger strike lies in a definition of myth as "a strategic mode of consciousness whereby we seek to negate a real world that has grown intolerable in order to transform it into an imaginary world which we can tolerate. We negate the world in order to better cope with what appears to be intractable problems" (Kearney, 1988, p. 223). According to O'Malley (1990, p. 137) the hunger strikes exposed the "contradictions at the core of the Catholic nationalist psyche. The revolutionaries won the War of Independence in 1921 but the pragmatists inherited it. The new Irish state was non-revolutionary.... Accordingly, the tradition of physical force, of an élite minority whose actions had the imprimatur of history and the sanction of dead generations, triumphed but did not prevail." If the secret of the civil rights campaign was that it moved republicanism out of the narrow world of a conspiratorial movement, the aftermath of the hunger strikes was to be the fusion of the military and the political whereby the IRA – in the name of the people and of the dead generations – was to find its place in the sun: "In 1976 the British government tried to criminalize the republican prisoners. In 1981 the republican prisoners criminalized the British government" (Adams, 1986, p. 87).

These remarks should not be treated as mere rhetoric, because there is no doubt that the hunger strikes discommoded the political and religious establishment. Feehan (pp. 20–3) records the international protests and media coverage which greeted Sands's death and concludes with a piece of hyperbole: "Is there any single case in the entire history of the world where the death of a 'criminal' was accorded such international admiration and sympathy?" Financial support from an IRA front group in the United States reached $250,000 in the first half of 1981 (compared with an average figure of $110,000 every half year over the previous seven years). The *New Statesman* (14 August 1981) highlighted the IRA's tactical advantage: "By her continuing inflexibility over the H Blocks, Mrs Thatcher has now achieved what the Provisional IRA always wanted. She has made politics in Northern Ireland into a straight confrontation between the British Government and the Provos, in which everyone else is rendered powerless or irrelevant." And in a survey of sixty-four newspapers in twenty-five countries throughout the world *The Sunday Times* (31 May 1981) concluded that the news was not good for the British government: "... world opinion has begun to shift away from the British government and in favour of the IRA. The image of the gunman has actually improved. And the general opinion is emerging that the time has come for Mrs Thatcher to begin negotiations with Dublin leading to eventual union with the South.... The sympathy which many countries felt for Britain after the

IRA had murdered Lord Mountbatten has largely disappeared as a result of the death of the hunger strikers."

But the hunger strikes also raised questions about what type of emancipatory movement is republicanism. Unlike Colombian political violence the Irish were demonstrating that it was more about death and sacrifice than about killing. It had more in common with the Shi'ite discourse of violence with sacrifice to the point of martyrdom and its ritualized nature as in the religious ceremony of "Ashura" (Picard, 1992, pp. 51–3); or in such extreme forms of resistance to colonization as the "national suicide" of the Xhosa cattle-killing movement in 1856: "an attempt to mobilize the deepest resources of culture and religion in order to undo the historical reality of conquest" (du Toit, 1992, p. 19). But it can also be seen as a challenge to the impersonality of man-made mass death. Following Heidegger the hunger strikes can be seen as a form of negation, a self-destruction rather than a collective devastation: "... devastation is the expulsion of memory, the historically weighted spiritual and useful objects which make up the traditions and material culture of Western man" (Wyschogrod, 1985, p. 177). The hunger strikes was about the retention, not the expulsion, of memory; it was about demonstrating that one was not swept up by the movement of history, rather that a "dynamically self-transcending and imaginative consciousness recognizes the power of memory to control history by becoming narrative consciousness" (Wyschogrod, 1985, p. 125). Wyschogrod (p. 126) quotes an inmate of Majdanek concentration camp: "Should our murderers be victorious, should *they* write the history of this war ... their every word will be taken for gospel. Or they may wipe out our memory altogether, as if we had never existed.... But if *we* write the history of the period ... we'll have the thankless job of proving to a reluctant world that we are Abel, the murdered brother." The hunger strikes were about writing history and retaining memory.

Their deaths were to change the strategy and tactics of Sinn Fein and the IRA. The Armalite *and* the ballot box came into their own. Even before his death Bobby Sands had been elected MP for Fermanagh and South Tyrone in a byelection on 9 April: "Your vote can save this man's life" was the highly charged slogan which was effective. And in the byelection following his death his agent, Owen Carron, was successful. In the meantime in the Republic's general election in June 1981 nine prisoners stood and two, Paddy Agnew and Kieran Doherty, were returned thereby preventing the Fianna Fáil leader, Charles Haughey, becoming Taoiseach. Elections were becoming infectious and euphoric and, according to Adams (1986, p. 151) were playing "a major role in changing the nature of Sinn Fein". He himself became the MP for West Belfast at the 1983 general election and in Belfast Sinn Fein became the major national-ist party. Beside winning West Belfast Sinn Fein were just short of a majority in the Mid-Ulster constituency. The SDLP feared being over-taken by Sinn Fein as the leading nationalist party.

But electoralism has its downside. With 13.4 per cent of the vote Sinn Fein peaked in 1983. At subsequent general elections in 1987 and in 1992 their vote dropped to 11.4 and 10 per cent respectively: by the 1990s in the Republic Sinn Fein could command slightly more than one per cent of the popular vote. And in 1992 Adams lost his West Belfast seat with all the international prestige and symbolism that went with it. In addition it caused tensions within the movement.

Traditionally republicans had been wary of granting any recognition to parliaments in Dublin, London and Belfast. There was the added compli-cation that electoralism interfered with the armed struggle. Ideally both would go hand-in-hand, but as early as 1983 there was the first of a number "of 'fraternal' calls from the expanding Sinn Fein political organ-isation for a 'refinement' of IRA activity to minimise adverse electoral repercussions" (Patterson, 1989, p. 177). In 1986, when the Sinn Fein Ard Fheis voted to remove the ban on attendance in the Dail, a rival organiza-tion, Republican Sinn Fein, was established despite the fact that support for the "armed struggle" was to be maintained, and that the end of absten-tionism had been supported by the General Army Convention (of the IRA). The rather hasty entry into the political process raises questions about how successful Adams in particular has been in moving beyond vic-timness to find a logical project which would lead this emancipatory movement towards emancipation. A recurring subtext in his personal man-ifesto, *The Politics of Irish Freedom,* had been the necessity to move away from the conspiratorial ethos. None could challenge the success that Sinn Fein had in Northern Ireland when it took as much as 40 per cent of the Catholic vote. And it was an electoral base with a social profile which has the capacity to challenge the constitutional nationalists, the SDLP, for some considerable time (cf. Irvin and Moxon-Browne, *Fortnight,* May 1989, pp. 7–9).

By 1992 the republican movement suffered from "voicelessness" and from a series of IRA "mistakes" – between November 1987 and June 1990 the IRA accepted responsibility for mistakenly killing twenty-two inno-cent civilians; and that some of their human rights' violations were described as "barbaric" and "particulary gruesome" by the respected inter-national human rights body, Helsinki Watch. Their loss of "voice" was as a result of government policy – from 1971 in the Republic and 1988 in the

UK when they were denied the use of the airwaves. Even within these constraints they maintained 10 per cent of the Northern Ireland vote, making them the fourth largest party in the province.

Time will tell whether or not electoralism is an extension to the development of the ideology of violence in Ireland. In some respects it arose simply as an adjunct to the hunger strike campaign when the republican leadership realized that it might win the battle but lose the war because it had not ensured popular support. But what it does demonstrate is the tension between pragmatic political action and political violence. The ballot box indicates the level of popular support, and for those who base their claim to unity on self-determination the ballot box has been telling them that only a few per cent of the Irish people are prepared to accept their *methods*. In addition, entry into the political arena assumes acceptance of accountability and consensus. But two exercises conducted in the 1980s highlighted the degree to which contemporary republicanism has been marginalized.

The first was the New Ireland Forum, an attempt by the three major constitutional nationalist parties in the Republic – Fianna Fáil, Fine Gael and Labour – and the SDLP in the north, to redefine the meaning of Irish nationalism in the late twentieth century, in 1983–4. Sinn Fein was excluded. One of the Forum's reports produced a demography of violence for the years 1969–81, highlighting the overwhelming concentration of urban violence, and concluded that nationalist areas "such as Derry, Strabane and Newry, already suffering from regional disadvantages, have been further set back by the campaign of bombing and destruction" ("New Ireland Forum", 1983, p. 8). In other words the IRA was causing greater damage to those it was supposed to be defending. And in its final report the Forum (1984, pp. 14–15) excoriated the

negative effect of IRA violence on British and Unionist attitudes [which] cannot be emphasized enough. Their terrorist acts create anger and indignation and a resolve not to give into violence under any circumstances. They have the effect of stimulating additional security measures which further alienate the nationalist section of the community. They obscure the underlying political problem. They strengthen extremist Unionist resistance to any form of dialogue and acccommodation with nationalists.

In an attempt to open out the dialogue, and in a search for accommodation, Sinn Fein and the SDLP entered into talks in March 1988 and closed it with a simultaneous release of party statements on 5 September 1988.

As the constitutionalist party the SDLP came under severe criticism from Northern Ireland's other parties and from the leader of the Progressive Democrats, Des O'Malley, in the south. They all believed that the talks could only give succour to the IRA and they failed to realize that the moral certitude of a closed organization was being prised open. They did not recognize the extent to which the concealed intentions of myth were being exposed and that a distinction was being made between a utopian concept of myth and the ideological, between the inclusive and the exclusive: "A positive hermeneutics offers an opportunity to salvage myth from the abuses of doctrinal prejudice, racist nationalism, class oppression or totalitarianism. And it does so in the name of a universal project of freedom – a project from which no creed, nation, class or individual is excluded" (Kearney, 1988, p. 275). During the talks the concept of self-determination and of Britain's intentions in Ireland were at the top of the agenda; but, above all, it was about the challenge the SDLP put up in its final document:

Solutions to the problem of division in Ireland have been postponed by nationalist/Republican concentration on the language of ideological rectitude rather than trying to face the political reality. The challenge is to change this reality by political dialogue and not to estrange it further by the continued futile and counterproductive use of force against fellow Irish people

The SDLP's central message was that they were "a party of realistic politicians, not a team of theologians. We must deal with factual reality." They recognized that every "mythology implies a *conflict of interpretation*"; and so they were engaged on "touching on a new understanding of myth: one we might best term *postmodern* by way of distinguishing it from both the_*revivalist* apotheosis of myth as a unitary tradition and the *modernist* rejection of myth as a mystifying dogma. A post-modern approach to myth construes it as a two-way traffic between tradition and modernity, rewriting the old as a project of the new" (Kearney, 1988, pp. 276, 278). In short, it was about the search for anticipatory memory.

Bobby Sands and his fallen comrades have entered the pantheon of the republican dead. His poetry has been published; hagiographies have appeared; streets have been named after him; he has become the subject of wall murals. The prisoners' valedictory statement will be part of the narrative, one of the texts, of the struggle: "Our comrades have lit with their very lives an eternal beacon which will inspire this nation amd people to rise and crush oppression forever, and this nation can be proud that it produced such a quality of manhood."

It will take its place alongside the writings and speeches of Wolfe Tone, Padraig Pearse and others. And Sands will have found his place in the Pearsean *religion* of nationalism.

On the day that Bobby Sands died a RUC Constable was shot dead. At his funeral the Church of Ireland Primate, Dr Robin Eames, asked rhetorically: "... where does the real agony lie? Is it with those who use the threat of the choice of death or with those who have no choice?" This perception, according to O'Malley (1990, p. 182), "once again reaffirmed Protestants' sense of their own victimhood and helplessness, invalidating their grievances, making meaningless the deaths of their coreligionists who gave their lives for the protection of the state, reminding them of the perilous state of their existence ...". In that respect the hunger strike serves as a paradigm of the Northern Ireland conflict – a society without a sense of empathy. Protestants, too, had their "chosen traumas".

The hunger strikes, then, have illustrated the degree to which both communities have fallen back on a mechanism which characterizes traumatized national groups – what Mack (1990, p. 125) calls *the egoism of victimization*:

The egoism of victimization is the incapacity of an ethno-national group, as a direct result of its own historical traumas, to empathize with the suffering of another group. It is analogous to the narcissism or self-centredness of some individuals who see themselves as having been so hurt or deprived in the past that they can attend only to their own needs, feeling little or no empathy for the hurt they inflict upon others. Similarly, ethno-national groups that have been traumatized by repeated sufferings at the hands of other groups seem to have little capacity to grieve for the hurts of other peoples, or to take responsibility for the new victims created by their own warlike actions. Victims kill victims through unendingly repeated cycles that are transmitted from one generation to another, bolstered by stories and myths of atrocities committed by the other people, and by heroic acts committed in defence of the nation and its values by one's own.

As late as December 1992, after more than twenty years of direct rule and various attempts at reforming the system, the secretary of state, Sir Patrick Mayhew, admitted that much remained to be done: "It remains generally, but not universally, true that unemployment, educational under-attainment, poorer housing conditions and other indices of disadvantage, are still relatively more widely to be found in the minority community than the majority." Added to that was a series of miscarriages of justice of Irish people living in Britain, such as the trials of the "Birmingham 6" and the "Guildford 4", that it was not really surprising that victimness had become a way of life.

VIII   CONCLUSION: BEYOND A "VICTIM-BONDED" SOCIETY

In November 1971 two girls were tarred and feathered in the Bogside for "fraternization", that is they had befriended British soldiers. The most rational explanation for the action was given by a man who had witnessed the incident: "This is no time to talk of civil liberties.... You get civil liberties in a political situation. This is no political situation. This is a war.... Have you any idea what we have gone through, you who make moral judgements from the comfort of Dublin and London?" (*The Irish Times*, 16 November 1971).

On 24 October 1990 Patsy Gillespie, a civilian from the economically-deprived Catholic ghetto of Shantallow in Derry, who worked in the kitchens of a British army camp, was strapped into a lorry containing 1,000 lbs of explosives and told to drive to a border check-point. When he arrived there the lorry was blown up by remote control killing him and five soldiers. Mr Gillespie was simply an ordinary civilian trying to fend for his wife and family in a harsh economic climate. He was *of* his community. It was the second time he had been used as a human bomb but he insisted in maintaining his dignity through work. An IRA statement justified its action in the language of patriotism: "We particularly appeal to the patriotism of a small number of nationalists involved in such work and ask them to set aside personal gain and cease to assist the British war machine."

Some of his neighbours found the statement as odious as the action. But the IRA persists, and Sinn Fein continues to draw on the electoral support of 10 per cent of the population. Nor was that a particularly isolated incident. Republicans have been conscious of the number of "mistakes" which occur on IRA actions. They are aware that they are open to the charge that they

bomb factories and shout about unemployment; they shoot a teacher in a classroom, kill school bus drivers, kill people on campuses and then lecture us about education. They kill, maim and injure and they carry out attacks in hospital precincts and then they tell us about protecting the Health Service. They rob post offices, leaving people without benefit payments, and then they preach to us about defending the poor. They talk about housing. When we deliver 65 million pounds of Euro Aid for housing Danny Morrison says it is a bribe to wean people away from republicanism. In short, homes for Catholics are bad for republicanism.

Those allegations were made by John Hume, the leader of the SDLP, at his party's 1985 Annual Conference. Hume has been particularly scathing about Sinn Fein/IRA pretensions. In his 1988 leader's address he pointed out that "people describing themselves as Irish republicans have killed six times as many human beings as the British army, 30 times as many as the RUC and 250 times as many as the UDR.... In the last 20 years republicans have killed more than twice as many Catholics as the security forces and in the last ten years have killed more than the Loyalists! Some defenders."

And yet they endure. One explanation lies with establishment insensitivity: the demeanour of Prime Minister Thatcher during the hunger strikes is an obvious example; the suspension of due process by the authorities is another. Republicans have been assisted, too, by loyalist rhetoric and action. It was the wholescale intimidation on some Catholic communities in 1969 which brought the invigorated IRA into existence in the first place. Catholics have noted the UWC strike in 1974, the "constitutional stoppage" in 1977, the creation of a "Third Force" in 1981, of the Ulster Clubs' movement in 1985 and Ulster Resistance in 1986. They note the language sometimes employed by some loyalist politicians and charges of collusion between the security forces and some loyalist paramilitaries in recent times. All of this is grist to the republican mill.

Above all, it is the fact that republicanism is "a central ideological component within the Catholic social consciousness", a consciousness which Burton (1978, pp. 120–2) sees as a combination of the politics of civil rights and of national liberation: "It is this significance of the IRA as a potential merging of the fundamental representations of Catholicism that stands in the way of the community's rejection of them." He finds it a remarkable ideology "that can express its revolutionary claims one week in a thinly veiled religious and mystical form and the next in a style and reasoning much closer to Lenin and Mao than Aquinas" (Burton, 1978, p. 75). It has to be said that with the passage of time it has leant less towards Lenin and Mao.

All of this can be translated into moral terms because the violence, they believe, is directed against a regime lacking in legitimacy. They are aware of the "normality" of violence. Theirs, they believe, is a mission to obtain a purer form of democracy and is so motivated that some are prepared to sacrifice their very existence to obtain such. Theirs is a form of "democratic violence" (cf. Honderich, 1976, pp. 90–116). Ultimately it is based on "memory", on how the past plays a role in the formation of myth by providing a collage of images, a series of memory bytes.

In the two decades between the tarring and feathering of the two girls, and the killing of Patsy Gillespie, a discourse community had been created whereby:

... people interpret certain negative conditions and circumstances and try to transcend them by thinking one's way past them. Our concern is when this process becomes collectivized and the interpretation of events, the doctrinal ways that people try to make sense out of randomness, or the contradictions they face or the predicaments they encounter in daily life are based on retrievals and projections, with events as metaphors and metonymies, narratives and texts, and in inversionary ways.   (Apter, 1992, p. 15)

But it may be a discourse community that has lost its way, that has given up on the project of a "society-in-becoming". There is no shortage of evidence of its sense of victimness. Following the murder of Sheena Campbell by the UVF in October 1992 Gerry Adams condemned elements in the media, the churches and some political parties which "demonize" Sinn Fein: "You can censor us, call us thugs and murderers, call us fanatics and lunatics, refuse to speak to us, imprison us, extradite us, ban us, torture us and kill us, but there will always be enough of us to ensure that one day you will talk to us. No other party has suffered like Sinn Fein, but we are still here" (*The Irish News*, 19 October 1992). Here you have the articulation of victimness and defiance, a simple belief that endurance in itself is enough.

But contrast that with the discussion document, "Towards A Lasting Peace In Ireland", presented to the 1992 Sinn Fein Ard Fheis by the Ard Chomhairle. It recognized that "[t]raditional sovereignties are eroding, jurisdictions in flux, boundaries altering" (Apter, 1992, p. 26). It alluded to the demand for political democracy in Eastern Europe, to German reunification, to economic restructuring under E.C. integration, and to an Irish republicanism which "has its roots in the crucible of Europe during the great French Revolution". It saw the political and economic transformation of Europe as providing "a golden opportunity for Ireland to finally resolve its British problem ...". It believed that the United Nations might be the agency to fashion a peaceful resolution; and that in the transitional period the U.N. could convene an "international conference on the democratic resolution of the conflict in Ireland".

Here was the tension between purveyors of meaning and of violence. One suggests that republicanism was moving out of its mode of fatalism, the other that "memory" would endure. There is some evidence to suggest that the former may be in the ascendant and that Adams has followed the path of seeking a logical projection. Alongside his deputy, Martin McGuinness, he has been pursuing for some years what has been called the peace process. He can point to some success for republicanism. Perhaps the most significant has been that he has demonstrated the existence of exchange relations between the worlds of violence and politics. The evidence lies in Britain's acceptance that it has no economic or strategic interest in the Union; in the admittance by the British government that it had had secret contacts with the IRA for years; in the Joint Declaration signed by both governments on 15 December 1993: "… it is a political statement of attitude and intent directed primarily at the IRA. The two heads of government have carefully shelved all the difficult longer-term issues … in order to make a bid for an IRA ceasefire" (Goodall, 1994, p. 1676); in the Irish government's removal of Sinn Fein "voicelessness", by permitting them the use of the air waves once more, and of the Clinton administration's 48-hour visa to enable Gerry Adams to put the republican case in the US in February 1994 – both in response to the peace process.

But this is a high-risk strategy for the producers of meaning. It is an acknowledgement that the producers of violence are not succeeding and that compromises may have to be fashioned with those whom they perceived as counter-revolutionary. It is an acceptance of the road of pragmatic political action. Hence the tension remains within and without the movement. Many in the former eschew the political and fear that it will lead to their demise. Besides, they wonder, why did so many of their comrades (including the hunger strikers) have to die? Whereas the latter fear the the peace process is war by other means. They cannot understand why the decision to renounce violence is so painfully slow. They, for their part, fail to understand the nature of emancipatory politics and the distance between history and memory.

REFERENCES

Adams, Gerry, *The Politics of Irish Freedom* (Kerry: Brandon, 1986).
Apter, David E. and Sawa, Nagayo, *Against the State. Politics and Social Protest in Japan* (Cambridge, Mass.: Harvard University Press, 1982).

Apter David E, "A View from the Bogside", in H. Gilomee and J. Gagiano (eds), *The Elusive Search for Peace: South Africa, Israel, Northern Ireland* (Cape Town: Oxford University Press, in association with IDASA, 1990).

——, *Democracy, Violence and Emancipatory Movements: Notes for a Theory of Inversionary Discourse* (Geneva: UNRISD paper, 1992), no. 44.

Arthur, Paul, *The People's Democracy, 1968–1973* (Belfast: Blackstaff Press, 1974).

——, "Diasporan Intervention in International Affairs: Irish-America as a Case Study", *Diaspora. A Journal of Transnational Studies*, vol. 1, no. 2 (Fall, 1991) pp. 143–63.

Bell, J. Bowyer, "Aspects of the Dragonworld: Covert Communication and the Rebel Ecosystem", *Intelligence and Counterintelligence*, vol. 3, no. 1 (1990) pp. 15–43.

——, *IRA Tactics and Targets. An Analysis of Tactical Aspects of the Armed Struggle, 1969–1989* (Dublin: Poolbeg Press, 1990).

Bruce, Steve, *The Red Hand. Protestant Paramilitaries in Northern Ireland* (Oxford: Oxford University Press, 1992).

Burton, Frank, *The Politics of Legitimacy. Struggles in a Belfast Community* (London: Routledge and Kegan Paul, 1978).

Cohan, Al, *The Irish Political Elite* (Dublin: Gill and Macmillan, 1972).

Darby, John, *Intimidation and the Control of Conflict in Northern Ireland* (Dublin: Gill and Macmillan, 1986).

Donoghue, Denis, "Inside the Maze – Legitimising Heirs to the Men of 1916", *The Listener* (3 September 1981).

—— (1991), *Warrenpoint* (London, Jonathan Cape).

du Toit, André, *Understanding South African Political Violence: A New Problematic?* (Geneva: UNRISD paper, 1992).

Edwards, Ruth D., *Patrick Pearse. The Triumph of Failure* (London: Gollancz, 1977).

Elliott, Marianne, *Wolfe Tone. Prophet of Irish Independence* (New Haven: Yale University Press, 1989).

Fairweather, E., McDonough, R. and MacFadyean, M., *Only the Rivers Run Free. Northern Ireland: The Women's War* (London: Pluto Press, 1984).

Feehan, John M., *Bobby Sands and the Tragedy of Northern Ireland* (Dublin: Mercier Press, 1983).

Garvin, Tom, *The Evolution of Irish Nationalist Politics* (Dublin: Gill and Macmillan, 1981).

Geertz, Clifford, *Old Societies and New States* (Free Press, 1963).

——, *The Interpretation of Cultures; Selected Essays* (London: Hutchinson, 1975).

Goodall, David, "Terrorists on the Spot", *The Tablet*, no. 25 (December 1993/ 1 January 1994).

Harris, Rosemary, *Prejudice and Tolerance in Ulster* (Manchester: Manchester University Press, 1972).

Hechter, Michael, *Internal Colonialism. The Celtic Fringe in British National Development, 1536–1966* (London: Routledge and Kegan Paul, 1975).

Honderich, Ted, *Political Violence* (Oxford: Basil Blackwell, 1976).

Irvin, C. and Moxon-Browne, E., "Not Many Floating Voters Here", *Fortnight*, no. 273 (1989) pp. 7–9.

Kearney, Richard, *Transitions: Narratives in Modern Irish Culture* (Manchester: Manchester University Press, 1988).

Keena, Colm, *A Biography of Gerry Adams* (Dublin, Mercier Press, 1990).

Lee, J. J., *Ireland 1912–1985. Politics and Society* (Cambridge: Cambridge University Press, 1989).

Loftus, Belinda, *Mirrors. William III and Mother Ireland* (Dundrum: Picture Press, 1990).

MacDonagh, Oliver, *Ireland: The Union and its Aftermath* (London: Allen & Unwin, 1977).

Miller, David W., *Queen's Rebels. Ulster Loyalism in Historical Perspective* (Dublin: Gill and Macmillan, 1978).

Miller, Kerby A., "Emigration, Capitalism and Ideology in Post-Famine Ireland", in R. Kearney (ed.), *Migrations. The Irish at Home and Abroad* (Dublin: Wolfhound Press, 1990).

Mack, John E., "The Psychodynamics of Victimisation among National Groups in Conflict", in Vamik D. Volkan, Demetrios A. Julios and Joseph V. Montville (eds), *The Psychodynamics of International Relationships*, vol. 1: *Concepts and Theories* (Lexington, Mass.: Lexington Books, 1990).

Moss, David (1989), *The Politics of Left-Wing Violence in Italy, 1969–1985* (London: Macmillan, 1989).

——, *Italian Political Violence, 1969–1988: The Making and Unmaking of Meanings* (Geneva: UNRISD paper, 1992).

——, "Analysing Italian Political Violence as a Sequence of Communicative Acts: The Red Brigades, 1970–1982", *Social Analysis*, no. 13 (May 1983), pp. 84–111.

Mulloy, Eanna, "Emergency Legislation: Dynasties of Coercion", *A Field Day Pamphlet*, no. 10 (Derry, 1986).

MacDonagh, Oliver, *States of Mind: A Study of Anglo-Irish Conflict, 1780–1980* (London: George Allen and Unwin, 1983).

MacStiofain, Sean, *Memoirs of a Revolutionary* (London: Gordon Cremissi, 1975).

New Ireland Forum, *The Cost of the Conflict Arising from the Northern Ireland Crisis since 1969* (Dublin: Stationery Office, 1983).

O'Faolain, Sean, "Hate, Greed, Lust and Doom", *London Review of Books* (May 1981).

O'Keeffe, Terence M., "Suicide and Self-Starvation", *Philosophy*, vol. 59, no. 229 (1984) pp. 349–63.

O'Malley, Padraig, *The Uncivil Wars. Ireland Today* (Belfast: Blackstaff Press, 1983).

——, *Biting at the Grave: The Irish Hunger Strikes and the Politics of Despair* (Belfast: Blackstaff Press, 1990).

O'Tuama, Sean and Kinsella, Thomas, *An Duanaire, 1600–1900. Poems of the Dispossessed* (Portlaoise: Dolmen Press, 1981).

Patterson, Henry, *The Politics of Illusion: Republicanism and Socialism in Modern Ireland* (London: Hutchinson Radius, 1989).

Picard, Elizabeth, *The Lebanese Shia and Political Violence* (Geneva: UNRISD paper, 1992).

Sinn Fein, *Where Sinn Fein Stands* (Dublin: 1970).

——, *Towards a Strategy for Peace* (Dublin: 1988).

——, *Towards a Lasting Peace in Ireland* (Dublin, 1992).

Townshend, Charles, *Political Violence in Ireland. Government and Resistance since 1848* (Oxford: Clarendon Press, 1983).

Wright, Frank, *Northern Ireland. A Comparative Analysis* (Dublin: Gill and Macmillan, 1987).

Wyschogrod, Edith, *Spirit in Ashes: Hegel, Heidegger and Man-Made Mass Death* (New Haven, Conn.: Yale University Press, 1983).

8 ETA and Basque Political Violence

MICHEL WIEVIORKA

I INTRODUCTION

The history of violence in Spain is a complex one. It has its ideological as well as its ethnic sources. Competing strands, Catholic, conciliar, monarchist, anarchist, communist, Trotskyist, socialist and that strange amalgam of corporatism, monarchism, and Catholicism represented by Franco, have all left their residue in a country in which localism and an extraordinary imperial history remain retrievable memories. Monarchy, republic, civil war, dictatorship, autocracy, democracy – these have succeeded each other at the state level with Spain perhaps today one of the more stable and increasingly prosperous countries in the European community. Such progress has eroded Basque nationalism. So have crackdowns on terrorists who have taken refuge on the French side of the border by the French government. But acts of terrorism continue and Basque nationalism and separatism remain a festering sore in the Spanish polity.

However, the political violence characteristic of Spain's Basque country is very different from the kind of political violence that comes from economic marginality. Rather, a little like Sikh violence in India its origins are connected to myths embodied in a discourse. But this mythic side has been eroded by economic gains. While Spain, in common with other European countries, is suffering from economic recession Basques continue to enjoy a relatively high level of economic prosperity. The question then is what keeps the movement alive and so little amenable to conciliation and mediation. Because the Basque case differs from most others where perceived injustice, loss, depatrimonialization, dispersion, etc., constitute a general context for violence, none of these factors are strategically relevant here. Examining it thus requires a different way of looking at political violence. For as a case it is puzzling, undermining a good many preconceived ideas and stereotypes.

To some extent one can apply discourse theory. Basques remain a discourse community if only in terms of their own language. Moreover, the discourse claims to a uniquely antique nationality. One such "authenticating myth" goes back to the eleventh century and "La Chanson de Roland". In the conventional version Roland, the nephew of Charlemagne, was defeated by the Arabs at Ronsevaux (which is in Basque territory). In the Basque version, however, Roland was defeated not by the Arabs but the Basques. Recountings give an illusion of historical pedigree within a discourse of multiple retrievals most particular in the nineteenth century when Basque became industrial. The name Sabino Arana, one of several folk heroes of this period has come down to us as one of the founding fathers.

Whatever the remaining utility of this putative history, the real development of ETA (Euskadi Ta Askatasuna – Basque country and Freedom), begins during the all-powerful Franco dictatorship and intensified almost in proportion to the decline of that dictatorship, and we see a progression. As Spanish society made the transition to democracy it became more violent and more separatist rather than less. Terrorism escalated just as democracy had indisputably established itself.

We can consider ETA's political violence from three different standpoints. It is first an effort to define or express the nation. It is in this context that it developed an historical pedigree, and mixes memory with desire within a retrieving discourse. It also represents a genuine social movement. Finally, it projects what it considers to be a revolutionary design. We can use these three dimensions to examine Basque nationalism both historically and analytically.

Today the content of these dimensions has changed radically. Indeed, Spain itself has changed and the larger political context has as well. It is no longer an oppressed nation as was the case of Spain under Franco's dictatorship. With freedom, the role of its key institutions have been altered. What had been a strong and determined Basque labour movement challenging the power of the Franco regime in a series of major struggles against the regime, as occurred in the mid-1970s, is very different from the labour movement today which has not only been split by the economic crisis but has lost its central focus in what is now a new post-industrial stage of Spanish society. Nor can revolutionary objectives have the same meaning or scope as when the world was dominated by the cold war and when communist and Marxist–Leninist ideologies played a ubiquitous leading role. Today few communist regimes are left. All those in Europe have collapsed. Marxist–Leninist thinking has lost its attraction.

These changes have of course deeply affected ETA. But that, all the more so, because the organization was, one might say, a sum of the three elements embodied within a discourse whose symbolic and ideological aspects were renewed by the practice of violence itself. Violence was not only the result of each of the three elements – the nation, the social movements and the revolutionary plan – but gave such violence purpose, directionality, within the framework of an integrated discourse. One can say that Basque nationalists represented a genuine discourse community, not least of all because of its real linguistic separatism.

Today such coherence is lost. Hence the movement relies more on violence to keep itself alive. The increasing uses of terror is its chief characteristic. Yet such reliance on terrorism has changed the character of the movement itself. Indeed, it has become counter-productive. For as a method terrorism has become blind where it was purposeful. It confuses means and ends. It bears little relation to the expectations and experiences of the people in whose name it is carried out. Terrorism has in fact broken up the original "synergistic" qualities of the three dimensions mentioned above. Basque nationalism then is increasingly dependent on violence for its own sake. The movement has lost its original meaning. As already indicated, when the principle of armed struggle was adopted by the first militants of ETA, they were neither desperate nor poor. The Basque region was neither an economically exploited region nor the victim of a centre which pillaged its wealth. On the contrary, industrially and financially, it was a major centre. It was indeed a key to economic growth in Franco's Spain. It was critical to the more over-all modernization process. Indeed, it attracted large-scale emigration. The recourse to violence, at least in its initial stages, was not therefore the result of crisis or poverty but rather prosperity and growth.

Precisely because of such prosperity there was a well-defined proletariat. What gave Basque nationalism its originally revolutionary appeal and impetus was its attractiveness to those who saw the future in terms of a radical "repossession" of wealth by the proletariat. The revolutionary class, the class with radical "brains" was neither poor nor excluded. The chief agent of nationalism was a strong labour movement capable of aspiring to the leadership of an already well-established industrial society. ETA's activities had always been based on strong nationalism. It was able to hitch this nationalism to the star of the labour movement.

As suggested, this nationalism has a long history which has succeeded in combining and synthesizing pre-modern and totally modern aspects. On the one hand, it is based upon what Clifford Geertz has called primordial links.[1] It is here that language and traditional culture become relevant in providing a sense of belonging to an ethnic or even racial community. On the other hand, its nationalism supported the creation of a modern state, capable of economic development, moving away from primordial links in order to involve in combat emigrants who had come from all over Spain to

take part in the region's industrial development. In this regard it repudiated racism and declared itself in favor of more universal values. Basque
nationalism, as formulated by ETA, combines what might otherwise be
considered, especially by political anthropologists, as opposites, the traditional versus the modern. But quite the contrary, these were originally
made mutually reinforcing. To use the words of Louis Dumont, it was
both holistic and individualistic.[2] It combined references to the earth and
to blood, akin to the German tradition of the nation, with the political will
to carry out a common project, more compatible with the French tradition
of the nation. Perhaps, however, as Alan Renaut suggests, one should
avoid radicalizing the opposition of these two concepts.[3] Nevertheless,
ETA's nationalism is a complex structure which does not allow for any
simplifying preconceptions.

Which perhaps accounts for the continuity and development of ETA.
Practically up until now it has been able to go through radically different
historical circumstances while maintaining the structural basis of its creed,
minor changes excepted. ETA emerged in opposition to a dictatorship that
was all-powerful, it grew during the dictatorship's decline and progressed
during the transition to democracy. The irony is that its violence escalated
as Spain became more democratic.

Yet it still remains true to say that one cannot really consider ETA
without taking into account the three dimensions indicated above. It
remains simultaneously an urge to nationhood, a genuine social movement, while projecting a revolutionary design. Analysing ETA does not
only mean understanding how an actor is created by elaborating an "inversionary discourse".[4] It also outlines a way of thinking which as action
expressed and takes into account aspects of each of the three dimensions'
meaning.

In so far as ETA bases itself on the nation, social movements and the
revolution, we will need to consider these three dimensions one by one,
including diachronic consideration of their transformation over a period of
time. Which leads to a more general hypothesis. The degree of facility
with which nation, social movement and revolutionary plan can be doctrinally integrated the more significant a limited and symbolic expression
and level of violence. The more difficult such integration, and the more
artificial the effort the more violence itself becomes the necessary substitute. Hence, the growth of terrorism is correlated with the dissociation and
the fragmentation of the three components.

This leads to another issue, which is that of the conversion to terrorism
as such and the consequences of what can be considered to be sheer blind
terrorism. If there is a confusion of means and ends, and actions bear no

relation to the expectations and experiences of the people then in effect it is the randomization of violence which results. This changes the nature of conflict from purposeful actions to hit and run tactics which people are not likely to support. ETA as it has existed over the past thirty years is in this sense not only randomizing its violence, but beginning to undergo a kind of historical exhaustion. Its trajectory is coming to an end.

To analyse this trajectory, field work was engaged in under the auspices of the Centre d'Analysa et d'Intervention sociologigues (CADIS), Paris, which, beginning in 1983, lasted several years during which time three long-term sociological projects were carried out.[5] The first was with a group of around a dozen former ETA militants, the second with a number of militants belonging to its political wing and frequently involved in clandestine activities, and the third with members of the Basque Nationalist Party, which functions along institutional lines within the framework of democracy and which, in the late 1950s, saw the emergence of the founders of ETA. This text does not describe work carried out by these research teams, which has already been published in a book, although some factual or historical information contained in the book is mentioned.[6] The reader should be aware that this text is not only based on information obtained using traditional methods, but also on research carried out in the field with the protagonists who have shaped political violence in Spain's Basque country for the past thirty years.

II   THE FORMATION OF ETA

"Gora Euskadi" – long live the Basque country: this slogan first appeared in 1959 on the walls of several towns in Spain's Basque region and it was the first public manifestation of an organization which no-one at the time imagined, not even its founders, would gradually occupy an important political and symbolic place.

(a)   The Crisis of the PNV

ETA was originally formed as a consequence of a crisis within traditional Basque nationalism, more specifically within the party which had incarnated it since the end of the nineteenth century, the Basque Nationalist Party (PNV).[7]

This party had played an important role against Franco at the time of the civil war and had then organized political opposition to the dictatorship from exile, setting up a Basque government. Its ideas combined nationalism based on the concept of a Basque culture, history and sometimes even race, with outspoken Catholicism and political trends along Christian Democrat lines. It was openly hostile to socialism, although that did not prevent it from showing firm support for the forces opposed to Franco's dictatorship.

At the end of the Second World War, the PNV had high hopes. The Axis Powers had been defeated, Germany and Italy had become democracies and, in spirit, Franco's regime was condemned to disappear as a result of pressure by the victors and United Nations decisions which were moving towards a boycott of Spain. However, everything changed very rapidly with the beginning of the Cold War and the new strategic policies of the United States, which decided to give Franco's Spain a central role in its diplomatic and military order: there was no room for the PNV in this new orientation; it soon became isolated, marginalized on the international scene where its independentist projects had no place.

The internal crisis was particularly acute because the Spanish Catholic Church, or at any rate its hierarchy, was also playing the card of the regime and because in the field in Euskadi the PNV was less and less present or capable of action. Repression by the dictatorship had led to the exile or imprisonment of the majority of its leaders and it had to operate at a distance, especially from France, thereby cutting it off from the situations being experienced on the spot and creating additional tension between the exiled leaders and the nationalists at home. More specifically, the new political and social situation helped to weaken the PNV, whose orientation was ill-adapted. The regime used force to repress the labour movement, banning strikes, controlling trade unions within a framework of constrictive corporatism and at the same time managing to obtain from the industrial middle classes in general and Basque in particular if not support at least a non-hostile attitude. The Basque bourgeoisie, which was often active within the Party, did not draw attention to its national feelings and the PNV's anti-socialism prevented it from envisaging any real rapprochement with the labour movement.

This is why at the beginning of the 1950s in Euskadi an internal confrontation within the PNV began to emerge, caused primarily by the young members who could not accept what they saw as a combination of impotency and archaism in their Party. The nationalist students who from 1952 onwards edited the journal *Ekin* (Action) were first and foremost critical of the older members who they reproached for their religious orientation and, above all, for their lack of action in the field; Ekin groups were set up in Guipuzcoa and Biscay, many young members attacked the functioning of

PNV's youth organization, EGI, and left it, and in 1959 these different elements combined to found ETA, which in the beginning was effectively the result of the crisis within the PNV.

In the past, the Party had already experienced considerable tension and even internal confrontation which had led to the ideological radicalism of some of its constituents: for example, those who in 1932 had already attempted to combine nationalism and anti-capitalism within the "Jagi-Jagi" movement. But the creation of ETA resulted from a much deeper crisis whose meaning was defined by young intellectuals who, in various Western European universities, had become acquainted with Marxist–Leninist ideologies.

(b)   The Protagonists' Discourse

The foundation of ETA was not only an organizational split which would continue PNV's traditional ideas in a new political form. It primarily involved a three-fold ideological mutation.

On the one hand, ETA nationalism, without really breaking with that of the older nationalists, was radically different. The young founders of ETA rejected the religious bias, which was central, and the racism, which was secondary, advocated by the PNV. They also adopted a more active position regarding the national consciousness. The nation was no longer seen as the heritage of the historical past, a culture that had been handed on, nor even the biological manifestation of the Basque race; it became a structure that was particularly necessary because, under Franco, repression sought to eradicate the Basque language and eliminate everything which embodied the Basque national specificity. The nation was threatened with disintegration and for the first ETA activists voluntarist measures were needed to allow the nation to survive and develop culturally. It is not therefore surprising under the circumstances that a man like Txillardegui appears both as an inspiration for the political renewal of the Basque nation and as an intellectual who played a role in its linguistic revival.

In addition, in comparison with the PNV, ETA's political and social orientation became radically different. In the early 1960s, the Basque country was the scene of labour mobilization, as in other parts of Spain where there was industrial growth. The major strikes in the Asturias in 1962, then in Biscay and Guipuzcoa, showed a labour movement that was capable of asserting itself despite the repression and of opposing it. It provided meaning, a reference point, the image of an opponent whose vitality was in marked contrast to the powerlessness of the PNV. For ETA's first leaders this gave food for thought and reason to develop so the ideological choice was made fairly rapidly: ETA became a movement that was politically left-wing and relied on the working proletariat to become the central focus for opposition to Franco's dictatorship. Its action assumed a new signification, it became a combination of Basque nationalism and a labour movement and it aimed to involve the industrial proletariat in its struggle for national liberation. This meant a two-fold reversal of the situation. Henceforward, the Basque bourgeoisie would become an adversary because not only the major employers, seen as a "pro-Spanish" oligarchy, but also the middle and lower-middle classes, even though they were patriotic, exploited the working class. The latter was perceived in a wide sense as including the "maketos", the large number of workers who had come from other provinces in order to work in Basque industry. ETA thus became the figurehead for a struggle that was both national and social and it gave a concrete demonstration of this in 1963 when it publicly marked its solidarity with the workers punished for having taken part in the 1962 strikes.

Finally, ETA also broke with the Christian Democrat leanings of the PNV by taking a completely different stand in the arena of political ideology and becoming increasingly extreme left-wing. This conversion owed a great deal to the influence of some of its leaders who had studied in France and Belgium and who had met different left-wing or Third World-influenced thinkers. Marxism–Leninism and revolutionary ideas penetrated ETA fairly rapidly and the experience of Cuba (Fidel Castro), Algeria (the FLN), China (Mao Zedong), Vietnam (Ho Chi Minh) and then the action of Che Guevara became important points of reference, as shown by the articles distributed secretly in the "ETA Journal" or the magazine *Zutik*. Revolutionary vocabulary became the norm in an organization which studied the classical authors, Marx, Lenin, Mao Zedong. This made ETA a movement with three dimensions: national, social and revolutionary. This three-dimensional aspect was originally an ideological structure that was not only weak but also of little practical effect. It took the form of declarations which portrayed Euskadi as a dependent and little developed society, the victim of internal "colonialism", although this did not correspond to the reality in provinces which were among the most industrialized in Spain and which, as we have seen, attracted an immigrant proletariat from other regions. But the message was effective: the declaration conveyed by ETA proposed a logic of emancipation on the basis of a moral design. This was similar to what David Apter calls "inversionary discourse".[8] But it is necessary to look at the special nature of this discourse. It was not based upon negation or criticism of the democratic categories embodied in a democratic state or regime. It opposed dictatorship, a highly oppressive and repressive power, and in reversing the categories on which democratic action is based it kept its distance from the concepts of one Party, the PNV, which also combated dictatorship.

(c)   The Principle of Armed Struggle

The three-fold ideological transformation constituted by the ETA had one extremely important consequence: in the early 1960s, ETA adopted the principle of armed struggle, here again breaking with PNV thinking.

In the beginning, the decision had few practical results, it was a voluntarist affirmation which was not founded on any capacity for action. The decision was based on an analysis of the situation. Faced with a dictatorship which was itself violently repressive, which resorted to imprisonment for political reasons, torture and execution, faced with state violence which went far beyond straightforward repression of political activists and was aimed at prohibiting any expression of national sentiments, armed struggle appeared as the only possible response, one which had proved itself over time with the Algerian FLN or Mao Zedong's Long March, and one which was exemplified in many national liberation struggles and guerrilla movements all over the world.

However, like other left-wing activists in western Europe, for a number of years ETA did not put this principle into practice. Armed struggle was an objective, an idea, an aspiration, the subject of heated discussion and childish squabbles, not a practice.

Some members were in favour of a guerrilla war such as that waged by the FLN, for example, Krutwig, who had put forward the formula of revolutionary war;[9] others somewhat later developed a theoretical model, that of the action–repression–action spiral, the idea being that any armed action would lead to increased repression, whose consequence would be to exacerbate the revolt and the violence, etc. However, with the exception of some minor operations, until 1967 armed struggle was only part of the movement's discourse: the only important acts were two relatively unimportant attacks in 1961 against a police station (in Bilbao) and civil government offices (in Vitoria) and a failed attempt to derail a train transporting pro-Franco war veterans going to San Sebastian to participate in a ceremony commemorating the Civil War.

ETA activists who took part in this initial stage in the movement's history told us during separate interviews that the lack of material means had made it impossible to put the principle of armed struggle into practice. However, this explanation does not suffice. During this period, ETA was not really ready to take the step, it hesitated to transform its declarations into action, it was dominated by the structure of its internal debates, by tension, especially between those who were situated at one extreme which was above all Marxist and labourist, and others who gave pride of place to the nationalist aspect and called the others "pro-Spanish" so as to underline clearly that they saw in the reference to the class struggle a danger of betrayal *vis-à-vis* the reference to the national liberation struggle. As David Apter says, the text started to be written, it preceded action but it foreshadowed it and called for it.

(d) Two Types of Logic of Armed Struggle

Starting in the mid-1960s, the tension between the two trends in ETA gives us the key to understanding the first armed acts, which corresponded to two main types of logic.

The first is the autonomy achieved by the purely nationalist wing of activity. In 1966, the military leader of the organization, Zumalda alias "el Cabra", opposed to the "pro-Spanish" majority, left ETA with a few dozen activists. He adopted an intransigent nationalism which rejected revolutionary ideas or references to the labour movement and formulated a project for military and psychological action. The "Cabras" got ready by stocking weapons and ammunition, drawing up plans of attack on specific targets, they trained and, in the mountainous region where they operated, they attempted to create a climate of insecurity for those representing or supporting the regime and to mobilize the region's youth using patriotic propaganda which called *inter alia* for the boycott of shops or bars owned or utilized by those collaborating with the regime. In some villages and small towns, their efforts influenced young Basques, but after two or three years the repression got the better of the group and it disappeared.[10] Its disappearance should not simply be seen as the military failure of a guerrilla movement. It is much more than that, it is the first expression – and we shall see that there were others – of a major phenomenon: in the Basque country armed struggle could only continue and resist repression if its protagonists retained the three-dimensional characteristics of the movement, the three-fold reference to the nation, as the Cabras had done, but also to the revolution and the labour movement, which they had rejected. The separation of one component, nationalism in this case, either leads to radicalization towards a militarization which is divorced from the experience of the Basque masses and limits itself to straightforward confrontation against repression or to a move toward other forms of combat in which violence has no place but which irredeemably move away from the movement. This was the case at the same time for the "pro-Spanish" who also left ETA or rather were expelled because they gave absolute priority to the class struggle. Those expelled – the "Felipes" – abandoned the principle of armed struggle, after hesitating between Trotskyism and Maoism they joined the Spanish communist movement, moving completely away from specifically Basque-oriented action.

The second type of logic of armed struggle, on the other hand, is based on the idea of linking the three major points of reference of the Basque movement. It corresponded to the setting up in 1966–7 of an organization which envisaged four "fronts" – military, cultural, political and economic (later called labour). Its aim was to associate in the same struggle the working proletariat, peasants and the national bourgeoisie, with the idea of eliminating the latter at a subsequent stage. The project took form at ETA's Fifth Assembly and for the first time it envisaged in practical terms a plan of action comprising propaganda, in particular to cover labour demands among ETA supporters, and first and foremost the pursuit of armed struggle: the objective was to blow up monuments and various symbols of the regime and at the same time to obtain funds by attacking banks and enterprises. The Military Front was responsible for procuring weapons, ammunition and explosives.

In fact, from 1967 onwards, a number of violent acts were committed; bombs in symbolic buildings associated with the regime, nails spread in front of the Tour of Spain cycle race and hold ups, while at the same time the organization recruited many young militants. The peak was reached in August 1968 when ETA assassinated Irun's Chief of Police, Meliton Manzanas, a well-known figure detested for his repression and a notorious torturer.

The first violent acts were therefore directed at the dictatorship and its symbols. They led to assassination in a specific context since the killing of Manzanas followed an episode in which an important leader of ETA, Txabi Echebarrieta, had been killed by the Guardia Civil at a police blockade and another militant had been arrested and condemned to a long term of imprisonment.

Above all, the assassination of Manzanas corresponded to a carefully considered decision, to a real internal debate. Those who for the first time resorted to assassination were not hot-headed or panicky terrorists and at no time did they envisage unbridled proliferation of such practices. Their decision was part of a process which for the time being was fully under their control and they were perfectly aware that their gesture would be understood by the Basque population. In this case, violence was directly linked to the experience and feelings of a large number of Basques. It had symbolic weight, because it was directed at an important symbol of dictatorship, but it did not allow the public expression of the complexity of the significations which ETA wished to control because it did not take into account the three-dimensional aspect; it first and foremost highlighted the emergence of an actor able to show concrete opposition to an oppressive and repressive regime.

III HISTORICAL BACKGROUND AND SOCIOLOGICAL ANALYSIS

We shall study in more detail the moment when ETA had just announced its existence as a figure capable of carrying out active and deadly violence. The historical background, as it has been reconstituted, is more a chronological description than a real analysis. This is why it is necessary here to study carefully the paradigms and methods of approach capable of helping us to understand the action better and especially the fact that it utilizes violence.

(a) The Limits of Traditional Reasoning

The historical background we have described underlines ETA's important characteristics. The birth of the organization came about through a split rather than an extension of traditional Basque nationalism; it involved the ideological structuring of a complex action through the formulation of a discourse based on three fundamental axes because it was founded on the concept of simultaneously speaking on behalf of the Nation, the Class and the Revolution. It was based on the apparently straightforward image of one single enemy, dictatorship, the Spanish state. However, although the more detailed versions of this description allow the history of the protagonist's tensions and internal debates to be retraced,[11] they leave many questions unanswered.

(b) Culture and Violence

The first question which springs to mind relates to the role of Basque culture in ETA's mobilization. This theme is often present in the spontaneous speeches by its militants, in popular references to a Basque nation. In its erudite form it can be found in several works which are more or less outspoken. For example, Juan Aranzadi suggested that there is a "Basque millenarism", a culture rooted in the distant past and capable of projecting itself into the future.[12] In a slightly different approach, Julio Caro Baroja strongly attacks the idea that the violence can be explained by historical or sociological "reasons" and at the same time puts forward an analysis of traditional Basque culture, which he shows operates according to dichotomous opposites such as good and evil thereby encouraging the recourse to violence.[13] As Antonio Beristain writes,[14] this culture has not had to confront modernity and has certainly not generated it; The Basque country did not experience the equivalent of the Age of Enlightenment or the German Aufklärung, still less any revolutionary episodes, and the traditional culture, mainly dominated by Catholicism, was not even shaken by a secular university culture because up until 1968 the only university was a Catholic one.

The Church's role was not only to exert a strong influence over the cultural formation of the Basques. Under the dictatorship, contrary to what was taking place elsewhere in Spain, the clergy, in opposition to its hierarchy, played an important role in what Francis Jaureguiberry called the "fabrication of rebels", the formulation of an ethic of resistance to oppression and of Basque national affirmation.[15] By organizing cultural and leisure activities for young Basques, priests not only made youth aware of the Basque cause but also helped to combat dictatorship.

Violence was cultivated in schools, through education, the Church, the family and cultural models which guaranteed a favourable terrain for the expression of what became with ETA the armed struggle. It is tempting to integrate the patterns which resulted from such cultivation in the form of syndromes, such as an authoritarian personality.[16] However, this would do violence to the complexity of the results. For one thing ETA was born within a party, the PNV, which had never advocated an armed struggle. It assumes continuity, a structural trait of culture, whereas ETA introduced a rupture. Moreover, ETA never had the slightest inclination towards clericalism and that from the beginning most of its militants were distant from the Church and often even from religion.

For them, the image of a "eskualdun fededun" (a religious Basque) was archaic, a figure about which to joke. In other words, the "cultivation approach" ignores the special conditions under which a movement such as ETA is formed, as well as the social, political or other relations which make possible its creation; it considers that violence is inherent in the essence, a historical being, instead of trying to find a meaning for it, seeing whether it corresponds to precise significations, orientations for action which are to be found not in the immemorial past but in a system of action that is very present.

It is possible that the culture created conditions favourable to the conversion to violence in Euskadi, but it is not an explanation for the violence, or only marginally so. In its initial stages, ETA was far from giving the image of an organization inspired by traditional violence. It was not part of the continuity of a culture in which violence arose spontaneously, on the contrary, it aimed at rational, highly moral and extremely modern action, only resorting to the armed struggle as a carefully considered instrument. The fact that its first armed acts incited echoes and sympathy among the population often rooted in Basque culture and its possible leanings towards violence does not in any way change the fact that sociologically they were far apart.

(c)   Frustration and Uprooting

A second question which needs to be asked concerns the social and psychological sources for the mobilization of activists in the ranks of the ETA. Two traditional approaches can be used here. The first corresponds to the concept of relative frustration, as it was adumbrated by James C. Davies and above all Ted Robert Gurr, for whom violence is the result of a gap between expectations and the possibility of seeing them met.[17] This type of approach has not, to our knowledge, ever seriously been applied to the Basque case and we shall content ourselves here with repeating the criticism of the theories which are based on this paradigm by James B. Rule, the most important being that "relative deprivation-thinking is perhaps even more susceptible than other theories ... to being interpreted in ways that are circular and hence unfalsifiable".[18]

The second approach does not ignore the concept of frustration, but lays special emphasis on the uprooting process. There is a common version, low on theory, among several observers who are hostile if not to the Basque cause at least to armed struggle and it forms one of the spontaneous explanations of violence. In this perspective, the protagonists of violence are formed in meetings of intellectuals, frustrated, corresponding to a type accurately described by Raymond Aron,[19] with uprooted individuals perturbed by social change and more particularly by the clash of modernity and tradition.

This reasoning is often applied to one particular region in the Basque country, Goyerri, which throughout the 1960s and 1970s provided many of the movement's activists. Goyerri is characterized by industrialization which has taken place side by side with rural styles of living without destroying them. In this area, where the Basque language has remained much more alive than elsewhere, many young people still belong to a peasant culture and live on the farm while at the same time finding work in the machine tool factories, which are usually on a small scale. They therefore find themselves situated half way between two ways of life and are ill at ease in both. At the farm, they feel out of things, having more or less broken with the values and ways of the traditional existence from whence they sprung, and at the factory they do not feel themselves to be truly integrated in the industrial society, not fully accepting to be workers and, for example, hesitating to take part in contestation. This reasoning has a number of variants; it has been put forward regarding the situation in the 1970s, which will be studied below, and the economic crisis which destabilized even further these proletarians who are half-farmer half-worker: in that situation not only are the proletarians torn between two systems, but the second system, which should have been increasingly able to accommodate them, is no longer able to do so because unemployment tends to exclude them from an industrial society to which they imagined they could belong and which would give them access to modern forms of consumption.

This type of analysis is highly questionable. At best it only covers part of the organization and leaves aside the large number of militants who have nothing to do with the frustration caused by the disastrous clash of tradition and modernity. It is true that, throughout the movement's history, many militants and leaders in ETA came from Goyerri or from similar backgrounds, in Biscay and even in Bilbao where large-scale industry makes wide use of workers who retain strong links with rural life. It also true that in an area like Goyerri, youth is relatively frustrated and uprooted and often joins together in groups of friends, the "cuadrillas", in fact typical of the Basque country as a whole, which create networks of solidarity that can quite easily and discreetly be used for the organization's recruitment. Nevertheless, too much importance should not be placed on the image of the dramatic clash between tradition and modernity. For many, the possibility of work in industry was seen as progress which did not prevent them staying harmoniously in the village or on the farm and if, in the area of Goyerri as elsewhere, some decided to join ETA, it was first and foremost as a reaction to the violence of dictatorship, to repression which prohibited public expression of ideas and above all any manifestation of belonging to Basque culture. The brother of one of ETA's historical leaders, Apalategui, explained at length that "the young worker receives his pay, in the evening he feeds his cows, works in the garden. He is one of the first to have a Vespa. If Franco had not been there, the situation would have been idyllic."

More generally, the approach mentioned above has the major disadvantage of depriving commitment to armed struggle of any meaning. It emphasizes social origin and a specific context, whereas in practice the organization's recruitment was from all classes and occurred in all situations; above all, it dissociates the signification of action and socio-professional or other characteristics from the actors, who in this perspective, are not influenced by any meaning but are only the fruit of a reaction to a situation which they are personally unable to control.

Later on, we shall see that ETA violence does tend to become meaningless and we shall explain this using the concept of inversion. For the moment, however, the history of the birth and initial stages of the organization on the contrary suggest the existence of orientation, the realization of significations, and make it impossible to give a leading role to the idea of a crisis being conducted through loss of its meaning.

(d) Instrumental Violence

In the 1970s, the frustration theories were severely criticized by authors such as Charles Tilly,[20] who mainly reproached them with not taking into account the fact that political violence was of an instrumental nature, that for the protagonist it constituted a way of achieving his objectives. From that point of view, analysis of armed struggle means reconstituting the protagonist's calculations, strategies and alliances, and examining the objectives he has set and the resources he utilizes to achieve them. This concept corresponds fairly closely to the discourse of the protagonist for whom organized violence is an instrument adopted rationally and it is hardly surprising that it was presented as such by a leading ETA militant, Mario Onaindia, whose name would become known worldwide in the early 1970s on the occasion of the Burgos trial and the intensive international mobilization to save those condemned to death, including precisely this activist.[21] In his book, Mario Onaindia presents ETA in strategic terms, through its capacity to make politico-military calculations, to foresee or respond to those of other organized actors, and through its efforts to bring the Basque population closer to ETA by inciting increasingly severe and blind repression, which it was expected would in turn incite awareness among the Basque population and rouse the national consciousness.

This form of approach is more appropriate if one seeks to understand the political and military stakes of the actor once he has really become established and included in a system of organized actors. Even here, however, its scope is limited because, as we shall see later in the history of ETA, violence was never limited to these instrumental dimensions. And as far as the period of ETA's formation is concerned, this view is extremely weak. It ignores the orientation of action, the meaning it expresses, the effort exerted by the protagonist over himself to deal simultaneously with significations which we know are three-dimensional, national, social and political, and ultimately it tends to confuse the meaning of the action with the practical objectives, the most profound signification with the more immediate goals. If violence is instrumental, for example, it is not easy to understand why it slackens off or is rejected by those who distance themselves from ETA on a nationalist basis, or why it escalates, as will be seen later, among those who wish to maintain the three-dimensional nature of the action. Let us state clearly: the instrumental paradigm provides a useful clarification, but it is not sufficient and even leaves aside some decisive aspects of the struggle. That is why it is necessary to turn to another method of approach.

(e)   Analysis of a Comprehensive Social Movement

The best works on the Basque experience show how Franco's dictatorship exercised indiscriminate repression which shaped a collective consciousness that was easily reflected in ETA practice. The dictatorship, by resorting to mass arrests and imprisonment, by restricting individual freedom, by prohibiting use of the Basque language, by making workers' social contestation extremely difficult, created what Francis Jaureguiberry called an "underground society" in which the three-fold oppression suffered, as a Basque, a worker and at least for some as a prohibited political person, united in a more or less confused way large sectors of the population in Euskadi.[22] The dictatorship in fact helped to unite against it differing sentiments and ETA aimed to incarnate these.

This is why an analysis must put a specific question, relatively distinct from those which allow the methods of approach mentioned above to be utilized: what is the link between organized violence, formulated by ETA, and the three levels of signification which it states it represents, how does one move from national consciousness, a social movement, a political design and their association to concrete utilization of armed struggle? Put like this, the question needs some clarification, especially regarding each of the meanings to which ETA relates.

(f)   Basque Nationalism

Basque nationalism, as formulated in the 1950s and 1960s, over and above ETA, among large sectors of the population, has two aspects which have to be distinguished analytically.

The first aspect is identity. It consists of a cultural affirmation, that of a community which was able to resist the destruction sought by Franco's regime and which contained many of the elements of traditional Basque society. It is expressed in collective activities, for example, societies for gastronomy, Basque folklore, sports events, in which the strength and virility of those who fell the most trees in a given time or who move the heaviest stones are admired. It is based on strong networks of solidarity, in particular among the young, whose "cuadrilla" get together in large numbers when it is time for the "poteo" – a round of the bars.

Basque identity is also based on a language, Euskera, whose defence is deemed to be central to the extent that, despite repression, it was taught secretly during the dictatorship in schools, Ikastolas, where education took place in Basque.

It is also founded on a history which goes back to the earliest times and whose largely mythical reconstitution allows the historical unity of the Basque nation to be affirmed, showing how it managed both to resist all sorts of invaders and to establish its own institutions in the past. For example, as Basque people well know, those who attacked the withdrawal of Roland's army at Roncevaux were not, as French history states, Arabs but Basques; it also refers to the original principle of the "Fueros" who for many centuries embodied the institutions of Basque society.

Finally, the affirmation of identity sometimes confines the Basque nation in a racial definition of itself, supported by scientific work which in fact shows that there is a certain biological, or at any rate blood group, characteristic.

All this could mean that the Basque national consciousness was an ethnic phenomenon, if there was not at the same time a second aspect, which could be called political. This second aspect involves a call for independence, therefore the creation of a state with all its modern components: police, judiciary, taxes, currency, army, diplomacy, etc. Nationalism here is not so much the affirmation of an identity – cultural and historic – as the desire to end a domination that is seen as foreign and to sever the links of servitude with Spain. This means total rupture with Madrid and the definition of non-negotiable claims.

The two faces of Basque nationalism did not follow exactly the same historical route and since the end of the nineteenth century they have maintained extremely complex relations. In some circumstances, they can be seen as dissociated: for example, a majority of Basques are satisfied to see their culture recognized and revived, their language spoken, their history taught, without worrying too much about an independent and sovereign state. However, under the dictatorship, these two aspects united, the struggle to affirm identity could easily be associated with the dream of a Basque state, for example, with the idea that only independence could provide the necessary conditions to safeguard the Basque language, history and culture.

(g) The Labour Movement

The labour movement strictly speaking is not basically different in Euskadi from that in other industrialized provinces in Spain, for example, in the Asturias. It should be pointed out that Euskadi has a middle class which was initially in trade then in industry, but also in banking; it never restricted itself to the local market and in successive waves it developed a powerful industry, in particular, in sectors such as steel, shipbuilding, engineering. In such a context, labour's consciousness is also potent, but under the dictatorship it encountered enormous difficulties in expressing itself and could not transform itself into a visible and structured labour movement. A corporatist system of control was installed by the regime and its functioning has been analysed remarkably by Juan Linz.[23] During the period 1910–40, the most influential trade unions were the UGT, ideologically very close to the Socialist Party, and Christian-based organizations very responsive to the paternalism of some sectors of the Basque bourgeoisie. Under the dictatorship, the UGT's influence declined, while that of the Labour Commissions (CCOO), linked to the Communist Party, increased substantially.

Repression and corporatism never really prevented the manifestation of the workers' consciousness, whether in clandestine activity or in the major strikes in 1962. From the point of view which concerns us, it can be seen that when ETA refers to the labour movement, it is not as a participant. Although workers joined the organization early on, they did not in any way see it as a labour organization and they realized that they would have to choose, abandoning militant and clandestine activities in or around the factory for political action which moved them away from it. What ETA gained from the labour movement was a meaning, a reference point; ETA wanted to be a political expression which did not only support the working class but was also capable of representing its demands and its opposition.

(h) Revolutionary Action

As we have seen, left-wing and extreme left-wing ideologies within ETA formulated revolutionary projects which corresponded to several models. Some related to guerrilla action, others dreamed of organizing or directing mass movements, while others related to communism, so different ideas coexisted or succeeded one another. Taken in isolation, this political dimension had two important characteristics.

The first is that, like the social and labour dimension, it is not specifically Basque and the political ideologies to be found in Euskadi are the same as those traversing Spain as a whole. This is why those who in ETA claimed kinship with a class or a revolutionary design to which they subordinated the national consciousness were taxed with being "pro-Spanish".

The second characteristic is that these ideologies were not opposed to others which one might term democratic. In the face of dictatorship, revolutionaries and democrats should not be opponents and they had good reason to identify themselves with a common struggle. If one goes outside ETA, dominated by left-wing and extreme left-wing ideologies, the Basque population is much less sensitive to the differences and debates on the type of regime which should replace the dictatorship or even to the nature of the process which would allow that to happen and much more sensitive to the very fact of dictatorship. It wanted to end the dictatorship more than to build political divisions. This had significant consequences: ETA's attacks against the regime were seen not so much as the work of militants oriented towards revolution, but more as the expression of a struggle against dictatorship. At its creation, ETA could therefore derive benefits from the political sympathies emanating from diverse horizons.

(i) A Comprehensive Basque Movement

We can now explain the concept on the basis of which we shall move forward in our analysis of ETA's armed struggle. The concept is that of a comprehensive movement, in other words, a movement capable of speaking on behalf of the Basque nation, of advancing labour contestation and of developing a political design based on revolution or Marxism–Leninism.

This movement did not exist anywhere else in Basque society outside ETA. The Basque population possessed a strong national consciousness, the Basque working class a strong social consciousness and the political aspirations, the desire to end dictatorship, were strong and widely shared. Although each of these dimensions involved practical action, and even more or less clandestine action, there was no unifying link, at least until ETA appeared. The latter was not directly the active expression of social or political struggles, and the national consciousness was the responsibility of other organizations, starting with the PNV, which remained a strong factor. But ETA spoke on behalf of the whole, it integrated what was dissociated elsewhere and projected the unified image of a comprehensive movement.

Nevertheless, it should be emphasized that this image was only really unified and harmonious seen from the outside. Within ETA, the different significations of action clashed, were in contradiction, so that the subsequent history of the armed struggle can be seen in the light of that tension and the different approaches pursued.

We can now explain the reasoning which will allow us to analyse the history of ETA from where we left off, namely, the first major action, the assassination of Manzanas. This reasoning consists of relating ETA violence and the internal debates and tension which centre around the three major significations of action. In order to understand the avatars of such debate and tension, we must take into consideration not only the ideological work within ETA, but the real and concrete developments in the national consciousness, the social struggles and the political forces in Spain in the 1970s and 1980s.

IV   ARMED STRUGGLE AND A DICTATORIAL STATE

To a certain extent, the assassination of Manzanas illustrates the theory of the action–repression–action cycle, leading to an immediate increase in repression, which was already impressive in Euskadi. It was not only ETA as such which was targeted, and assimilated to banditry by the regime, but also the society as a whole in its role of contestation. To demonstrate, take part in strikes, even to participate in simple work stoppages, to meet, was to disturb public order and could lead to an accusation of "military revolt" Arrests, torture, imprisonment, proliferated and ETA, which had just enrolled a large number of new activists, saw its organizational structure weakened following the arrest of numerous leaders and the majority of its leaders were obliged to take refuge "on the other side", in other words, in France.

(a)   The Movement's Peak

ETA was, however, to experience its golden age in the early 1970s and provide the most effective image in its history of an organization fulfilling the overall symbolic role of a comprehensive movement able to transform that symbolic force into concrete action. Despite the tension and splits, which we will return to later, and despite the repression, ETA ceased being primarily a small group and became a structured organization with several hundred militants. Initially, it demonstrated its support for workers on strike in Biscay (February–March 1969) and practically suspended the armed struggle until July 1970 when it attacked banks and carried out a commando raid which seized a large sum of money from the Sestao shipyards. ETA announced that the money would be handed over to the families of workers killed by the police during a demonstration in Granada. This gesture perfectly illustrates the relationship which ETA intended to maintain with the labour movement because it marked active support for workers, even outside Euskadi. Six months later, on 17 January 1971, another commando kidnapped an industrialist, Zabala, whose enterprise was on strike; the workers' action was particularly spectacular because it took the form of a hunger strike. ETA transmitted its demands: Zabala would be released if wages were increased and a commitment was made not to punish the strikers. Within a few days, the enterprise's management agreed to ETA's conditions and Zabala was released. Even more than during the preceding operation, it underlined ETA's commitment alongside the workers and against the bourgeoisie. It had kidnapped a Basque employer, a man who spoke Basque. Unlike the PNV, ETA could not be accused of collaborating with the bourgeoisie on the pretext that it was Basque.

In addition, ETA's political affirmation included counter-attacks by its militants when they were arrested. Each trial provided the opportunity for proclaiming out loud nationalist and revolutionary convictions and gave a platform from which the regime was denounced. As we have seen, the Burgos trial was the peak from this point of view and it made ETA known all over the world;[24] moreover it was a success because the authorities, subject to strong international pressure and unable to prevent large-scale mobilization of Basque and Spanish public opinion, transmuted the death penalties into terms of imprisonment, which was seen as a retraction and a sign of weakness.

ETA did more than underline its determination against the regime and help the labour movement. It was effectively capable of expressing jointly the three great significations of the struggle, to speak unequivocally on behalf of the nation, the working class and the revolution, and in 1972 and 1973 the result of its action was spectacular. On the one hand, on several occasions its acts reaffirmed its commitment alongside the labour movement through the bombing of the premises of corporatist trade unions linked to the regime and the kidnapping of another industrialist, Huarte, also freed after payment of a ransom and once the demands of the workers on strike in an enterprise he headed had been met. On the other, it took direct action against the dictatorship, while at the same time clearly stating that it was doing so because it rejected national dependence. It placed explosives in tourism offices and, above all, on 20 November 1973, it carried off an operation of considerable importance by assassinating Admiral Carrero Blanco, the only leader in the regime likely to assure continuity when General Franco died.[25]

At the beginning of the 1970s, ETA thus appeared to be the central focus of opposition in the Basque country, it gained a large audience and symbolized without any apparent contradiction all the Basque public's hope and expectations, which it concretized. That ability to embody a comprehensive movement corresponded to a specific historical context which needs to be defined in political and social terms.

Politically, the dictatorship had weakened, particularly since its counterpart in Portugal had collapsed in 1974 and the regime of the colonels in Greece had also collapsed. Repression of course continued very actively, but it was increasingly less able to circumscribe the contestation which agitated not only the Basque country but the whole of Spain. ETA evolved during the period of the Franco regime's crisis and its peak was at a time when the regime was disintegrating, when it was still capable of repression but its weakness was becoming increasingly apparent.

Socially, the years 1970–4 corresponded to two no less important phenomenons. On the one hand, there was an incredible upsurge in labour struggles, the last great mobilization before the disintegration of the labour movement at the end of the 1970s. The struggles were very combative and gave rise to an organizational trend which had its counterpart during the same period in Italy. The "assembly" trend during the period 1974–6 was in many ways revolutionary, it increasingly took place in the open, overtaking the trade unions, particularly the CCOO, which had been so important in the preceding phase manifestly dominated by the difficulties of clandestine activity.

In addition, new social movements emerged outside the industrial sector, mainly following the announcement of a Spanish nuclear energy programme in 1973 which planned four nuclear power stations in the Basque country. The mobilization was initially limited and very local, but it was indicative of increased complexity in the area of social combats, which were no longer restricted simply to labour action.

The combined effects of social combats and the regime's crisis seemed to give ETA wings and it was widely perceived as the only focus of federation and integration of all forms of opposition. That perception was largely shared because ETA, seen from the outside, appeared to have full control over its own action. The most violent acts had in fact not been numerous, but they had been highly significant and well understood not only by the Basque population but also by Spanish and even international public opinion, so that ETA appeared as a profoundly legitimate and moral force. It had not yet committed any useless or unbridled violence, it seemed to be in control, only to use arms or explosives in extremely limited and always symbolic cases. It was in direct harmony with the expectations of the population to which it related. The declarations and the acts, the meaning and the practice, the ends and the means, appeared to coincide.

(b)   The Other Side of the Coin

Even though ETA had reached its peak, the image just given is too partial. It corresponds in fact to what could be perceived from the outside, away from the organization or the company of those who to a greater or lesser degree knew its inner workings. The other side of the coin is much less harmonious and the relations within ETA were far from corresponding *in toto* to the perception from outside.

These relations were primarily governed by the tension between those militants who identified themselves with the nationalist wing of action and others who put the class struggle, revolutionary and Marxist–Leninist ideologies first. As a rule, the former were more inclined to armed action, the latter much less so, and the balance between the two sides was perpetually unstable.

In 1969 and the beginning of 1970, ETA's leadership managed to avoid excessive internal tension. But in 1970, the organization split. As a majority, the militants who embodied a revolutionary line called for a new General Assembly, the sixth, which ended in a split. The minority remained faithful to the decisions of the previous assembly and formed ETA (V); the majority aimed to draw closer to other social and political actors on the Spanish scene and set up ETA (VI). They rejected nationalist theses and the principle of armed struggle and in 1972, after heated ideological debates between the left-wings of various tendencies, they disappeared as a collective actor.

ETA (V), in fact ETA, then gradually rebuilt itself. It was this wing that organized armed action, rebuilt its machinery. In doing so, it refused to confine itself purely to nationalism and sought a new ideological formula which would allow it to retain identification with what we have called a comprehensive Basque movement while affirming its identify as a revolutionary figure linked to workers' struggles. In fact, it operated according to a Leninist principle, it wanted to be the vanguard of a national and socio-political liberation movement.

The reconstitution was marked by new tensions which this time opposed the "military" elements in the organization, partisans of violent action whose successes attracted many young people, and the Workers' Front militants, who realized that on the field it was contradictory to try to practice armed struggle and at the same time participate in the increasingly less clandestine social combats which were taking place in the factories. Armed struggle isolated its militants in clandestine activities, prevented them from taking part in open action such as trade unions or assemblies, it obliged them to take decisions without endorsement from the workers, without discussions with them, and it attracted repression. The militants of the Workers' Front were very vulnerable, much more so than the "military" elements, who were protected by their absolute secrecy and who increasingly lived in France, on "the other side", in safety when they were not taking part in operations.

In 1972 and 1973, the tension between these two extremes was more or less controlled by the organization, which was in fact in the hands of the "military". A balance seemed possible between armed struggle and open mass action, the presence of militants in the field, especially in social struggles. But in 1974, a new split occurred when the majority of the Workers' Front militants left. For them, armed struggle was an obstacle and not a help to mass action, the context was that of a strong labour movement and it called for the creation of a political party and not a secret organization which practised violence. They founded a political party, LAIA (Revolutionary Patriot Workers' Party), which gave rise to another revolutionary group. They did not exclude recourse to armed struggle, but *de facto* dissociated themselves from it.

This departure did not resolve the internal tension within ETA, which turned towards new internal debates opposing two concepts of action. The question posed was in fact the relationship between mass action and armed struggle, no one questioning these two forms of intervention, and the movement discussed how to link them.

Some considered that it was unwise to integrate the two forms of intervention in one organization and proposed that they should be dissociated, which meant only keeping within ETA a military mechanism and leaving other organizations, parties and trade unions the task of carrying out mass action. These were the "milis". The others, on the other hand, called for dual action within the same organization under the control of a leadership which simultaneously controlled work among the masses, and thus ETA's presence in social and political combats, and armed struggle, which continued to be viewed as necessary. These were the "poli-milis". And once again, ETA experienced a split, but this time two organizations rose out of the separation: the military ETA (ETA [m]) and the politico-military ETA (ETA [pm]).

At first sight, the position of ETA (m), which had less members, appeared to be weaker than that of ETA (pm), which wanted to be present on two fronts: carrying out active work among the masses as well as the armed struggle which was the sole objective of ETA (m). ETA (pm) seemed to correspond better to the situation, dominated by the exhaustion of the Franco regime and the increase in social combats. ETA (pm) even appeared to be much more capable of adapting itself to different situations, being visibly present in the arena of mass action if repression decreased, and concentrating more on the armed struggle if it increased and made open action difficult. However, ETA (m)'s arguments had great force: armed struggle did not have to concern itself with the risks of mass action, each element had its own autonomy and its own rhythm and above all clandestine activists did not involve themselves with the militants of mass action and so were less likely to suffer the effects of repression.

During the period 1975–6, ETA (pm) was on top. It structured itself so as to integrate to the greatest possible extent the dual orientation it had adopted, by deciding not to allow the organization's "Fronts" any autonomy; it decided upon a geographical division of Euskadi in which each zone had one person responsible who directed military and political activities, and it decided to use arms in the light of an assessment of its effects on mass action. Nevertheless, ETA (pm) set up a purely military structure, with special commandos (the "bereziak" commandos) who were responsible for carrying out large-scale operations on targets which went beyond the responsibility of zone leaders. Simultaneously, its militants participated in the formation of a new trade union, the LAB, of revolutionary inspiration.

Even though ETA (pm) developed, it encountered serious difficulties. The dictatorship was politically exhausted and just before the death of General Franco in November 1975 it was only able to hang on through increased repression. The repression was facilitated by the very principle which was the basis of ETA (pm). The police were easily able to identify the militants carrying out political work in the field in the open; and since military activity was not dissociated from mass action, they were able to trace the leaders. ETA (pm) was thus practically dismantled in a few months, many of its leaders were arrested, and several were killed in the course of confrontation with the police. This had an important consequence: the mechanism had to be renewed rapidly, with militants who were less well trained and less experienced than in the past, very often more frustrated and more ready to resort to armed violence than their predecessors. At the time of Franco's death, approximately 500 members of ETA (pm) were in prison and many more were living in France; only one military commando was still functioning and the organization's leadership underwent a profound crisis.

This crisis represented the first step in a lengthy process in which ETA (pm) and its successors became committed to practices which foreshadowed a new phenomenon: the trend towards terrorist inversion.

V   THE TERRORIST INVERSION

We have not employed the word "terrorism", which does not apply to the Basque experience, at least until the mid-1970s. Now, in order to clarify the rest of ETA's history, it is necessary to introduce this concept and give it a precise sociological meaning.

(a)   Myth and Terrorism

What is terrorism? Frequently, specialist literature comes up against an obstacle which it does not really try to eliminate. It explains that one person's terrorists are another person's freedom fighters and proposes a definition which does not in fact allow the question to be answered: how is it possible to chose between the subjectivity of the protagonist and that of his enemies or those he intimidates? With very few exceptions in history, "terrorists" never define themselves as such and do not accept the qualification from those they oppose. Many actors have endeavoured to propose a technical definition of terrorism, *inter alia* allowing it to be distinguished from other forms of violence, war and revolution, and even political violence. They have emphasized the disproportionate nature of the effects of this particular form of violence compared to the means it utilizes, the privileged relations with the media, or the fact that it constitutes the weapon of the weak. They have sometimes laid emphasis on its frenzied character, developing for example the image of mechanisms which go out of the actors' control or of a diabolical machine. However, if the notion of terrorism is to help us analyse ETA's armed struggle, it can only be on the basis of a completely different perspective.

We shall in fact define terrorism as a phenomenon which, in varying forms, combines two main principles. On the one hand, terrorism is an instrumental act, it is the result of decisions, calculations and strategic choices by its protagonists. From this point of view, it can be highly rational, carefully elaborated. But on the other hand, and contemporaneously, it is a violence that is particularly deadly and unrestrained because it refers artificially to a meaning, a series of significations which it aims to embody in a more or less abusive manner.

The most extreme terrorism is not necessarily able to utilize calculations and strategies because it is dominated by the second dimension, which it pushes to the extreme. It speaks in the name of a people, a nation, a social movement, without the people, nation or social movement, if they exist, being able to recognize themselves in it; it replaces them in a totally fictitious way. Violence then claims to have a meaning, but that claim is a form of self-proclamation and the meaning, that is to say the social, national or other movement with which the actor identifies himself, either has no tangible existence or is in practice embodied by collective figures which have nothing to do with the terrorists who speak in their name.

As it is thus appropriated by terrorists, meaning becomes a myth, a representation which combines in an imaginary fashion elements which are not reconcilable in reality, a construction which brings together in a single principle significations which could well have no genuine expression or correspond to practices that differ from those which created the myth.

In terrorism, the myth is closely linked to the violence. The more the actor operates on a voluntarist basis, the more he seeks to give form to the mythical representation with which he identifies, and the more the transition from the imaginary to the real means inordinate efforts, increased violence. From the moment when armed struggle ceases to be in direct relation with the concrete experience of those it defends, helps or represents, also from the moment when it has to deal with significations that are not only distinct but also increasingly distant from each other, violence provides a mythical method of resolution and increasingly becomes the only way to exist for the actor. This is why it is necessary to make a theoretical association between terrorism, in its extreme manifestations, and the myth on which it is based, as was perceived in his own way by Georges Sorel, who combined in the same reasoning the mythical call to a general proletarian strike and the call to violence, defined as a vital force, a constituent of workers' action.[26]

(b) The Inversion

If one considers the extreme forms of terrorism, one can see that the practice reverses the principles and the significations on which it is based. In the name of a certain concept of humanity, the protagonist acts as a barbarian and within the organization itself, suspicion, use of force, lies, replace community warmth and solidarity. The order of the means and the end is reversed, and instead of being an instrument, the use of weapons becomes the object of action. One speaks on behalf of the labour movement and one kills trade unionists, in the name of the nation and one utilizes violence which revolts the national community, in the name of the masses and one ignores them or flatters their basest instincts. One declares support for a scientific concept of progress, and one forbids any exchange of ideas, any theories, any criticism etc. The most total forms of expression of terrorism are a negation which, as we have seen, do not exclude the recourse to instrumental rationality, but go beyond it in a spiral of unrestrained violence which can only be stopped by repression, the destruction of the protagonist, maybe his self-destruction, prison, exile or death.

The protagonists of armed struggle never directly resort in a single step to the extreme forms of terrorism, and the process leading to it is always chaotic, with moments of acceleration and others where it appears to have stopped, with steps backward as well as splits and ruptures within the movement concerned. It is not a linear progression and corresponds in fact to complex mechanisms which we have called inversionary mechanisms, giving this concept a significance which should not be confused with that of "inversionary discourse", as defined by David Apter[27] – we shall come back to this later.

In our vocabulary[28] inversion is the ideological and practical effort through which an actor reinterprets the experience of those whose demands and aspirations he claims to represent and transforms this interpretation into concrete, structured and organized violence. It is delineated, clarified and intensified according to the changes affecting the actor himself and his reference population. As far as the actor is concerned, important transformations relate to the way in which activists are replaced, according to the success of the repression and deaths or imprisonment, individual departures and splits. In many experiences, including that of ETA, the renewal sees militants who are increasingly less well trained politically, increasingly eager to utilize weapons, replace the first generations who were generally more concerned to resort to self-limitation of the recourse to armed struggle and to develop more elaborate political theories. On the part of the reference population, the changes are due to social movements, either because they inevitably decline or, on the contrary, they become more important unexpectedly, but also to political aspirations or attitudes towards national liberation projects. As a rule, the more there is weakness or decline in the social or political movements of reference, the more the protagonist of armed struggle runs the risk of becoming carried away by terrorist inversion, in other words, wanting at all costs, against a background of fundamentalism and rupture, to maintain the high level of the project's image for the movements concerned. The trend towards inversion is particularly strong when the protagonist preaches the struggle of the classes and the labour movement at a time when the latter is disintegrating and losing its social focus.

One possible but not inevitable dimension of terrorist inversion is growing political heteronomy, in other words, the subordination of the actor become terrorist to forces which give him a new meaning at the same time as they help him and make use of him. This phenomenon was embodied in the experience of terrorism in the 1970s and 1980s through the internationalization of violence, especially in the Middle East and the Palestinian movement. The latter's most radical factions attracted activists from all over the world, particularly from Germany and Japan. The most extreme heteronomy can be seen when the terrorist-actor becomes almost a mercenary at the service of one or more sponsor-states.

Here, it should be stated quite simply that the Basque experience, even during the episodes which most clearly underlined its inversion, never progressed to the stage of political heteronomy. It was able to develop contacts with many organizations involved in armed struggle, utilize what was virtually diplomacy, maintain relations with representatives of a number of States, Nicaragua and Libya, for example, help or be helped by foreign groups. But at no time did ETA seek the signification of its action outside its own discourse and it was never subordinated to any other force but itself – quite simply because its nationalism had always prevented it from this type of deviation, which was much more common in struggles of a purely revolutionary inspiration without a national liberation dimension.

Inversion is a process which transforms the actor so radically that it leads to extreme tension at the same time as it attracts persons or groups who had kept their distance up till then. In other words, it cannot be dissociated from fusions or splits. From the moment when it is deployed, it destabilizes the organization carrying on the armed struggle, it creates a spiral in which the points of reference constantly become confused or in which the original discourse hardens or is retracted, where the end and the means are confused or inverted. Inversion, as we understand it, is a process of *losing signification* which is not the same thing as "inversionary discourse" in the sense of David Apter,[29] which defines the process and method by which an actor affirms himself by violating the rules and principles of the state and its hegemony.

Inversion is the actor's effort *vis-à-vis* himself, while "inversionary discourse" implies his rupture with an order or hegemony. This is why inversion is often the possible but not inevitable consequence of "inversionary discourse".

(c) Reformulation of the Basque Issue

From the beginning of the 1970s, everything changed, in Spain and in Euskadi, whether it was the political system, social combats, or the treatment of the national question. Within that transformation, which is explained below, could ETA still occupy alone the symbolic place of the various forms of contestation which propelled Basque society? The answer is no, or with increasing difficulty, and the image of a comprehensive Basque movement, to which it corresponded relatively faithfully, started to become a myth at the same time as the violence it organized assumed a new and more deadly character.

The myth which ETA increasingly defined was quite simple: the organization wanted to be both the foremost embodiment of Basque history and culture, the spearhead of a struggle for independence, the epitome of revolutionary action and the expression of the social demands which arose both in industry, with the labour movement, and in the new social movements, especially the anti-nuclear and feminist movements. The more this representation became unrealistic or only corresponded to increasingly restricted sectors of society, the more the inversion process was amplified and finally took over ETA Following the history of the organization now means following its progress towards inversion and the series of trends which led ETA towards terrorism.

VI   THE PARADOXES OF THE POST-FRANCO ERA

In September 1975, the Caudillo signed the death sentences for the ETA militants Txiki and Otaegi and in November he died, opening up a period of profound upheaval which ensued and we shall first of all study that which most directly concerned the Basque country.

(a) Transition to Democracy

The institutional system which was installed after Franco's death was a constitutional monarchy, sanctified by parliament's adoption of a new

Constitution in December 1978. Spain thus became democratic and the principal expression of this was the formation of a political system, which assumed a special form in the Basque country.[30]

Three Basque parties took part in open politics, not to mention numerous smaller groups. The oldest was of course the PNV, which obviously benefited from democracy. The Party, created in 1895, had in the past experienced internal tension and many difficulties between the two wars with the radical anti-capitalist movement at the national level called the "Jagi-Jagi," with the creation of ETA in the 1950s, with the ETA peak in the early 1970s and the haemorrhage of its youth organization, EGI, which massively went over to the ETA. But the PNV had managed to survive; it was based on networks which had remained powerful, on solid community links, on the design of building a nation step by step. It had strong popular backing and emerged as the main Basque political force, capable of dialogue and negotiation with a centralized Spanish Government. It was even seen as the only Basque alternative to ETA's violence, which many thought no longer had any meaning in the new historical context of the restoration of democracy.

In practice, the relations between the PNV and ETA remained complex. Even though ETA was the result of a rupture with the PNV, all through Franco's dictatorship the latter had constantly aided the armed struggle, behaving rather as a father with his son. The PNV had often felt very close to ETA, sharing the same repression and the same clandestinity. But the time of democracy had arrived, and from 1976 to 1977 onwards the relations between the two organizations became tense. Some members of the PNV found it difficult to adjust to the new situation, had doubts about the stability of the young democracy and therefore hesitated to distance themselves from ETA; others considered that armed struggle, due to its very existence, gave them a weighty argument in the political arena: what the Spanish government would not grant in the course of peaceful negotiations could be demanded by using explosives. This is why the break between the PNV and ETA is not as clearly defined as one might expect, at least from the PNV side. ETA for its part continued to appeal to the nationalist sentiment of the PNV in order to seek help from its militants if necessary: for example, to facilitate the transfer to France of an activist threatened with arrest. In ETA, however, and in the most radical sectors of Basque society, the PNV was reproached with being satisfied with limited measures which did not bring about national independence but a degree of autonomy, with not calling for the immediate creation of a Basque State, and, in addition, with being a reformist or even middle-class force. Nevertheless, when the dictatorship ended, the PNV could open up shop, impose itself as the most important political force, with 26.9 per cent of the votes in the 1979 elections, and become a part of the government in Vitoria, capital of the Province, head several municipalities and have deputies in the Cortes (the parliament in Madrid).

Two other Basque political forces emerged during the same period, both as an extension of ETA. Euskadiko Eskera (EE) brought together militants who wished to keep alive the three-fold banner of social struggle, the nationalist combat and revolutionary action, while at the same dissociating themselves from the principle of armed struggle, with which nevertheless they did not completely break until the beginning of the 1980s. It wanted to make full use of democracy, while at the same time situating itself on the far left-wing of the political stage. Its policies were difficult to implement for fundamental reasons. On the one hand, its revolutionary and class positions were not homogenous and several left-wing or independent elements coexisted as best they could within the party. In addition, its nationalism oscillated between a very hard independentist position and other more flexible positions, more open to the idea of action which would obtain growing autonomy step by step. Finally, and above all, the integration of significations akin to those of ETA, but eliminating the principle of armed struggle, turned out to be very fragile, as was demonstrated by a sociological study which we carried out with a dozen or so of its members, all former ETA militants, all strongly opposed to the idea of armed struggle but powerless when it came to stabilizing the image of action with high ambitions: the reference to the myth of a comprehensive Basque movement becomes ambiguous if it is not amplified by violence – we shall return to this later.

The second new political force was Herri Batasuna (HB), which is not a party but an assemblage of several organized groups (HASI, ASK, JARRAI, etc.), a gathering with close ideological links based on the same three-dimensional references. Unlike EE, however, HB was "pro-rupture", it recognized the need for armed struggle and wished to be the legal point of assembly for all those who called for a break with Spanish institutions. This is why HB was a candidate in the elections, but did not take up its seats, or only intermittently, in the Spanish and Basque parliaments, where it nevertheless had a number of members elected at the municipal level. In fact, HB was closely linked to ETA in a direct relationship which made it ETA's legal political wing. The two organizations functioned in perfect harmony in accordance with a structure which gave the leading role to ETA. The latter was the vanguard, which alone carried on the only struggle that the system could not assimilate or accept, the armed struggle. In the light of day, the amorphous HB took over, exerting political control over all sorts of sectoral combats, including those of the workers and the trade unionism of LAB, "a pro-rupture" trade union, combats on behalf of women, the anti-nuclear movement, the promotion of the Basque language and culture or support for political prisoners. In the view of the militants and supporters of HB, armed struggle alone could concretize a global project for national and social liberation, it alone could give generalized coverage to practices which would be fragmented without it or in any event unable alone to call into question the system of domination exerted by the Spanish government, the Basque and Spanish oligarchies and their political arms. It has already been mentioned that in the 1979 elections the PNV obtained 26.9 per cent of the votes, it should be added that EE obtained 7.8 per cent and HB 14.8 per cent.

The total number of votes shows that in the Basque country approximately one voter in two recognized himself in the nationalist-based parties. It also implies that the same proportion voted for parties with a Spanish bias. By far the most influential of these parties in Euskadi, as elsewhere in Spain, was the Spanish Workers' Socialist Party (PSOE), which united those who voted left-wing and embodied trends that were increasingly favourable to Spanish centralism. Under Franco, the clandestine PSOE had been relatively open to the Basque cause and even envisaged a federal Spain, granting a large measure of freedom to a number of republics, including the Basque region. After the death of the Caudillo, a leader like Venegas still embodied broad acceptance of Basque nationalism. However, from 1978 onwards, the PSOE became increasingly reserved and even hostile to anything which went beyond a certain level of autonomy.

This formation of a democratic political system created unprecedented conditions for ETA. Under the dictatorship, armed struggle could concretize or bring closer political aspirations which were more or less distinct, but all hostile to the regime. With the transition to democracy, these currents drew apart. Democrats and revolutionaries became opponents rather than allies and armed struggle became the subject of debate and conflict among those who up till then had accepted it. In the beginning, these debates and conflicts were extremely confused and unstable. For example, should one participate in the democratic renewal or continue to support a "pro-rupture" position, should one vote or remain aloof from the elections taking place in a Spain which did not accept the idea of independence for Euskadi?

These parties could well recommend abstention, as was the case in 1978 for the PNV, HB and EE in the elections concerning the adoption of the Constitution, and at the same time put forward candidates for other elections. Their candidates could well adopt different behaviour in different institutions, participate in municipal affairs and refuse to sit in the Congress or the Senate, as was the case for HB.

During this transitional period, positions were often unstable, the guidelines were also unstable and, above all, the legitimacy of violence was less obvious.

(b) Nationalism and Tension

Under the dictatorship, the two faces of nationalism appeared to complement each other harmoniously and there was a direct link between calls for the promotion of Basque culture and, more politically, for national independence. Here as well, everything changed, especially after 1979 when the Statute given to the Basque country granted the Province considerable autonomy: a government, a parliament, a police force with limited competence but which it was proposed to increase, media operating in the Basque language (radio and television), etc. Some of the nationalists welcomed this autonomy, without however considering that it sufficed, but they saw it as a first and important step along the path which would in the end lead to independence through negotiations. Others, however, considered that it was meant to deceive and was simply "window dressing"; that no gains were sufficient except for independence as such. The latter were in favour of armed struggle, the others opposed it in the name of democracy.

This dissociation cannot simply be seen as a break between currents that were more concerned by cultural identity and other more political currents aimed at setting up a state with all its components. However, the new institutional provisions satisfied the majority of the cultural demands. It was now possible in Euskadi freely to educate one's children in Basque, write, publish and communicate in Basque and even obtain jobs in the public sector which were closed to those who only spoke Spanish. The transfer of competence provided for in the 1979 Statute went hand in hand with progress in the cultural field for some, but for others it would in the end lead to dissociation; because of their "pro-rupture" stance, ETA and HB could no longer embody all aspects of nationalist demands.

(c) The Decline of the Labour Movement

At the time of the transition to democracy, the workers' struggle appeared able to play a leading role, they mobilized a strong labour movement which, as we have seen, went further than the trade union organizations which had carried on the conflict under dictatorship.

Even before the death of Franco, the "assembly" trend had provided the image of an important grass-roots mobilization and the trade union scene revived with the strong growth of two organizations. On the one hand, ELA moved away from its original ideology, Christian and basically fairly close to the policies of the PNV; it developed in a manner relatively similar to that of the CFDT in France during the same period and pursued action aimed at exerting pressure on economic policies. On the other hand, LAB followed the "pro-rupture" trend, defended revolutionary-based policies and embodied a labour consciousness which was anxious and deeply angered. Finally, the UGT, which had no Basque identity, appeared to be on the upswing.

However, this growth in the labour movement quickly slowed down. The economic crisis had a catastrophic effect on Basque industry, which was often the most affected, and unemployment reached impressive levels (22 per cent of the active population in 1984 in the Bilbao region). In such a situation, the labour movement disintegrated. The "assembly" trend disappeared early on, in 1977, and the councils and assemblies were nothing but arenas for political manoeuvres; trade unionism weakened just at the time when it had been recognized (recognition of free trade unions in 1977, right to strike, etc.). This development had important consequences for the armed struggle. Several years before, ETA had not only supported the workers' struggle but had also identified itself with the highest ideals, speaking of the class struggle which would overturn capitalism and build a more equitable society. Henceforward, the workers' combat would turn towards corporatism, the limited defence of jobs, explosions of anger or rage, or institutionalized negotiations or political pressure. It became increasingly erroneous to speak of a social movement, an action capable of questioning the more general orientations of collective existence, or to refer to a historical role. The gap widened between the discourse ETA, as well as HB and LAB (which only obtained an average of 5–10 per cent of the votes in professional elections) intended to maintain, and the much less glorious reality of the workers' combat.

As we have seen, at the same time new social movements emerged, mainly the anti-nuclear and feminist movements.

In the beginning, the anti-nuclear movement represented limited opposition to the Spanish government's project to implement a programme which provided for four, then only two, nuclear power stations in Euskadi, at Lemoniz and Ea. The movement grew in 1976 and became a complex ensemble of meanings. It protested against the undemocratic conduct of the decision-makers, especially the technocrats of Iberduero SA, the enterprise which has the quasi-monopoly of the production and distribution of electricity in Spain. It called for a new concept of progress and development and had an important ecological component.

The women's movement was strongly influenced by similar organizations in Europe and North America. In the mid-1970s, it evolved a cultural creed which called on the one hand for equality between men and women and on the other for a different relationship between men and women.

These new social movements were based on values which were no longer those of the industrial society and their goals were noticeably different from those of the labour movement. They outlined a new social structure for which ETA was not really prepared. Much more than the labour movement, they rejected subordination to external political forces, heteronomy. They were also much more responsive to pacifism, to the non-violence which some of their opposite number, notably in Germany, had made their creed. They were also very fragile. This is why ETA was able to draw closer and, on the one hand, achieve at least in part the subordination of the women's struggle in Euskadi, and, on the other, take the place of the anti-nuclear combat, which it would in fact destroy, as we shall see later. For the moment, suffice it to say that in the new social scene, ETA either had to identify itself with a social movement which only existed in its discourse, or to absorb the women's struggle while at the same denying it, or resort to arms against Iberduero SA to obtain the withdrawal of the nuclear programme, causing the greatest wrong to the genuine anti-nuclear militants who did not accept violence.

On all sides, ETA found itself in a much more difficult situation than during the dictatorship. Created under an authoritarian regime, armed struggle could no longer situate itself by reference to opposition to oppression and repression, even though this did not disappear from one day to another, and its protagonists had to chose between democracy and revolutionary violence, cut off from the aspirations of broad sectors of the population. Rooted in a cultural and political nationalism which could have conferred considerable legitimacy on it, it was henceforward opposed to all those who noted the progress brought about by a large degree of autonomy which could be extended pursuant to negotiations. Identified with a class struggle that had been particularly active for a number of years, it now ran the risk of pursuing the discourse while the reality evaporated and new types of conflict arose. In this completely new context, the significations to which ETA referred became mythical and it adopted exacerbated violence which in fact became a shift towards terrorism. Paradoxically, the armed struggle would develop at the same time as democracy was being established. ETA now embarked upon a logic of action which could only lead in the end to terrorist inversion, which is the counterpart to the weakening and disintegration of the social, national and political struggles which dictatorship had unified and which armed struggle, even if limited, embodied.

VII   FROM ARMED STRUGGLE TO TERRORISM

The processes of change which have just been mentioned did not take place contemporaneously, they did not follow a linear and regular pattern. They were taking shape even before Franco's death and continued after the democratic transition phase, even when democracy was solidly implanted in Spain. This is why the first signs of the terrorist inversion which emerged in ETA can be seen from 1973 to 1974 onwards.

(a)   The First Signs of Inversion

As from 1973 to 1974, the internal tension within ETA basically opposed two concepts of the same action, which it was generally considered should be both military and mass, but it also covered a still minor phenomenon which would be important later: the tendency of the most "military" towards autonomy, towards ignoring the considerations regarding mass action. This could lead to action in purely strategic terms, dissociated from the experiences of the Basque people, its expectations and the opposition which it was genuinely capable of implementing – and it therefore corresponded to a logic of inversion. This phenomenon grew when the military leader Txikia "fell" – he was a strong personality, capable of maintaining an internal balance, of thinking in both political and military terms – but above all when the military elements of the Labour Front split in 1974.

The first important manifestation of the autonomy of the military logic was the attack in Correos Street in Madrid. A blind act, in a cafeteria, where a bomb exploded and killed several people. This attack had nothing in common with the symbolic, specifically targeted, previous attacks.

Within ETA itself, there was considerable unease, and the leaders understood perfectly that this was the type of excessive action which happened when the preparation of an armed attack was not made under political control and did not in any way correspond to popular feelings and expectations.

Even in the Basque country, who could welcome the death of customers sitting in a cafeteria in Madrid, who could see any direct link with the national and social liberation struggle?

As we have seen, in 1975 there were two ETAs, that of the "milis" and that of the "poli-milis", the most numerous and the most capable of action. In ETA (pm), the problem of the trend towards terrorist inversion, even if it was not formulated thus, started to be perceived and a leader like Pertur perfectly embodied this concern with regard to the risk of a shift towards purely military action. During this period in which repression came down strongly upon ETA (pm)'s militants and the majority of its leaders were in France, in this period of radical mutations, the organization entered into a crisis and adopted behaviour which was both new and disturbing.

ETA (pm) needed money and decided on kidnapping with ransom demands. In the past, the kidnapping of industrialists had had a strong symbolic weight, well understood by the population; it had basically been a way of helping workers directly in their struggle. Kidnapping would now change its meaning and do away with that signification.

This is why the kidnapping of the industrialist Luzuriaga aroused heated controversy even within sectors that were favourable to ETA, to such an extent that a communiqué by a number of Basque left-wing organizations (LAB, LAIA, etc.) dissociated them from this act which was prejudicial to the prestigious image of the movement. A minor but significant event showed clearly that the organization was shifting towards a terrorist logic: the leader who had most clearly demonstrated his hostility to the kidnapping, Pertur, was given the responsibility for drafting the communiqué claiming responsibility for it.

A second kidnapping, that of the industrialist Berazadi, led to discussion and highlighted similar tension, which was particularly noticeable because the affair went on for a long time as the family resisted paying the ransom. In addition, the Basque left-wing was highly criticized, particularly since it was now the post-Franco era and a time of transition towards democracy. Once again, it was the leader most hostile to the kidnapping who was entrusted with managing the affair, that is to say negotiating in France with the emissaries of the industrialist's family – which had the perverse effect of seeing him designated by the Spanish press as the brain behind the kidnapping. Once more, the weight of the military logic, even though it was supported by a minority of militants, at least among the leaders, went a great deal further. They wanted to bring the affair to an end because they considered that the negotiations between Pertur and the industrialist's family had gone on too long and in April 1976 Berazadi's body was found, he had been killed with a bullet in the head.

The "berezis", those who pursued a predominantly military logic, therefore placed ETA (pm) before a *fait accompli* and the murderous gesture, which could probably have been avoided, led to a prolonged crisis within the organization. Pertur and his collaborators gave up their responsibilities but then suspended their resignation at the request of the "berezis", who proposed to discuss the issue at a meeting of the leaders – they considered that the internal conflict should not be brought out into the open but should be resolved by the leadership. On the eve of the assembly, two of them came to "arrest" Pertur and sequestrated him, reproaching him with having passed confidential information to the exterior. They held him prisoner and prevented him from appearing at the first meetings of the leadership. These meetings were extremely lively, the "berezis" providing explanations which were not accepted by the majority of the participants. The assembly concluded with the apparent defeat of the "berezis", who were ordered to liberate Pertur. A disciplinary commission was decided upon and those who had organized Berazadi's murder were excluded from the leadership. These events took place on the French side of the border and they did not stop at that. While Pertur and some close companions went into isolation to consider the preparation of the next general assembly of the movement, the "berezis" did not remain idle. On the contrary, they enticed Pertur into an ambush on 23 July 1976 and this time eliminated him definitively. His disappearance was presented as an act by the Spanish extreme right-wing and responsibility was laid on a para-police group which had not hesitated to cross the frontier to operate on French territory. An intensive press campaign orchestrated by the ETA and its well-wishers denounced the terrorist practices which the new Spanish regime allowed to operate. The truth was only established with difficulty by Pertur's family, notably by one of his aunts, who possessed letters he had written just before his disappearance, which he had virtually predicted. Just when these were to be made public, one of the two presumed assassins was the subject of an extradition request by the Spanish government and so the declarations of Pertur's family were obfuscated: how was it possible to state that a person who press campaigns presented as a Basque national hero, Apalategui, who should be protected and not handed over to the Spanish authorities by the French, was in fact probably the murderer of one of the most prominent leaders of the same movement?[31]

Pertur's death was an isolated episode which would not recur for a number of years. But this dramatic episode shows clearly that ETA, whose legitimacy remained important, had embarked upon a new era marked by trends towards terrorist inversion. This could be seen from the exterior with the absurd attack in Correos Street, or with the new significations which the kidnapping of industrialists assumed. They are far more impressive seen from the inside. The solidarity born of the common struggle and clandestinity had turned into internal violence and murder; the political debates, the conflict of ideas and projects had been reduced to the use of force and the practice of the *fait accompli*. The heroes, seen from the inside, the resistance fighters, the combatants, or at least some of them, had become abject, cynical and even psychologically disturbing persons as Pertur himself had noted before paying the price with his life in what was in a way his political testament, the draft project for the forthcoming general assembly prepared a few days before his disappearance: "History shows", he wrote, "that many deviations, especially when they are linked to ambition and abuse of power, are closely related to psychological disturbances if not, more specifically, to neurosis, paranoia or other mental illness" whose origin in his view could undoubtedly be found in the trend towards the autonomy of the logic of arms, the transformation of a militant into a soldier and the growing stranglehold of the "military" over the "political" in the organization.

(b) Stabilization, 1976–85

Nevertheless, ETA did not pursue an accelerated process of inversion and after the major crisis which arose with the death of Pertur it even appeared capable of becoming more stable and retaining considerable legitimacy in Euskadi.

This stabilization first of all involved a sort of transfer in which there was a reclassification between ETA (pm) and ETA (m), as well as regular departures of militants who left ETA (pm) at the same time as they abandoned the armed struggle, either for strictly political combats or simply for a more peaceful existence, made legitimate in their eyes by the new political situation, which was both democratic and open to a certain degree of national autonomy. The "berezis" left ETA (pm) fairly rapidly to join ETA (m). Euskadiko Eskera (EE), which had originally been called Euskal Iraultzale Alderdia (EIA), received a large number of militants who had maintained links with ETA (pm), but it gradually moved away from armed struggle. ETA (pm) itself, once the "berezis" had gone, adopted the line advocated by Pertur; it considered that the installation of a bourgeois democracy in Spain made it possible to envisage mass action and that armed struggle should only take place to guarantee the victories achieved by open non-violent struggle. Above all, it gave priority to the creation of a political party – EIA, which in fact led to EE In the early 1980s, ETA (pm) announced an indefinite truce and then the end of the armed struggle. Its leaders appeared openly at a press conference and only a few militants, the "octavos" (who based themselves on the decisions taken at the Eighth Assembly) continued the armed struggle and clandestinity, fairly soon joining ETA (m) – we shall once again simply say ETA – or in turn abandoned action to return to social and possibly political life.

This reorganization should not hide the essential, which is the relative organizational and ideological stabilization of ETA. In accordance with a formula which would not change after the end of the 1970s, the organization was governed by a committee of about ten, installed in France and therefore safe from Spanish repression. In passing, it should be said that the latitude given to ETA by the French authorities is surprising. It is essentially based on a tacit agreement between the local and national police authorities and ETA. The organization operated discreetly in tolerated clandestinity, finding in France a "sanctuary", and not operating at all on French national territory. Above all, up until 1984, the presence of ETA in France prevented any creation on the French side of a comparable organization and paralysed any inclination which existed on that side of the Pyrenees to develop an armed struggle: Iparetarrak emerged in 1979 but only showed itself to be violent later, in 1982, exactly when the tacit agreement between the ETA and the French authorities started to be broken.[32] It should be added here that one justification often put forward by the French for this agreement was that it was preferable to have an ETA leadership which was known to the police, with a solid political formation, experienced, rather than a leadership which was constantly renewed as a result of repression and so was less responsible as well as less predictable.

The committee which headed ETA took military decisions whose implementation was entrusted to operational commandos which were independent from each other and which enjoyed a large degree of freedom of movement in conducting their operations. As a maximum, ETA had a dozen commandos ready to function, each with four or five members. In addition, the committee was in relation with a very dense network which ensured the circulation of information with the Basque country, especially with sympathetic organizations on the spot, the HB group, and the press, committees for an amnesty, which dealt with political prisoners, etc.

The movement's ideological stability was also more or less established from 1977 or 1978 onwards and one of its expressions was the KAS (Koordinadora Abertzale Sozialista) platform, which proposed a five-point programme covering almost all the "pro-rupture" trend: amnesty and liberation of all Basque political prisoners in Spain, legalization of the independentist parties (which effectively took a long time to be granted to HB), expulsion from the Basque country of all police and military forces of the Spanish state, improvement of the living and working conditions of the working classes, greater autonomy than that provided for in the 1979 statute – which in fact meant independence. This platform is consistent with what we know about the myth to which ETA adheres and about its concern to embody three-dimensional action.

Until the mid-1960s, therefore, it would appear that ETA had been able both to establish an organizational model which functioned well and to pursue a programme for the social and national liberation struggle. Does this dual stabilization mean the end of the inversion process which had begun with the 1975–6 crisis and the death of Pertur?

(c) Halfway Down the Slope Towards Inversion

At first glance, and paradoxically, ETA emerges strengthened from the democratic transition and the figures are impressive. In France alone, several hundred militants had found refuge and were more or less on call, and around forty leaders formed the central nucleus of the organization. Armed action proliferated, but on a scale which bore no relation to what had occurred during the preceding decade, assassination of those collaborating with the regime, the Guardia Civil or soldiers, kidnapping with ransom demands, robberies and hold-ups, sabotage. The practice of the "revolutionary tax" became general, entrepreneurs were obliged to pay their tithe to ETA if they wanted their business to function normally. However, in many ways, ETA had changed and its relationship with Basque society had also changed. Prisoners, ETA militants, were no longer feted as before when they returned to their village or neighbourhood after they had been freed, there was a genuine lassitude among many activists and above all it was no longer possible to maintain the image of a direct link between the various aspirations of the population and armed struggle.

This phenomenon, which is the sign of inversion, first of all appeared in the social movements. The labour movement had been significantly weakened by the economic crisis, which itself had been exacerbated by the disastrous floods in 1983 which had destroyed an important part of Euskadi's industrial structure, and it disintegrated. ETA, together with the LAB trade union, could only embody one aspect of the social movement; it was in fact representative of a "pro-rupture" trend which was both defensive and imbued with labour's anger so that it differed from the negotiating trend in EE or UGT; it only represented a small minority of workers and was in conflict with other sectors of the labour movement.

The relationship is even more negative if one considers the anti-nuclear movement. At the beginning of the 1970s, for a short time ETA had been in favour of the nuclear energy programme. It saw the possibility of giving

Euskadi modern installations which would allow it, once political independence had been obtained, to benefit from an independent source of energy. However, when the anti-nuclear struggle began, ETA reversed its position to participate in the struggle and even play a leading role. At the end of 1977, it announced that it would participate concretely in order to respond to what it called the "terrorism" of Iberduero SA, which had commenced the construction work on the nuclear power station at Lemoniz. It did in fact manage to cause significant material damage to the power station. Other action followed and in January 1981 a decisive step was taken when ETA directly attacked the persons involved by kidnapping the chief engineer responsible for the work at Lemoniz, Ryan. ETA gave the Spanish government and Iberduero one week to announce their decision to withdraw from the project and, not obtaining satisfaction, it assassinated Ryan. It relapsed in April 1992 by assassinating the director of the Lemoniz project, Pascual.

The Lemoniz power station would finally not be built and a superficial assessment might see in this decision a total victory for ETA. After all, to our knowledge its action has been the only one in the world which actually directly prevented the implementation of projects under a nuclear energy programme. But from the point of view of the anti-nuclear movement, ETA was seen to have behaved as a destructive force.

The growth in anti-nuclear committees (CAN) was dynamic until 1981; their progression was halted by the murderous action of ETA. The anti-nuclear movement was effectively demobilized by the recourse to a violence which transformed social conflict into war, democratic mobilization into terrorist acts and clashed forcibly with Basque public opinion which, for the first time, unequivocally mobilized and demonstrated in the street in February 1982 to show its opposition to the armed struggle. By introducing an instrumental violence from outside, ETA replaced the anti-nuclear movement, spoke on its behalf but against it, and put the movement out of touch with the Basque population. The anti-nuclear movement might perhaps have weakened by itself, as the French experience showed, where it disintegrated from 1980–1981 onwards, firstly as a result of the violence of the repression and then of the political changes which saw the socialist and communist left come to power.

Nevertheless, it cannot be denied that in Euskadi the ETA contributed to the collapse of the struggle and the demobilization of its supporters: why militate, build up grassroots action when it is sufficient to commit a few murders in order to resolve the issues, how could one commit oneself alongside the civilian society when arms were taking up the contestation?

From 1982 onwards, the CAN were dissolved or turned into small sectarian or hyper-ideologized groups.

In the case of the women's movement, the result was the same but the process differed. ETA, but above all its political wing HB, aimed to embody this movement like all the other forms of popular contestation in Euskadi and an organization close to the HB, Aizan, grouped feminist militants. But in its more general concepts, as in its internal functioning, the ETA–HB combination was not in fact really open to feminism. The latter was rhetorical, an ideological discourse which was in fact quite far from the real practice of these organizations, outside demagogic efforts which never went very far. Revolutionary militancy, more or less labour-based, is ill-adapted to specifically feminist demands, it is based on a largely "machist" culture which is indifferent to the aspirations of the women in the movement when they talk of establishing new relations with men; it usually defines specific roles which confine women to certain more or less inferior tasks and make it difficult for them to affirm themselves as participants in the more central debates. In that sense, ETA appears as a figure which obliges feminism to subordinate itself totally to the national liberation and revolutionary armed struggle – which is a way of rejecting it and hampering its development.

Inversion is also seen in a very different way if one considers ETA's relations with industry. During the preceding phase of its history, ETA intervened to make known its support for the workers' combat and to help the capitulation of management in open conflict with strikers. Henceforward, its position is different. Basque employers, which had often given financial help to the independentist movement or militants in trouble under the dictatorship, was now terrorized by ETA which extorted a revolutionary tax. Its response was sometimes to leave, to make new investments outside Euskadi and even to disinvest. It also responded by leaving the rural areas, where many generally small enterprises were located, for the towns, which were anonymous and where their families were less threatened. The effect of the armed struggle was therefore to impoverish the country, or certain areas, to paralyse economic modernization and efforts to overcome the crisis. These effects were exacerbated by the destructuring of the social relations resulting from action by ETA and those who benefited from it. In many enterprises, the relations between management and personnel were bedevilled by a diffused climate of violence which prevented negotiation, even if it was conflictual negotiation, and sometimes even led to personal threats. In such a context, foremen and managers avoided responsibility and it became difficult for the enterprises to keep functioning. In the beginning, ETA's action took place within the framework of a class relationship, to the benefit of those contesting and against the managers; it became a disintegrating factor in this relationship by preventing its establishment, it spoke artificially on behalf of the labour movement but in reality its main function was to ensure the entry of funds and its major effect was the weakening of enterprises as well as their actors, both managers and workers.

In the past, ETA had expressed its determination to end the dictatorship and it could embody authentic liberation designs against a particularly repressive regime. But here again, far-reaching changes took place. The new regime had of course not abandoned repressive practices, there were still many political prisoners and it was not difficult to establish that torture still functioned all too often. However, henceforward the relation between ETA and the authorities and their repression took on a totally different meaning. The state was no longer the instrument for prohibiting expression of struggles which had a signification in themselves, the obstacle or the enemy against which arose the actors who embodied the nation, the revolution, the proletariat, it was no longer part of a system of action in which ETA was but the outward manifestation of these actors and it was no longer only defined by its confrontation with ETA. In this confrontation, ETA, instead of expressing and epitomizing several forms of contestation, increasingly expected that repression would feel the effects of public opinion's sympathy. It no longer relied on the signification which it formulated, but on the price paid by its militants in carrying out the armed struggle, on its victims, its martyrs, its members tortured and imprisoned. Its political weapon became its victims, rather like the action of the terrorists of the Red Army Fraction which, through suicide, had tried to mobilize German and international public opinion against a state which it denounced as brutal and oppressive. It developed a death cult, a martyrology, a victimology, which replaced signification.

This phenomenon was of special importance in the prisons where ETA exerted over its members a control that sometimes tended towards terrorism and was opposed to anything which might lead to negotiated relations that would allow those who so wished to leave the armed struggle. The theme of prisoners and their conditions of imprisonment became central to ETA's propaganda and HB's discourse and, it might even be said, became the goal of the armed struggle, whereas in the beginning it had only been a consequence. From that point of view as well, ETA was moving down the slope to inversion: repression and its excesses was increasingly relied upon to maintain and regain popular support, even if it sometimes had to provoke, instead of trying to fulfil popular demands through armed struggle up to the level of the state, as it had done in the past.

The main reason why the notion of terrorist inversion deserves to be applied to ETA is due to its most visible and direct manifestations: the proliferation of violence which had lost its ethical signification and its symbolic weight, affecting persons who were not all, far from it, obvious enemies of the Basque cause. Bomb attacks caused victims among the population in a totally indiscriminate fashion, injuring individuals whose only crime was to be present in the bank or enterprise which ETA had decided to blow up, individuals were assassinated on the slightest suspicion or following a minor accusation, for example, a baker, a plumber, a stonemason, and "errors" became commonplace. ETA spoke of accidents, exactly as the dictatorship used to do. Recruitment, which had never ceased, brought into the organization young people with no political background, who were simply hungry for action and little control was exercised over them so they might have eight or ten deaths on their conscience. Sometimes joining ETA did not even correspond basically to an ideological commitment but to the desire to avoid being arrested by the policy for delinquency.

This did not, however, prevent ETA from being the only organization in Euskadi capable of carrying on an armed struggle which elsewhere in Spain was also being pursued by other left-wing groups, particularly the Autonomous Commandos. This should not give the idea that it was pure terrorist logic, that the inversion had reached its conclusion. ETA's "pro-rupture" nationalism largely corresponded to the aspirations of a population which voted for HB with average levels of 20 per cent of the votes; within PNV and among its voters, there was resistance to a complete break with ETA, at least ideologically, autonomy was practised, but the dream was independence and it was stated that Madrid only really retracted when the threat of armed struggle became a reality and the Spanish government would never grant total independence.

In addition, the economic crisis had significant effects in the poorest districts where anger and rage were utilized by the HB. more than by any other party and where the most active manifestations of the associative structure were directed by militants sympathetic to ETA, which utilized to its benefit the demands of the most radical sectors of the population, especially the young who increasingly appeared to be marginalized by the crisis.

Finally, official repression was amplified, without it being possible to ascertain what really were the links between this extension and the police, through the action of the Spanish Basque Battalion of the ATE (ETA Anti-terrorism) and above all the Anti-terrorist Liberation Group (GAL), whose aim was to terrorize the terrorists. From 1983 onwards, it carried out a number of attacks against Spanish Basques exiled in France – there were twenty-three assassinations, several kidnappings and numerous wounded between 1983 and July 1986 on French territory. GAL often utilized mercenaries and when they were arrested almost all of them stated that they had worked in collaboration with Spanish police officers – although it was never really proved. This counter-terrorism struck real blows against ETA, even if it was often blind or not well-targeted. It also, paradoxically, strengthened popular support which had been waning.

ETA's image over the period studied is complex. On one side, it could not be denied that the organization was shifting towards a logic of terrorist action. On the other, however, it is difficult to say that it had really done so. This is why Basque public opinion appears to be so unstable, capable of demonstrating against the armed struggle but also of showing its sympathy for an organization which still retains a certain degree of legitimacy.

VIII   TERRORISM AND POLITICS

From the mid-1980s onwards, a new era in the history of ETA began, with a significantly weakened organization which carried out increasingly deadly and much more blind acts than at least some of those in the past.

(a)   A New Context

This transformation marked a definite step along the path towards inversion and it took place in a context which was totally new.

The first factor in the development was the reversal of French policy. From 1984 onwards, the French government opted for an economic realism which departed from its previous position and simultaneously decided for the first time to grant the requests for extradition of the "etarras" (Basque militants – the expression is pejorative) made by Madrid. This new line of conduct was subsequently defined with ups and downs: France was no longer a sanctuary for ETA and over the years that followed more than a hundred expulsions or extraditions took place, as well as many arrests, some of which were important, for example, those of Josu Ternera (January 1989), ETA military leader, or Santi Potros (30 September 1987), one of the organization's leaders. Police action in France was sometimes more apparent than effective, as for example during the "raid" in Bayonne (October 1987), which was a media operation without any significant concrete results, but overall it noticeably destabilized ETA.

A second factor for change was the evolution of Basque society. Although the national consciousness did not diminish in Euskadi, the other elements which gave ETA's action its three-dimensional aspect underwent radical changes which all went in the same direction. On the one hand, as in the rest of the Western world, the labour movement's decline was consolidated. On the other, the new social movements such as the anti-nuclear and feminist combats appeared to have exhausted themselves. Basque youth showed less and less interest in political struggle and it was affected by a phenomenon which concerned the whole of Spain, "pasotism", in other words individualism which was hostile to any form of collective commitment and which led to focusing on oneself, to a certain narcissism, over-emphasis on the consumption of cultural assets.

Moreover, slightly later in the Basque country than in other Western European countries, communist and above all left-wing ideologies were losing ground and the reference to democracy replaced that of revolution. With the exception of nationalism, the significations which underlay the armed struggle in the past had all been weakened or diminished, thus making ETA's rhetoric increasingly artificial because its discourse, without being completely mythical, was moving further away from the concrete realities which it aimed to represent and epitomize. Nationalism itself was more divided than ever between the partisans of a gradual acquisition of autonomy and uncompromising independentism, the former seeing that the 1979 Statute had in fact allowed Basque political forces to govern the Province and obtain real power.

Under those circumstances, ETA was much more fragile than before, less convinced of its legitimacy and vulnerable to repression.

(b) Negotiate?

Henceforward, ETA and its fellow organizations, starting with HB, were subject to frequently strong tension between two opposing trends. On the one hand, the new historic situation appeared to be favourable to the negotiated abandonment of the armed struggle, while on the other those who refused this policy resorted to increased violence which became much more blind and unrestrained than in the past for both practical and political reasons. The success of repression had been such that ETA's military commandos often preferred to carry out bomb attacks, especially car bomb attacks, which had the advantage of minimizing the risks, especially if the bomb was set off by remote control from a distance, but they also had the disadvantage of indiscriminately wounding and killing people who became victims simply because they had the misfortune to be on the spot at the time of the explosion. In addition, the response of those who rejected any form of negotiation consisted of a capacity for intervention which, whenever progress appeared to be made in contacts between the Spanish government and ETA emissaries, resorted to extremely violent acts to overturn the efforts of those who presented themselves to Basque and Spanish public opinion as desirous of finding a solution to the armed struggle.

ETA thus seemed able to embark upon the negotiation process. In 1986, its leader, Rxomin Iturbe, expelled from France to Gabon and then Algeria, entered into contact with Madrid's representatives and rumours persisted of the progress of the discussion. He died in a car crash in Algeria, but discussions continued with his successor at the head of ETA, Antxon Echeveste, transferred to Algiers by France. Evidently not everyone within ETA accepted this development and two spectacular attacks showed that a hard-line tendency continued to exist within the organization, hostile to any negotiated compromise with the Madrid government. The first occurred in Barcelona in June 1987 and killed twenty-three people in a supermarket where a bomb had been placed; the second led to the breakdown of the negotiations in Algiers, killing eleven people in Saragossa in December 1987, including five small girls aged from 4 to 7. ETA proudly claimed responsibility for the attack so as clearly to mark the rejection of negotiations by those who had perpetrated it, whereas after the Barcelona attack it had publicly expressed its "regrets" for what it acknowledged to be a "serious mistake".

In January 1988, for the first time in its history, ETA announced a provisional truce, which perhaps demonstrated its weakness and undoubtedly underlined the desire of at least some members of its leadership to negotiate with Madrid. However, just a month later, it kidnapped a wealthy entrepreneur, Emiliano Revillan, who was held for almost nine months, which would indicate the opposite trend. The end of the 1980s was dominated by a contradictory process of secret negotiations which continued, together with extremely violent acts which proliferated and hampered the negotiations. The violence, often in the form of car bombs, was aimed primarily at the police and the Guardia Civil; it also wanted to reach tourists and give a negative image of Spain, which was preparing the Barcelona Olympic Games (1992); that was why several armed operations took place there or nearby, in particular, the attack in Sabadell in December 1990, which killed six people; this is also why nearly every summer, when the tourist season started, ETA announced and carried out attacks against

Spanish trains and railways. The violence was just as impressive as the success of the repression. ETA was disorganized, the majority of its commandos had been dismantled, included that led by a Frenchman, Henri Parot, arrested in 1991 while he was preparing to commit a series of attacks and who it was learned operated as an "itinerant commando" in exclusive and direct liaison with the new head of ETA, Artapalo. To facilitate the reinsertion of prisoners who in prison had decided to leave ETA, the Spanish government dispersed them all over Spanish territory so as to separate these prisoners from others who still followed the "hard" line. In addition, HB, which had suffered electoral setbacks, on several occasions projected the image of a party concerned to play a greater role in democratic life and in November 1989 it decided to end its boycott of parliament; this which must also be seen as a gesture towards opening and a trend favourable to the search for a negotiated solution. Two of its most important leaders, both deputies, were victims of an attack in November 1989 which killed Iñaki Esnaola and seriously wounded Josu Muguruza, precisely at the time when HB had just announced its decision – and although GAL was quickly suspected of responsibility, some people wondered whether the attack had not been perpetrated by the hard line within ETA.

Against a background of increasingly close contacts between France and Spain, which had become a full member of the European Community and was participating in a joint security policy (notably within the framework of the Trevi Group), ETA and the "pro-rupture" trend, weakened, fluctuated between negotiations and intensifying the armed struggle, whose objective seemed increasingly to be to prevent the success of the negotiating trend.

Violence was not only more blind, but more and more it turned against those who, among the Basque population, were suspected of weakening *vis-à-vis* the cause, of abandoning or betraying it. One event particularly shocked public opinion: the assassination of a young woman, "Yoyès" in September 1986, killed in her home village in front of her son, because ETA reproached her with having "repented" and deserting the organization. This was not an isolated event and constant pressure was exerted, especially in the prisons, on Basque prisoners. Furthermore, although ETA had up till then avoided attacking the Basque police, the Ertzaïna, in May 1989 it placed a car bomb near Bilbao killing three people including a member of the Basque police. Each year, ETA proved itself capable of causing dozens of victims, and at the same time not only did it lose some support but among the population the idea grew that it was necessary to demonstrate publicly, as Basques and as democrats, their rejection of armed violence. For example, in November 1989, a singer who was well known in Euskadi, Imanol Larzabal, organized in San Sebastian a "concert against fear". He had been a militant close to ETA and had made the headlines in 1985 by helping two "etarras" to escape, hiding them in the loudspeakers during a concert given in their prison; his rapid transformation was symbolic of the changes taking place in Basque opinion.

ETA was not, however, completely isolated. It still enjoyed a large degree of sympathy, partly because it embodied an independentism which remained potent, a nationalism without concessions in which many still believed, at least deep in their hearts, and partly because, however irrational it might seem, it appeared as the only recourse in the eyes of those sectors of the population who had been marginalized economically, victims of rising unemployment, poverty and the crisis which democracy was powerless to resolve. In a certain manner, it derived benefit from everything with which democracy could not deal, on the one hand the national rupture, on the other the growing social duality which divided those "in" from those "out". ETA had become a terrorist organization, but it was not just that, it retained a genuine capacity to speak in the name of national and social aspirations. It had taken a major step backward down the slope to inversion, but it could not be restricted to that single image.

IX CONCLUSION

Is the ETA experience coming to an end? In many respects, one might think this. The general conditions of its existence have all evolved in the same direction, unfavourably. The social movements which ETA aimed to represent are weakened, have even disintegrated, and it has become the spokesman for the marginalized rather than the highest expression of contesting social protagonists; the nation at least in part is tired of armed struggle and violence and many convinced nationalists are favourable to an institutional and reformist policy. Spanish democracy has been consolidated and we are now far from the remote and uncertain era of the transition and the risk of a military *coup d'état*. France has been increasingly resolute in refusing to offer a "sanctuary" to ETA activists, and on the Spanish side repression has increased.

Although it is possible to defend the hypothesis of a historical decline of ETA, nothing permits the affirmation that its experience has come to an end. Popular support has diminished, but it has not entirely disappeared and there is still a reservoir of militants and activists. This is why we shall not conclude with a historical diagnosis, which is far too risky even if everything points to the decline of ETA, and our conclusions will be reserved for theoretical considerations.

(a) A Modern Protagonist

Does ETA fit within post-modern political systems? Our answer would be resolutely negative. ETA is a modern movement in the sense that its projects and the myth which underlies it are seeking with increasing desperation to integrate the constituent elements of modernity, as it was invented in Europe at the end of the Middle Ages.

ETA's aim is to combine reason, political and economic development, with an identity, the nation together with its language and its history. It dreams of a nation-state, it wants to establish a national society, it refuses even the idea of a dissociation of economy and culture. For ETA, the Basque state must be given all the components of a modern state, currency, diplomacy and an army. At least in the beginning it was not carried by marginals, the poor, it did not act on behalf of the deprived, it arose in a context of economic growth in which the theme of exclusion or duality had no place, even though later it tried to mobilize those left behind by the crisis. It does not speak in the name of pariahs, but tries to combine various demands, social and cultural, outlining the mythical image of a society reconciled to itself, abolishing any principle of social division and born along by the spirit of progress which, in its view, will ultimately be embodied by the independent state it aims to establish. Its Marxism–Leninism protects it from the worst loss of identity, from the call to undivided focus on the community and the rejection of reason; its nationalism, in many ways the heir to nineteenth century European nationalism like some national liberation movements in the twentieth century before their abolition in totalitarian regimes, remains responsive to the idea of modernization.

It is thus modern, but with increasing difficulty, attached to a myth which combines the classical components of modernity, and increasingly terrorist precisely because the myth itself is becoming progressively obsolete.

(b) ETA and Democracy

ETA was set up against dictatorship, in a context which prevented even envisaging the idea of a dialectic or an opposition between an "inversionary discourse" model, within the meaning given by David Apter,[33] and a model of institutional democracy. In that historical context, the two models could co-exist, but instead of defining the actor-contester and his enemy, they both helped to define the actor alone.

Faced with dictatorship, ETA's action could bring together both revolutionaries of all tendencies and nationalists desirous of ending Franco's oppression but also of establishing democracy.

Then came the death of Franco and the era of transition. From then on, a superficial observer might have thought that the armed struggle would disappear since it no longer had any signification having been deprived of its enemy. However, as we have seen, a completely different process took place and it has two principal aspects.

On the one hand, the transition to democracy strengthened the movement instead of weakening it; for a few years it provided the opportunity to gain a much wider audience. ETA found its second wind by exteriorizing what it had internalized during the preceding period, the idea of institutional democracy, although it had up until then always been a minor part of the organization, henceforward it had no place. The transition to democracy created the condition for the dialectic mentioned by David Apter[34] and what is remarkable is that ETA plunged into this dialectic and endorsed it wholeheartedly. ETA in fact does embody the "inversionary discourse" theorized by David Apter, including its three levels, which is opposed to the discourse of institutional democracy, which it rejects.

In addition, this distinct trend followed by the actor weakened, at least at two levels. It led to considerable tension within the organization between the "milis" and the "poli-milis", it caused splits, it generated a series of internal crises which each resulted in the departure of activists who turned to institutional struggles or simply were tired of an armed struggle which devoured their personal lives and wanted to participate peacefully in a modern world, even eschewing any political activity; it also caused internal violence: for example, the assassination of Pertur.

Furthermore, the effect of this trend within ETA was to widen the broadening gap between it and the PNV. Until the transition to democracy, this party had never really severed its links with ETA. It viewed the armed struggle organization as its heir, perhaps excessive but nevertheless courageous and combating for the same cause. For the PNV, ETA militants were like unruly children, always welcome when they came to seek help, a shelter, a way to escape repression, and with whom joint action was not necessarily excluded.

However, the PNV did not hesitate to chose the institutional path and in the Basque country to become a party within the government, in power in Vitoria from the end of the transition. The currents then separated, even though certain events sometimes brought them closer again, and ETA's independentist nationalism and Marxism–Leninism were opposed to PNV's nationalism open to negotiation and institutional democracy.

It is necessary to clarify this. Although ETA is clearly defined through its opposition to institutional democracy, those who supported the latter and those who, within the group of parties united under the HB, constituted its legal and political wing, were not excluded from institutional life. HB was clearly present in the most open debates and it had an important press medium, *Egin*. It took part in elections and played the card of local democracy. Many of its members were elected to sit on municipal councils and it headed several municipalities. Its position at the national Spanish level was more complex and its candidates generally, but not always, adopted an attitude of boycott. HB was situated in the intermediate zone where the strength of the "pro-rupture" positions also helped to exert influence in the institutional arena, to negotiate and to come together with other parties, and where violence often appeared as an instrument, brandished as a threat or effectively utilized in mechanisms within the framework of a logic of institutional democracy.

It is not possible to dissociate ETA from HB, even though the latter sometimes experiences extreme tension between its political participation and the requirements of the armed struggle to which it is overall subordinated. This is why it is equally impossible to consider that ETA can be limited to a straightforward "inversionary discourse" logic and why it is also necessary to admit that it is not extraneous to what David Apter called an "exchange model", in which violence functions according to a strategic method.[35]

(c) "Inversionary Discourse" and Terrorist Inversion

As formulated by David Apter, the concept of "inversionary discourse" describes the radical opposition of one actor to the categories of democracy and to the state which implements them.[36]

As I have formulated it, the concept of inversion relates to the more or less artificial relation which an actor has with those in whose name he acts, class or nation, for example. Here, inversion is a reversal in which the actor's ideology is as far removed as possible from the experience of those he says he represents and it changes the nature of the ideological matrix from which it came at the same time as the violence becomes more blind and increasingly terrorist.

Both of these concepts are useful when analysing the ETA experience.

The first describes clearly the foundation of the movement, which resulted from the rupture with the more prudent attitude of the PNV and the call to an armed struggle. It is particularly apt in the case of the context, which has just been recalled, namely, the transition to democracy. During its whole trajectory, ETA behaved as a "pro-rupture" force and from that point of view it is perfectly compatible with the logic of "inversionary discourse", whose concept also throws light on the most recent period, simply with the limits mentioned in the previous paragraph.

The second concept, inversion, in the sense in which we have presented it, is not applicable to the first years of ETA's history, the time when violence was limited, extremely moral, understood and supported by large sectors of Basque and international public opinion. The more democracy predominated in Spain, the more the labour movement disintegrated and the new social movements, especially the anti-nuclear and feminist movements, declined, and the more terrorist inversion came to the fore. This did not mean that "inversionary discourse" had weakened. On the contrary, it became harder. It promoted the image of an implacable struggle to the death, substituting increasingly blind violence for the previous legitimacy and moral values which ETA could claim to embody.

The two concepts should not be opposed. The first defines a principle of opposition. It situates the protagonist in relation to the state and institutional functioning. The second defines a principle of identity which is perverted. It situates the protagonist in relation to the population he claims to represent. The first is directed upwards, the second downwards.

In Basque experience, as in many other experiences, the protagonist's trajectory first of all goes through a phase in which he situates himself in comparison with the values of democracy and the institutions – with the special feature that this phase is preceded by the moment of foundation which takes place against a dictatorship. Then the protagonist, increasingly caught up in his logic of rupture and motivated by a social and political transformation over which he has no control, embarks upon a chaotic spiral of inversion in the sense we have defined. If "inversionary discourse" was the point of departure, terrorism with the randomization of violence has become the point of arrival.

NOTES

1. Clifford Geertz, "The Integrative Revolution. Primordial Sentiments and Civil Politics in the New States", in C. Geertz (ed.), *Old Societies and New States* (London: The Free Press of Glencoe, 1963) pp. 105–57.
2. Cf., for example, Louis Dumont, *Essais sur l'individualisme* (Paris: Seuil, 1987).

348   The Legitimization of Violence

3.   Alain Renaut, "Logiques de la nation", in *Théories du nationalisme* (Paris: Kimé, 1992) pp. 28–46.

4.   On the theory of inversionary discourse, cf. David E. Apter, "Democracy and Emancipatory Movements: Notes for a Theory of Inversionary Discourse", *Development and Change*, vol. 23, no. 3 (1992) pp. 139–73; and David E. Apter, *Democracy, Violence and Emancipatory Movements: Notes for a Theory of Inversionary Discourse* (UNRISD Discussion Paper, 1993).

5.   On the principles of the method for the sociological project, cf. Alain Touraine, *La voix et le regard* (Paris: Seuil, 1978).

6.   Cf. Michel Wieviorka, *Sociétés et terrorisme* (Paris: Fayard, 1988).

7.   Cf. Francisco Letamendia, *Les Basques. Un peuple contre les États* (Paris: Seuil, 1977).

8.   Cf. David E. Apter, op. cit. (1992).

9.   Cf. Fernando Sarrailh de Ihartza (pseudonym of Federico Krutwig), *Vasconia* (Buenos Aires: Norbait, 1962).

10.   Cf. the anonymous work which relates this experience, *Barro y asfalto* (Cuaderno Barrokan: Euskaldunak Derrok Bak, n.d.).

11.   Cf., for example, Francisco Letamendia, "Ortzi", *Historia de Euskadi: el nacionalismo vasco y E.T.A.* (Barcelona: Iberica de Ediciones y Publicaciones, 1971); and Jose Mari Garmendia, *Historia de E.T.A.* (San Sebastian: Haranburu, 1980) 2 vols.

12.   Juan Aranzadi, *Milenarismo vasco* (Madrid: Taurus, 1982).

13.   Julio Caro Baroja, *El laberinto vasco* (San Sebastian: Txertoa, 1984).

14.   Antonio Beristain, "Los terrorismos en el País Vasco y en España", *Violencia política en Euskadi* (Bilbao: Desclée de Brouwer, 1984), pp. 169–95.

15.   Francis Jaureguiberry, *Question nationale et mouvements sociaux au Pays Basque sud,* doctorate thesis, Paris, EHESS, 1983.

16.   Theodor Adorno et al., *The Authoritarian Personality* (New York: Harper, 1960).

17.   Cf. James C. Davies, "Towards a Theory of Revolution", *American Sociological Review,* 27 (February 1962), pp. 5–19; Ted Robert Gurr, *Why Men Rebel* (Princeton, N.J.: Princeton University Press, 1970) p. 17

18.   James B. Rule, *Theories of Civil Violence* (Berkeley Calif.: University of California Press, 1988).

19.   Raymond Aron, *L'opium des intellectuels* (Paris: Gallimard, Coll. Idées, 1968, 2nd edn).

20.   Charles Tilly, *From Mobilization to Revolution* (Reading, Mass.: Addison Wesley, 1978).

21.   Mario Onaindia, *La lucha de clases en Euskadi (1939–1980)* (San Sebastian: Hordago, n.d.)

22.   Jaureguiberry, op. cit.

23.   Juan Linz, "An Authoritarian Regime: Spain", in Eric Allardt and Yrj o Lillunin (eds), *Cleavages, Ideologies and Party Systems* (Helsinki: The Academic Bookstore, 1964) pp. 291–341.

24.   Regarding this trial, cf., for example, Gisèle Halimi, *Le procès de Burgos* (preface by Jean-Paul Sartre) (Paris: Gallimard, 1971).

25. For an account, cf. Julien Aguire, *Operación Ogro. Como y por que ejecutamos a Carrero Blanco* (San Sebastian: Hordago, 1977).
26. Georges Sorel, *Réflexions sur la violence* (Paris: Geneva, Slatkine, 1981), reprint.
27. Cf. David E. Apter, op. cit. (1992, 1993).
28. For a first presentation of this concept, cf. Michel Wieviorka, "Un outil pour l'analyse de la violence politique. La notion d'inversion", *Etudes Polémologiques*, no. 37 (January 1986) pp. 191–213.
29. Cf. David E. Apter, op. cit. (1992, 1993).
30. Cf. Juan Linz, *Conflicto en Euskadi* (Madrid: Espalso Calpa, 1986).
31. Regarding this episode and this period, cf. Michel Wieviorka, "Vie et mort de Pertur, militant basque", *Passé-Présent*, no. 3 (1983), pp. 183–99; for a document by one of Pertur's close collaborators see Angel Amigo, *Pertur, E.T.A. 71–76* (San Sebastian: Hordago, 1978)
32. Regarding Iparretarrak, cf. Jean-François Moruzzi and Emmanuel Boulaert, *Iparretarrak. Séparatisme et terrorisme en Pays Basque franÿais* (Paris: Plon, 1988).
33. Cf. David E. Apter, op. cit. (1992, 1993).
34. Cf. ibid.
35. Cf. ibid.
36. Cf. ibid.

9 Violent Exchanges: Reflections on Political Violence in Colombia

MALCOLM DEAS

I HOW VIOLENT IS VIOLENT?

We conclude these essays with a perplexing example, where political violence as a form of exchange itself comes to be normal. An aspect of political life regarded as underground in most countries (even in Italy where the Mafia has penetrated the highest places), political violence in Colombia is open, visible, accepted, and persistent. With *Sendero* words are things, reified, and symbolically dense. With *La Violencia* words are vacant. Events are the real thing – they are what they are. At this point discourse, and discourse analysis, simply fade into irrelevance.

Which for our purposes makes the case particularly significant. For it shows how political violence can feed on itself as a phenomenon in and of itself.

One would think this would provide, at least, the virtues of a certain harsh clarity. No mysteries, no story-telling, no theory, no mytho-logic. Political violence simply is what it is. Yet nothing about Colombian violence is clear, not even the extent of its political component.

****

Colombia has at times been a violent country, but it is not easy to be precise about how violent Colombia has been. The historical statistics of crimes against the person have not been established, and probably never will be. The enterprise would present the usual large range of archival and statistical problems that criminal statistics always present, even in the case of countries as statistically advanced as France and Germany.[1]

It is therefore prudent to begin with such a low-key statement as "Colombia has at times been a violent country", perhaps surprisingly low-key to those who know Colombia only by its current reputation. I begin that way also because it is my impression that at times it has not been a particularly violent country. There have apparently been periods when the level of violence has apparently been low. Some ornithologists who travelled extensively in the second decade of this century recorded expressly how secure they felt, against assault or even minor theft.[2]

Perhaps they were lucky, or perhaps Colombians were not much interested in attacking ornithologists, but even such impressionistic contemporary evidence should not be too rapidly cast aside, as it almost always is by an historiography that has in recent years been dominated by a desire to find historical antecedents for recent violence: historians often find only what they are looking for.[3]

It is also always difficult to define the exact extent, or even the approximate extent, of *political* violence in the republic. It requires agreement on the definition of the political, and a frequently unobtainable precision in the knowledge of who did exactly what to whom. It should be noted at once that political violence is not necessarily either revolutionary or repressive. The definition of the political proportion in violence has been particularly difficult in recent years.

This hesitant beginning has a deliberate intent: Colombian phenomena are not in the least simple. Colombian homicides cannot be dismissed, accounted for, explained, even sketched by such a phrase as "a high-degree of frontier-like random killing", though indeed there has often been violence on Colombian frontiers, and though I understand the impulse, even the frustration behind the phrase, the desire somehow to get the seemingly amorphous violence of Colombia out of the way, to get to grips then with phenomena that present clearer political profiles, more linear narratives, more defined texts: but, too much haste with the Colombian case underestimates what it can offer in the search for more satisfactory theories of political violence. The hasty also run the risk of casually reviving just the sort of theory that these chapters are trying to supersede – theories that seek to explain violence as a product of marginality and relative deprivation, or even simple theories of violence as a phenomenon of the frontier. Certainly, there is some correlation in Colombian history between frontier and violence. Yet by no means all frontiers have been the scenes of a high-level of random killing, even in Colombia. Very few frontier killings are random. They may appear to be random to the metropolitan visitor, the dude, but not to the inhabitant of the frontier.[4]

Colombia has *at times* been a politically violent country. That too is true. It is common to begin to support that statement with a list of the nineteenth-century civil wars. First there is the list of known national conflicts since the emergence of the republic from the Wars of Independence, which were themselves quite bloody and lengthy and complicated: there were wars which could claim to be national in 1830–1, 1839–42, 1851, 1854, 1860–2, 1876–7, 1885, 1895, 1899–1902. To this list can be added a much longer one of the local conflicts – Colombia was for extended periods a federal republic – and these are conveniently listed in G. Arboleda's *Las rebeliones locales en Colombia*, which arrives at a total for the century of fifty.[5]

These are the more-or-less formal conflicts, opened with some sort of declaration and closed by some sort of submission.[6] Some of them are mere *golpes*, which implied little fighting: Arboleda's list is diminished by no less than sixteen rebellions if one excludes changes of government in Panama, which was until 1904 part of Colombia. Though the local traditions of government were clearly unstable, Panama was not a particularly violent place: few died in Panamanian coups. All the same, in most of the rest of these confrontations armed force was used, people did die – sometimes, it seems, in proportionately large numbers – and were outraged, humiliated, forced to hide or to migrate. Their property might be expropriated or destroyed. These were real little wars. They were about who should exercise power – their political nature is undeniable. They were fought between Liberals and Conservatives, or between factions – Liberals versus Liberals, and, more occasionally Conservatives versus Conservatives.[7]

There is some point in insisting on the essentially political nature of these conflicts, as the historiography of this part of the world is prone to deny the purely "political", or at least to try to force it into other frames – regional conflict, agrarian conflict, class conflict. This insistence in itself has an effect, that of picturing the national history as a series of frustrations. What, if anything, these conflicts solved is forgotten or overlooked, and so they are held to have solved nothing, and this paradoxically further justifies present conflict.

To these formal wars, the last of which took place at the turn of the century, have succeeded periods of intense partisan competition that have left numerous victims. The first such period is generally held to be the years immediately after forty-five years of Conservative hegemony came to an end in 1930.[8] The second is the years 1946–53, which began with the fall from power of the Liberal Party and ended with the installation of a brief military government, which lasted until 1957.

The period from 1946 to 1953 is now referred to by Colombian historians as that of the "classic violence" – "la violencia clásica". It is classic in the sense that it is seen by Colombians to have involved sectarian or partisan violence in its purest form and to its widest extent. The statistics of how many died are, as we have noted, speculative, which does not prevent them from being continually cited. Indeed, they acquire a specious plausibility by being cited over and over again. All the same, whatever the number was, many died.

Many have died since 1953, though conflict gradually ceased to set Liberal against Conservative. Successive governments intermittently fought bandits, guerrillas and "self-defence groups", some of whose leaders at least were of communist, Maoist or Castroite persuasion. The country was relatively peaceful in the mid 1970s, but has become more violent again. Continuous peace-making efforts since the early 1980s have met with only partial success. One recent authority I have to hand gives, for the period 1980–90, the sum of "165,000 violent deaths, 321 massacres, 168 of them in 1988 and 1989".[9] These are far higher figures than those of Peru. The index of violent death in Colombia is in Latin America only matched by El Salvador and Guatemala.

This is the most skeletal review of Colombia's politically-violent past. It is not being offered as the explanation of anything – tradition is the lamest of explanations. (Though it is interesting to see how Howard Zehr is forced to fall back on it, *faute de mieux*, in his study of European homicide.)[10] It cannot of course offer much of an explanation at this stage, as it itself remains unexplained. Nor has it yet been established that this Colombian past is exceptional.

Does Colombia have a more *politically*-violent past than other countries? Has it been violent politically in comparison with other Latin-American republics, often, and sometimes mistakenly, conceived as being all of them inheritors of recently violent politics? Has it been violent in comparison with other countries within the Western political tradition, not to cast the net too wide?

The answer is not clear to me. The score of nineteenth-century civil wars would be high for Venezuela, Bolivia, Argentina, Uruguay, Mexico and most of Central America, to name only the most obviously belligerent parts of an unsettled half-hemisphere.(From this impressionistic list I am currently inclined to omit Peru.)[11] For the twentieth century, Mexico was certainly more politically violent than Colombia up until the 1940s. Guatemala and until recently El Salvador, as already mentioned, seem proportionately at least as violent, or more violent.[12] Despite the lip-service frequently paid to comparative history, it is rarely attempted, even within Latin America, where a common language and a common imperial heritage should make it a less far-fetched and more plausible undertaking. This short excursion merely indicates that a past of civil wars is no sure predictor on its own for a violent late twentieth century. Such a past may be a necessary condition, but it is not a sufficient one.

Venezuela has not been a politically violent country by most conceivable indicators in the twentieth century, nor has Argentina. Both have recently known violent episodes – Venezuelan riots and attempted coups, and the Argentine guerrillas and repression in the 1970s. Both series of events came after long periods of relatively unviolent politics – not necessarily democratic, not necessarily stable, but not violent. The analysis of both Venezuelan riots and *coup* attempts and the Argentine cycle of subversion and repression may benefit from a knowledge of each country's history, but a reference to a tradition of nineteenth-century civil war does not look to be a hopeful start.[13] Something in those two countries had happened to their nineteenth-century traditions: their past politics are severed from the present in ways that Colombian traditions are perhaps not, by massive immigration and by discontinuities in the history of party, to name but two characteristics absent in Colombia, but present in both Venezuela and Argentina. In neither Venezuela nor Argentina has the argument of nineteenth-century precedent been recently employed in explanations of political violence. In both countries such argument would be regarded as unlikely to yield much.

A close examination also leads one to doubt that there is a single or uniform nineteenth-century tradition at work here, even in civil wars. An Argentine war was not necessarily like a Venezuelan war, and a Venezuelan war was not exactly the same as one in Colombia.

One can begin to isolate the peculiar nature of Colombian political conflict in the nineteenth-century compared to that of some of the other Latin-American republics. It seems to have involved more strata of the local society, and to have involved them more frequently and repeatedly, than was commonly the case elsewhere. Nor did the conflict ever resolve itself in Colombia with the victory of one side or the other of the Liberal–Conservative divide, once such a common feature of Spanish-American politics. I treat this point further below.

I shall suggest that this peculiar nature is part of an explanation of the persistently high level of political violence in Colombia, but I am still far from certain that in the nineteenth century Colombia was, in terms of the number of dead, a particularly violent country.[14]

II SOME COMPARISONS

A comparison further afield, between Colombia and Italy, seems to me useful, and will perhaps be provocative. Though I have found in reading

David Moss's *The Politics of Left-wing Violence in Italy, 1969–1985*,[15] certain parallels with Colombian experience, and observations that can be adapted to illuminate Colombian phenomena, it is more the Italy of John Davis's *Conflict and Control in Nineteenth-century Italy*[16] that stimulates this comparison.

Post-Risorgimento Italy was certainly a politically-violent country, and by no means only in the South. Moss makes an interesting passing reference to this history, and to one of the founding fathers of small-group semi-irregular insurrectionary warfare, the bearded and cigar-smoking Giuseppe Garibaldi, a figure too often forgotten by twentieth-century analysts of subversive violence:

> The establishment of successive political frameworks – Liberal, Fascist, Republican – is associated in historical and mythological narratives with the enterprise of small armed minorities: Garibaldi and The Thousand, the March on Rome, the Resistance – a sequence which offers elements to render more plausible the seriousness of the threat to political stability posed by tiny groups of military officers or the Red Brigades.[17]

He does not, however, feel the need to draw at all heavily on these aspects of Italy's historical tradition in his analysis of left-wing violence in the last twenty years. Perhaps it is a vein he could have explored further.

The historian must certainly be aware that much divides the Italy of Davis from the Italy of Moss: a World War, the experience of Fascism, another World War, defeat. In that sense far less cuts off the Colombia of recent decades from the Colombia of the War of the Thousand Days, 1899–1902. Traditions can be broken, or severely interrupted, or at least their weight can be diminished – we have already hinted at this in the cases of Venezuela and Argentina – but the general point I wish to make here is against the common version of the Colombian argument from tradition, that Colombia, having been a politically-violent country, is *by that heritage alone* condemned to continue being a politically-violent country.

The argument is crude, but frequently deployed. It is surprisingly easily adopted by foreign commentators, who would be reluctant – who are reluctant – to adopt it in similar simple form about Italy, where political violence was perhaps more widespread in the last century and more intense than it was in Colombia. (Those who doubt this assertion should read Davis's book, which recalls such startling events as the military bombardment of parts of Milan, as late as 1898.)

Colombia's fatal past is therefore not fully or satisfactorily stated, or analysed – here the analysis is hardly begun – as merely a violent nineteenth century. If that past is relevant – and I think it is – it is because Colombia's nineteenth century was violent in a particular way, one which differed from that of other Latin-American republics, and from that of Italy too, though both with other Latin-American republics and with Italy there are many suggestive parallels and contrasts to explore.[18]

The lack of a break in tradition may also be relevant. To take only one aspect of that, Colombia does stand out as peculiarly left alone by her neighbours and the rest of the world, even within Latin America, a region where international conflict has not been pronounced. Colombians, the argument can be sketched, can continue to fight each other so much because they are not called upon to fight anyone else. The internal politics of many other republics have been decisively altered at one time or another by the experience of foreign war – that is true for Peru, Bolivia, Chile and Argentina, but not for Colombia.

Some further comments on this nineteenth-century heritage have their place here, and may help in our attempts to find new ways of bringing the protean and amorphous subject of political violence into sharper focus.

One new way, which the Colombian experience certainly leads this commentator to emphasize, is really an old way. The broad focus on which some other commentators are likely to insist, which forms indeed part of their definition of political violence, is on conflict between the state and its opponents. Some rightly wish to advance beyond the uneven emphasis placed on the analysis of the opponents to the neglect of the nature and varieties of state response: there are many pregnant questions raised by Moss, Apter, Arthur and others here. They are questions certainly relevant to the Colombian case. But there is a much larger matter that is barely hinted at, but which to most historians bulks large: that is, political violence in the pursuit of power where the state has only the most tenuous claim to a monopoly of force. Such violence is directed against political rivals, who may or may not be in power. Who holds the state apparatus in a given conjuncture is certainly not irrelevant in such conflicts, but it may not be so central to them. The parties in contention may be much more equal, in force and in legitimacy, than the more modern focus on state/opposition frequently seems to imply.

The political violence of nineteenth- and much of twentieth-century Colombia is, in this sense, a violence between equals, or near-equals. The protagonists, ideologues, narrators, text-authors, exegetes of this sort of violence are in no sense marginal figures. Some were national heroes, and many combined in their political careers all sorts of political method and talent, and some such figures still live in Colombia, and by no means do I refer only to survivors or graduates of revolutionary organizations: the "traditional parties", the Liberals and the Conservatives, possess them too. It is in part this common historical resort to violence – and some of it is quite recent history – that makes it difficult in Colombia to generate a political atmosphere in which violence is convincingly rejected. To give one small example, a recent work on the violence in the Eastern Plains in the 1940s and 1950s contains a reference to a legal dossier involving charges against one Hernán Durán Dussán. This eminent Liberal, a former Mayor of Bogotá and presidential "pre-candidate" in 1990, now takes a hard anti-guerrilla line. Nevertheless, in the matter of condoning violence he has in the Colombian phrase a *rabo de paja*, an ignitable straw tail. This is perfectly well-known in the Eastern Plains, the guerrilla-frequented source of his steadiest votes.[19]

III   THE PRIMACY OF POLITICS

A favourite quotation among Colombian guerrillas is Clausewitz's opinion that war is a continuation of politics by other means. Clausewitz was invoked daily in the orientation lectures inflicted on the captive audiences of the *Fuerzas Armadas Revolucionarias de Colombia*, the FARC, by its chief resident ideologue Jacobo Arenas.[20] All Colombian politicians must be familiar with the phrase.

On reading the works of my colleagues in this symposium I find this element of rivalry, so crucial to an understanding of Colombian political violence, largely absent. The vision of Hobbes, of the nature of political competition in the absence of the sovereign, or under a weak sovereign, is not much a part of their discussions.

I am not so sure that this is at all an archaic or negligible aspect in any modern study of political violence. Moss raises the question, when considering political violence in post-1968 Western Europe, why do we have to look at Germany, why at Italy, why not France? My line of suggestion does not offer much for the German case – it is hard not to shrug there and point out that all German violence could be fitted into one Colombian week-end, but anything violent that happens in Germany is bound to attract an inordinate degree of attention – but it does perhaps have some bearing on events in the weaker state of Italy. The state apparatus is there altogether less powerful, less convincing; violence is to some extent directed, at least symbolically, at rivals. I think too it has even more relevance to South Africa. 'Black on black' violence is a struggle for power between blacks that the government is powerless to contain. That powerlessness obviously needs to be explored. It is surely impossible to define political violence in such a way that this sort of violence is excluded – not only impossible, but undesirable. The enemy, the political target, is not always the obvious enemy, the state. These are old-fashioned points, but my guess is that they are still ones that must be part of any analysis that is to avoid the danger of excessive sophistication.

There are some others I would like to make about the more distant Colombian past before looking at more recent Colombian violence in comparative perspective, and with the distinct theoretical incentives that this symposium provides.

The first is to acknowledge years of frustration not only with the "argument from tradition" but with the simpler versions of some other common lines of analysis – social injustice, marginality, agrarian discontent – of both Colombian and foreign writings on the theme.[21] Colombian authors are more easily excused for their lack of a comparative appreciation than are the foreigners, for the conditions of intellectual and political life in Colombia have made it difficult to escape from certain perspectives, particularly when foreigners have been eager, despite the scantest research, to suggest to Colombians, with all the authority that they have until recently enjoyed, what they ought to think: countries like Colombia have lacked theoretical defences.[22]

Considering once again the nineteenth-century republic, I have come to some tentative conclusions. They are expanded in my comparisons between the Colombian and the Peruvian cases.

The first is easily stated in simple form: Colombia was not politically violent because it was a society of caste, of inequality, of manifest social injustice, of oppression. Of course, it was no egalitarian paradise: caste, inequality, injustice, oppression were all present. They were in most countries – including the United States, and in parts of the United States to a degree more severe than in Colombia. But in many respects Colombia was a more mobile, freer, less caste-bound, less deferential, more democratic society than its neighbours.[23]

I am aware that I am writing for readers unfamiliar with the social history of Colombia, and they must take what I say on trust. But certain facets of this society and its politics are incontrovertible, and are relevant to its subsequent development, and to the analysis of the extent and the nature of political violence in Colombia.

It is, broadly, a *mestizo* society. Carl Gosselman, a Swedish official envoy of the 1820s, noted the widespread diffusion of political conversation in Colombia, and defined the *mestizos* as the political class *par excel-*

lence. This did not exclude a dominant creole element in high politics, but the politics of provincial Colombia, of small-town Colombia, Gosselman discerned to be in mestizo hands. Many other nineteenth-century commentators confirmed his observation, among them some from other parts of Latin America. These last observations are particularly valuable, as they do not suffer from the combination of indifference and condescension that is the common note of contemporary European and North American comment.[24]

My second observation is summed up in the phrase that the French historian Maurice Agulhon in his *La République au Village,*[25] applies to the Provence of the 1840s: "democracy arrives before modernity". "Politics arrives before material progress" would be a justifiable paraphrase. The degree of partisan involvement among the Colombians, and its vehemence, sometimes shocked visitors, not only from the old world, but even some from the post-Jacksonian United States. They felt that somehow it had to be meaningless, that because these people were miserably poor and provincial and unqualified by literacy or property, their political involvement was somehow unreal.

It was real enough to the protagonists, in a great many dimensions. These included not only the arts of survival – who could do what to whom at a local level did depend to some degree on the outcome of political conflicts at higher levels – but also the senses of family and local identity, and a degree of personal identity and ideological commitment as well.

The latter is frequently ignored, or even denied, by those who wish to dismiss the popular element in past political struggles, to frame them exclusively in terms of manipulation – an essential element in the efforts of the revolutionary apologists of the 1960s, 1970s and 1980s. Past politics has to be dismissed as manipulated, the product of false consciousness, "unreal" – there modern ideologues coincide with the dismissive nineteenth-century travellers. This error of appreciation has quite a lot to do with underestimating the difficulty faced by any would-be "cosmocrat" in Colombia of establishing authoritative revolutionary narratives and texts, and the failure to appreciate the difference in atmosphere that makes it hard to conceive in the Colombian case of the successful emergence of a movement like *Sendero Luminoso.*[26]

However, it does suggest parallels between Colombia and Northern Ireland. In the Colombian case there is no irredentism, nor is there a religious cleavage of the same sort, though the Catholic Church has played an important role in the republic's political history, predominantly on one side of the sectarian division between Liberals and Conservatives. "Sectarian" has long been an indispensable adjective in the vocabulary of

Colombian political comment – and attitudes towards the Church do differ between members of the two currents.

There were few neutrals left in Colombia at the end of the nineteenth century. Surviving indian populations, which are not of great weight in the republic, did participate in civil wars, and cannot be considered apolitical, though their behaviour – generally supporting central government, whatever party is in power – does seem to differ from the more consistently partisan responses of mestizo Colombia. There each district or *vereda*, every family, was conscious of its political allegiance – it was Liberal or Conservative. Many Latin American republics passed through phases of Liberal– Conservative antagonism, and Colombia is not unique in that. But nowhere else was the political mobilization – much of it defensive, be it noted: a standing-to-arms against intruders[27] – so prolonged, nor so internalized by such a high proportion of the population, nor, as we have emphasized, so uninterrupted by any extra-national interference or concern.

In Mexico, for example – violent enough in other ways – there is no proclaimed conservatism after the French intervention. In Venezuela nobody is a *godo*, a Conservative, after the Federal War of 1858–63.

Colombian and Venezuelan politics, when one takes a view either side of the Santander–Táchira border between the two countries, do share certain similarities. In both Santander and Táchira there was in the last century vigorous local faction-fighting, and there were a number of prominent figures who had political careers in both countries. But on the Venezuelan side the Conservative–Liberal antagonism disappears. Something else is lacking, at least during the long periods of dictatorship that constitute most of Venezuelan history: the frequent gearing of local political destinies to national political change, which is such a feature in Colombia.[28]

Similar cultures exist either side of this border – both Santander and Táchira grow coffee, raise cattle. The racial composition is similar. There has always been much cross-border migration and intermarriage. Venezuelans went to Colombian schools, Colombians traded through Venezuelan agents and ports. But the similar cultures come to experience different politics. In the Colombian version sharp sectarian conflict is maintained – Santander politics had a fierce reputation even within Colombia. Changes at the national level from the dominance of one party to that of the other have violent local repercussions. Frequent elections keep local antagonisms alive. Public administration is partisan and discriminatory. There is heavy clerical involvement in politics, many "Carlist" priests – the Santandereanos even borrow the term. The ownership of arms is common: Santander was notorious for this sixty years ago, when carrying arms was rare in the rest of the republic.

On the Venezuelan side local antagonisms are also strong, and the fate of local factions does depend too on the outcome of rivalries at the level of national government. But the conflict is Liberal versus Liberal – different coloured Liberals, *azules* or *amarillos*, blues or yellows, but Liberals none the less. Church involvement is much less important – Venezuela is a much less catechized country than Colombia. For long periods – Antonio Guzmán Blanco's near quarter-century of dominance, Juan Vicente Gómez's twenty-seven years – there is much less scope for local conflict. It does not entirely disappear, but it is most effectively muted. Gómez's rule broke what traditions of party were left; on a famous occasion early in his government he deliberately failed to respond to a toast to the Liberal party, and the invocation was not repeated. Gómez too virtually disarmed the country, Táchira included. It was a serious matter to be found in possession of a firearm; those who still dared to possess them buried them, and did not dig them up. By the time of his death in 1935 the Venezuelan penchant for political violence had been much diminished.[29]

By contrast, the early 1930s on the Colombian side of the border were the most violent years since the last civil war: the Conservatives in many parts of Santander resisted by force the hand-over to a Liberal government after they had lost the elections of 1930. The distribution of arms to the already well-armed faithful by the outgoing Conservative governor was notorious.

IV   TRACTS AND TEXTS

It is easier to set out the prolonged nature of Liberal–Conservative antagonism than it is to describe its multifold local consequences on the map of the country, and on the character of Colombian political allegiance or identity. Colombia was not at all at the end of this intense process of politicization a land without heroes, narratives, or even texts and exegetes. It might be said to have had all too many, but as well as having their local variations, they were heroes, narratives, texts either for Liberals, or for Conservatives. You steeped or were steeped in liberalism, or in conservatism. Folklore, folkloric expression, was frequently partisan – this even appears in some anthologies, though I should imagine much politics is expurgated; folklore held a particular attraction for Conservatives, who also held beliefs about the loyal and catholic nature of certain peasant populations.[30]

It is also unwise to suppose that certain texts in the most literal sense of the term were not widely diffused. In the summer of 1991 I was allowed to inspect the contents of a trunk by the widow of a minor Conservative politician – a *campesino* of rural Boyacá, a peasant by some definitions, though he might not have called himself one – which contained her husband's papers: little catechism-like party documents from the 1940s and 1950s, old party newspapers, membership cards, convention lists, modest historical works, biographies of nineteenth-century party heroes, attacks on masons, atheists, communists: plenty of texts, in short. All showing signs of having been studied, carefully kept, miles from anywhere, a little ark of Conservative orthodoxy and identity, of comfort and prestige. We should remember that such documents are all the more powerful and prestigious when they are comparatively rare.

By "sectarian" we usually mean an uncompromising depth, or at least fixity, of involvement. The sort of identification with party achieved in Colombia appears to me uncommon. It was aided no doubt by the prolonged Liberal–Conservative antagonism in the country's history, but also by the politically permeable nature of Colombian society – contrast Ecuador, or Peru – and by the necessity of looking after oneself, one's family, one's district in that uncertain political context.

Identification with party is an expression of solidarity: it is hard to conceive of "good" reasons for changing one's allegiance. What could such "good" reasons be?[31]

Though some regions suffered more than others in the civil wars which, along with the more peaceful but not always entirely peaceful habits of electioneering, settled the political map of the country, most places suffered to some degree, if not from fighting, then from recruiting and arbitrary measures of one sort or another.[32]

Some regions were more deferential than others, but the general picture of Colombian society is not one of deference. As has already been stated, the government institutions of this country have always been weak, and for the most obvious of reasons. It has not been able to afford anything stronger, at least not during the republic's formative years – and thereafter that weak institutions can become something of a habit, a tradition.[33] (It is not, for example, national *poverty* that now accounts for the inefficiency of much of Italian government. The Italians, according to some sources, have a higher per-capita income than the British.)

The class-structure of Colombia is neither simple nor uniform, and the relations between class and politics likewise. J. A. Soffia, the Chilean diplomat of the 1880s to whose thorough sociological account of

Colombian politics we have already referred, observed that the Colombian upper-classes played little direct part in politics, which were too rough and too dirty, and attempted to secure their interests by keeping on even but distant terms with the politicians immediately concerned. He defined most of the officer corps – the small army played a significant role in politics at this time – as of humble origin. Civil war offered a career open to a certain sort of talent.[34]

So did politics. The Colombian political vocabulary, Colombian political discourse throughout the history of the republic, has frequent recourse to anti-oligarchic rhetoric, to denunciation of "señorial" dominance. This is, as a dispassionate French historian might be tempted to observe, a characteristic of the Colombian *longue durée*. Both parties have used this rhetoric. Colombian Conservatives can be as violent in their criticisms of the *status quo*, and as anti-oligarchic, as Liberals.[35]

But rhetoric should never be confused with objective analysis. It frequently has been, and still is: most foreign commentators received the M-19 movement's account of its motivations – the opening up of a closed political system, the creation of new political space, the freeing of a "blocked society" – with a great deal less scepticism than they would have treated similar pronouncements from the Red Brigades, or even from the Uruguayan Tupamaros.[36] (Nobody before the Tupamaros gave repression a pretext and a chance ever thought of Uruguay as an oppressed country.)

This rhetorical tradition may well contribute to Colombia's continued propensity for political violence: it diabolizes, polarizes, and it can be used by both sides of the partisan divide, or by all three sides if one includes, as one ought, the Marxist left in its various guises. The Liberal Jorge Eliécer Gaitán was its most famous practitioner, but he was not its only one; the Conservative Laureano Gómez discerned a Liberal oligarchy too. The rhetoric has a life of its own. It does not have to match reality, and it is not frequently checked against reality.

How does one check whether a society is "blocked", for example? Is it evidence enough that it is blocked if one feels blocked? Was Colombia exceptionally blocked, averagely blocked or not blocked enough? Too many Colombians would find such a line of questioning almost impertinent, so prevalent has the language become.

But the point I am labouring here is a rather more simple one: Colombian violence cannot be satisfactorily accounted for as a revolt against an oligarchy: the desire to open up a closed political system, for the creation of new political space, seem to me to be unsatisfactory explanations.[37]

So far I hope I have succeeded in setting out at least some of the reasons why Colombian politics had a violent potential. This was fully realized – to the surprise of many Colombians, who had prematurely concluded that the nineteenth-century inheritance had been overcome – after 1946, in the years of the "classic violencia".

Partisan conflict, exacerbated by the assassination of Gaitán on 9 April 1948, first sought the form of the old civil wars. One of the curiosities of this early period, along with the reappearance of the model 1874 Gras rifles that had already seen service in the last wars of the nineteenth century and the Santander violence of the 1930s, was the search for veterans of the last civil war who might impart their formal military knowledge to a new generation, and the widespread illusion that a properly-constituted Liberal "Estado Mayor", a General Staff, existed somewhere in the Eastern Plains.[38] Though there were many contacts between the leading national figures of the Liberal party and the guerrillas, the upper echelons had by now lost their vocation for taking to the hills or the plains themselves – such a course had always, even in the nineteenth-century, been the choice of only a minority. The virtual absence of any upper-class leadership in the countryside may also have contributed to making the "classic violence" more violent.

"La Violencia" in consequence expresses the fragmented, relatively formless nature of what ensued.

It has produced a large literature, some of it of high scholarly quality. There are a number of detailed local monographs. There are oral histories, almost all of humble protagonists. There are histories of individual guerrilla bands, of individual bandits, or guerrillas, detailed accounts of how the early Liberal–Conservative conflict later evolved, first under the military government of Gustavo Rojas Pinilla, 1953–7, and afterwards under the power-sharing Frente Nacional, 1958–74, into ostensibly revolutionary guerrilla warfare or "peasant self-defence". Anthropologists, historians, novelists, political scientists, sociologists and lawyers have all contributed. One recent study even attempts a semiotics of massacre and mutilation.[39]

There is also propaganda put out by the guerrillas – FARC, M-19, EPL, ELN[40] – and by sympathetic journalists and writers, though the quantity is surprisingly small for so many years of activity. I provide in the final note a select and commented bibliography to guide the reader through this literature, but I shall make no attempt here to resume the extraordinarily complicated history of political violence in the years since 1946, as I want to concentrate on certain themes in response to the work of some of the other contributors to this volume, and to some of the suggestions of its editor.

V   CONTEXTUALIZING VIOLENCE

The history of these years is extraordinarily complicated for all sort of reasons. Violence varies in its nature and intensity according to region, and over time. A few shots fired to influence the elections in Boyacá in 1946, say, makes quite a different affair from a massacre of peasants in Tolima in 1953. The guerrilla of Efraín González, a Conservative with good convent and emerald-mining connections in Santander and Boyacá, is quite different from the Castroite ELN, in composition, intention, action. Much remains mysterious, even after seemingly exhaustive scholarly examination.

Take massacres: one's first reaction is to analyse them in terms of antagonisms between the *veredas*, the rural districts of highland central Colombia, and to map them according to the political colour of the *vereda*, to hypothesize that they were more likely to occur in *veredas* which were not politically homogeneous – it can be seen that between 1946 and 1958 many districts were violently made uniform in their politics by the killing and expulsion of the minority or weaker party, and that *veredas* where politics were mixed were particularly prone to be the scene of massacres.[41] One can ponder their exemplary nature – a massacre is a particular sort of boundary-mark. One can even in Tolima find traces of a tradition: in the War of the Thousand Days there were massacres in that Department, and guerrilla leaders are said to have marked the boundaries of their territories with executions.[42]

All the same, one has still got virtually nowhere in answering the question why in certain parts of Colombia peasant fears and antagonisms under certain political conditions find expression in this extreme and to some degree ritualized form. Massacres are not that common. They do not feature much in the history of Venezuela, of Ecuador, of Bolivia, or until recently of Peru – at least not on the Colombian scale, or in the Colombian number, and as far as I can discern not in the Colombian manner – troops or police firing on peasants or miners, a pattern of Peruvian killing, or Bolivian massacres of former days, is quite a different phenomenon. Colombian massacres, despite the fame Gabriel García Márquez has given the *Masacre de las Bananeras* of 1928, are not usually carried out by the government. The antagonisms of *veredas*, the early politicization of rural Colombia, the weakness of state authority and its partisan deviations – all these are necessary parts of an explanation. But one still has not got a sufficient explanation.

Clearly, much of this violence was not revolutionary. Most Colombian violence today is neither revolutionary nor political. The question will naturally be raised, to what degree then can "classic" Colombian violence be analysed in political terms at all. How political was it?

As I have already noted, there is a pronounced tendency in the early literature of the 1960s to reject political explanations. My memories of that time are that Colombians who tried to insist to foreign enquirers that "politics" was at the root of it failed to convince. Their questioners wanted some other answer: violence had to be about land, or about social injustice, or coffee, or it even had to derive from the genetic inheritance of the Pijao indians – "politics" would not do. I can still detect today among some commentators a desire to define the political in terms that will exclude at least the early sectarian phase of Colombian conflict, that phase prior to the emergence of groups that at least made some attempt to emulate Mao or Castro – attempts which, as I shall describe, included at least one "long march" planned in part in deliberate emulation.

The squeamish have at times groped for phrases like "pre-political", adjectives like "primitive" when faced with this sort of politics, but I am not inclined to follow them. There are certainly many similarities between Colombian and Northern Irish politics, which are not commonly – or at least openly – called pre-political or primitive. A number of Colombians take a lively interest in Northern Ireland, even to the extent of reading books about it, which would confirm the existence of certain parallels. Northern Irish party allegiances, what to my English eye is the non-deferential nature of political life in the province – "Je suis leur chef, il faut que je les suivre"[43] – which used to so confuse and and disappoint successive British governments, when they expended so much useless effort on persuading leaders to be reasonable: these party allegiances seem familiar to a student of Colombia. Other similarities may emerge.

I argue that it was "politics" that was the root of Colombian violence, a "politics" not reducible to something more acceptable to a certain cast of academic mind, such as land tenure, relative deprivation, or marginality. Once political conflicts got under-way, much else entered in: robbery, banditry, land-grabs (most, it seems from the one adequately-documented study, by medium-sized proprietors against other small- and medium-sized proprietors),[44] acts of private vengeance, even Marxist revolution.

Here emerges one comment from the Colombian vantage point on some of our other cases: violent acts do not show up well against a background of violence. The currency of violence gets devalued. Particular "discourses", if you like, are drowned in the general noise.

In the days of the theory of the "foco", Guevara and Debray wrote of the "small motor" of the guerrilla which set in motion the "larger motor", the disintegration of the existing power structure. In the 1960s and 1970s there were attempts to apply this theory – and other variants, Maoist, Moscow-line, Uruguayan – afresh in Colombia. Their impact was undoubtedly blunted by the sheer quantity and variety of previous violence. Certain groups tried to begin operations with violent local or national "spectaculars": the attack on Simacota by the ELN is an example.[15] But it is hard that way to achieve much *frisson*. Some subsequent violent "spectaculars" have also met with disproportionately little success, either in exciting public alarm or in getting across the particular message or messages the movement concerned had in mind.

Take the extraordinary example of the seizure of the Palace of Justice in the centre of Bogotá by the M-19. This was no peaceful sit-in even at its beginning – the M-19 invaded the place with a sizeable arsenal, killing security guards as they went in – and it ended in a full-scale military assault, with the deployment of light tanks, and in the deaths of many unfortunate members of the Supreme Court, of many of its staff and of most of the assailants.

It is hard to get more spectacular than that. Yet it is not easy to see what had changed politically when it was all over. Surely such a disastrous event must have had political consequences, but what were they?

Some of this lack of political consequence may have been accidental. Had the army made a better job of retaking the Palace of Justice and rescuing the judges, its prestige would have been much enhanced and its political power likewise, but the army failed to achieve "an Entebbe", to use the expression of the time, and emerged with its prestige somewhat tarnished. President Betancur was not in a strong position before the affair – he was widely thought to have made too many concessions to the guerrillas, who had responded in bad faith – and he was not in a strong position after the affair either. The M-19 suffered heavy physical losses, and the reaction of public opinion to this particular violent experiment was entirely hostile, but the movement did not disappear. It continued on its erratic course towards some sort of deal with the government, and eventually made one with a sense of timing that gave it a surge of renewed popular support.

Nobody now remembers the ostensible message that the seizure of the Palace of Justice and the Supreme Court hostages was meant to get across. Few at the time paid much attention to it. The M-19 demanded a public trial of the President, to be held under their armed supervision. They were also to have many hours of guaranteed television time.

Violence certainly has its short-comings as a medium of communication, and they are the more apparent the more violence there is. As David Moss has written: "Power to establish what violent acts are symbolic of is as critical as the ability to carry out the acts themselves."[46] The M-19 entirely failed to establish what the taking of the Palace was symbolic of, though the government's retaking of it was also from that point of view less than a complete success: "What are you doing?" asked a reporter of an army captain briskly engaged in directing the siege of the building: *"Pues, defendiendo la democracia, maestro"*. "Defending democracy, chum" was not quite what it looked like.

The M-19 combined a talent for improvisation, indeed even a theory of improvisation, with gross misjudgements of what it was doing, or at least most questionable rationalizations of what it was doing. The theory of improvization was expressed by its most flamboyant early leader, Jaime Bateman, when he compared making the revolution to cooking a *sancocho*, a stew: it has to be done with love, you put in a bit of this then a bit of that, you taste as you go along. (Bateman was probably not aware that this same image of the *sancocho* had been used a century or more ago by the black Radical Liberal General David Peña, the author of a notorious nineteenth-century "spectacular", a seizure of the city of Cali during which distinguished Conservative ladies had been made to sweep the streets).[47]

The M-19 at times appears to have done things primarily to see what would happen, and then to have trimmed its course and its pronouncements accordingly. Many of its members were previously in the FARC, and gave as their reasons for quitting that organization inactivity and boredom.

Another example of M-19 misjudgement and improvisation was the kidnapping of the Conservative politician Alvaro Gómez, a violent act in itself and the more violent for the ruthless killing of Gómez's bodyguard. Again, the general public was not much concerned with the ostensible reasoning behind this kidnapping at the time, concluding, perhaps accurately enough, that the movement was just after publicity and another bargaining-counter. Afterwards the reasoning has again been rapidly forgotten, as with the Palace of Justice.

It is curious to recall it. The movement had concluded that its way forward politically, out of the slump in its fortunes that followed the Palace of Justice and some further military debacles, was to kidnap an "oligarch". This would somehow bring about the fusion of the armed forces, the M-19 and "the people".

How this miracle was to be precipitated by kidnapping Gómez will forever remain a mystery. Events did not follow this unlikely prediction. Gómez, who does not consider himself an "oligarch" – who does? – but a popular politician, did indeed turn out to be remarkably popular and demonstrations and demands for his release were many of them spontaneous and sincere.[48] After much dialogue, which in the long run did contribute towards an accord between the government and the M-19, Gómez was released unharmed, though suffering somewhat from the "Stockholm syndrome": he succeeded in establishing some rapport with his kidnappers, and he even temporarily changed his views on agrarian reform. His supposed representativity as an "oligarch", the fusion of the armed forces and "the people" – all that was forgotten and cast aside.

There is thus a great gulf between the message intended, the effect intended, and what is achieved. In Colombia, there is much competition between the politically violent, and the presence of much unpolitical violence drowns out messages and makes the desired significance of violent acts yet harder to discern. The public, when it is not indifferent, reacts with multiple speculations, many of them Byzantine, most of them plausible. When Gómez was kidnapped, all sorts of theories at first flourished about who had done the deed, and why. They were not all political, but they were most of them plausible: it was hard to rule any of them out, and the M-19's claim to authorship was widely doubted.

As David Moss mentions in the Italian case, there are internal as well as external audiences. Messages of a violent sort are directed not only at governments or the general or local public but at rivals, would-be defectors, informers, dissidents. Much of this traffic obviously gets through loud and clear to those to whom it is directed, but it sounds muffled and enigmatic to the ears of the rest of the country.

The lack of protest that commonly follows Colombian killings is also at first disconcerting. One hypothesis is that this lack of protest results not only from intimidation and prudence, or familiarity, but from the clear understanding in the vicinity of the deed that somebody broke the rules of the game, did something de-stabilizing – broke "the peace in the feud", if I understand that phrase rightly.

This background will not, I predict, seem familiar to a Peruvian. Peru does not have such a violent republican history as Colombia, though it has its share of civil wars and violent episodes.[49] Its party structure is more fluid, its ethnic divisions more marked. It should be illuminating to explore how and why Sendero Luminoso differs from Colombian revolutionary movements, as it is described by Carlos Iván Degregori in it origins, and by Gustavo Gorriti Ellenbogen.[50]

I have already alluded to the difference in context between the two countries. Peru did have some brief guerrilla experiences, and some relatively widespread land conflicts, in the 1960s. To a Colombian observer, or one looking for widespread and prolonged violence, those outbreaks look trivial in comparison with Colombia's guerrillas, almost as trivial as the Venezuelan experience, a series of mild excursions too often misleadingly held to provide the Colombians with a model of how to deal with such troubles. They were brief, too theoretical to take root, and easily suppressed by the Peruvian armed forces, without much bloodshed.

Counter-insurgency theories, of French rather than North American origin, the need for government action in the sierra to pre-empt further guerrilla attempts, formed part of the doctrine of the Velasco government after 1968, and the policies of that government are some of them seen at work in Ayacucho in Carlos Iván Degregori's *El surgimiento de Sendero Luminoso*. There are clearly some connections between the abortive guerrillas of the 1960s and what came later – the experience forms part of the debates which themselves are part of the formation of Sendero Luminoso. But Sendero does not emerge against what a Colombian would consider a background of political *violence*. The Peruvian authorities have somewhat more justification for being bewildered and surprised by the onset of armed struggle than one might conclude from a casual reading of the criticisms of government intelligence and analysis made by Gustavo Gorriti Ellenbogen. (He seems wise after the event, or at least naïve about intelligence: not the acutest policeman or soldier imaginable could have predicted Sendero Luminoso in 1979.)[51] Before passing on to explore further differences between Colombian movements and Sendero – differences in structure, ideological formation, political context, political control, discipline, tactics and strategy, attitude to publicity, attitude to violence and death; the list of differences is a long one – I will dwell a bit longer on this first difference and its consequences.

VI   FIELDS OF PEACE: FIELDS OF VIOLENCE

A movement which aspires to use violence creatively must look for a relativel peaceful field of action. At first the Colombian M-19 did this. With a countryside already occupied by earlier practitioners of violence, or at least by the memory of such earlier practitioners, some of them active since the 1940s, rural operations were less attractive than urban. Hence the movement's opening act – the robbery in Bogotá of Bolívar's sword. This sword was not an object previously held in much account by Colombians – after all, Bolívar was a Venezuelan, to many Colombians a soldier of not altogether progressive views, and he had left behind more than one sword. Removing this particular sword from its unguarded and insecure glass case in the not much frequented Quinta de Bolívar was easy enough. But the action at least had novelty: it made a change from the distant and desultory ambushes of the FARC.[52]

The other famous early operations of the movement were also urban: the kidnapping and later execution of the labour leader José Raquel Mercado, the robbery of a large quantity of arms from the Canton Norte barracks of the army in Bogotá, the seizure of the Dominican Embassy on Dominican National Day, with a large number of Ambassadors inside.

All these actions attracted great publicity. At the time of the Mercado kidnapping, the country was still not accustomed to such acts. Commercial kidnapping was still in its infancy, and this was the first metropolitan political kidnapping – Mercado was taken and later killed as a traitor to the cause of the workers. The episode caused the government considerable anguish, and despite his shortcomings as a union leader a popular cult sprang up around Mercado's tomb, which shows that at least some workers remained unconvinced of his treachery. The robbery of weapons from the army through a tunnel dug from a nearby house was also a great publicity success inside Colombia, and the seizure of the Dominican Embassy was for a couple of weeks news reported around the world.

So the M-19 kept the ball rolling. These events were not particularly violent, though they were not without violence, and there was some violence in the government's response, particularly the torture of suspects by the army after the arms robbery. Some bombs were placed in Bogotá, against foreign concerns, though no one was killed. The leaders of the movement had not been at all sure whether to kill Mercado or not, and at this stage in the movement's evolution that execution looks a bit of an aberration. Nobody was killed in the arms robbery – not a shot was fired, not a charge blown. Nobody was harmed in the Dominican Embassy seizure, in part thanks to the extraordinary patience shown by the government of President Julio César Turbay.

The purpose of these actions was not particularly clear. The Mercado kidnapping, designed to gain the movement prestige and influence with labour, was a failure, and nothing like it was tried again. The arms theft was too successful: the M-19 at that time could not possibly employ the number of weapons it seized, and was also unprepared for the vigour of the army's reaction. Most of the weapons were quickly recovered and a high proportion of the movement's members were arrested. As is usual in Colombia, most of them were fairly rapidly released, the military courts that by civilian decision tried them being no more efficient in gaining convictions in this sort of case than the civil courts.[53]

Nonetheless, it was ostensibly to force the government to end this repression that the Dominican Embassy was seized. The movement's other aims were temporarily lost in this circularity. Keeping the ball rolling meant making the cause up as one went along. Events become causes – the Dominican Embassy seizure has to take place because of what happened after the Canton Norte arms theft. Thence for a while the leaders went to Cuba, thence to the countryside – it appears that no Colombian revolutionary group can conceive of a strategy that does not have setting up a rural guerrilla in it somewhere; then purchase of more arms abroad, the adventure of the ship *Karina*, and an incursion into the jungles of the southern border with Ecuador; a restless pattern of *tomas*, temporary seizures of small pueblos, often with large losses to the movement; then the erratic course of peace-making: a meeting abroad with President Belisario Betancur (an even greater master of publicity than the leaders of the M-19), truces and the breaking of truces, further *tomas*, the invasion of the Palace of Justice in Bogotá.

In the course of composing this *sancocho* the M-19 became increasingly violent. Many died from its activities, and it suffered heavy losses itself. The sound of gunfire was in some phases music in its leaders' ears, and a music which to them was a necessary part of the movement, as expressed in their latter-day paradox of "*peleando para la paz*", "fighting for peace".

As this notion emerges from one of their documents, the argument is that concessions from the government in the peace-making negotiations (these began under Turbay, intensified with Betancur's election in 1982 and have continued ever since) must be seen to be the result of armed pressure from the movement. Hence the sound of gunfire must continue up until the moment of signing any truce or agreement.[54]

There appears to be a sort of willed self-deception at play here, as well as the desire to deceive the imagined spectator. The leadership knows that the process of negotiation obeys other determinants, that fighting has to be severely rationed if other gains are to be made, that armed pressure makes it harder, not easier, for the government to make concessions. All the same, if they cease firing too soon they will look defeated. This particular fly on the chariot wheel therefore fires off its guns to proclaim that it is raising all this dust. It hopes that the dust will hide its weakness – the movement was certainly not negotiating from strength – and the dust gets into its own eyes: one should not underestimate the degree of confusion, muddle, self-deception and military sentimentality present.

By the time it chose to abandon violent acts – with the patient and detailed assistance of a government determined to make peace with at least one guerrilla movement, even if it had to go to considerable lengths in preserving that movement's life in order to do so – the violence of the M-19 had ceased to convey to the country even the semblance of a coherent message. The M-19 had not been economical with violence. It had failed to maintain its distinction from other violent actors – drug barons, kidnappers, other guerrillas. It had gained the reputation that it was willing to contemplate any sort of deal.

It had always believed in the merits of personality, publicity, improvisation, typified by Jaime Bateman, its principal *vedette* in the early days. No fool, Bateman had a Communist background and had become convinced that the FARC and the orthodox party had no real intention of making the Colombian Revolution. He was, despite what was to follow and despite his lack of any coherent vision of a post-revolutionary future, a cerebral revolutionary tactician. But he was no "cosmocrat". His reputation was for *pachanga*, a good time, and panache. He must have known how he was reported. His revolutionary trappings included light aeroplanes, credit cards and pina coladas.

A journalist at one interview was astonished to hear him begin the interview with a nursery rhyme: "Los pollitos dicen, pío pío pío, cuando tienen hambre, cuando tienen frío." What could this be? Some code? No, the leader explained. There was a photographer present, and the best way for a man to look natural and serious was to recite "Los pollitos dicen ...". Bateman's remains were identified – he was killed in an air-crash in Darien and the wreck lay hidden in the jungle for many months – by the presence of his up-to-the-minute electronic portable typewriter.[55]

The M-19 was, in its own eyes, simply more active, more imaginative, more Colombian, warmer, more idiomatic: *mamaba gallo, ponía conejo* – it mocked, it showed superior cunning. It put no message across because it came to have no message, only style. Styles catch on, but styles never last. They have their moments, and the M-19 showed how well it could exploit them, even after the disaster of the Palace of Justice, in what it made of the Gómez kidnapping and its subsequent agreement to make peace. But moments do not last. The movement's subsequent descent into opportunism has not been its least spectacular phase. Its recent list of candidates for the Senate was made up of persons of all sorts of antecedent and condition, including at least one prominent Conservative landowner, and at one point its candidate for Mayor of Bogotá was an octogenarian television priest of decidedly authoritarian, not to say "Carlist", temperament.

These details have already extended the grounds for comparison between Peru and Colombia further than the long previous existence in Colombia of political violence of many types that deprives new practitioners of the chance of novelty.

Not only is the Colombian background violent: it is politically saturated. Much useful oral and local history has recently been written in Colombia, and most of it explores the origins of the violence and its development in the 1940s, 1950s and 1960s.[56] These works are interesting in all sorts of ways, some of which their authors do not suspect. They are often artistic, artful. They are sometimes nostalgic. They revel in the extraordinary complexities of local tradition and of personality, though this may sometimes get in the way of the particular line of revindication concerned.

A number of them concentrate on the emergence of the FARC from the at first predominantly Liberal resistance to the Conservative onslaught of the late 1940s in the Western Cundinamarca–Tolima region.[57] They describe how a Communist-led movement of armed rural self-defence first came into being there, what the government did to it, where its peregrinations led it, what heroes and doctrines it produced. A deal of myth-making is sometimes at work.

Oral history in Colombia is in many ways sophisticated; it has become quite the local genre, but the practitioners remain highly selective in what questions they ask and to whom they ask them. They are much more inclined to interrogate Liberals and Communists and guerrillas than Conservatives, members of the armed forces or government officials, who are thus to some degree diabolized, at least denied variety or personality. Nevertheless, the effort to construct, *post hoc*, a politically usable narrative of this struggle is in itself interesting, and not necessarily invalid. It can even make a contribution to making peace, if the books find the right readers. Much can be extracted from it for our purposes.

Political saturation: the traditional Liberal–Conservative allegiances are heavily present. The leadership may leave a lot to be desired in all sorts of ways, and it is a constant Liberal complaint that the national leadership is not present enough in these local struggles – it leaves the rural following with insufficient guidance and support – but the sense of a relative vacuum, the disappearance of any pre-existing traditional authority, that one gets from Carlos Iván de Gregori's account of Ayacucho (and which is also present in Davis's account of the post-Risorgimento *mezzogiorno*) is absent.[58]

Such authority was never much present in this particular region anyway – it can be categorized as at least semi-frontier, and though some large enterprises, coffee and cattle estates, are present, their owners are not men who have traditionally exercised local political authority. The protagonists in the local conflict are Liberals and Conservatives, and a few Communists – the Communist Party has been active in the region since the 1920s. They are all aware of the geographical and familial patterns of alliance and solidarity, and from the oral accounts it can be seen that most of them are capable of recounting their antecedents in detail.

The protagonists in their different ways all attempt to organize, to employ existing organizations, to manipulate existing institutions – the alcaldes, the judiciary, the police, the army. They use their contacts and sympathetic organizations outside the region, in Ibagué, the capital of the Department of Tolima, and in Bogotá, the capital of the Department of Cundinamarca and of the republic. Neither city is far away. Their life histories show that some of them had previous experience outside the region. Some have done military service. The region itself has been the scene of previous agrarian conflict: there have been strikes, *sindicatos*, leagues, colonization projects official – and therefore probably political in the party sense – and unofficial. No *tabula rasa* here, even if saturation is perhaps too strong a word.

VII   NARRATIVES AND DISCOURSE

The detail need not concern us, at least not the detail of the narrative, the personalities, the regional history. Certain themes are of more general interest.

These protagonists read. One can list the works that crop up – *Les Miserables*, Emil Ludwig's biography of Napoleon, a work on the Soviet Union by the "Red Dean" of Canterbury (also read by Fidel Castro after Moncada), *How to be a Good Communist* by Liu Shaoqi. Some study, some intermittent "poring over texts" did occur, and as the Communist-led movement was cut off by the Liberals and cut itself off from the Liberals, political orientation naturally became more systematic. Thoughts became, through a combination of indoctrination and experience, "clearer", as the subjects usually put it.

Conditions were far from ideal even for achieving a "brotherhood of the text" on an elementary level. There were few intellectuals in the guerrilla at this time, perhaps not a single person who could properly qualify as such, though the details of schooling attended and of the background of those concerned show that "peasant" is not a complete characterization. There were small landowners, peasants, but also small traders – the pre-revolutionary background of Pedro Antonio Marín/Manuel Marulanda Vélez/Tirofijo, the longest-lasting and still-surviving leader of the FARC, notwithstanding frequent assertions that he is a peasant, is that of the son of a small landowner who turned successfully to rural commerce, selling agricultural goods and buying produce, including coffee. Though his father had only twenty hectares, one of his uncles was a more substantial landowner.[59]

Most had some years schooling and those with curiosity read some books. One notices a certain independence of mind, an eclecticism: no ruling text, no ruling intellectual figure, an insistence that they learnt primarily from events. Scales fall from the eyes after, for example, such a prime case of army treason as the trapping of a column and its arms by soldiers posing as deserters at Rioblanco, not after the reading of some little book. These men become "curtidos", tanned, by years of resistance. They are not easily persuaded to accept anyone's theoretical instruction. Those who wanted to instruct them had to become rather like them, if they were to get anywhere at all, and the ascendancy of intellectuals and party theorists has never been complete.

Despite fierce antagonisms, with frequently ferocious results, the atmosphere is not truly manichean: these narratives of men who often started out as Liberals and for a time became sectarian Liberals even contain references to some good Conservatives. In many areas in the years before the violence it had been quite common for Liberals to invite Conservatives to be *compadres* of their children, and vice-versa. Many testify that this sort of relationship held up in the years of sectarian violence, and that Conservative *compadres* did protect their Liberals as far as they could. Likewise Communists distinguish between "advanced Liberals" and "oligarchic Liberals" and treasonable Liberals. There are even good and bad police, not all *chulavitas*, *chulas*, as the politically-recruited Conservatives were termed, and good and bad soldiers. A number of revolutionaries had done military service, and the army was not a strange institution for them – they even mention introducing into the guerrilla *la milicia chilena*, the order and tactics of the Colombian army derived from the Chilean military mission of 1907.

Offers of truce, or of amnesty, are not often rejected out-of-hand. They are carefully weighed, and carefully managed even if rejected. Sometimes a show of acceptance, the hand-over of a careful selection of weapons, mostly but not all useless, has been considered the wisest response.

The FARC has in its "foundational narrative" a number of marches. This seems to be a pattern in other Colombian movements as well – defeats and marches, individual and collective, also figure in the history of the ELN. These marches are both real and symbolic. Marching away from real persecution and danger, the exodus of whole small communities, was sometimes the only possible recourse. There are examples of the same in previous civil wars, and a number of settlements have their origins in such forced migrations. But there is also present a consciousness of the symbolic value of such episodes. Alape records that an early march in Tolima was in part inspired by a leader who had read Jorge Amado's *The Knight of Hope*, his version of the 1930s journeyings of the Prestes column in Brazil. A later exodus found inspiration and justification in the to us more obvious model of Mao's march, specifically recommended by a visiting ideologue.[60]

These marches are proudly described. They have about them some of the puzzling nature of that original flight out of Egypt, in which the Children of Israel "went ten days' journey in forty years". The marches are recalled in detail, with all their logistical difficulties and their sufferings. They produce heroes, veterans, solidarity, organization, sacrifice, legend.

It is tempting to speculate further. The marches have their stations of suffering. The marchers cross over into other lands, they enter new valleys, they found new settlements, whose names acquire resonance, little echoes of Yan'an: El Davis, Seúl (a clearer echo of Korea), La Uribe. The survivors are the stronger and purer, and they have carried with them something essential with which they will later return, after a necessary spell in the wilderness: Exodus, Odyssey, Anabasis, journey to the headwaters.

The scene being Colombia, however, there is more than one march, few apart from the marchers are aware at the time what is going on, the destinations are remote and irrelevant, the overall strategy unclear, and one is reminded of the nineteenth-century Argentine General Lucio V. Mansilla's *aperçu* that the frontier is where old politics take refuge, not where new politics are born.[61]

Nonetheless, the exodus from the "independent republic" of Marquetalia in 1964, the later evacuation of El Pato, the shift over the Eastern Cordillera onto its eastern slopes and down into the Llanos is the founding epic of the long armed struggle phase of the FARC, which lifts it out of localized *"autodefensa campesina"*, "peasant self-defence" – at least in theory, for the FARC long remains an essentially defensive and unambitious organization. (It is, as we have noted, their conviction that the FARC never really intends to make the revolution that leads some of its impatient members into founding the M-19.) The new doctrine, and the epic, are elaborated in the comparative peace of the late 1960s and

1970s. In the face of new rivals – the Castroite ELN, the Maoist EPL – the FARC must provide the Moscow-line Communist Party, which in Colombia is a legal, cautious, non-vanguard Party that has a history of alliances with the Liberal Party and much at stake in union organization and urban politics of a conventional nature, with visible revolutionary credentials.

This the FARC does, largely in these years under the direction of the Party. (Circumstances have since altered the balance of authority; the guerrilla has become much richer and more independent, while the urban Party has declined.) For these purposes, making the most of the symbolism of the march had obvious attractions.

The "university" at the end of the march was, however, a poor thing compared to Yan'an. Ideological guidance was provided by the Communist Party, chiefly in the shape of Jacobo Arenas, a figure whose intellectual vanity clearly exceeded his capacity, and who became increasingly out-of-touch and even nostalgic in the intellectual isolation of the FARC headquarters of La Uribe – relatively comfortable for some years though that was, especially for the upper end of the guerrilla hierarchy. Arenas appears to have yearned for debate with other Colombian notables: once communications were established for "dialogue" with the government, under the presidency of Belisario Betancur, he would insist that some hapless official in Bogotá should read him the editorials and opinion columns of *El Tiempo* over the radio telephone, while he would continually interrupt with comment and argument. Arenas died of a heart attack in 1990. A belated attempt to humanize the FARC–CP leadership in the face of changing world conditions – "one of the great and grave defects of biographies of revolutionary leaders all over the world ... is to present their subjects as perfect, without error or stain" – is C. Arango Z.'s *Jacobo: Guerrero y Amante*.[62] In its pages he appears all too human.

Even in life Arenas enjoyed little intellectual prestige outside the more naïve sectors of the Communist Party – he was not a leading party intellectual, merely a sort of field-intellectual or commissar. Most intellectuals must have found his increasingly antique meanderings embarrassing, despite the references to Clausewitz and however attractive to a certain cast of mind observations such as one of his last, that Gorbachev was obviously a CIA agent, may have been. He was too blinkered, too folkloric, too rhetorical to be taken seriously. Though exceptionally placed geographically and equipped with fatigues, horses and sub-machine gun, he is an example of the failure of the Colombian revolutionary left to produce intellectual figures of any enduring prestige.

Nor was he the guerrilla's central figure. That remained Marulanda.

Here again there is a contrast with Peru. Peru produces at least the occasional political guru. In this century it has produced two – three if one is to include Abimael Guzmán.[63] The first two – and again from the Colombian vantage point they both seem useful for an understanding of Sendero – are José Carlos Mariátegui and Victor Raúl Haya de la Torre. Mariátegui was Latin America's most distinguished Marxist, the author of many texts that excite much exegesis, a "monumental" thinker. Haya de la Torre was also the author of a series of original doctrines, ostensibly revolutionary, ostensibly Peruvian, and the founder of the *Alianza Popular Revolucionaria Americana*, APRA, a political movement that endured persecution, that worked through a cell-structure, that embraced and commanded all aspects of life, or at least aspired to, and that exacted exceptional devotion from its members.

I can think of no Colombian figures equivalent to either of these two, and that may have something to do with the lack of any Colombian equivalent to the third, Abimael Guzmán. Colombians have always been rapid and fluent assimilators, expanders and modifiers of foreign theory and doctrine. It is no lack of talent, wit or intellectual ability that is at work – the country has produced some formidable Conservative systematizers, and plenty of able publicists of all sorts of doctrines.

Perhaps the techniques of cultural and intellectual history are not yet sufficiently developed to account for the Peruvian appearance and the Colombian non-appearance of a Mariátegui or a Haya de la Torre. It may have something to do with the relative ease and frequency of intellectual–political careers in Colombia, the continual co-optation of dissidents that has always eroded the Colombian left, though Mariátegui's early conventional career, which included a spell as editor of a horse-racing paper, was hardly a failure. It may be also the absence of "oligarchy", at least in obvious and imposing form, and the lack of the grand racial and regional differences that mark Peru, even the lack of a grand vice-regal colonial past, the lack of historical tragedy, or tragedy in the grand dimension.

There is no great catastrophe in the Colombian past on which to meditate. Colombia has consequently lacked historical system-builders or tragedians: its historiography is rich in memoir, anecdote, incident, sketch; it is intimate, conversational, personal – even, as I have hinted, in its recent revolutionary versions. But there are Peruvian notes that are not sounded in the successor state to the humbler, later, less fabulous Viceroyalty of New Granada, itself the successor of a minor imperial presidency that modestly administered the conquered cacicazgos, chieftaincies, tribes, and petty princedoms of muiscas, quimbayas, ansermas, taironas.

Likewise, though the APRA Party in its infancy attracted some attention among Colombian politicians, such a movement would have had no prospect of success in Colombian circumstances. In Colombia a figure with the pretensions of Haya de la Torre would have been ridiculed, or co-opted. Gaitán, who certainly had high national ambitions, eventually chose to work them out within the Liberal Party. It would not have occurred to any ambitious Colombian to launch such a project as APRA, except as a temporary tactical move. The equivalent political territory in Colombia was already occupied, by the ever-divided, ever-vigilant, ever-open, ever-argumentative Liberal Party – or by those sectors of the Conservative Party that never entirely forgot or neglected the populist strands that can be derived from the Spanish theory of empire. (This is not just lyricism: Quintín Lame, the most prominent indian leader of this not very indian republic, was for most of his career a Conservative, and from time to time enjoyed the esteem and assistance of national Conservative leaders; he was a student of the laws and structures of the colonial past and even wrote about them.)[64]

The two countries offer different political contexts, and though there are certain common elements – the expansion of provincial secondary and higher education comes to mind, with the Universidad Industrial de Santander, an early nucleus of the ELN, attempting the part of the Universidad Nacional de San Cristóbal de Huamanga – the Colombian environment is not a good breeding-ground for most aspects of the Sendero mentality as described by Carlos Iván Degregori.[65]

It is too communicative, fluid, un-manichean. It does not, and here it contrasts with Ireland as well as Peru, place much emphasis on martyrdom, on suffering and dying for Colombia. Those who die in Colombia are not often portrayed as suffering, and the blood of the martyrs receives rather perfunctory attention.

There is no "quota" of revolutionary dead, such as Sendero is said to exact. The ELN remembers Camilo Torres – another failed "cosmocrat" – especially when its leaders are being interviewed by journalists from abroad, but he is not an obsessive point of reference, nor is he a constant source of inspiration. His death is portrayed as the result of his lack of tactical experience, a mistake, not a sacrifice, and his works are not much read. (The ELN texts, when they touch on what books *Elenos* read, refer to García Márquez – *La Hojarasca* and *Cien años de Soledad* (which "recount Colombian history in an agreeable way") – Che Guevara or the propaganda of the organization itself, "some little works of José Martí", one or two Soviet novels like *How The Steel Was Tempered*, novels of the Mexican Revolution, Clausewitz, Mao, Bolívar.

"All these little books would go into the rucksacks.") The leaders of the movement talk more of killing, in a practical and economical fashion, than they do of dying.[66]

Overall, the impression is that Colombian guerrillas want to live. Life within the guerrilla gets more comfortable as you rise in the hierarchy. The rank-and-file is predominantly youthful, and hence not so aware of mortality. There is a turn-over: guerrillas retire. Colombia must contain many more retired than active guerrillas. The FARC sometimes sets them up in small useful businesses, the ELN settles families, and seems to have an elaborate "civilian camouflage" and rest-and-recreation organization. In propaganda and interviews there is some emphasis on normal life going on, of the guerrilla as a way of life, now stable, achieved after various phases of persecution, peregrination, ideological error and disciplinary excess, varying with the movement concerned. A recent text of the ELN has extensive passages about love, marriage and child-care.[67] The FARC advertises improved material conditions – jeans, canned beer. At one time it was rumoured that the ELN provided Nike trainers. One of the few documents of the Maoist EPL – it at one time adopted the Albanian line and named one of its fronts after Enver Hoxha – contains a little guerrilla tale, like one of the *costumbrista* sketches in the nineteenth-century literature of the republic, in which Rosendo successfully courts Fanny and finally marries her in a pretty rural fashion, despite attempted interruptions by government forces.[68]

Not only do they want to live. They frequently seek a measure of personal and material success. Given the country's history, these aspirations are not entirely unrealistic. The "combination of all forms of struggle" has in recent years appeared as a formulation of the Communist Party, formerly Moscow line, in distinction from the ELN's ostensible conviction that power is to be taken through the local version of "prolonged people's war", but it has, as we have noted, often characterized both Liberal and Conservative careers. One sort of reputation can be translated into another.

Though "reinsertion" into unarmed politics has its hazards, particularly vulnerability to revenge, it can be achieved. One suspects that it is usually there somewhere in the Colombian guerrilla mind, even in its ostensibly most intransigent forms. The EPL work to which I have referred again surprises the reader, after the *amores* of Rosendo and Fanny, with a discussion of the movement's differences with the Barco government over the provisions for a constituent assembly and the details of a proposed system of municipal referendum. Hardly "Albanian". (The movement, or at least part of it, has subsequently made its peace and participated in the recent Constituent Assembly. At the time of writing the chief menace to its "reinserted" members comes from their un-reinserted former companions in arms.)

The difficulty facing the guerrilla is how to trade one sort of political capital for another – when to do so, how to judge the market, what sort of goods to go for.

The works to which I have referred are accounts, in the terms of this symposium, of the formation of "symbolic capital". This capital is acquired through suffering original persecution, through endurance, by *hazañas*, or deeds of daring, through the falling into error and the emergence from it, through the deaths of exemplary combatants, the years and years of survival.

One imagines that survival takes up a large proportion of physical and mental effort, and that its achievement, and slight improvements in material conditions and security, are the source of a continued current of self-satisfaction, an indication that one is somehow on the right lines. The longer one has managed to go on, the longer one is prepared to go on – at least, in some of these cases. Some old guerrillas, like old soldiers, simply fade away, but some, like Moses, persist, resigned that they themselves may never see the Promised Land.[69]

One can detect different qualities in this symbolic capital from one movement to another. The M-19, with its emphasis on daring, imagination, improvisation, *élan*, gesture (an emphasis that had brought its career as an armed movement to the verge of total defeat), found it easier than most of the others to choose its moment, make peace, be filmed letting off its remaining ammunition and throwing its arms into a furnace, and then to launch itself as a new political movement, with substantial initial success at the polls. The first leader in this evolution was assassinated, but the second has managed to establish himself as a national political figure, and members of the movement have "captured some space", and do occupy some places in the several levels of the political system.

In order for this "transformation of symbolic capital" to occur, the government in the last stages of the process had to sustain the vestiges of the movement and preserve it from at least the most obvious appearances of defeat. It did so with the rivals of the M-19 in mind, because it was determined to show in the case of at least one armed movement that making peace was possible. The lengths to which it was prepared to go seem extraordinarily generous to European eyes. In some ways more has been offered than in the recent settlement in El Salvador. The leader of the M-19 movement was made Minister of Health. After the initial euphoria, to many this looked like cynicism on the government's part and opportunism on the movement's, and this weakened the force of the desired example and even eroded the "capital" the movement received in the exchange.[70]

VIII   REAL RATHER THAN SYMBOLIC CAPITAL

The real and symbolic capital acquired differs, as has been noted, from movement to movement, and considered in this light each must contemplate a different exchange in considering whether to abandon the armed struggle. The FARC, the "senior guerrilla", would require in the process much more historical recognition – the Communists have some claim to be the third traditional party in the country, their historical consciousness is much more elaborate, their discipline is firmer, their real capital – zones of control, resources, arms, organization – is larger. (It would be out of place here to explore in detail the business side of their operations, which has become the more notorious through involvement with drugs but which has always extended into many fields, many of which they are reluctant to abandon.) The ELN has its own history, not so long but distinct, its own zones of influence – there is conflict where they overlap with the FARC, despite the existence of the *Coordinadora Guerrillera Simón Bolívar* – and its own more intransigent devotion to armed struggle, its own way of life.

The reader will note that these comments have so far hardly touched on many of these aspects. To many of those involved the intermittent presence of guerrillas, even their own sometimes transitory involvement, may seem far more "normal" and undramatic than it does to even the most guerrilla-weary academic observer. People are not perhaps "in" or "out" of these movements in the way one at first imagines. Recruitment to some of them is now quite highly organized, through youthful "support militia". In new zones recruits are even to start with pay. Service appears sometimes to be for a certain length of time: the guerrilla is in its rank and file comparatively youthful, and, as emphasized before, there must be many ex-guerrillas in the country. It is said that some movements issue to their departing former members the *libreta militar*, the national army certificate that testifies that the bearer has done his military service. One doubts that these guerrilla reservists are all attentively awaiting recall. In many areas of the country, the equivalent of the "no man's land system" operates, so that actual conflict is limited and normal life goes on. Divisions on the ground, in the functioning of guerrilla and government authority, are blurred. In parts of the eastern *piedemonte* the FARC's and the ELN's political practices could be defined as "armed clientelism" – they operate by exercising tutelage over the traditional party politicians, the state apparatus and the state resources, which, when they also include oil royalties, are a major source of guerrilla funds. They have recently been urging their puppet politicians from the traditional parties not to announce any change of allegiance. Heavy political camouflage is preferred.

Nor have we said much about government response. This is remarkably understudied. The literature is usually content with perfunctory denunciations of oligarchy, landowners, repression, militarism and imperialism. The historiography of the early phases, the sectarian times of the "classic violence", is predominantly Liberal or Communist. The oral histories largely ignore Conservatives, local officials, local politicians, soldiers, clerics, police, landowners and oligarchs. Few of these have written memoirs. Government policies of some importance, such as the early amnesties of the 1950s and the military operations of the 1950s and 1960s against the groups that were to become the FARC, have been studied hardly at all, and then one-sidedly, only from the guerrilla side. They naturally appear inadequate, heavy-handed, ill-judged, ineffectual.

No doubt government operations were often as violent or as ineffectual as they have been pictured, but they still need analysing and explaining. For example, it is not, despite the protestations of those who write guerrilla history, altogether clear why the government of General Rojas Pinilla in the mid-1950s launched a large-scale military operation against the Villarica region of Cundinamarca–Tolima, complete with aerial bombardments and tanks. A tank looks strange and out-of-place in a mountainous coffee-growing region. Who gave the orders, and why? What did those who gave the orders have in mind? The area did not contain many properties of influential oligarchs. The one influential oligarch with whom I have spoken who owned coffee property in a region of Communist influence told me that his family was entirely opposed to army intervention and considered their interests best served by a local compromise. Some evidence suggests an agreement between the army and the Liberal guerrilla, now fallen out with the Communists, an alliance that helps to explain the obstinate persistence of the Communist guerrillas. The Liberals had too many intimate local enemies, and if they were going to make a pact with the army there could then be no question of the Communists being allowed to accept an amnesty as well. Communists would then have no *garantías*, guarantees, to use the nineteenth-century word.

My impression is that this military response more obeyed an institutional *macartismo*, McCarthyism, in the armed forces, reinforced by participation in the Korean War. This was also the case in the attacks on

Marquetalia and the other "independent republics" in the 1960s, after the success of the Cuban Revolution, when "the Andes" were going to be the "Sierra Maestra" of South America. The government initiative then did a great deal to produce the enemy it had in mind, which hitherto had been only the embryo of an embryo.

Here one can return to a comparison with post-Risorgimento Italy, to make the response of the weak Colombian state more familiar and understandable. It is also good to remind Europeans and North Americans that this repressive aspect of the Colombian response is not some exotic tropical phenomenon, not entirely a matter of lawlessness on the wild Andean frontier.

There is even a rhetorical similarity between the limitations common in the Italy of the years between the Risorgimento and the First World War and the Colombia of the "classic violence". Italian intellectuals commonly distinguished between the social order and the political order, between the "real Italy" and the "legal Italy", in exactly the same terms as Colombian intellectuals and politicians have done. One suspects that this is more than just chance. Jorge Eliécer Gaitán, whose assassination in 1948 is often, though not altogether accurately, taken as the start of the violence, was a student in Italy in the 1920s, a favoured pupil of Enrico Ferri, one of the leading figures in the Italian sociological–legal school, which much influenced not only his practice as a criminal lawyer but also his political thinking and his political activity.

Italians lamented that they were the most criminal society in Europe, and they produced the most sophisticated school of criminology. Colombia produces many students of violence, with the same rather disappointing harvest of certain or practical conclusions. Kidnapping used to be known as an Italian speciality. President Núñez, in the more innocent Colombia of the 1880s, referred to it as "the Sicilian crime." It remains an Italian crime, but Colombian cases are now much more numerous.

These parallels may seem merely picturesque, decorative. Nevertheless, a reading of Italian history of this period suggests many themes that invite profounder comparison, which seem to me to be of likely interest to many more countries than Italy and Colombia, and which no work on political violence can ignore without itself running the risk of seeming merely decorative. Some of these themes are unmanageable within the space of this essay, perhaps unmanageable at any length, but I hope it will be useful at least to note them down. My order follows roughly their appearance in John Davis's study.

He explores the first half century of the attempt to establish in Italy a constitutional monarchy based on the rule of law. There are all sorts of gaps between desire and reality, and there is a great deal of political violence.

The government is weak. In many parts of the country its legitimacy is uncertain. It does not rest on a traditional and accepted social order. Many notables are alienated from it at the start, dislike its intentions and obstruct its officials. The influence of many of these notables is at the same time being eroded by rapid and unprecedented economic change. The impression is that even if such figures had been prepared to act as pillars of the new state they would have been weak pillars. There are manifold material and political weaknesses in the state institutions. The judiciary is miserably paid and overloaded. The majority of cases fail to reach a judgement, and judges are mostly venal, subject to pressure and threat, resentful – "fifteen years' service before you can afford a restaurant meal and a few shirts". The legal profession was overcrowded: it was frequently observed that Italy boasted the largest number of law graduates and of illiterates in Europe. There was much friction between the judges and the police, endless confusion: "the dividing line between legality and illegality was nowhere in Europe more uncertain than in Liberal Italy". Davis concludes:

> The evidence would seem to suggest that the criminal law and its procedures proved ill-suited and unreliable as an instrument of authoritarian government [or even, one might add, of authority. MDD]. The record of attempts to obtain convictions through the criminal courts was very poor, while the courts also provided opportunities for challenging the use of arbitrary measures. As a result, the authorities were obliged to pursue their objectives by circumventing the law.[71]

The state even when it takes arbitrary measures is ineffective – it ends by exposing its own weaknesses. This culminates in the crises of the 1890s, which include that military occupation of Milan already mentioned – 80 killed, 450 wounded. The repression under Crispi, inspired by the anarchist menace, threatened to end in the repression of all forms of opposition, and this brought a wide reaction against it, and it had to be abandoned.

The apparatus at hand, besides the judiciary, is unequal to the task anyway. The police are few: "it is a well-known fact throughout the whole world that the lower ranks of the police are drawn inevitably from amongst the most immoral, the most corrupt and the most venal sections of the population."[72] They do not enjoy the confidence of any class in the society. Italian police history at this time is filled with the sort of incident familiar to the student of Colombia: in one mounted gendarmerie, "the majority of the recruits deserted to the brigands with their horses and muskets, while the remainder astonished the General by their refusal to pursue even known brigand leaders, and by their preference for negotiations, which inevitably ended in cash payments and amnesties."[73] The army is frequently involved in policing operations, and its principal task is internal security. It is recruited and garrisoned according to the needs of internal order. It did not particularly like these police functions, and performed them in a consistently heavy-handed fashion, but it did not particularly favour the most obvious alternative, which was an increased budget for the police. Various forms of vigilantism, paramilitarism and private order-enforcement are visible; in the former Papal States one exponent of popular vigilantism and of the arming of peasants summed up his activities with the phrase "Without the people you can't make revolutions", a simple notion that in Colombia would certainly have been endorsed by the backers of the paramilitaries of the Middle Magdalena Valley.[74]

The results: endless improvisation and arbitrariness; an extraordinarily high level of impunity: Davis gives some Palermo figures for 1887: 104 armed robberies, 5 arrests; 99 cattle thefts, 1 arrest; 232 murders, 1 arrest. Italy recorded more than 4,000 homicides a year, sixteen times the British rate, 40 per cent undetected – the Palermo detection rate was obviously much lower. She had a prison population twenty times that of Britain. Davis also notes a tendency towards the "criminalization of opposition", a necessary concomitant of the exercise of arbitrary power to which this weak liberal state was often reduced.[75]

These features are not strange to an observer of Colombia. They will raise in the minds of the readers of this collection inevitable questions.

How many of these phenomena can properly be accounted to fall within the notion of political violence, or the sub-category of revolutionary violence? How is the transition managed from the Italy of Davis, a more inviting parallel for a student of Colombia and perhaps Peru, to the Italy of Moss, more the locus of attention of the students of "modern" minority, "left-wing" violence, with its more surreal, less everyday transition from the will to the deed. It will all have seemed a long distance away from the tradition-bound, ritual field-game, a confrontation of forces severely limited by shared values, shared notions of how far either side can go, that has been taking place around Tokyo airport, and which a nineteenth-century Italian or a twentieth-century Colombian would hardly look upon as violence at all.[76]

I have already argued more than once that it does not seem feasible to exclude "messy" phenomena from any discussion of political violence, if it is not to exclude far too much. Perhaps most of the political violence in the world takes place in contexts like these Italian and Colombian ones, even most of the political violence that aspires to the "clarity" of the Red Brigades or to the affirmation of traditional righteousness of those Japanese farmers.

IX   CONCLUSION

Revolutionaries cannot choose their context. I am not convinced that there is such a vast difference between the minds of members of the Red Brigades and those of South American or Central-American revolutionaries. The Argentine case is here particularly pertinent as a link, for in many ways Argentina is much more like Italy than it is like Colombia. The *montoneros* and the ERP can be compared to the Red Brigades – loosely, of course, but they do emerge in an Italianate, highly urbanized, educated society. They also considered themselves Latin American. Some of them admired the Colombian Camilo Torres. Geographical location was part of what multiplied their sense of revolutionary possibility beyond the Italian scale, involving far greater numbers in the revolutionary cause than was possible – or conceivable – in Italy, though the "objective" possibilities of success were perhaps just as scant in one republic as in the other.

Certainly the case which follows, that of Peru, seems to match more closely David Apter's theoretical insights than does Colombia. This Colombian lack of fit can be made explicit in these conclusions, through comment on his Chinese reflections, contained in summary form in his article "Yan'an and the Narrative Reconstruction of Reality."[77] All quotations from this article.

"People make stories out of events". In Colombia there are many competing stories, as doubtless there were in the embryonic stages of the Chinese Revolution. No dominant story or story-teller emerges in Colombia, and in the literature of the *Violencia* the stories are now ends in themselves, almost studied like folklore, and folklore and its study is on the whole conservative, unrevolutionary.

No violent group acquires sufficient "symbolic capital" to "overcome". Only enough to demand a share, not enough even to claim to overthrow society and system.

There is little evidence for the successful conquest of individualism. That was less than perfect even in Yan'an. The early years of Colombian violence were individualistic and localist to a degree that recalls, perhaps exceeds, the fighting phase of the Mexican Revolution, and this individualism and localism persists, and is not effectively hidden by organizational façades such as the *Co-ordinadora Guerrillera Simón Bolívar.*

Mao was able to place himself in Chinese history in ways for which no Colombian equivalent is available, and which no Colombian political imagination has been able to fabricate. There is no grand imperial past, there are no histories or myths of peasants becoming emperors, no grand strategists. The historical sequences in Colombian narratives are predominantly local – the narratives are little interested in what is happening to the nation, even perfunctory where one would expect some Marxist insistence. There is little about imperialism, for example. This reflects Colombia's relative autonomy, even though what little there is on this theme must deny that autonomy.

Similarly, the "inversionary" is less evident than a less ambitious antagonism. The rhetoric of *oligarcas* and *pueblo*, oligarchs and people, brought though it was to the highest pitch of intensity by Gaitán, may seem at first sight inversionary enough, but it does not carry the true conviction that the world must be turned upside-down. *Exclusion must end:* that is not, in its essence, an "inversionary" notion. Turned upside-down, would poor, politicized, mestizo Colombia have looked so very different? Perhaps not.

Violence offers ample opportunity for storytelling. It generates despair and yearning. People come to believe that only drastic solutions will work, that any authority is better than none, and that the available ensemble of would-be leaders are wanting. ... Such conditions are on the whole propitious for totalizing cosmocrats, those who successfully create their own political cosmos, whether political, religious or both, and who in the context of high uncertainty retrieve myths of a golden past and project the logic of a millennial future.

Not all violence. Prolonged violence has not convinced Colombians that only drastic solutions will work, or that any authority is better than none. The available ensemble of would-be leaders, wanting though the leaders may be, changes little. There is no golden past, no millenial future. Certainly one might have expected Colombian conditions to be propitious for millenarianism. Though some such movements have sprung up, and in areas particularly affected by violence – the *encostelados* of Tolima are an example – they have not flourished, if that is the right word.

What has already been said about the difficulty of finding Colombian parallels to the figure of Guzmán can also be applied to Mao in his

Yan'an phase. Those techniques of constructing authority, the importance of culture and learning and writing, the great presence and the simple appearance, the condescension, the discipline imposed and self-imposed: they can be translated, it appears into Peruvian, but not into Colombian. Colombia lacks traditions of authority, or at least of authority with range.

This is an awkward, sceptical and inconclusive chapter. It has insisted on a strong definition of violence, and on raising and confronting an intractable question, the same that comes at the end of Stephen Wilson's exhaustive *Feuding, Conflict and Banditry in Nineteenth-century Corsica*: "Germane here is the uneven incidence of feud and conflict across societies. Why do people in some societies normally settle or try to settle their differences by using force, while in others violence is either absent or deliberately avoided?" [78] It has certainly not answered that question, but the reader may at the end of it agree that we know much less about political violence than we think we do.

NOTES

1. A convenient introductory collection of essays is C. Bergquist, R. Peñaranda and G. Sánchez (eds), *Violence in Colombia. The Contemporary Crisis in Historical Perspective* (Wilmington, 1992). However, like so much else written on Colombia, it is rare that the contributors to this work introduce any comparative perspective, and for all its interest it cannot be said to provide a satisfactory answer to the question why Colombia is such a violent country, within the Latin-American context.

    The statistical problems posed by Colombian violence from the 1940s on are examined in P. Oquist, *Violence, Conflict and Politics in Colombia* (New York, 1980). There must remain some doubt that estimates from multiple interviews with a sample of families affected – the method employed to reach a total – can arrive at anything more than a crude estimate, but the author thereby supports the estimate of 200,000 dead for the 1940s and 1950s, now sanctified by constant repetition.

    For the statistical pitfalls that dog the historical examination of European homicide, see H. Zehr, *Crime and the Development of Modern Society* (London, 1976).

2. F. M. Chapman, "The Distribution of Bird-life in Colombia", *Bulletin of the American Museum of Natural History*, vol. XXXVI (New York, 1917) p. 9.

3. A personal experience: in a historical congress in 1984 held in the Universidad Nacional, Bogotá, I suggested that the agrarian conflicts of the 1920s and 1930s in the central coffee-growing regions of the country, Cundinamarca and Tolima, were "not particularly violent". This opinion excited protests, and I was asked how many deaths I regarded as "particu-

larly violent". More people are now killed in a week-end in Medellín than died in all those confrontations. What struck me was the immediate rejection by the audience of my view: perhaps part of the protest was against a foreigner taking local suffering lightly, but the audience *wanted* a violent past. The excavation of past conflict, preferably violent, has been the dominant mode in Andean history locally and abroad to such a degree that it is widely accepted as natural even by historians who would regard such dominance with suspicion if they found it prevailing elsewhere.

4. The country's history and geography present a variety of frontiers. The best known colonizing region, Antioquia, whose south-eastern frontier was the subject of James Parsons's classic monograph *Antioqueño Colonization in Western Colombia* (Berkeley, 1949), also colonized Urabá and the mining regions to the north-east of the Department. Parsons's picture of a prosperous and relatively democratic frontier society in the south-east was much challenged by radical historians in the 1960s and 1970s; though dented, it has by no means been destroyed. Antioqueños are less proud of the other frontiers, which have a more violent history. Both the latter regions remain violent today.

Two useful introductions to Colombian frontiers are C. LeGrand, *Frontier Expansion and Peasant Protest in Colombia, 1850–1936* (Albuquerque, 1986), and J. J. González Arias *et al.*, "Un país en construcción", *Controversia*, no. 151–2 (Bogotá: CINEP, 1989).

5. G. Arboleda, *Las revoluciones locales en Colombia* (Popayán, 1907) p. 60.

All these wars from 1810 onwards generated a sizeable literature, and this literature contains certain suggestions. The Wars of Independence were not particularly intense in New Granada, what is now Colombia. Again, I must be impressionistic. There was bitter fighting in some parts, particularly in the south, and the Spanish reconquest was not gentle, but the struggle in New Granada was less devastating and violent than in Venezuela. For Venezuela see, for example, G. Carrera Damas, *Boves. Aspectos socioeconómicos de la guerra de Independencia* (Caracas, 1968). The duration and the destructiveness of the republican civil wars also varied, as did their incidence in different parts of the republic.

I make these qualifications here because the reader is too often invited by a simple recital of the list to accept that here is a sustained tradition of violence, and that little else is needed to explain the persistent violence of the last decades. Yet metropolitan Spain suffered far greater violence. As Bolívar is said to have remarked: "Where there are Spaniards there will be no lack of executioners." There is nothing in the Colombian civil war tradition to match the scale of massacre of the Spanish resistance against the French or of the later Carlist Wars. Nor was there anything in Spanish colonial repression in these parts, either in the colonial era or even in the Wars of Independence, to match the thoroughgoing atrocities perpetrated by the British in Ireland. (Compare the relatively gentle methods used to suppress the Comunero Rebellion in New Granada, and the lack of serious fighting involved, with the means employed by the British to put down the Irish Rebellion of 1798, which included wholesale hangings with no semblance of trial and the use of tar caps to turn peasants into human torches.) National and racial stereotypes are still sufficiently prevalent, in my experience, for these comparisons to come as a surprise to the reader fed on notions of South American savagery.

For the Comunero Rebellion see J. L. Phelan, *The People and the King* (Madison, 1978); for the Irish Rebellion of 1798, T. Pakenham, *The Year of Liberty* (London, 1969), and R. Kee, *The Green Flag*, 3 vols (London, 1989) vol. I, *The Most Distressful Country*. It is remarkable how little the last two narratives *explain* the intense level of violence in the events they so vividly recount.

6. The legal framework of nineteenth-century civil wars has recently attracted interest, and has been the subject of two works: A. Valencia Villa, *La humanización de la guerra. Derecho internacional humanitario y conflicto armado en Colombia* (Bogotá, 1991), and I. Orozco Abad, *Combatientes, rebeldes y terroristas. Guerra y derecho en Colombia* (Bogotá, 1992). Both authors in the interests of current peace-making seek to salvage certain aspects of the country's nineteenth-century tradition, the rules of the game that prevailed when even eminent figures in the "traditional parties" "combined all forms of struggle", to use the current formula of the Colombian Communist Party. The authors have unearthed a strong tradition of the internal application of the *Derecho de Gentes*, and of specifically defined and specifically treated political crime.

7. Arboleda notes the greater frequency of revolts of Liberals against Liberals in his *Las revoluciones locales*, p. 60: Liberals *v.* Conservatives, 2; Conservatives *v.* Liberals, 14; Liberals *v.* Liberals, 34. His conclusion is also interesting: ". . . only 15 have succeeded and in the rest, although the rebels laid down their arms the moral victory was theirs, for the peace treaties were followed by the resignation or deposition of the sectional Executive Power".

8. It must be remembered that these years of Conservative rule were neither uniform nor unchallenged – there was always intense factionalism among Conservatives, and the period contains the two civil wars following Liberal risings in 1895 and 1899–1902.

The years immediately after 1930 are now the subject of scholarly attention, and it is becoming increasingly clear that political violence was indeed then intense in certain parts of the country, and that after 1945 the Conservatives were consciously set on avenging what they had suffered at Liberal hands at that time. In the fifteen years between 1930 and 1945 political mobilization had certainly made some advances, for example in the numbers voting and listening to the radio, and this time the fighting was to be more widespread and prolonged. Given what is noted elsewhere in this essay about the possible influence of foreign wars on internal conflict, it is worth noting that a short conflict with Peru in 1932, the "Leticia Affair", is held to have arrested or at least diminished sectarian conflict at that time.

See J. Guerrero, *Los años del olvido. Boyacá y los orígines de la Violencia* (Bogotá, 1991); M. V. Uribe Alarcón, *Limpiar la Tierra. Guerra y poder entre esmeralderos* (Bogotá, 1992). There is a remarkable contemporary diary of some Santander violence contained in B. N. Muñoz, *Crónicas de Guaca. La ruina de un pueblo* (Cúcuta, 1937); see also M. Serrano Blanco, *Las viñas del odio* (Bucaramanga, 1949), for an account of the same region by another acute Conservative participant observer, and S.

Reflections on Political Violence: Colombia   393

Tello Mejía, *Sangre y sotanas. García Rovira al desnudo* (Armenia, 1934), for a Liberal view.

9. Guerrero, *Los años del olvido*, p. 29. Of the total of homicides it is probable that the *political* account for less than a tenth. There are no official estimates for political deaths, so one in ten is only an informed guess. It would include deaths in confrontations between the armed forces and guerrillas, and deaths of political activists.

10. "A tradition of violence is of course difficult to quantify. However, the highest homicide rate in France (20.98 persons tried per 100,000) occurred, as might be expected, in Corsica, another area with a reputation for violence. And a very high correlation obtained between homicide rates at the beginning and at the end of the period; 66 per cent of the variance in homicide rates in 1900–4 can be explained simply on the basis of rates during the 1830s. Traditions of violence, then, were better predictors of homicide rates than any other variable measured . . ." (Zehr, op. cit, pp. 117–18).

11. The recent collection of essays edited by C. Aguirre and C. Walker, *Bandoleros, abigeos y montoneros. Criminalidad y violencia en el Peru, siglos XVIII–XX* (Lima, 1990), does not convince this reader that Peru was a particularly violent place. (See note 44 below.)

12. On the intricacies of Guatemalan violence see the outstanding collection of essays in R. M. Carmack (ed.), *Harvest of Violence. The Maya Indians and the Guatemalan Crisis* (Norman and London, 1988).

13. It is interesting all the same to recall the Argentine experience of government-directed terror under Rosas, which had few parallels elsewhere in Latin America, a point further explored in note 44 below) and to note that the organization behind the coup attempt of Colonel Chávez in Venezuela has claimed to act in the name of three guiding heroes: the inevitable Bolívar, Bolívar's eccentric tutor Simón Rodríguez and the radical caudillo of the mid-century Federal War, Ezequiel Zamora – all nineteenth-century figures.

14. Number of dead is perhaps not such a good indicator, quite apart from the difficulty of establishing reliable figures. Killing people can be an expensive matter. It was not easy in the nineteenth century for Colombians to kill each other in large numbers. The country was poor, the armament employed was primitive, much of the population lived dispersed, and it was always hard to concentrate large numbers for a battle. As was common elsewhere, most civil war deaths were from disease. See the remarkably complete and lucid analysis of civil war in M. Ospina Rodríguez, *Exposición que el secretario de Estado en el despacho del Interior y Relaciones Esteriores del Gobierno de la Nueva Granada, dirije al Congreso Constitucional el año de 1842* (Bogotá, 1842), reprinted in G. Wise de Gouzy (ed.), *Antología del pensamiento de Mariano Ospina Rodríguez*, 2 vols (Bogotá, 1990) vol. I, pp. 471 *et seq.* One can imagine other indicators of conflictiveness besides the numbers of dead, though one can imagine too the enormous difficulties one would have in constructing indices from them.

Nevertheless, there is something to be said for calling attention to such a basic indicator as numbers of victims in a field of study where reputation and reality so often diverge – nebulous description attracts nebulous explanation.

One statistic of recent Colombian violence indicates an extraordinarily rapid increase over the past decade in deaths by firearm. There is much evidence that large numbers of sophisticated arms have entered the country in the wake of the drug traffic, though guerrillas and emerald miners and merchants have also made their contribution to the flow. The last "emerald war" is said to have led to 3,500 deaths, and emerald miners have spent heavily on arms. See M. V. Uribe Alarcón, op. cit., pp. 99 et seq.

15. David Moss, *The Politics of Left-wing Violences in Italy, 1969–1985* (London, 1989).

16. John Davis, *Conflict and Control in Nineteenth-Century Italy* (London, 1988).

17. David Moss, "Analysing Italian Political Violence as a Sequence of Communicative Acts: The Red Brigades 1970–1982", *Social Analysis*, no. 13 (May 1983). See also his *The Politics of Left-wing Violence in Italy*, pp. 11–12.

There is also an important South American connection here. Garibaldi first won fame in the wars of the River Plate, and his military and political techniques were first worked out in that field of action. His career had a profound influence in Latin America, as I have sketched in a brief article "Garibaldi in South America" in *History Today* (December 1982). He is part of the Latin American revolutionary tradition, as well as of the Italian, and his influence can be seen in figures such as Bartolomé Mitre, Benito Juárez, and Eloy Alfaro (see my introduction to E. Alfaro, *Narraciones históricas*, 2nd edn (Quito, 1992), and last and by no means least in the small-boat expeditionary Fidel Castro, whose Granma venture emulates the descent on Sicily of Garibaldi's Thousand, though that sacred number was in Castro's case reduced to the even more sacred number of a surviving twelve. One of Garibaldi's sons fought in the early stages of the Mexican Revolution.

18. Some of these will be further examined below.

19. See R. Barbosa Estepa, *Guadalupe y sus centauros. Memorias de la insurrección Leanera* (Bogotá, 1992) p. 117. This does not imply anything particularly sinister or out of the ordinary about his career.

The list of grander figures from the last century and the beginning of this century who combined all forms of struggle would of course be much longer and more impressive, and it should be remembered that some of those who were prominent in the last civil war were still influential figures in the 1920s and 1930s. The scarcity of leaders who could claim innocence on this score is lamented in M. Ospina Rodríguez's *Esposición* of 1842, p. 488, under the heading "La ineficacia de la sanción moral, respecto de los delitos de rebelión": ". . . the number of those who in all circumstances have defended the cause of the law is small; the force of public opinion against that crime has lost its vigour, and its action is ineffective." Ospina had himself been involved in the conspiracy to assassinate Bolívar in September 1828.

20. J. Arenas, "Curso de Estrategia", mimeo (La Uribe, n.d., *c.* 1990).

21. Let me emphasize that I do not reject such lines of analysis as having nothing to contribute; I reject their primacy and their adequacy. One runs the risk then of being thought a defender of the *status quo*. This seems to me to be in itself revealing. My personal conviction is that on balance violence

in Colombia has favoured the *status quo*, that its effect has been more reactionary than progressive, but to argue that position in detail is beyond the scope of this essay. There is no more a clear correlation between violence and poverty in Colombia than there is in Italy, cf. remarks of David Moss, "Italian Political Violence 1969–1988: The Making and Unmaking of Meanings", draft mimeo (1992), p. 23. This is also too large a subject to explore here in any detail, but it was remarked during the "classic violence" that certain rich coffee-growing zones were much affected; recently guerrilla activity has been notorious in Arauca (petroleum) and Urabá (bananas).

22.   This has certainly been a contributing factor in Latin American revolutionary violence. The intellectual climate of Europe, and even of some institutions in the United States, tended to favour some sort of revolution in Latin America for many years after the Cuban revolution, a "solidarity" that was given a late second wind by the Sandinista revolution in Nicaragua. This solidarity was undoubtedly important to many Latin American intellectuals, who looked with pathetic deference on such figures as Jean Paul Sartre, despite their profound ignorance of the region. Creole cultures defer to the metropolis. Many European writers and journalists who would have regarded the Red Brigades as way beyond the pale of political rationality hesitated to form the same judgement of the Uruguayan Tupamaros or the Argentine Montoneros, and regarded Colombian guerrillas as quite natural. Guerrillas do read the papers. They also exploit journalists – the Colombian *Ejército de Liberación Nacional*, the ELN, remembering Herbert Matthews of *The New York Times* and Fidel Castro, took great pains to secure early coverage from a Mexican journalist, and even held up a train for him. See R. Arenas, *La guerrilla por dentro* (Bogotá, 1971), for details. (The archetypes of the guerrilla-visiting journalist in this part of the world are John Reed, who "rode with Villa", and Carleton Beals, who discovered Augusto Sandino; they are the Edgar Snows of Latin America.) A more recent event that exposed the massive bias of foreign reporters was the Nicaraguan election that the Sandinistas lost.

23.   See for example the highly critical essay by Miguel Samper, *La miseria en Bogotá* (Bogotá, 1867), which opens with the following observation: "The streets and plazas are filled with beggars, who exhibit not only their wretchedness, but an insolence that should provide much food for thought, because alms are *demanded*, and if they are not given, then he who refuses is exposed to insults nobody thinks to check. . . ." Poor and "remote" societies are not necessarily "feudal" or "undemocratic"; "democratic" was indeed sometimes a term of criticism for these "disordered tropical republics". A mid-nineteenth century Chilean criticism that caused much resentment in Colombia, rebutted in M. Ancízar's pamphlet *Anarquismo y Rojismo en la Nueva Granada* (Santiago, 1853), contrasted Colombia's excessively progressive politics in their setting of poverty with the right-thinking conservatism, social order and wealth of Chile. Less nonsense about democracy there.

24.   Gosselman's observations are particularly important because they too are comparative: besides being an unusually conscientious and sober writer, his travels took him all over South America. See his *Viaje por Colombia, 1825 y 1826* (Bogotá, 1981), together with his *Informes sobre los Estados*

Sudamericanos en los años de 1837–38 (Stockholm, 1968). For later confirmation of his views see the passages on politics, particularly provincial politics, in I. F. Holton, *New Granada. Twenty Months in the Andes* (New York, 1857); the reports of the Chilean Minister in Bogotá in the early 1880s, J. A. Soffia in R. Donoso (ed.), "J. A. Soffia en Bogotá", *Thesaurus*, vol. XXXI, no. 1 (Bogotá, 1976); R. Gutiérrez, *Monografías*, 2 vols (Bogotá, 1920–21) vol. I, pp. 90–2 (late 1880s); my "La presencia de la política nacional en la vida provinciana, pueblerina y rural de Colombia en el primer siglo de la república" and "Algunas notas sobre la historia del caciquismo en Colombia", both in *Del poder y la gramática. Ensayos sobre historia, política y literatura colombianas* (Bogotá, 1993).

25. Maurice Agulhon, *La République au Village* (Paris, 1968).

26. The movement has of course not gone unnoticed in Colombia, and like all well-publicized *líneas* it has its Colombian imitators, at present visible on several university campuses. But they have yet to produce a Guzmán.

27. Paul Arthur's phrase "a tranquility of communal deterrence" suits Colombian circumstances between hostilities.

28. An excellent study of Táchira is A. G. Muñoz, *El Táchira fronterizo. El aislamiento regional y la integración nacional en el caso de los Andes (1881–1889)* (Caracas, 1985).

29. The best source for Gómez's methods of government are the hundred or so numbers of the *Boletín del archivo histórico de Miraflores*, in which recent Venezuelan governments have generously exposed the presidential activities of their predecessors since the late nineteenth century. Gómez and his correspondents had a low opinion of the Colombian government's ability to control anything; it was a "lyrical" government on which little reliance could be placed.

30. See the title essay in my *Del poder y la gramática*, (Bogotá, 1993), for an exploration of the link between Conservatism, folklore and violence.

31. Forced "conversion" was a feature of the early "classic" violence: Liberals were forced on pain of death to abjure their party allegiance and to carry certificates that testified that they had done so. This was naturally felt to be the depths of humiliation. Compare the conversions of protestants to catholicism and the issue of protection documents in the Irish rebellion of 1798, as described in Packenham, op. cit., p. 192: "In desperation many of the threatened Protestants begged to be allowed to be received into the Catholic Church. The rebels actively encouraged conversions: 'If you will go home and turn Christians,' they would say, 'you will be safe enough.' Catholic family retainers implored their Protestant masters and mistresses to ask the parish priest to christen them as it would be 'the saving of them all'." For Balkan examples of similar practices, particularly in Macedonia, see G. Kennan, intro., *The Other Balkan Wars. A 1913 Carnegie Endowment Inquiry in Retrospect with a New Introduction and Reflections on the Present Conflict* (Washington, 1993), particularly pp. 77–8: "The Holy Synod argued that since force had been used to convert the pomaks to Islam, force might fairly be used to reverse the process. The argument is one proof the more that races whose minds have been molded for centuries by the law of reprisal and the practice of vengeance, tend to a common level of degredation." And p. 108: "A *comitadji*, early in the first war, pointed a rifle

at his breast, and said: 'Become a Bulgarian, or I'll kill you.' He forthwith became a Bulgarian for several months and conformed to the exarchist church." For Colombia, A. Molano, *Los años de tropel*, pp. 115 *et seq.*

32.   A gazetteer of Colombian civil wars is E. Riascos Grueso, *Geografía guerrera colombiana* (California, 1950). The political map of the country as revealed and consolidated in twentieth-century elections is exposed in P. Pinzón de Lewin, *Pueblos, regiones y partidos* (Bogotá, 1988).

33.   For the nineteenth-century fiscal background to governmental feebleness see my "Los problemas fiscales de Colombia en el siglo XIX" in *Del poder y la gramática*. An English version of that study appeared in *Journal of Latin American Studies*, vol. 14, pt 2 (November 1982).

Feebler than other states in the region? Certainly feebler than most, feebler far than Argentina, Chile, Uruguay, Venezuela, Peru (at times), and faced with far severer problems of order than most. For an impression of comparative government incomes, taxation per capita, expenditure per capita etc, see the doubtless not entirely reliable but stimulating compilation of comparative statistics by F. C. Aguilar, *Colombia en presencia de las repúblicas hispano-americanas* (Bogotá, 1884). A feebler state, and a more politicized population: Aguilar, who was a priest, noted with dismay the large number of newspapers of doubtful political and moral character.

The self-reliant may prefer a weak state, and as John Stuart Mill noted in his *Political Economy*, lack of government may do less harm to an economy than perverse government policies. This remains true of recent years: in Colombia land values do not necessarily fall in violent regions, and the country's growth rate has been the steadiest in Latin America.

34.   See Donoso, op. cit.

35.   For examples and comments, for the nineteenth century see the "Discurso preliminar" in A. J. de Irisarri, *Historia crítica del asesinato cometido en la persona del Gran Mariscal de Ayacucho* (Bogotá, 1855), the pamphlets of Julio Arboleda against the Liberal governments of the 1850s, collected by G. Andrade González in *Prosa de Julio Arboleda, Jurídica, Política, Heterodoxa y Literaria* (Bogotá, 1984), and the comment of the American traveller Isaac Holton: "I saw the camera of Mariquita in session. It has a strong Conservative majority, while the Governor is of course a Liberal. What I saw here teaches me not to translate the word *Conservador* by Conservative: there are no Conservatives in New Granada except fanatic Papists. All the rest deserve the name of Destructives, and might be classed as Red Republicans and Redder Republicans; and the Redder men may belong to either party, but, except the *Gólgotas*, the reddest I know are the Conservatives of the Province of Mariquita" (*New Granada. Twenty Months in the Andes* (New York, 1857), p. 334). (The *Gólgotas* were the youthful upper-class Bogotá Liberals of that date.)

Earlier in this century it was a common Conservative argument that the party's superior right to govern derived from its more representative and authentic character: Conservatives were poor but essentially Colombian; Liberals tended to be rich and cosmopolitan.

36.   M-19 signifies *Movimiento 19 de abril*, the 19 april in question being that of 1970, when the populist movement ANAPO, whose figurehead was General Gustavo Rojas Pinilla, President 1953–7, was deprived of a narrow elec-

toral victory, on a minority vote against a divided "official" coalition, by the government's recourse to fraud.

37. Perhaps the point is worth emphasizing because European and North American attitudes are so critical of Latin American societies, which have usually presented them, such is their historical destiny, with a palpably failed reflection of themselves. Self-abasement feeds external criticism which feeds self-abasement: some of this feeds violence.

38. For details see E. Franco Isaza, *Las guerrillas del Llano* (Bogotá, 1959); R. Barbosa Estepa, op. cit. Franco Isaza describes how one civil war veteran was persuaded to drill Liberal guerrillas waving a sword.

39. There are a number of bibliographies of Colombian violence (see end references). There is, however, as yet no equivalent commentary to J. Whyte's complete and dispassionate *Interpreting Northern Ireland* (Oxford, 1990), though it is time such a work was attempted for Colombia.

    Any select bibliography of the subject, however short, ought to include the following outstanding contributions to the era of "classic violence", besides some of those already mentioned: G. Sánchez y D. Meertens, *Bandidos, gamonales y campesinos* (Bogotá, 1983), and other collections of essays by G. Sánchez; C. M. Ortíz, *Estado y subversión en Colombia. La violencia en el Quindío, años cincuenta* (Bogotá, 1985); D. Pécaut, *Orden y violencia, Colombia,1930–1954*, 2 vols (Bogotá, 1987); A. Molano, *Los años de tropel* (Bogotá, 1985). The finest novel of that era remains E. Caballero Calderón's *El Cristo de espaldas* (Buenos Aires, 1952); it is a work that bears comparison with, and calls to mind, the Italian classic of 1946, Carlo Levi's *Christ Stopped at Eboli*.

    The study of massacre and mutilation referred to is M. V. Uribe, "Matar, rematar y contramatar. Las masacres de la violencia en el Tolima, 1948–1964", *Controversia*, nos 159–60 (Bogotá: CINEP, 1990). Much mutilation is truly "inversionary".

40. *Ejército Popular de Liberación*, Maoist/Albanian, and *Ejército de Liberación Nacional*, Castroite.

41. A process familiar enough in parts of Belfast or Derry. Cf. Darby (1968), quoted by Paul Arthur: "The power of intimidation springs from its essentially defensive nature. Local minorities were driven by violence and fear to move to other communities in which they could become part of a majority. They were often willing to encourage the expulsion of ethnic opponents from their new community" (see Paul Arthur's chapter in this volume).

42. See C. E. Jaramillo, *Los guerrilleros del novecientos* (Bogotá, 1990), for the Tolima practices of the War of a Thousand Days.

43. This was Ledru-Rollin's resigned reply to someone who in one of the Paris *journées* of the 1848 Revolution asked him why he was going out into a street filled with marching protestors. It often came to my mind when reading about Prime Ministers O'Neill or Chichester-Clark in the early years of the current Northern Irish troubles.

44. C. M. Ortíz, op. cit. Naturally, in a rural society political conflicts have results that often express themselves in changes in land ownership. But it is more hazardous than many commentators think to prove that to bring about those changes was the motive of conflict. Expelling people of another political colour from a *vereda* is not necessarily a conflict about land, even

though land may change hands as a result. One gets the impression from Ortíz's work that land-grabs were almost an afterthought in the Quindio of the late 1940s and 1950s. A parallel from Belfast will make the point clearer: houses changed occupants as a result of sectarian violence, but nobody argues that housing problems rank high among the causes of that violence.

45. For a first-hand account of the beginnings of the ELN in the Department of Santander, which includes a pertinent discussion of the geographical thinking of the founders, see R. Arenas, *La guerrilla por dentro* (Bogotá, 1971) p. 42. The area chosen for beginning operations had certain physical advantages and "some experience of armed activity, as the inhabitants had collaborated in one way or another with the Liberal guerrillas, years previously". This was, however, a mixed blessing in the national context, as the new guerrilla could be portrayed by the government as merely a continuation of local tradition. This diminished the "gearing" of the "small motor".

It is not hard to list some other obvious differences between Santander and Ayacucho: the impatience of the Colombians, the attractions from the start of the Castroite guerrilla model, the strong presence of a local power structure in the departmental capital of Bucaramanga, plenty of politics, plenty of personalities, a thirst for publicity.

46. D. Moss, "The Kidnapping and Murder of Aldo Moro", *Archives européennes de sociologie*, vol. XXII, no. 2 (1981) p. 271.

47. For Bateman and the M-19 in general see P. Lara, *Siembra vientos, recogerás tempestades* (Bogotá, 1982); for Bateman in particular see P. Ariza *et al.*, *Bateman* (Bogotá, 1992). For David Peña, M. M. Buenaventura, *El Cali que se fue* (Cali, 1957) pp. 62–78; M. Sinistierra, *El 24 de diciembre de 1876 en Cali*, 3rd edn (Cali, 1937); I am grateful to Beatriz Castro for drawing my attention to Peña's use of the *sancocho* comparison.

48. It is interesting to note that lethal or personal attacks on prominent politicians, even prominent regional politicians, have been comparatively rare in Colombia. Their increase in recent years may obey more the growth in the drug traffic, which knows few inhibitions, than a strictly political cause. Generals do not shoot at Generals. Even privates do not shoot much at Generals.

49. Of course no country is without these, and in every country there is a small scholarly industry devoted to keeping such memories green. One Latin American publishing house of fair respectability even used to run a series on violence in Latin America, country by country. Unfortunately the effect was to make everywhere look as if it were cut from the same lump of cheese, in much the same way as tends to happen with the more intensive sort of regional study, where the high degree of magnification reveals seemingly indistinguishable microbes at work.

This is one fault of the interesting collection of essays edited by Carlos Aguirre and Charles Walker, *Bandoleros, abigeos y montoneros. Criminalidad y violencia en el Peru*, siglos XVIII–XX (Lima,1990). Its neo-Hobsbawmian pages refer from time to time to "baths of blood" and "innumerable bloody shocks", but because its authors are too keen to quote the rhetoric of past officials and because they at times fail to control a similar rhetoric of their own – "This book is also a homage to those men and women of Peru who have lost respect for, and fear of the norms and institutions that condemned them to servitude" – the reader at the end has no clear picture of how violent a country Peru has been, or of how continuous Peruvian violence has been, though he or she certainly knows more about the contents of Peruvian criminal archives. References to E. P. Thompson and his theory of moral economy tempt one to comment that certain techniques can make even eighteenth-century Surrey look a violent place; though not yet suburban, it was hardly wild. The Aguirre and Walker book is not concerned with some of the more political episodes of violence in Peru's past, such as the Trujillo massacre of 1932.

One embryonic conclusion that emerges from a reading of these essays is the possibility that the indian communities in their exercise of social control effectively limited some varieties of violence, an hypothesis that would tally with the greater violence of mestizo Colombia. The forms that *political* violence takes may bear relation with those of "ordinary" violence: in Peru, occasional, communal or pseudo-communal (it is well established that Sendero is not an indian movement), apocalyptic; in Colombia more continuous, individual, *veredal.*

My impression remains that Peru has not had such a violent republican past – at least, that a violent republican past as an antecedent for Sendero awaits much more precise exploration and evaluation.

Little has yet been written to compare the different forms violence has taken in these societies, and the different myths resulting. This might be both possible and fruitful, beyond the initial sketches in this essay, for it appears to me that patterns do persist. It may be possible to establish that there is more to the Argentine similarities between the Dirty War and the terror of Rosas than coincidence. There is some apparent similarity in the theory of the two periods, too: Rosas justified his dictatorship with arguments about the weakness of "natural" authority in Argentina in the face of anarchy, and used techniques of government – the wearing of ribbons, of scarlet waistcoats – that were designed to make neutrality impossible. The Argentine armed forces aimed to make neutrality impossible again in the 1970s.

Twentieth-century Peruvian political violence may perhaps centre around the periods of exclusion of APRA, a party with a guru, a mystique, a cell-structure, periods of catacombs and martyrdoms. There are no close parallels in the history of Colombia. The Chilean government has historically from time to time been extremely and competently repressive, a tradition the Chileans prefer to forget – hence the usual portrayal of Pinochet as an aberration in the "most European" of Latin American polities. (That argument of course depends on a distant and sentimental version of what happens in Europe.) Venezuelan history presents long cycles of stable and authoritative, when not authoritarian, government, broken by shorter periods of instability, in which authority first evaporates and is then re-focused. The Irish style of violent action has a number of founding fathers, but one of them must certainly be Michael Collins, whose inventive and dashing techniques have influenced small groups in many other countries besides Ireland, Southern and Northern. See T. Pat Coggan, *Michael Collins* (London, 1990).

These different forms of violence must generate expectations, which must condition events to some degree: what can happen anywhere may be surprising to many, widely deplored by many, seemingly irrational to many, but to some degree perhaps it has to be familiar, to strike some chord in some, perhaps in many. Few political analysts can avoid that musical metaphor, however prosaic they try to be.

50. C. I Degregori, *El surgimiento de Sendero Luminoso* (Lima, 1990); G. Gorriti Ellenbogen, *Sendero* (Lima, 1991).

51. Why should anyone have believed that Guzmán meant what he said? Moreover, governments these days, even in Latin America, are not what they used to be when up against such conspiracy. The Austrian Empire could send conspirators to the Spielberg, and Liberal Italy could maroon opponents on small offshore islands, and both could leave them to rot for years without trial. But before he went underground and began the armed struggle Guzmán had the protection of the law, and of good lawyers – and he had not done anything for which a court would have convicted him.

52. Bolívar has enjoyed a surprising revival as a symbol of revolution. The Colombian guerrilla co-ordinating body is the *Coordinadora guerrillera Simón Bolívar*. Colonel Chávez's *golpistas* in Venezuela refer to themselves as Bolivarians. In the Colombian case it is perhaps the lack of a suitable Colombian that is at work – the leading Colombian figure of Independence, Francisco de Paula Santander, though a General, was not particularly keen on armed struggle, and these words of his adorned the Palace of Justice that was assaulted by the M-19: "Colombians, arms have given you independence, but laws will make you free." He is too identified with the legalistic traditions of the republic and with the Liberal party, both of which are still very much alive. In Venezuela it is almost impossible not to invoke Bolívar in practically any cause. Colonel Chávez is also like Bolívar a voluntarist, a believer in the supreme importance of the will. The use of Bolívar's name appears to me to be bogus and ineffectual in both cases.

53. Large numbers of Colombian guerrillas have been captured and brought before courts, but few have spent long in jail. Colombian law favours the accused, and is subject to delays and confusions innumerable which lead to the collapse of a high proportion of cases. Guerrillas employ lawyers, and have funds set aside to pay them. They also threaten judges. The vagaries of politics prevent states of siege and states of exception from lasting, though they are frequently imposed. Though the Colombian left believes that the armed forces are always eager to try civilians, this is not the case. It is usually civilian despair of the civil courts that produces military jurisdiction, and this has commonly proved an ineffectual remedy. Military judges may be less intimidated, but military court procedures are no more effective than civilian ones, and the few convictions arrived at have failed to stick. Sentences are not only rare, they are usually short.

54. See M-19, *Corinto* (Bogotá, 1985). For a description of peacemaking with the M-19 see my "Un día en Yumbo y Corinto" in *Del poder y la gramática*.

55. See G. García Márquez, "Bateman, un misterio sin fin", in P. Ariza *et al.*, *Bateman* (Bogotá, 1992) pp. 455–63.

56. See, for an example, A. Molano, Los años de tropel (Bogotá, 1985); Siguiendo la corte (Bogotá, 1991); J. Aprile-Gniset, La crónica de Villarica (Bogotá, 1991); A. Alape, Las vidas de Pedro Antonio Marín, Manuel Marulanda Vélez, Tirofijo (Bogotá, 1989); E. Marulanda, Colonización y conflicto. Las lecciones del Sumapaz (Bogotá, 1991).

57. See especially the works of Alape and Aprile-Gniset. This is essentially the FARC's "revolutionary moment", and implies the transformation of a localized agrarian movement into a Communist-guided revolutionary guerrilla. (There is much implied criticism of this in the recent literature: some think that the agrarian movement had been better left as an agrarian movement, and contrast the successful pragmatism of the Sumapaz leader Juan de la Cruz Varela with the revolutionary persistence of Manuel Marulanda, Tirofijo.) Equally, the bombardment of Villarica in 1955 is its "chosen trauma", the event that makes any immediate peace impossible. For a more formal history of the FARC see E. Pizarro Leongómez (with R. Peñaranda), Las FARC (1949–1966). De la autodefensa a la combinación de todas las formas de lucha (Bogotá, 1991).

58. The complaint of abandonment, of being forgotten, of the absence of the state is one of the most constant in Colombian political rhetoric. It needs to be taken with a large pinch of salt. An interesting recent example is contained in the otherwise informative work of M. V. Uribe Alarcón on the emerald zone, Limpiar la tierra (Bogotá, 1992). The absence of the state is diagnosed as part of the problem, but at the same time the work shows that the majority of the inhabitants of the area are determined to keep the state out of it with all the means at their disposal.

In the comparison with Sendero, I have recently been reminded by Julio Cotler (Seminar, Universidad de los Andes, Bogotá, February 1993) of the importance of recognizing that Sendero is in its origins essentially a political party, not a guerrilla. No Colombian guerrilla has a similar trajectory, not one has its origins in such a lengthy period of essentially political preparation, and not one has taken similar care in the non-military preparation of its cadres and rank and file.

59. See Alape, op. cit.

60. For marches see J. J. González Arias and E. Marulanda Alvarez, Historias de frontera. Colonización y guerras en el Sumapaz (Bogotá, 1990), and E. Pizarro Leongómez, op. cit.

61. Lucio V. Mansilla, Una excursión a los indios Ranqueles (Buenos Aires, 1871). This work is unrivalled as a contemporary dissection of frontier politics in the Americas.

62. C. Arango Z., Jacobo: Guerrero y Amante (Bogotá, 1990).

63. Four, if one includes Hernando de Soto, author of El otro sendero – a title whose total significance exceeds its author's intentions. Five, if one includes the leading "Theologian of Liberation". And one should consider also the poet César Vallejo and the novelist José María Arguedas.

64. D. Castrillón Arboleda, El indio Quintín Lame (Bogotá, 1973). This judicious work contains a photograph of Quintin surrounded by his captors after one of his small Cauca rebellions. Quintin is seated in the middle, smoking a cigar. His captors have a proprietorial air, but the central and dominant figure is undoubtedly Quintin. It is clear from the picture that the game will

continue, and anything like an execution or assassination is out of the question.
65. For the Universidad Industrial de Santander and the origins of the ELN see R. Arenas, *La guerrilla por dentro*. His account can usefully be compared with Carlos Ivan Degregori's description of the Universidad de Huamanga. There are many significant differences.
65. For the reading, ELN, *Camilo camina por Colombia* (Navarra, 1989). Arenas, op. cit., describes killing policemen for their arms.
67. ELN, op. cit.
68. F. Calvo, *EPL* (Bogotá, 1985).
69. Such resignation is expressed by the cura Manuel Pérez, the leader of the ELN. See *Camilo camina por Colombia*.
70. The possible government cynicism would be a calculation that the movement would lose support more rapidly participating in government than if it were confined to opposition.
71. Davis, op. cit., p. 260.
72. Ibid., p. 132.
73. Ibid., p. 133.
74. Ibid., p. 139. For the paramilitaries of the Middle Magdalena see C. Medina Gallego, *Autodefensas, paramilitares y narcotráfico en Colombia. Origen, desarrollo y consolidación. El caso "Puerto Boyacá"* (Bogotá, 1990).
75. Davis, op. cit., chs XI and XII.
76. See D. Apter and N. Sawa, *Against the State. Politics and Social Protest in Japan* (Cambridge, Mass., 1984).
77. *Daedalus*, vol. 12, no. 2 (Spring 1993) pp. 207–32.
78. Stephen Wilson, *Fending, Conflict and Banditry in Nineteenth-century Corsica* (Cambridge, 1988) pp. 415–16.

BIBLIOGRAPHY

Three bibliographical introductions to Colombian violence are R. W. Ramsey, "Critical Bibliography on *La Violencia* in Colombia", *Latin American Research Review*, vol. 8, no. 1 (1973); G. Sánchez Gómez, "*La Violencia* in Colombia: New Research, New Questions", *Hispanic American Historical Review*, vol. 65, no. 4 (1985); G. Cardona Grisales, *Para un estudio de la violencia en Colombia* (Bogota, 1989) Documentos Ocasionales, CINEP, no. 55, a work with 1,807 entries, though unfortunately many of them have only the most remote connection with the subject. There are also ample bibliographical notes in C. Bergquist, R. Peñaranda and G. Sánchez Gómez (eds), *Violence in Colombia. The Contemporary Crisis in Historical Perspective* (Wilmington, 1992).

Some indications to guide the beginner have already been given above in the notes of this essay, but a more formal list of recommendations may be a help.

Four useful readers besides the last-mentioned are G. Sánchez Gómez and R. Peñaranda (eds), *Pasado y presente de la violencia en Colombia* (Bogotá, 1986); G. Sánchez Gómez (intro.), *Once ensayos sobre la violencia* (Bogotá,

1985); A. Alape, *La Paz, La Violencia: Testigos de excepción* (Bogotá, 1985); O. Behar, *Las guerras de la paz* (Bogotá, 1985).

There is still much indispensable information in the first systematic work to be published on the subject, G. German Campos, E. Umaña Luna and O. Fals Borda, *La Violencia en Colombia*, 2 vols (Bogotá, 1962–4).

The following dozen works should also be included in any select bibliography: E. Franco Isaza, *Las guerrillas del llano* (Bogotá, 1959), an account by a leading protagonist of the Liberal guerrillas in the Eastern Plains in the "classic" era; A. Molano, *Los años del tropel. Relatos de la violencia* (Bogotá, 1985), the author's first and most varied oral history; J. Henderson, *Cuando Colombia se desangró* (Bogotá, 1984), a study of violence in Tolima; C. M. Ortíz Sarmiento, *Estado y subversión en Colombia* (Bogotá, 1985), which analyses violence in the Quindío region in the 1940s and 1950s, and J. Arocha, *La violencia en el Quindío* (Bogotá, 1979), which does the same for the less sectarian but still violent 1960s; D. Pecaut, *Orden y violencia: Colombia, 1930–1954*, 2 vols (Bogotá, 1987), a complex sociological meditation, also available in French; P. Oquist, *Violence, Conflict and Politics in Colombia* (New York, 1980), particularly valuable for its statistical efforts; G. Sánchez Gómez's recent essays, *Guerra y política en la sociedad colombiana* (Bogotá, 1991); Comisión de Estudios sobre la Violencia, *Violencia y democracia* (Bogotá, 1987), a valiant attempt to bring notions of prevailing violence up to date; on the assassination of Gaitán and the 9 de abril of 1948, A. Alape, *El Bogotázo: Memorias del olvido*, and the more speculative H. Braun, *The Assassination of Gaitán: Public Life and Urban Violence in Colombia* (Madison, 1985); an outstanding study of civil war in detail is C. E. Jaramillo, *Los guerrilleros del novecientos* (Bogotá, 1991).

A recent short history of Colombia is D. Bushnell, *The Making of Modern Colombia: A Nation In Spite of Itself* (Berkeley, 1993).

Index